HISTORIC PHOTOS OF OUTLAWS OF THE OLD WEST

TEXT AND CAPTIONS BY LARRY JOHNSON

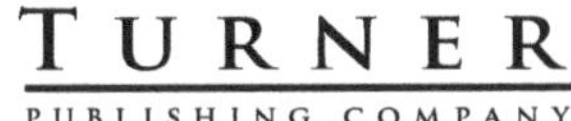

This is the stately town of Cheyenne, Wyoming, in 1876, which had shed its wilder days and become a proper capital city. It was at this time that Calamity Jane was working in the worst sort of whorehouse and convinced Wild Bill Hickok to allow her to join his expedition to Deadwood as a prostitute in exchange for whiskey.

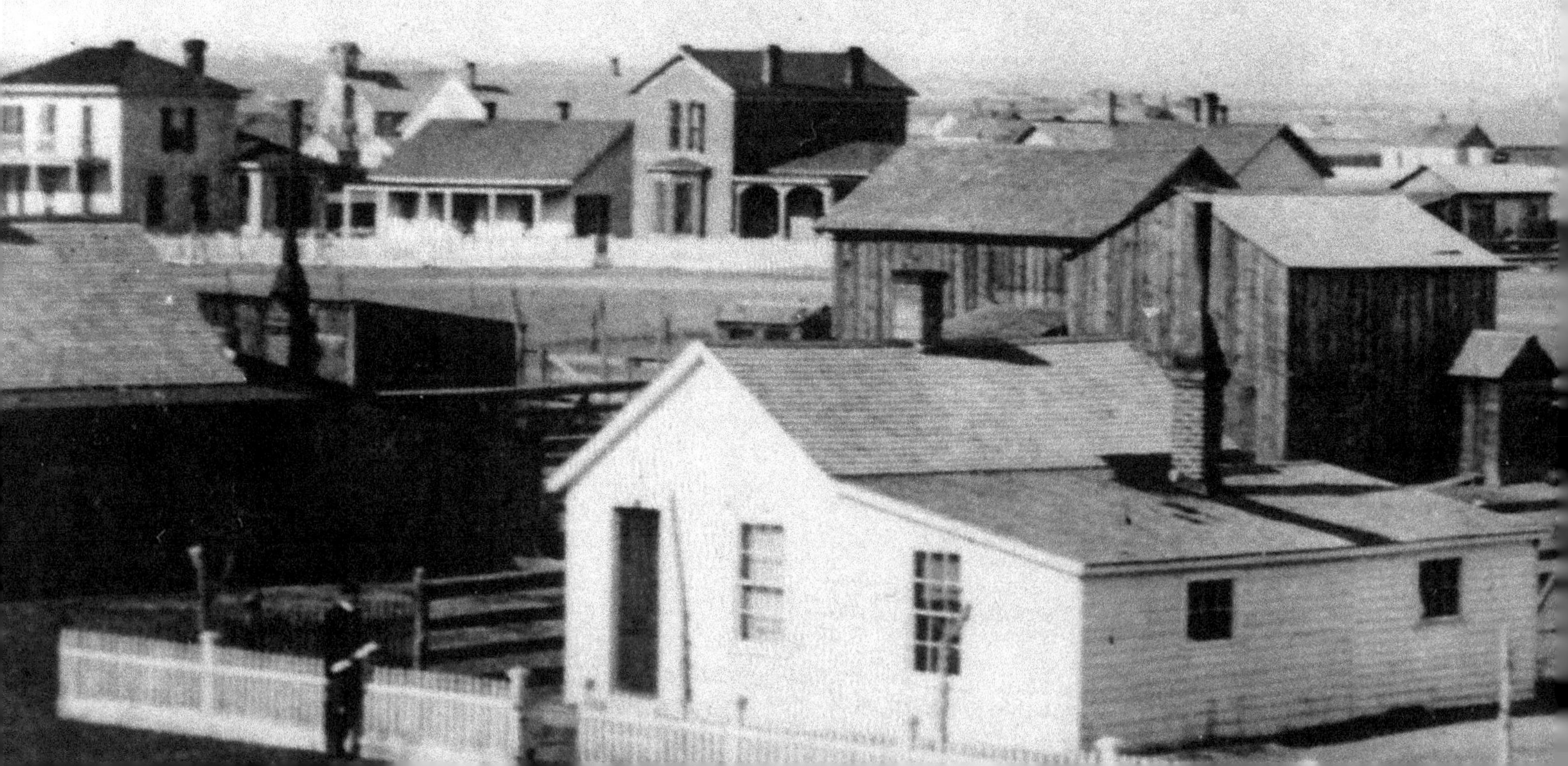

HISTORIC PHOTOS OF
OUTLAWS OF THE OLD WEST

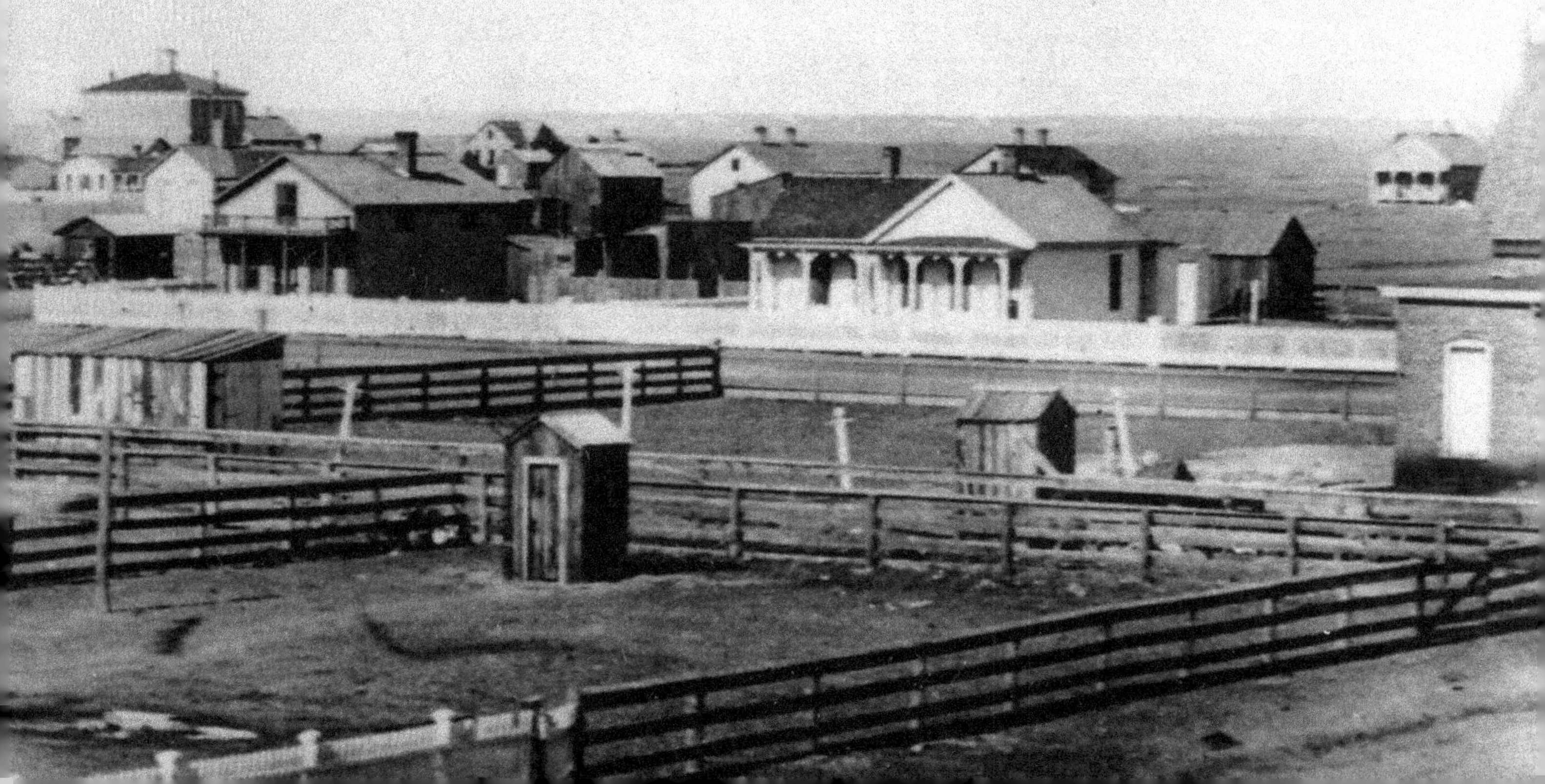

Turner Publishing Company
www.turnerpublishing.com

Historic Photos of Outlaws of the Old West

Library of Congress Control Number: 2010926751

ISBN: 978-1-59652-579-5

Printed in the United States of America

ISBN 978-1-68442-118-3 (hc)

Contents

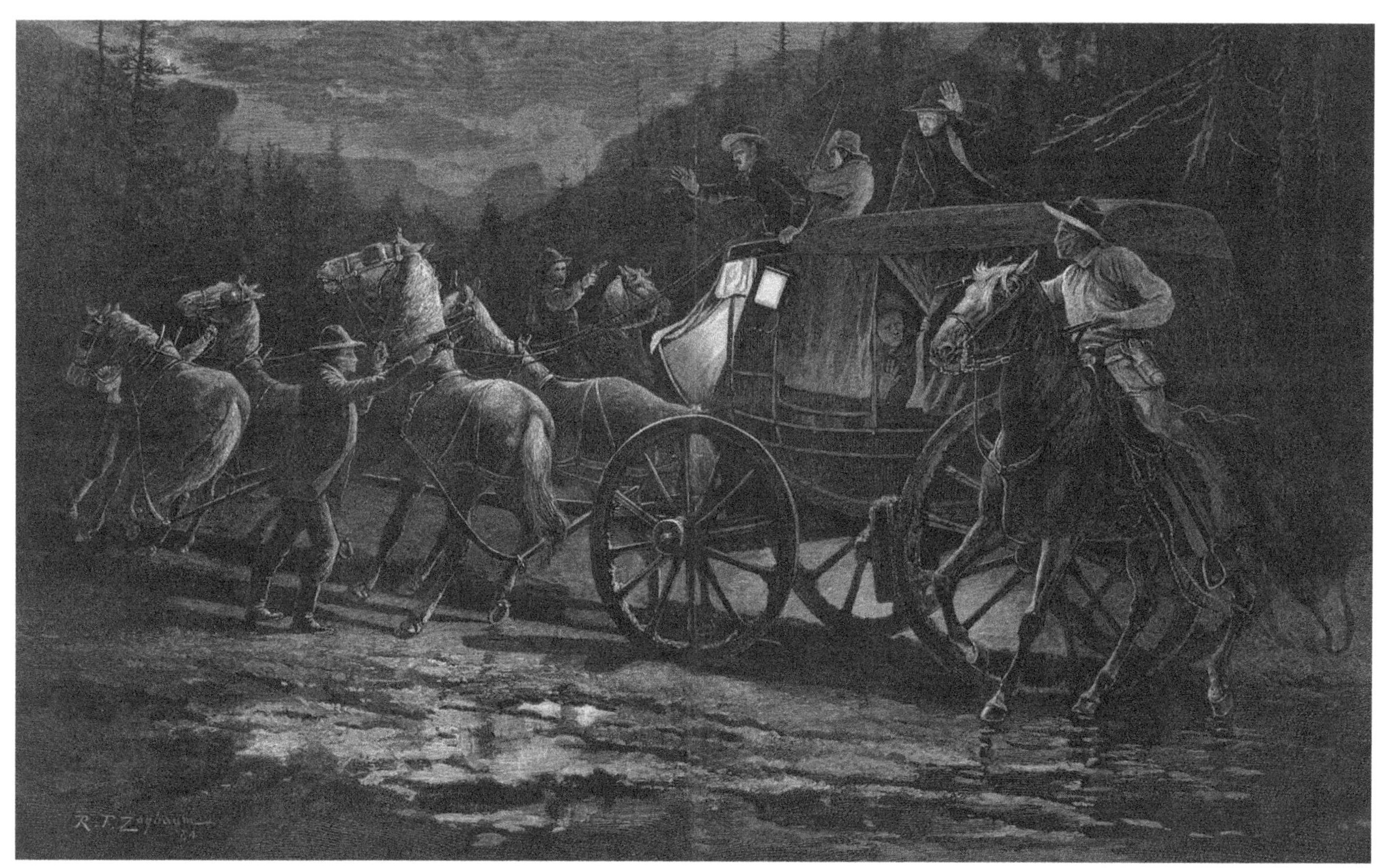

Although robbing stagecoaches fell off significantly with the arrival of the railroads to most parts of the West, the risk of hold-up was still on the minds of travelers in mountainous areas where the stages slowed to a crawl while negotiating high passes. This drawing from 1885 depicts the hazard that travelers could face.

Acknowledgments

This volume, *Historic Photos of Outlaws of the Old West,* is the result of the cooperation and efforts of many individuals and organizations. It is with great thanks that we acknowledge the valuable contribution of the following for their generous support:

Denver Public Library, Western History Collection
Kansas State Historical Society
Library of Congress
National Archives and Records Administration
Oklahoma Historical Society
Western History Collections, University of Oklahoma
Wikimedia Commons

For my dad in memory of the countless hours of Westerns we watched together.

PREFACE

For the historian, writing about outlaws of the Old West always presents a challenge. Most of the available sources are suspect and unreliable. Newspapers, which are invaluable resources in some areas of history, are of dubious reliability when researching crimes in the lawless West. Firsthand accounts are spotty and the testimony full of holes. The writings of early historians often disagree and are rife with errors like misspelled names and incorrect dates. And then there are those interviews done in the 1930s with pioneers who knew Jesse James or Mysterious Dave Mather; always in the back of the mind is the old adage of the 1960s—if you remember it, you probably weren't there.

Modern research methods, digital records, and databases have helped dispel some of the myths and filled in some of the blanks of the outlaws' lives, but the question remains—do we *really* want to know the truth? Is it even good for us to know the truth? It seems that one of the many legal traditions the United States inherited from our English forebears is our uneasy affection for our outlaws. It goes all the way back to Robin Hood. Those of us on the lower rungs of society find hope in knowing that a few among us are not afraid of our oppressors and have found the strength to fight the king or the railroad or the evil corporation or the encroaching government bureaucracy. We know the outlaws robbed and killed and stole, but the advocacy they represent is a powerful emotion.

Although their misdeeds were frequently exaggerated, it is possible to construct a composite profile of the outlaw. Most of the early outlaws of notoriety were former Confederate soldiers. Some returned home after the war to find it burned out; some returned home and found life oppressive under the thumb of the occupying Union forces and the carpetbagging Reconstructionists; some were restless after having seen other parts of the country; and some likely suffered from what we now identify as post-traumatic stress disorder. Even those who were not former soldiers typically experienced some sort of disruption in their youth, which is usually credited, whether or not it should be, for sending them down an errant path.

The typical outlaw usually started out an honest man. Some, like Butch Cassidy, made a youthful error in judgment and were made criminals by the rough-and-tumble frontier justice system, or their responses to it. Many started out as cowboys who were either tempted by the wild life at the end of the trail in places like Dodge City or began cutting a head or two from the herd to sell on the sly and ended up going to prison for rustling. If an outlaw started out as a farmer, he might end up choosing crime as his answer to a national economic depression or the ruthlessness of the railroads, which he blamed for making it impossible to earn a living at his chosen vocation. A typical gunslinger likely got into the killing business by accident, usually after a drunken brawl or a fit of anger.

Some outlaws planned on doing just enough crime to get them through a rough patch or to get together enough of a stake to turn legitimate. Jesse James tried at least twice to return to farming and Butch Cassidy got his nickname after he quit train-robbing for a while and worked as a butcher. But they almost always ended up dead or in prison by the age of thirty.

It's important to remember that part of the myth of the outlaws is that the West was violent. Certainly there were pockets of violence, but life in the West was no more violent statistically than life in the teeming cities of the East. More than likely, the perception developed because in the West life was rawer, lacking the veneer of society or the security of an established legal system. Likewise, in regard to outlaws, there were a few sociopathic killers, but they did not kill in great numbers nor were they overrepresented in the population. Most outlaws hid in remote areas and struck isolated targets, generally leaving the common man to his business.

This book is about the photographs. Some of the mythology is perpetuated in the captions and some new truths put forth as well. Viewing these photographs allows us to look these fellows in the eye and assess their character—something we probably wouldn't have been allowed to do in real life and live to tell about it.

—Larry Johnson

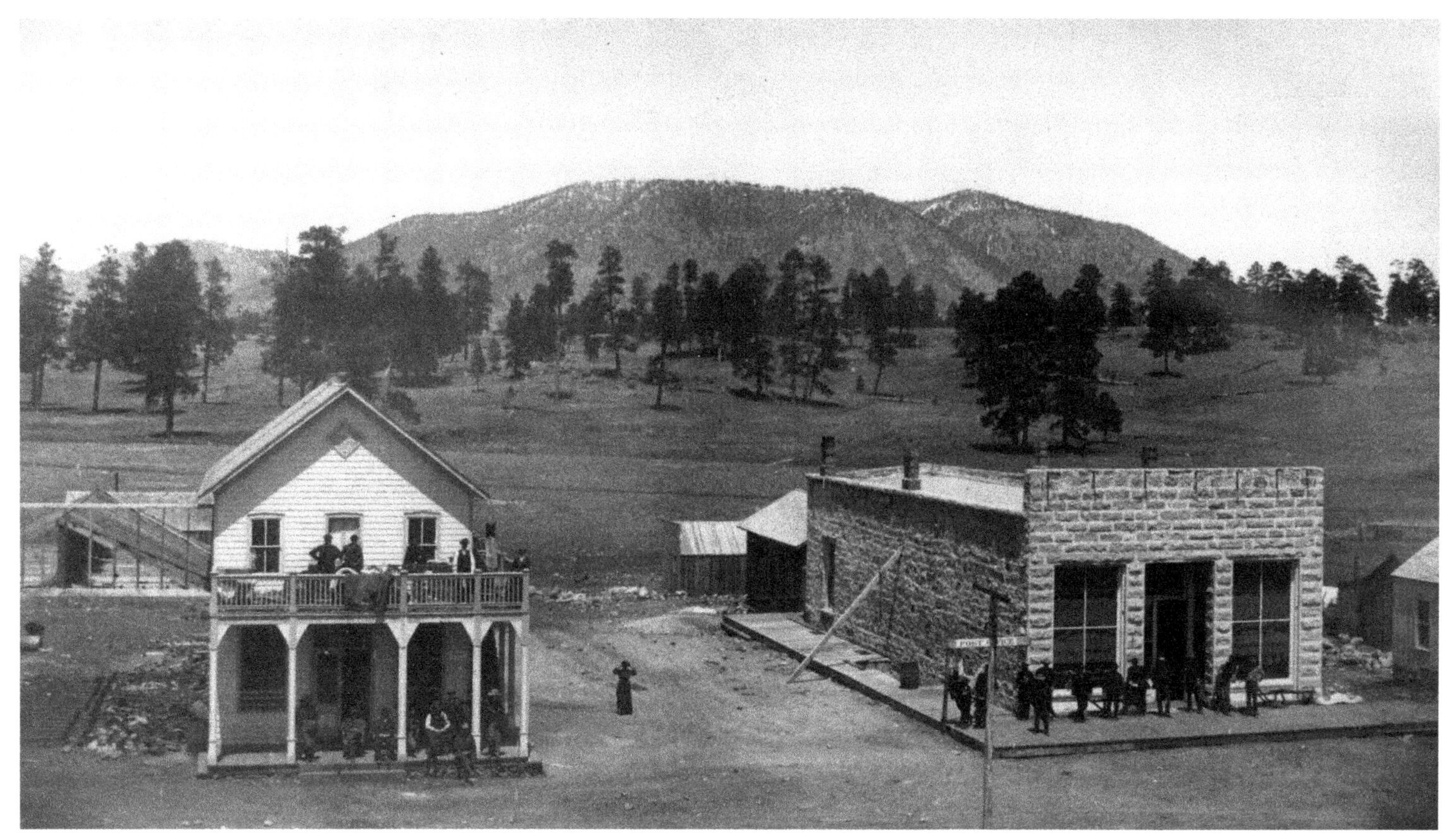

Around 1890, a local editorialist wrote of Flagstaff, Arizona, "Shooting, killing and robbing seemed to be the order of the day. Our authorities, however, buckled on their armor and away they went for the outlaw element." The most notorious outlaw operating in that area was train-robbing murderer Jim Parker, who was hanged in 1897.

We Were Driven To It

(1853–1876)

Whatever one thinks of the now romanticized Confederate general Robert E. Lee one hundred and fifty years after the Civil War, it's difficult to deny that he performed a great service to the fractured nation when he instructed his defeated army, "We must accept the situation. These men must go home and plant a crop, and we must proceed to build up our country on a new basis."

Lee made these comments in the face of the very real possibility of a decades-long guerrilla war in the South against occupying forces from the North. For the most part this did not happen, but in the western states the old divisions of the Civil War informed the actions and motives of many citizens, especially the outlaws. The best-known example of this is the James-Younger Gang. They learned their "trade" in the saddle from men like Confederate lieutenant colonel William Quantrill and "Bloody" Bill Anderson during their guerrilla raids along the war's western front. Over the ten succeeding years, they defined many of their own raids on banks and trains as strikes against former Union officers or Reconstruction profiteers. Other feuds were sparked by these festering wounds. For example, some of the trouble in early Dodge City erupted because many Texans felt they were mistreated by the ex-Union leadership in the town.

Outlawry in the late 1860s and 1870s was also inspired by haphazard settlement patterns in the West. Whether it was a gold rush in the mountains or a cow town on the Great Plains, the pattern often progressed from a rapidly populated camp of workers seeking instant riches; to the arrival of opportunistic purveyors of vice—gambling, prostitution, and whiskey—who sought to separate these workers from their earnings; to the larger corporate interests that moved in to organize the effort, invest the needed capital, and reserve most of the profit for the officers and shareholders; to finally the civilizers who came to build homes and businesses and schools. The outlaw existed in the fluid period between these stages, often in the absence of laws and organized governance. Some were men who had lost everything and turned to crime out of desperation, while others simply found it easier to steal the hard-won wealth of others than to work for it themselves. With few exceptions, most outlaw actions in this period were episodes of banditry perpetrated by lone men or small groups against stagecoaches and mining companies, since trains and banks were practically nonexistent in the West of this day.

After 1849, thousands of gold seekers flocked to California, giving rise to friction with the region's small Hispanic population. Joaquin Murrieta was a *californio* who is supposed to have protested the injustices done by these settlers in the 1850s, by rustling and robbing them as a sort of Robin Hood. Conventional historical accounts have Murrieta hunted down and killed in 1853, but his legend lived on in stories such as the Zorro tales.

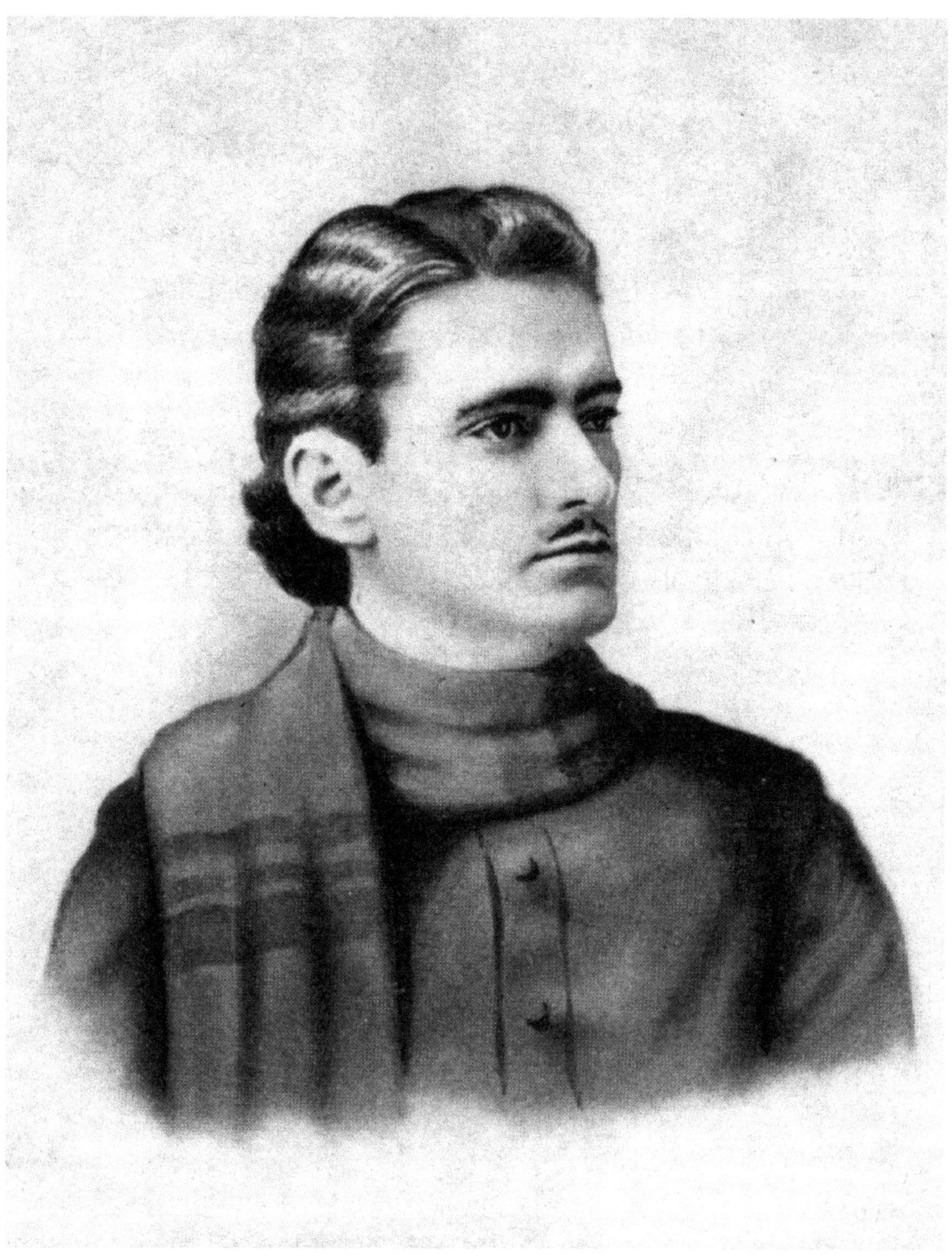

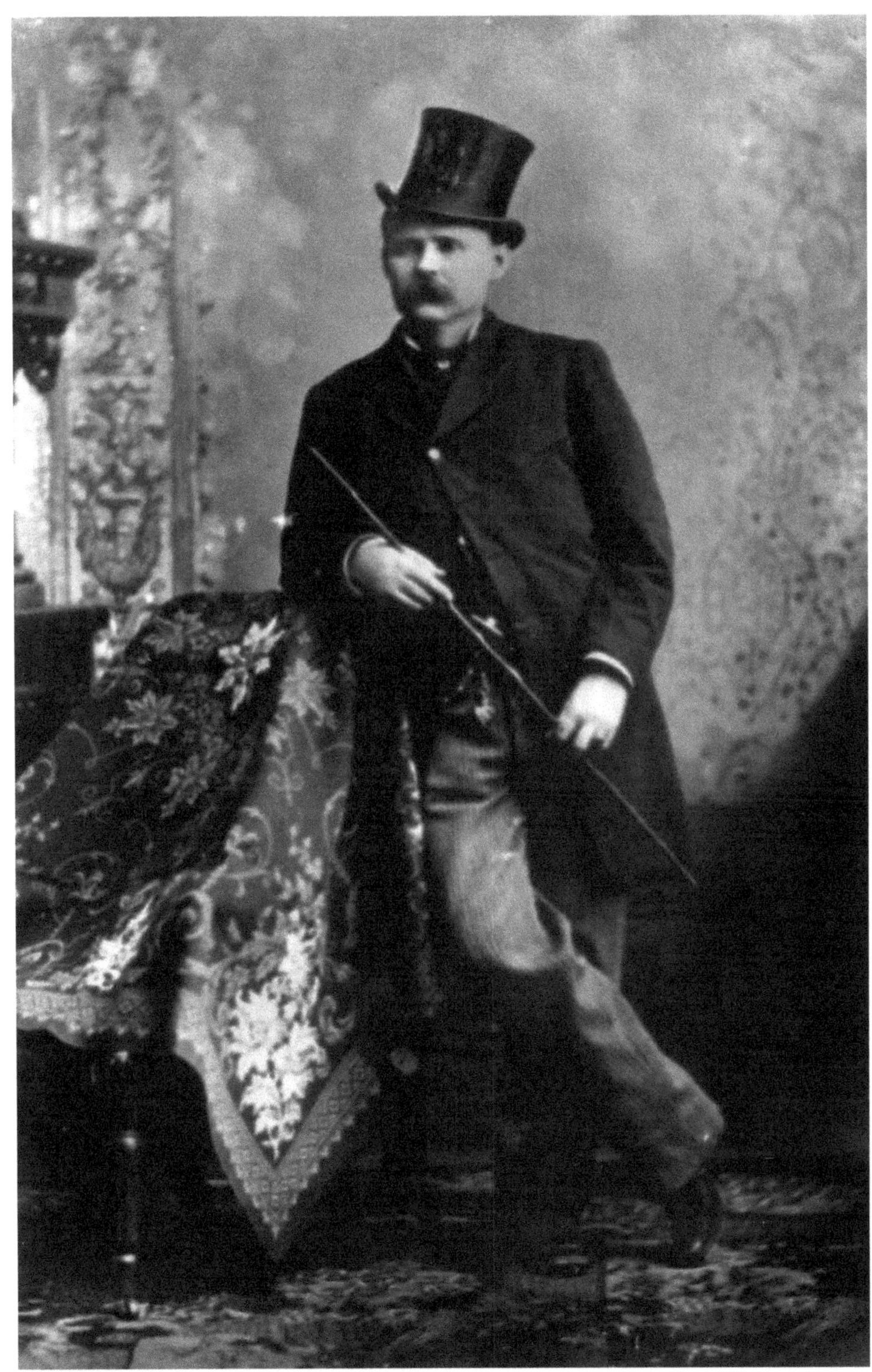

Ben Thompson (seen here in 1862) was probably a decent man inside, but trouble always seemed to find him—and he always resolved trouble with a gun. More a gunfighter than an outlaw, most of his myriad episodes of gunplay were accidental or done, he claimed, to keep someone from getting killed. His nominal vocation was professional gambler, and here he's seen in the dapper apparel of that role. He ran saloons in Ellsworth, Kansas, Leadville, Colorado, and Austin, Texas, and usually operated with a free hand. As outlaw chronicler Eugene Cunningham wrote, "The police walked clear of Ben and made no bones about it, because of his long, red record as a gunman."After a 20-year career knocking around cow towns in Kansas and Texas, he was murdered in San Antonio in 1884.

Though Confederate raiders operating out of Missouri often receive the lion's share of scorn for depredations against the population of Kansas, Jayhawkers from Kansas brought an equal measure of violence and destruction to the border counties of Missouri. Marshall Cleveland was once an officer in the Kansas Seventh Cavalry, but resigned his commission to be a horse-thieving raider. He was killed by soldiers of the Sixth Kansas Cavalry in 1862.

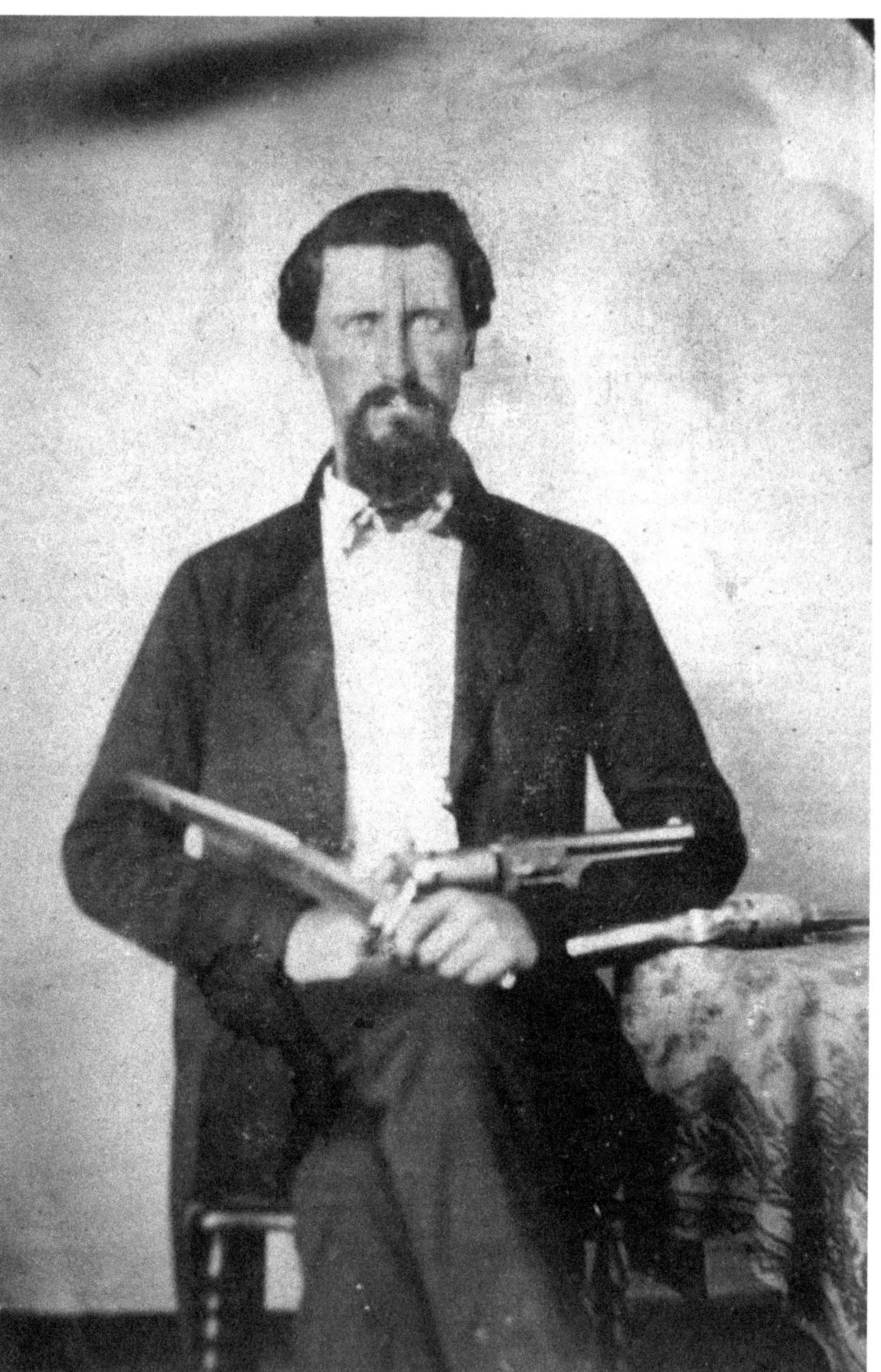

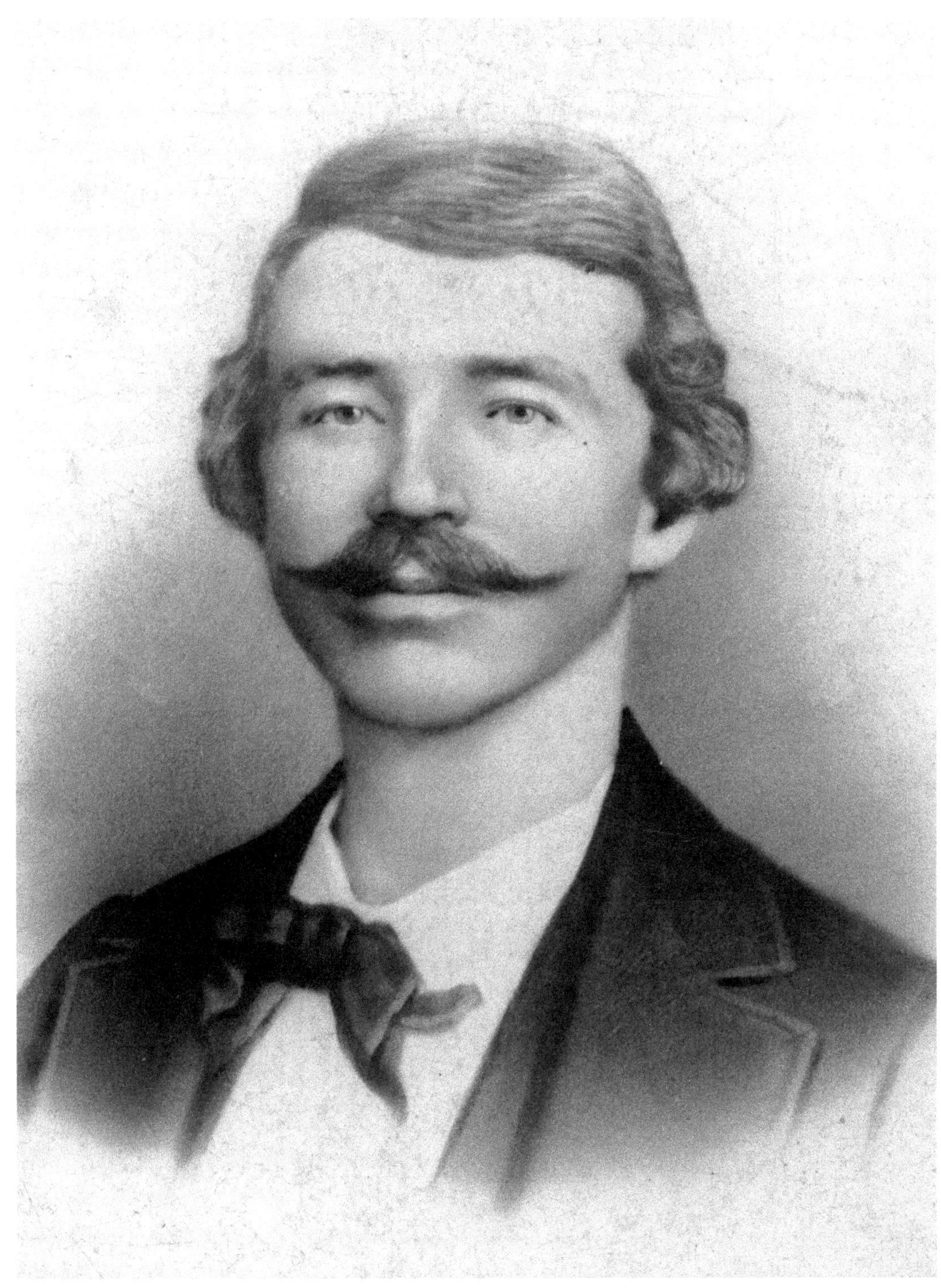

William Clarke Quantrill was quite possibly the original sociopathic gang leader of the Old West. Under the aegis of the Confederate States, he cut a swath of violence through Unionist towns in Kansas and Nebraska. Most notably he unleashed an orgy of murder and mayhem on Lawrence, Kansas, in 1863, burning it to the ground and killing nearly every male in the town—185 in all.

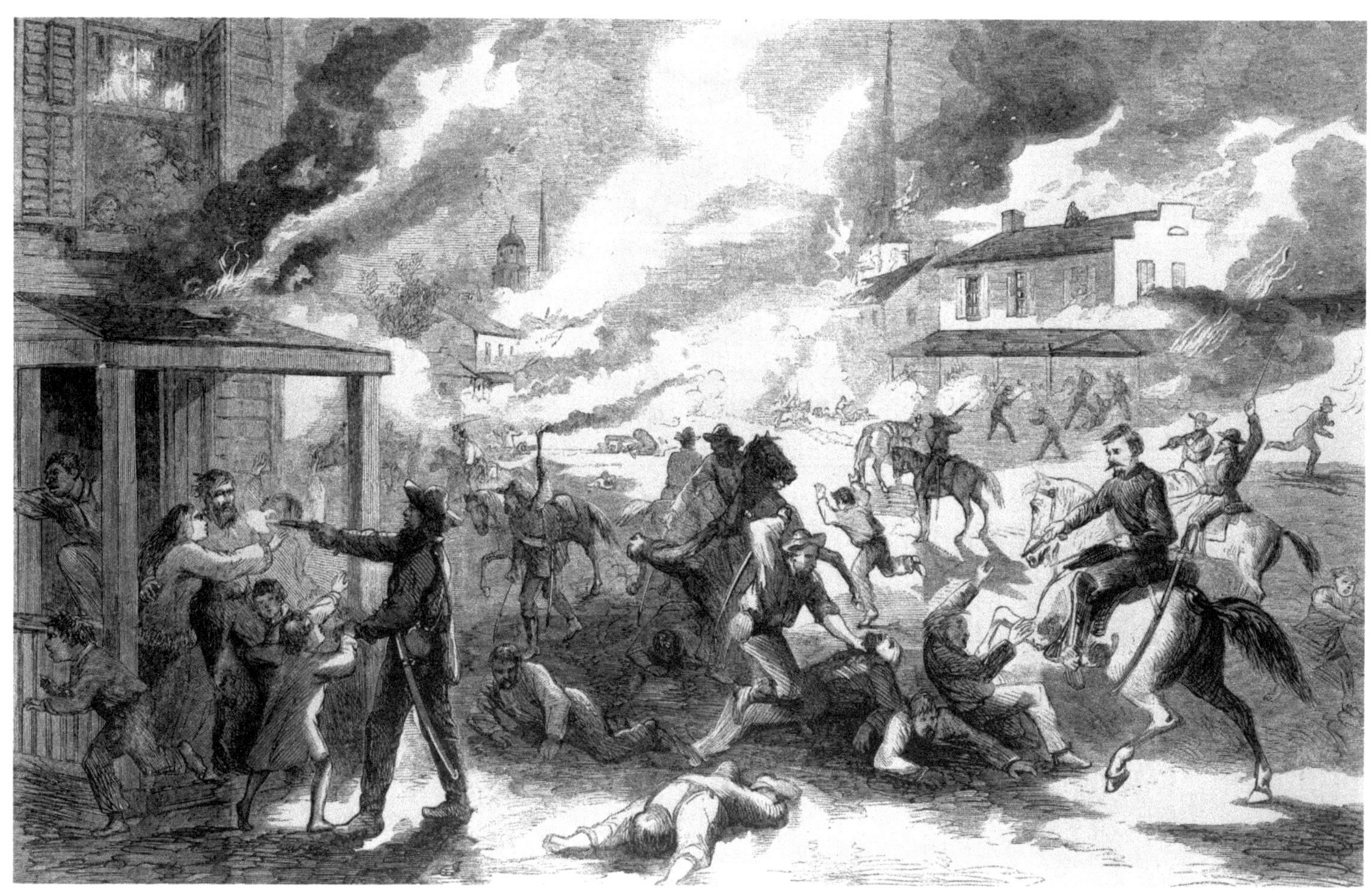

This artist's rendering of the destruction of Lawrence by rebel guerrillas accompanied news of the story in *Harper's Weekly.* According to witnesses, "The citizens were massacred by the light of their burning homes and their bodies thrown into wells and cisterns. In one case, 12 men were driven into a building where they were shot down and the building burned over their bodies."

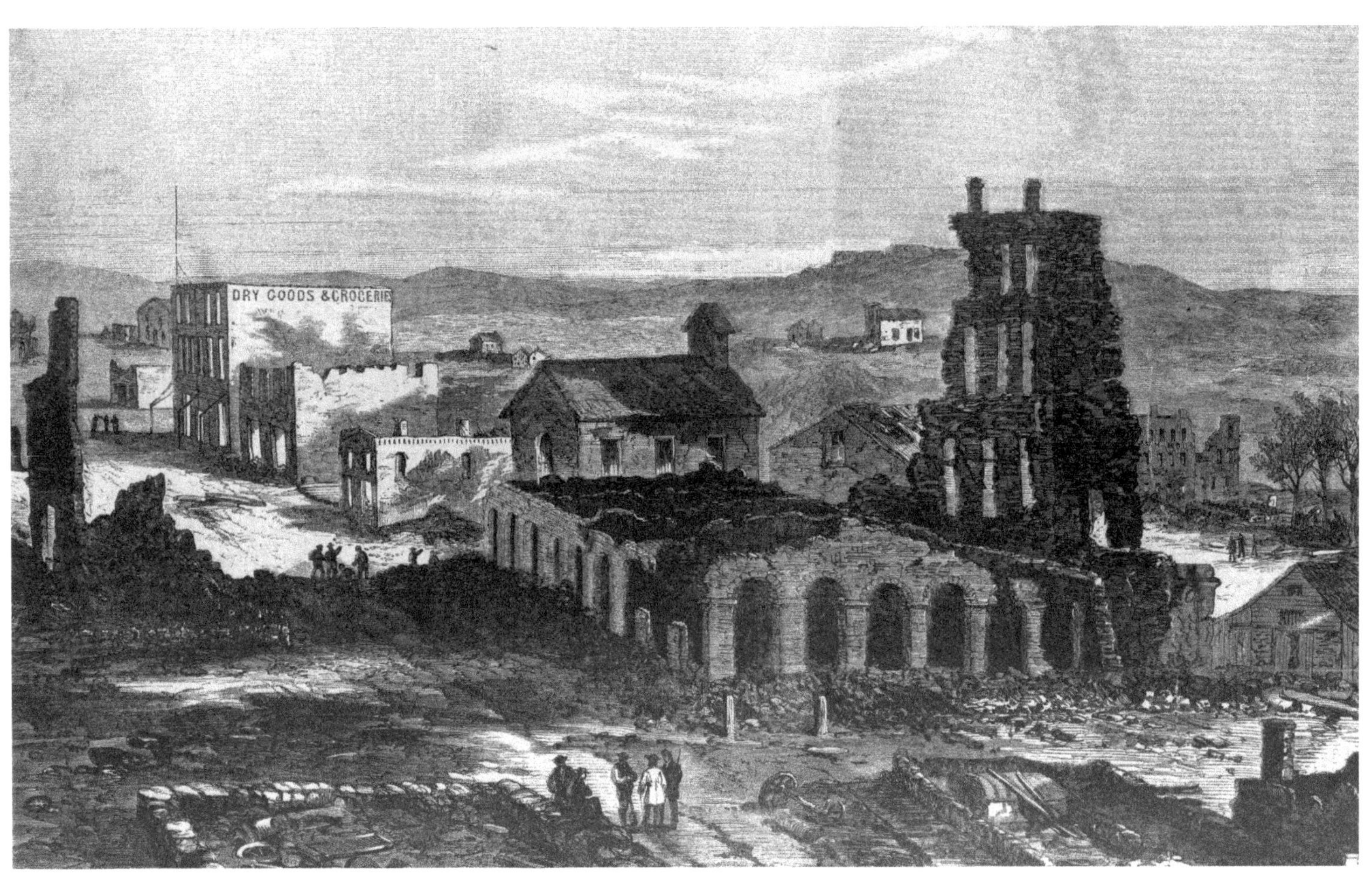

This sketch of the ruins of Lawrence was made soon after the attack. The motive for the attack was a medley of personal, political, and ideological revenge by the guerrillas, two of whom were 20-year-old Frank James and 19-year-old Cole Younger.

Despite his long life, Frank James (seen here ca. 1865) never adequately explained why he took to banditry in the Midwest after the Civil War, saying only, "We were driven to it." There was no doubt, however, that his career began in 1866 when he assembled a gang of men to rob the bank in Liberty, Missouri. They rode away with $60,000.

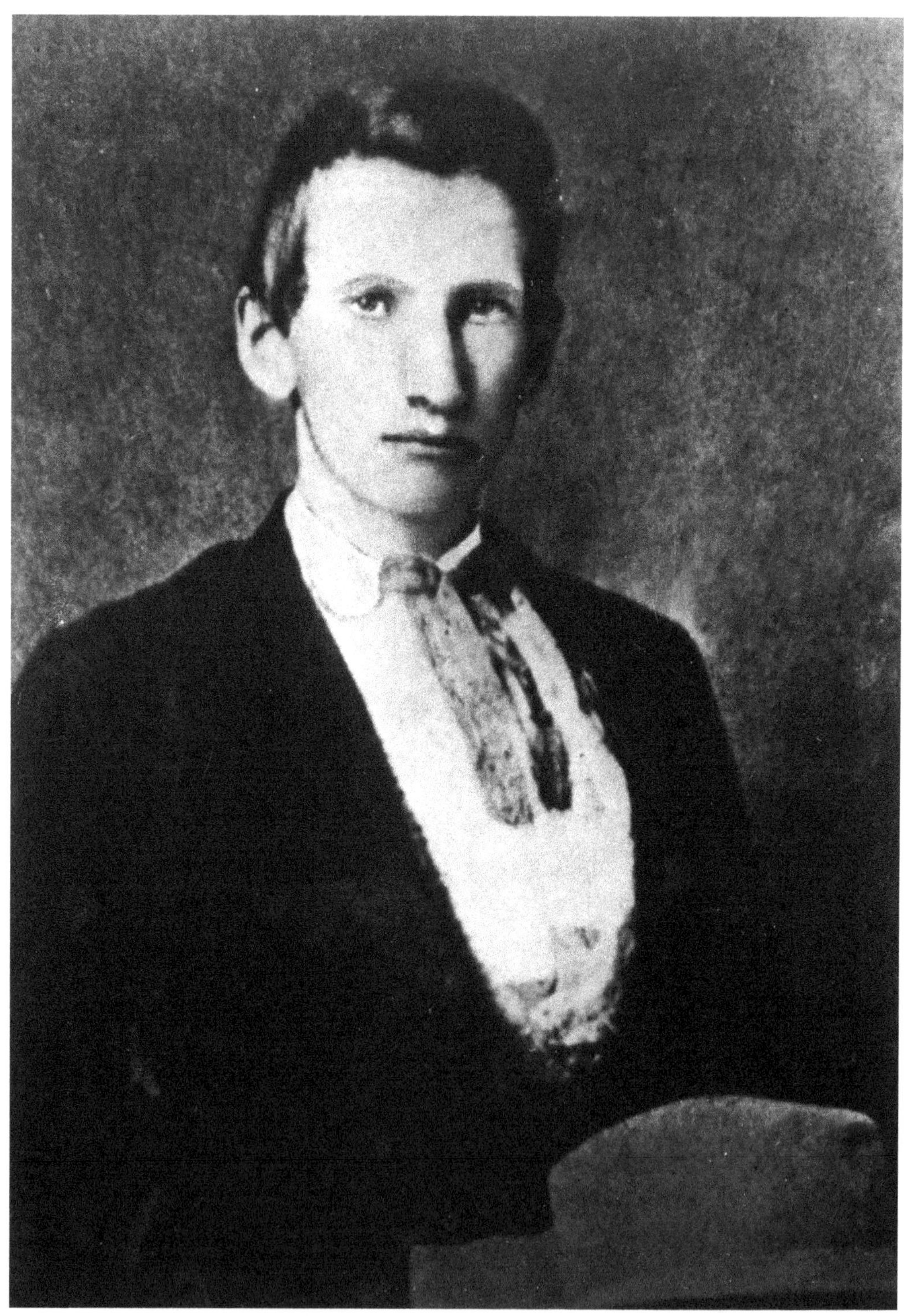

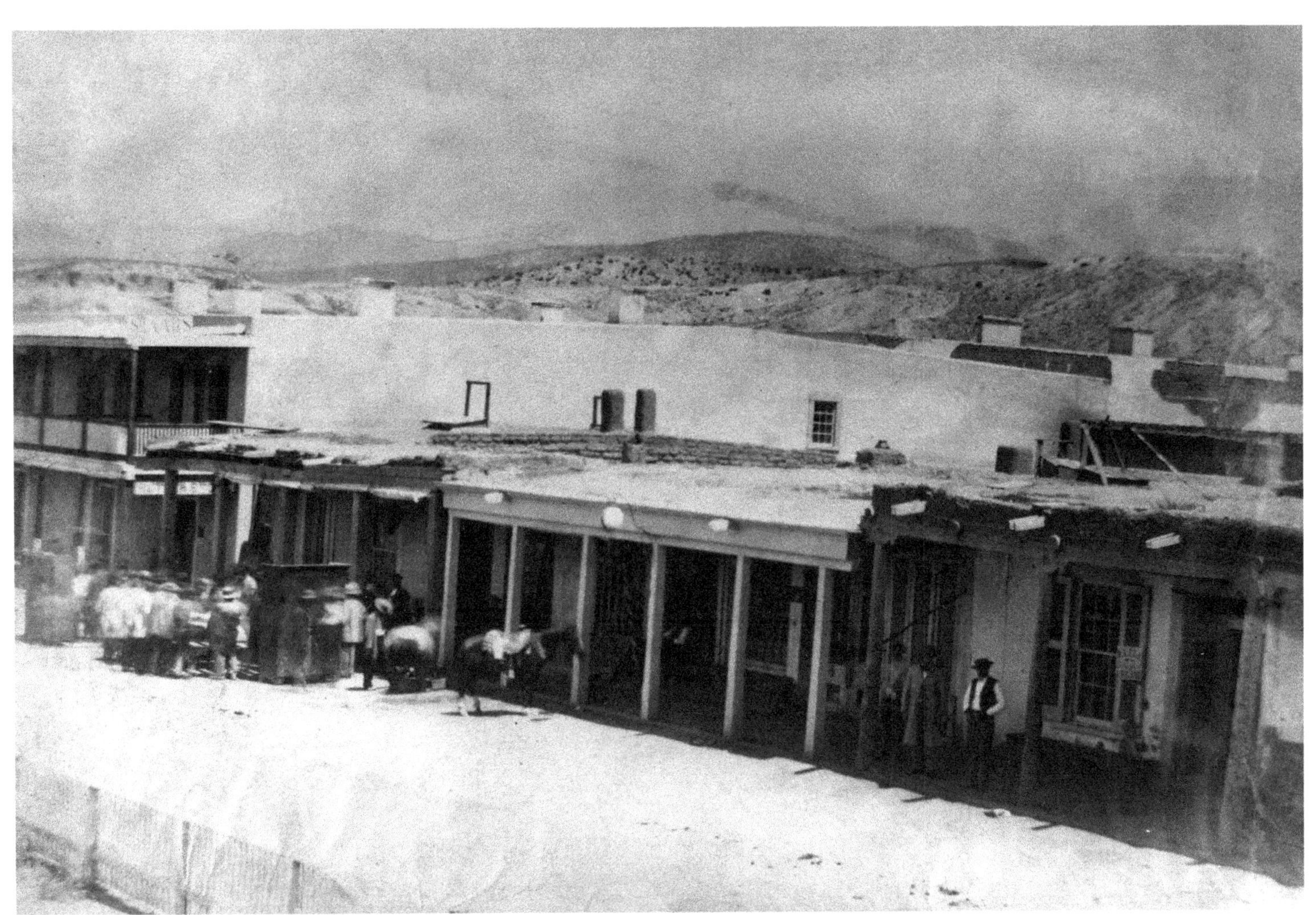

As capital, Santa Fe, New Mexico, was largely spared the violence of outlawry deposited on the territory's southern and eastern sides. What it lacked in violence, though, it made up for in corruption. Beginning in 1866 (when this view was recorded), the Santa Fe Ring of lawyers, politicians, and businessmen fueled many of the range and trade wars which marked life in 1870s and 1880s New Mexico.

Clay Allison was definitely a volatile man prone to violence without much provocation—much of it alcohol-fueled—but many of the most fantastic stories told about him are legendary. The most prominent of these was that he decapitated a murderer and placed the head on a pike. He was somewhat a vigilante, but he was well liked by many in Colfax County, New Mexico.

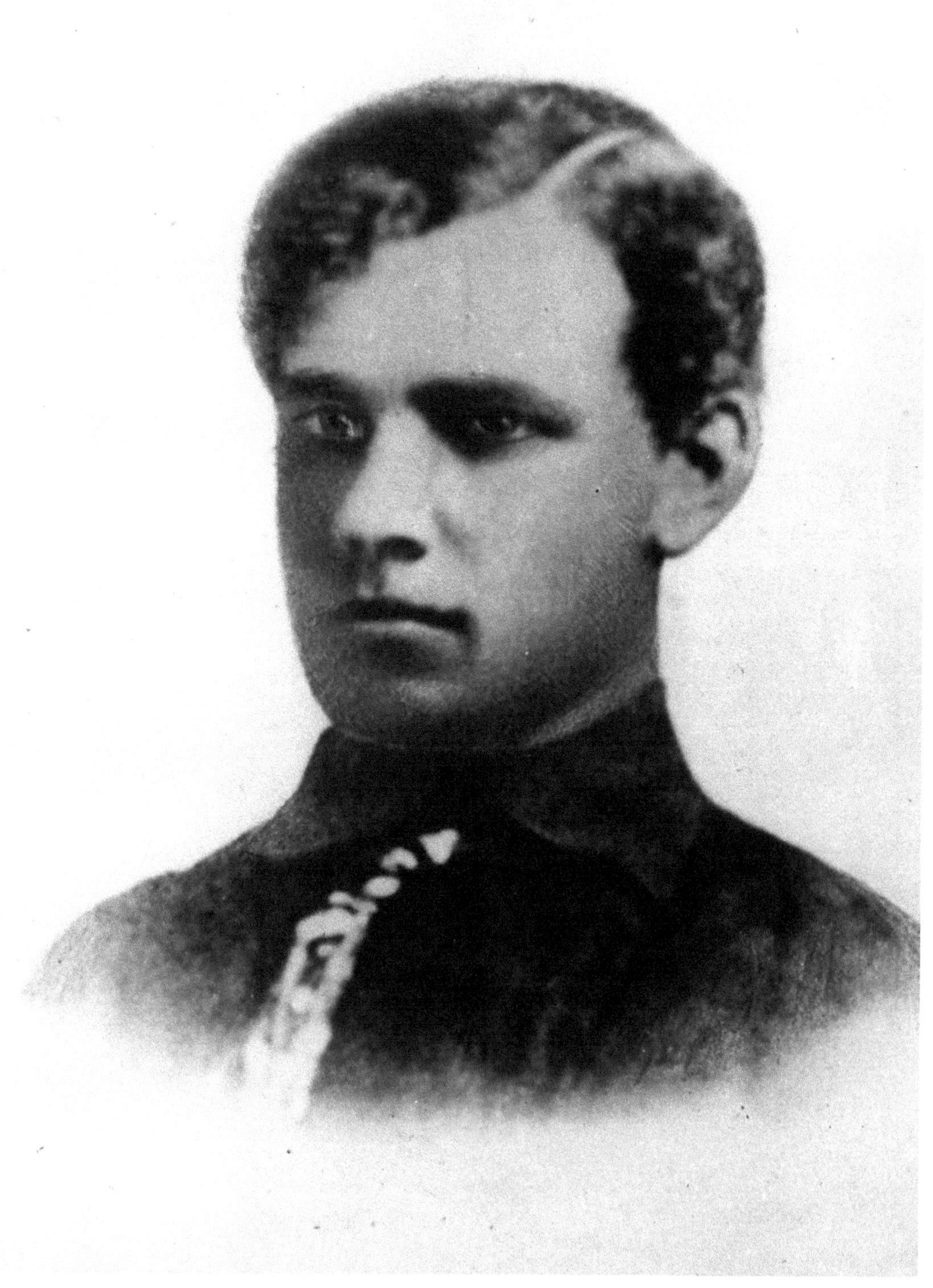

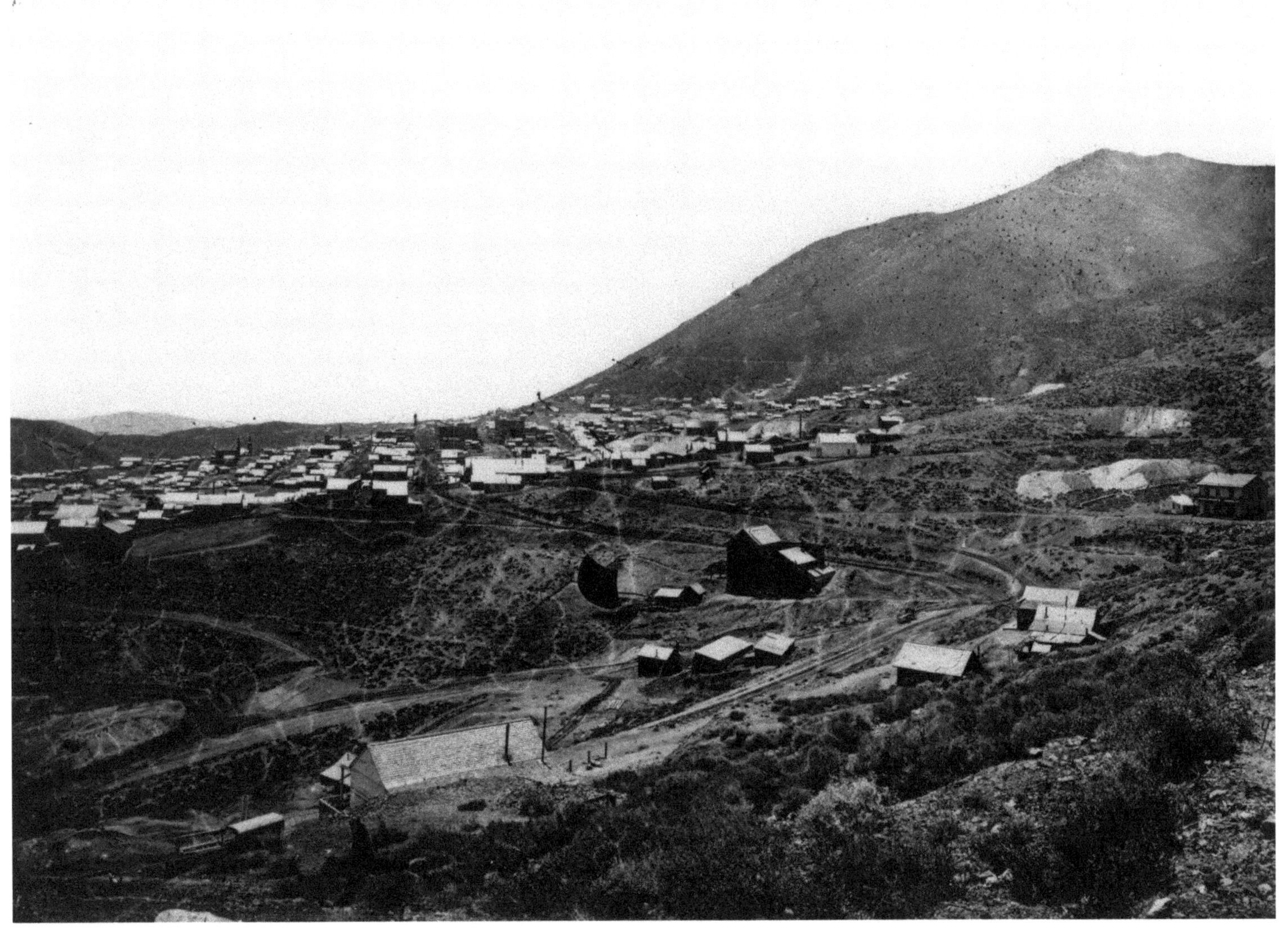

This hilltop photograph of mining boom-town Virginia City, Nevada, was made about 1867. Old-timer Emerson Hough remembered, "The wild license of the place was unspeakably vitiating. Fights with weapons were incessant. Pistols flashed, bowie-knives flourished, oaths filled the air. This was indeed the reign of unbridled license, and men who at first regarded it with disgust and terror, by constant exposure soon learned to become a part of it."

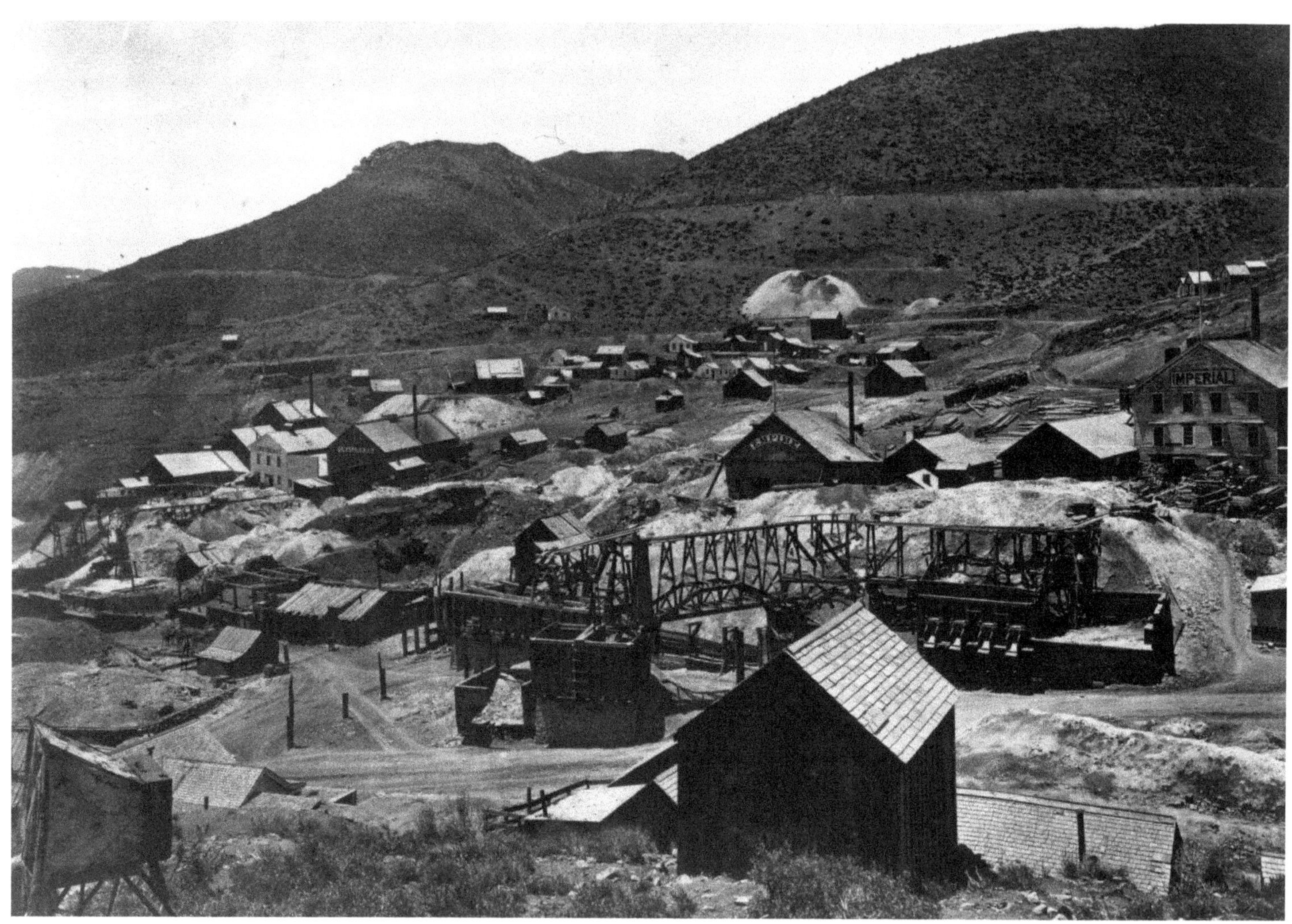

The town of Gold Hill, Nevada, in the Comstock Lode area. Nevada chronicler Sam P. Davis recalled that the stagecoaches hauling bullion out of the town were frequent targets for highwaymen, but "the passengers were seldom molested. The stage drivers didn't consider the fighting of robbers any part of their duty. . . . The general community hated the Wells-Fargo Company because of its extortions and only laughed when its stages were robbed."

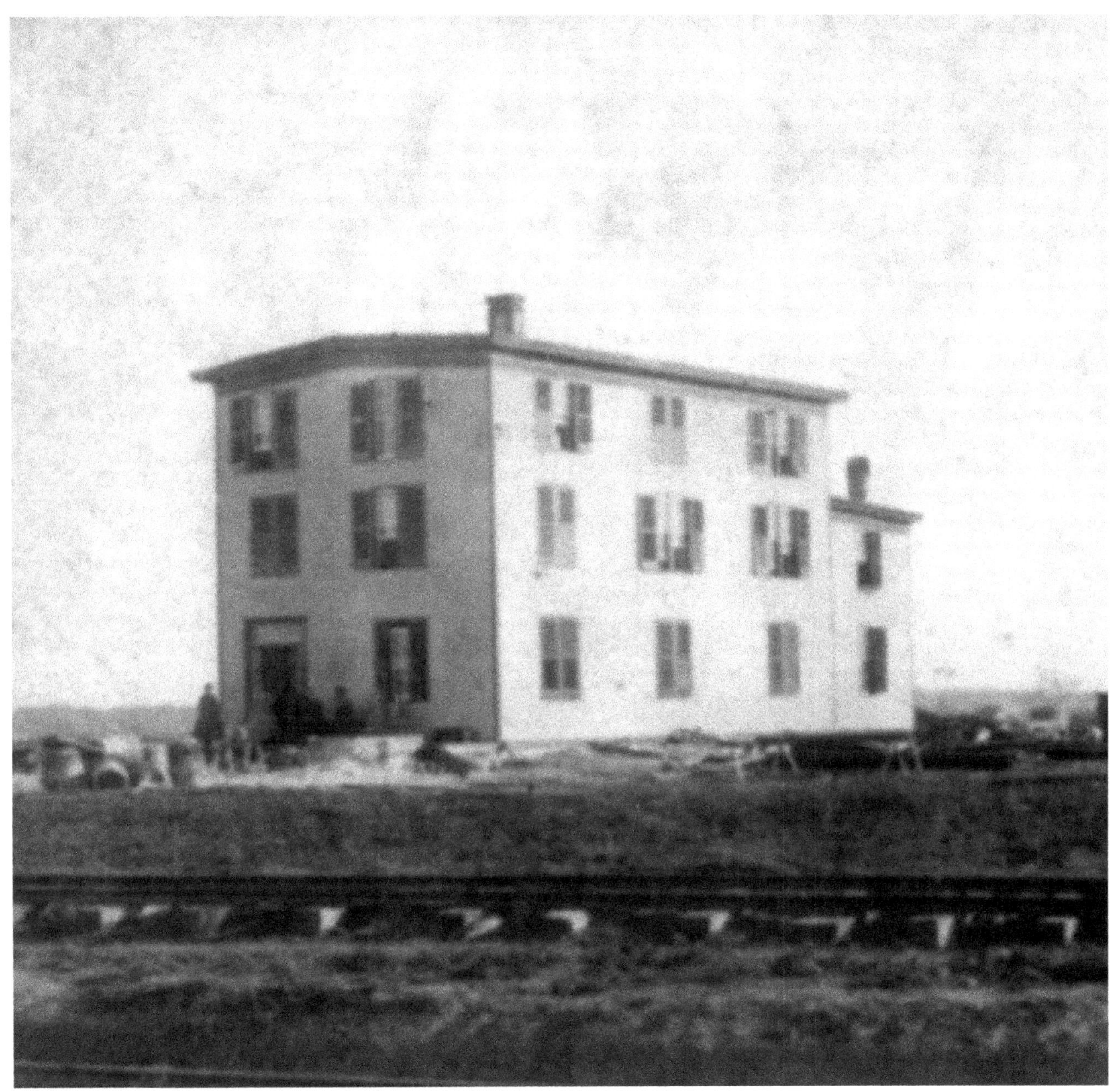

Not long after Joseph McCoy built this drover's cottage for his stockyards in 1867, Abilene, Kansas, became the original Old West cow town and one of the wildest. Both cowboy and badman when he arrived in town on the lam from Texas, John Wesley Hardin had already killed at least eight men by his eighteenth birthday.

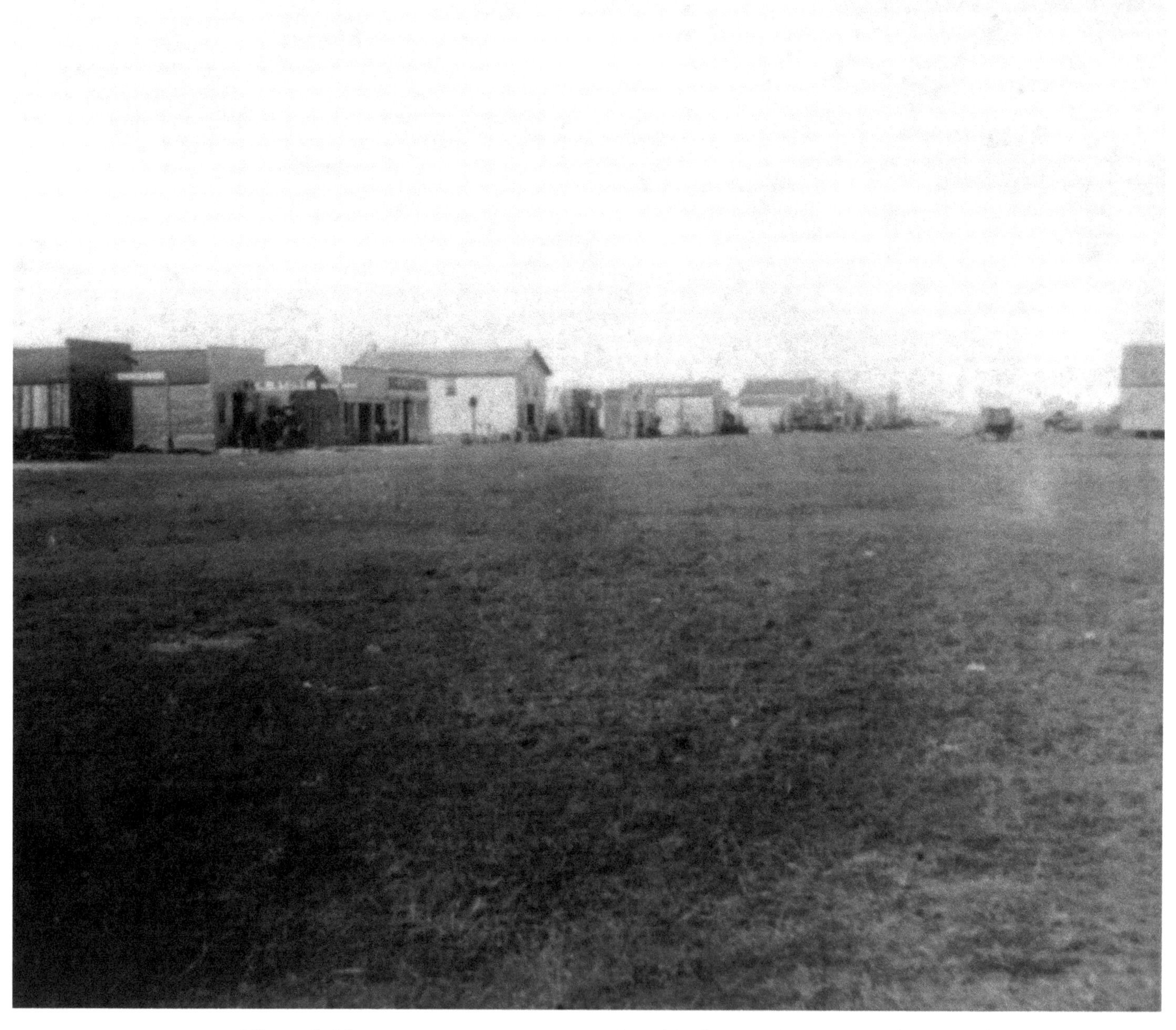

Ellsworth, Kansas, was not yet a cow town when this photograph was snapped in 1867, but when the Kansas Pacific Railroad arrived in 1872, Ellsworth was just as wild as its famous sisters Abilene and Dodge City. A year later, Sheriff Chauncey Whitney was accidentally killed during an argument with outlaw Ben Thompson, which set off a bloody battle between townsfolk and Texas cowboys.

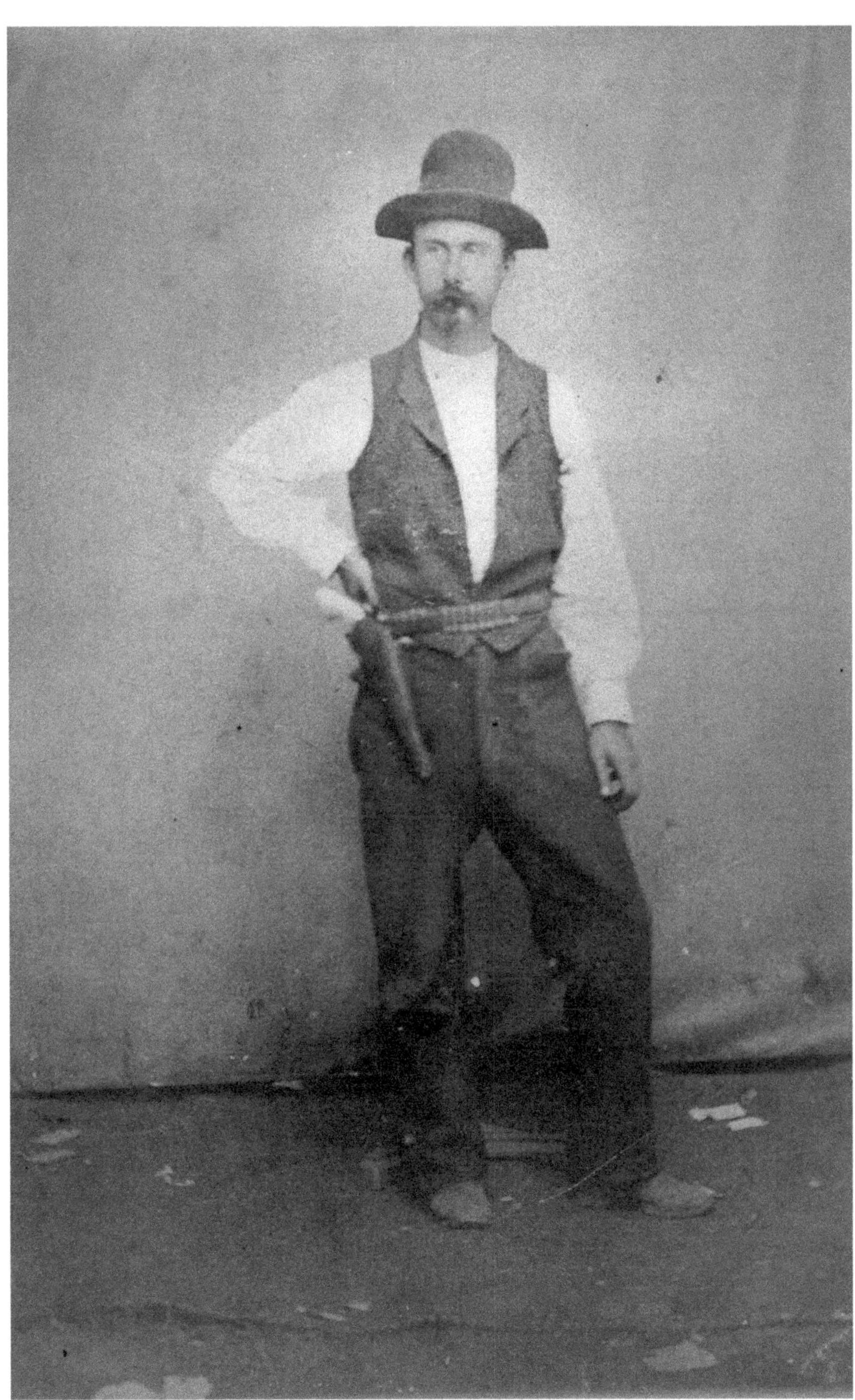

A former stage driver, Billy Brooks was a city marshal in Newton, Ellsworth, and Dodge City, but in 1874 he was caught stealing mules and was strung up by a mob of vigilantes. Later a story came out that Brooks was contracted by one stage company to run another out of business, and that after he was caught the rival stage stirred up the mob to hang him.

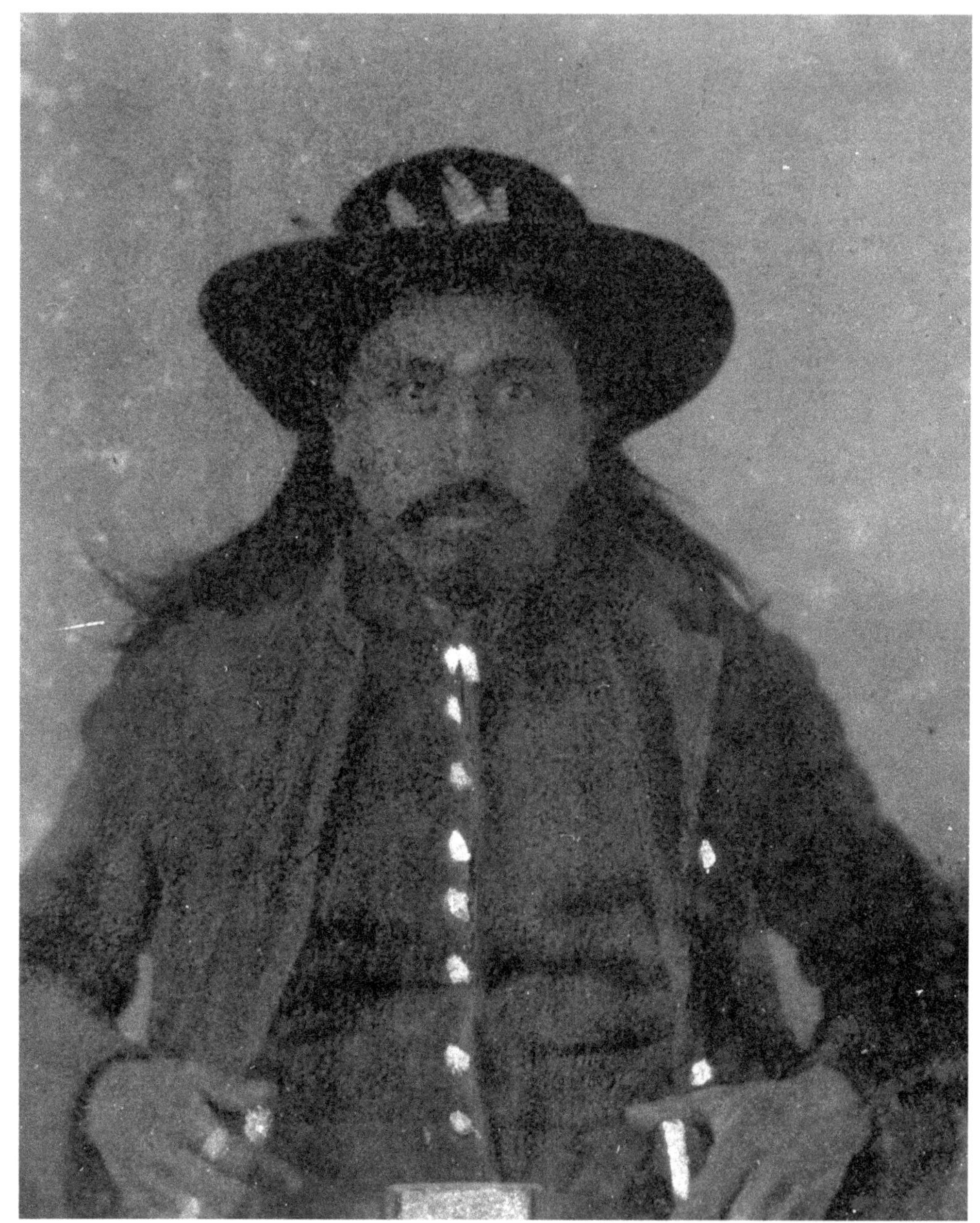

Undoubtedly one of the most colorful figures in Oklahoma history was Zeke Proctor, around whom the Going Snake Massacre of 1872—actually an epic gun battle in which eight deputy U.S. marshals were killed—was centered. For most of his life he was called an outlaw, but after receiving a pardon from President Grant, he became a Cherokee sheriff and a two-term deputy U.S. marshal.

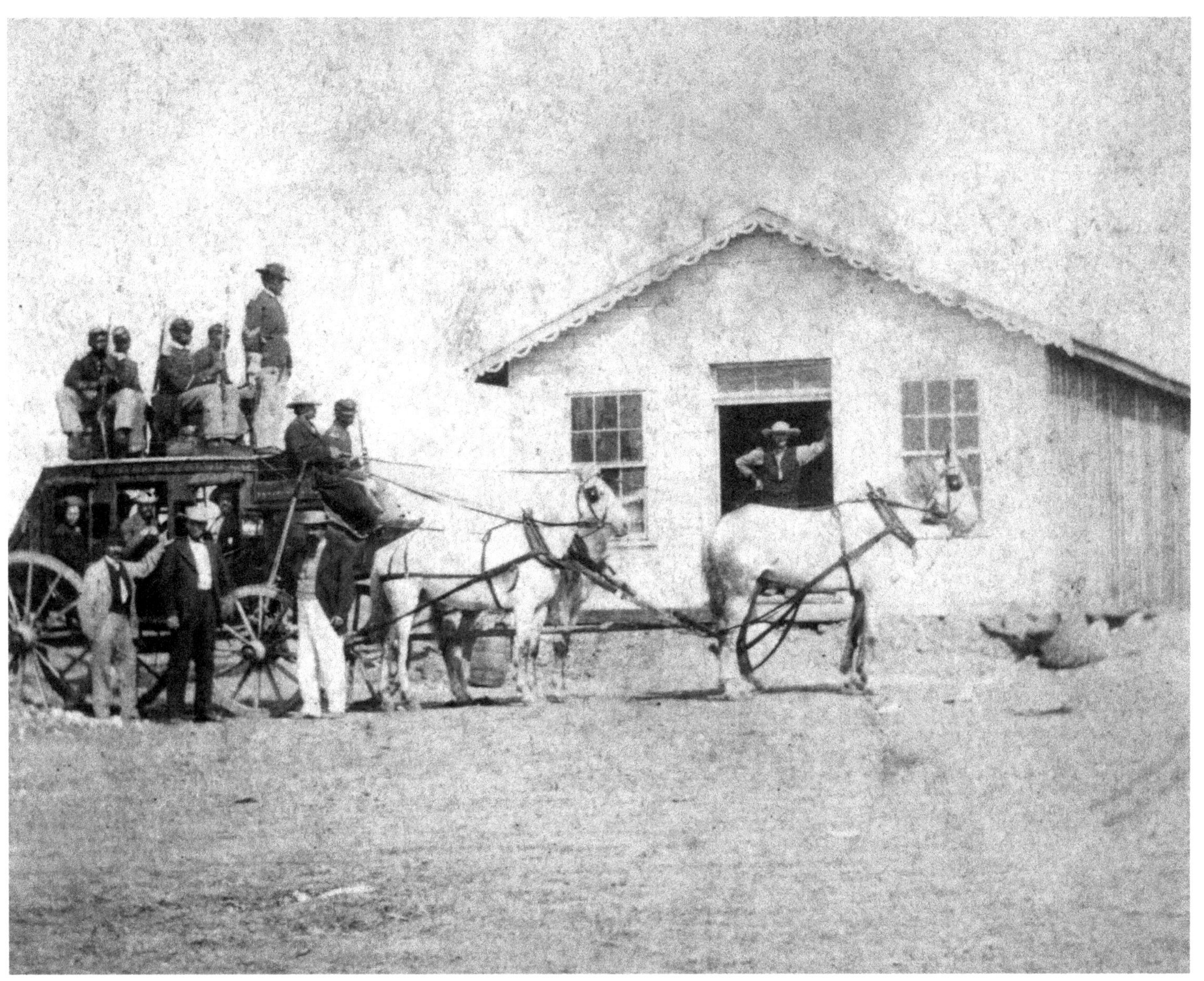

Overland stagecoaches were an extremely dangerous mode of travel in the Old West, presenting lucrative prizes for highwaymen and Indian raiders of the plains. Stops like this one at Fort Hays, Kansas, in 1867 allowed travelers to find a brief respite before setting out on another treacherous leg the next morning.

On the night of October 18, 1868, Laramie, Wyoming, suffered the throes of mob violence as vigilantes strung up the town's criminal ringleader and two of his associates at a saloon. A contemporary newspaper story contradicts modern opinion, but it is believed the three men seen here are Ed "Big Ned" Wilson, Con Wagner, and Ace Moore.

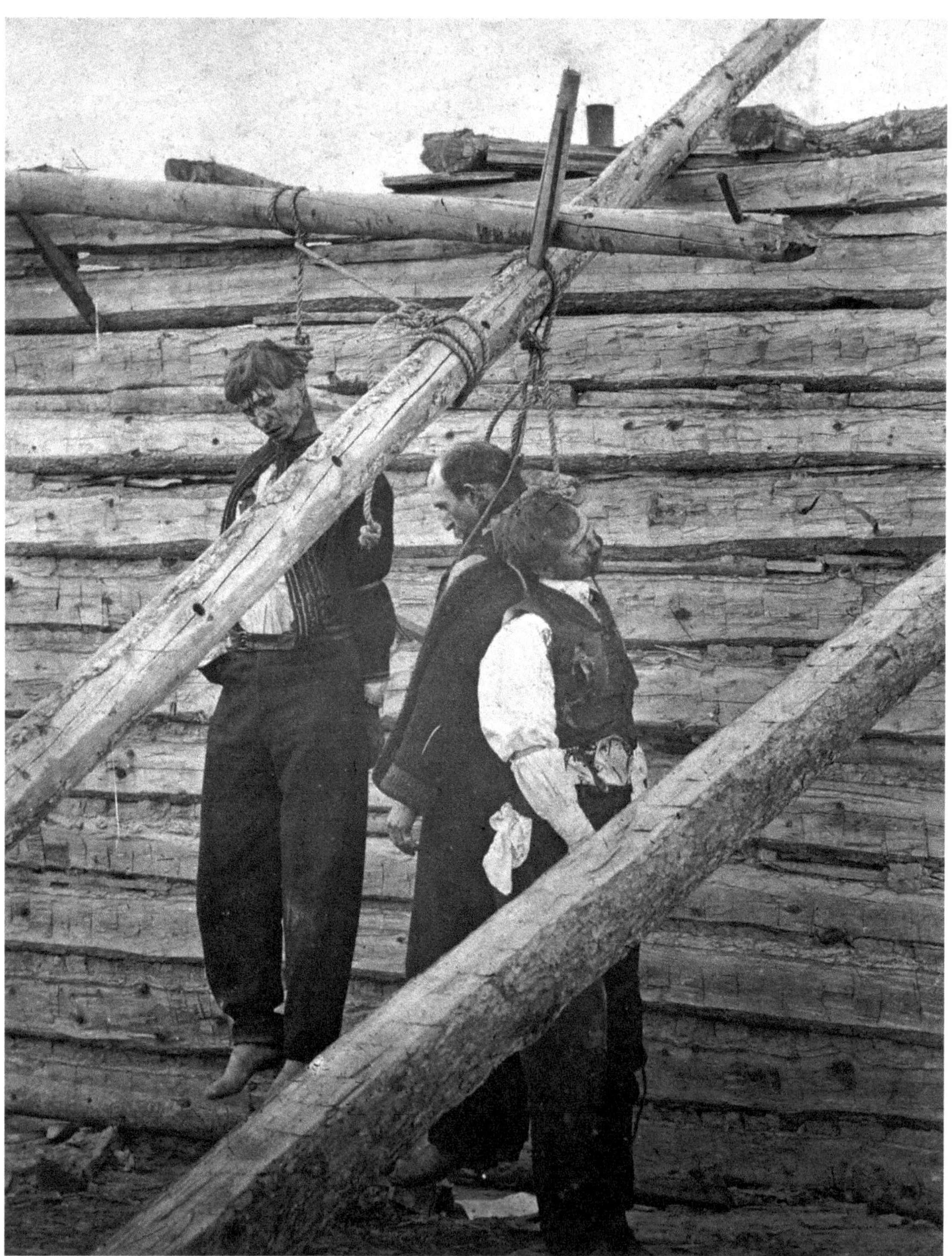

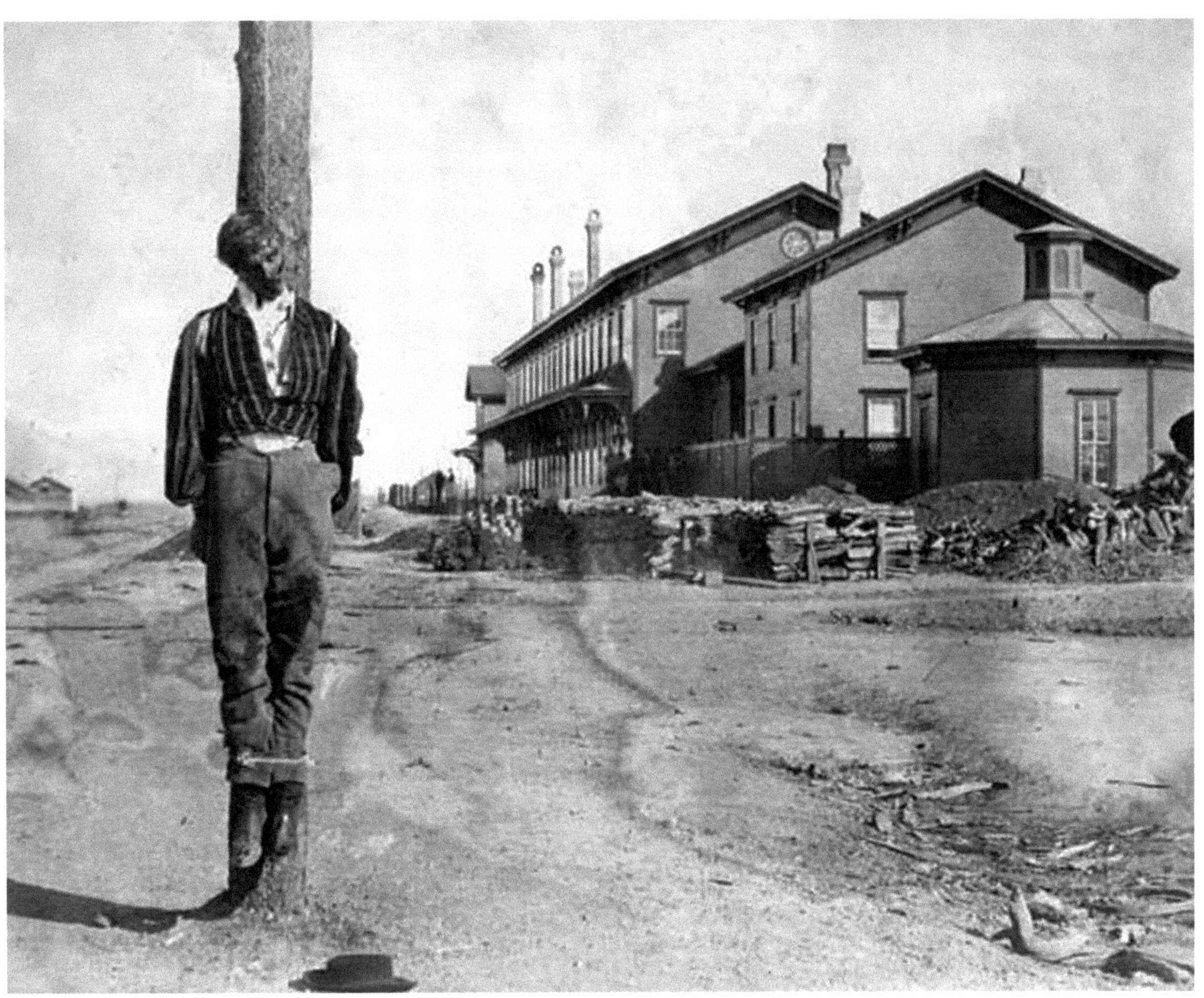

The next morning, as Laramie's vigilantes scoured the town for other lowlifes, most of the badmen promptly skedaddled, except for one the local paper described as "'Big Steve' Young, who defied them to do their worst." They did.

About the same time as the citizens of Laramie strung up "Big Steve" Young, their former mayor suffered the same fate at the hands of the citizens of Denver. Late out of prison for attempted murder in Wyoming, he murdered a Colorado man while robbing him. As he was being hauled to prison, a mob of nearly a hundred men stopped the wagon and attached him to a convenient tree.

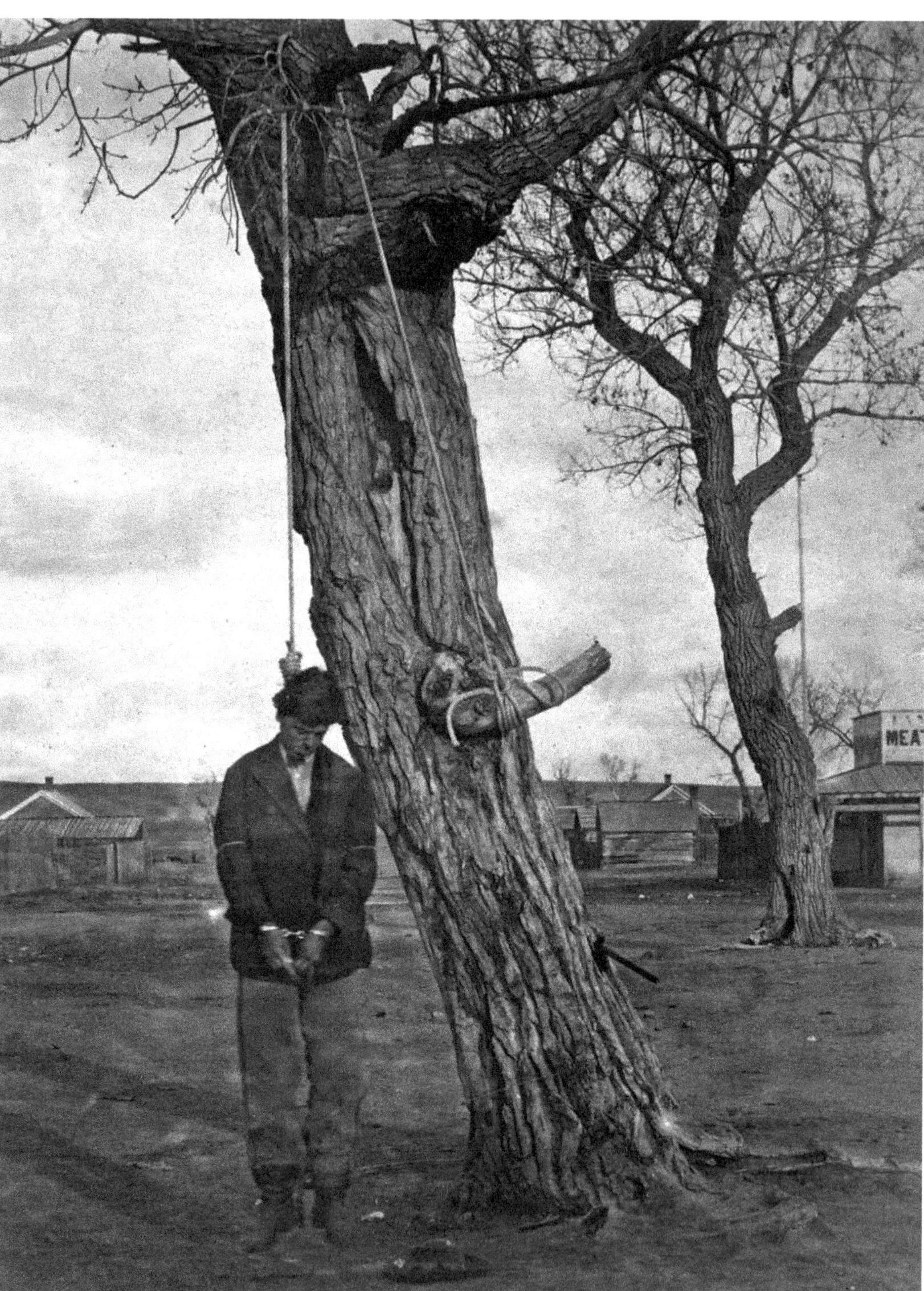

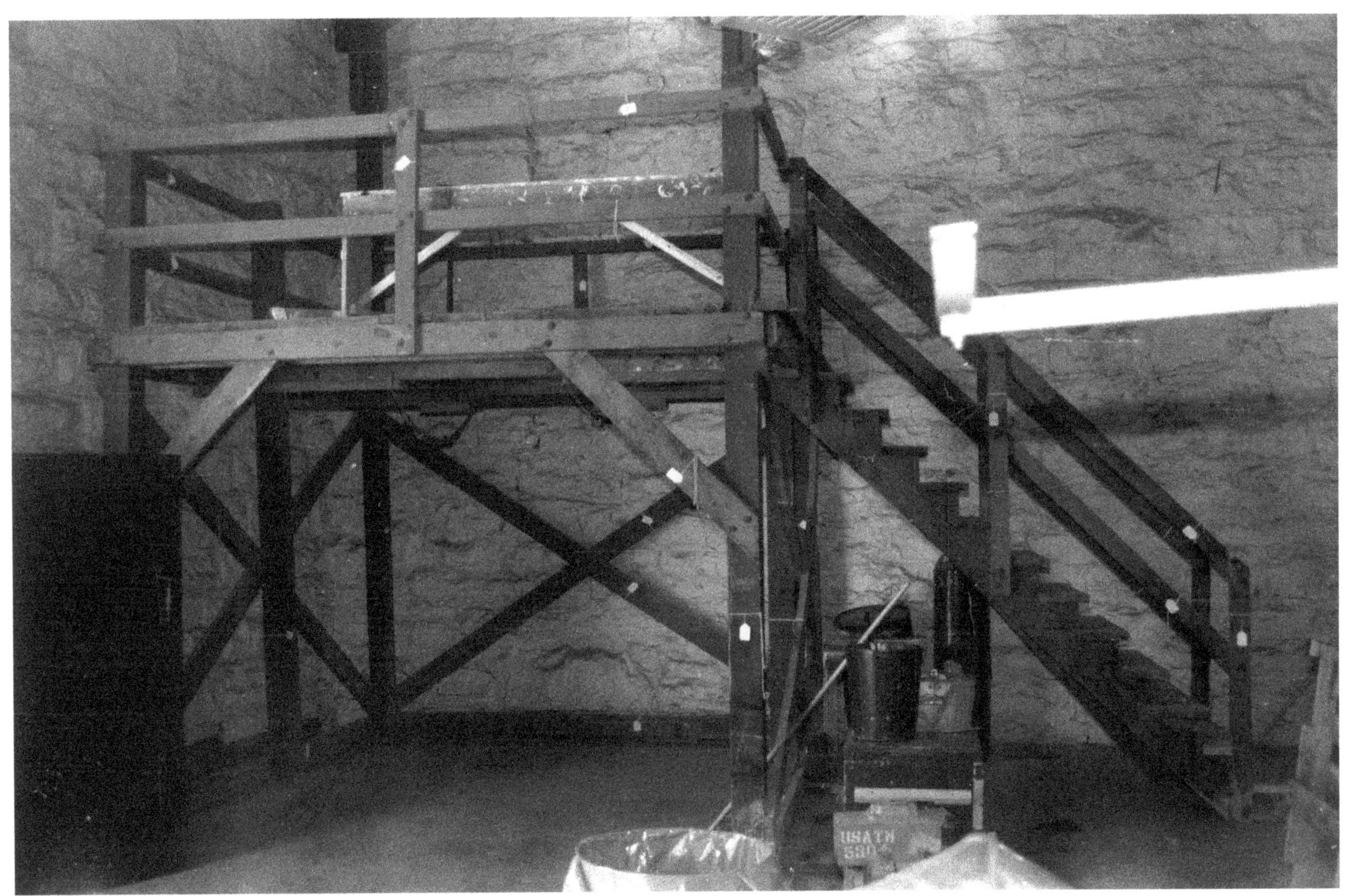

This photo depicts the gallows at the Kansas State Penitentiary in Lansing. Despite the violence of its cow towns and the many bank and train robberies visited upon its population, Kansas rarely exhibited the desire to execute its prisoners. Convicted murderer William Dickson was hanged from these gallows in 1870 and it would be 60 years before they were used again.

In late 1869, Frank and Jesse James rode into Gallatin, Missouri, about 50 miles from their hometown of Kearney, to rob the Davies County Bank (seen here). Jesse had a personal vendetta against the bank clerk there and upon entering the bank, Jesse murdered the man in cold blood while Frank took $500 from the drawers.

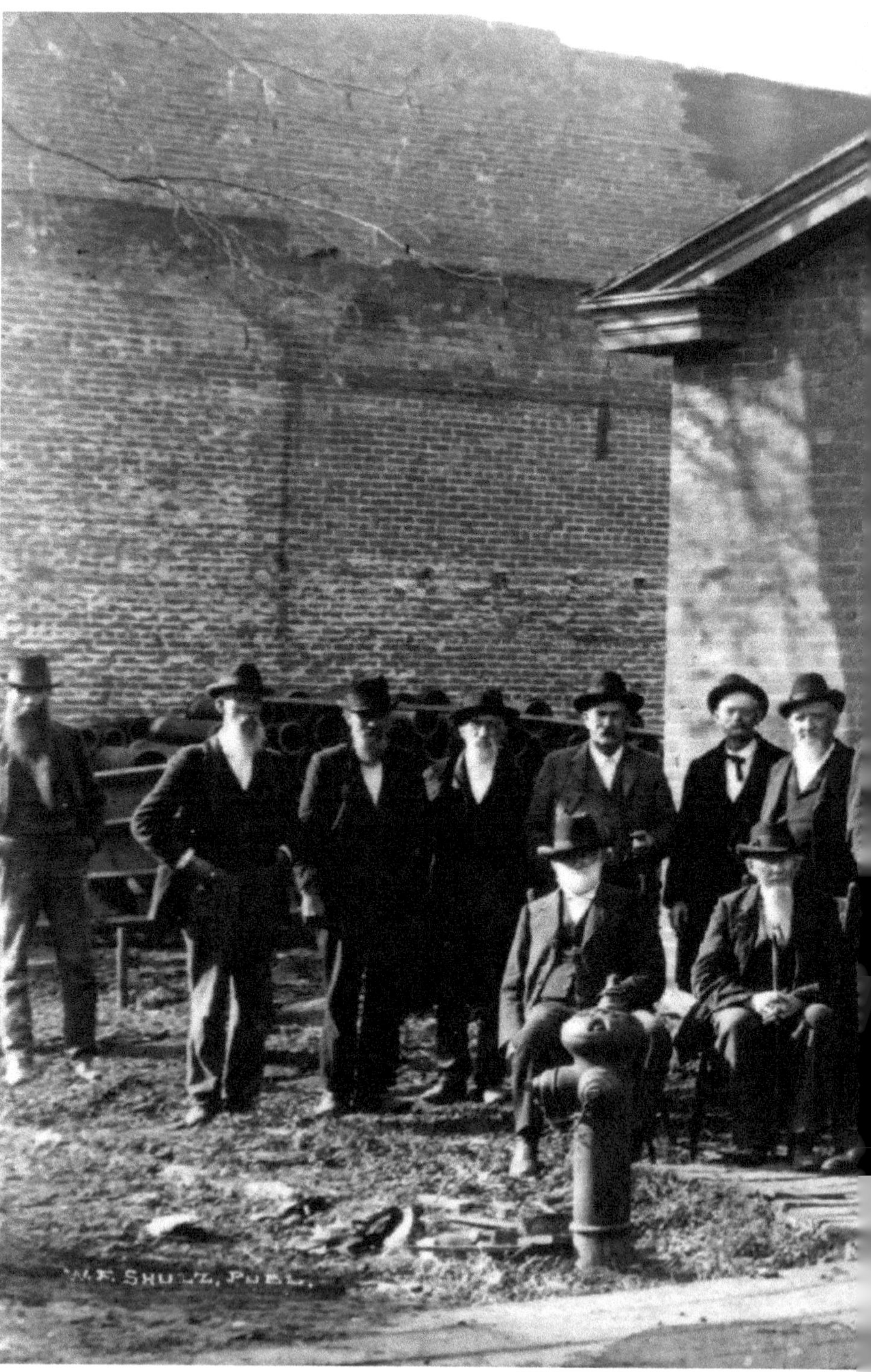

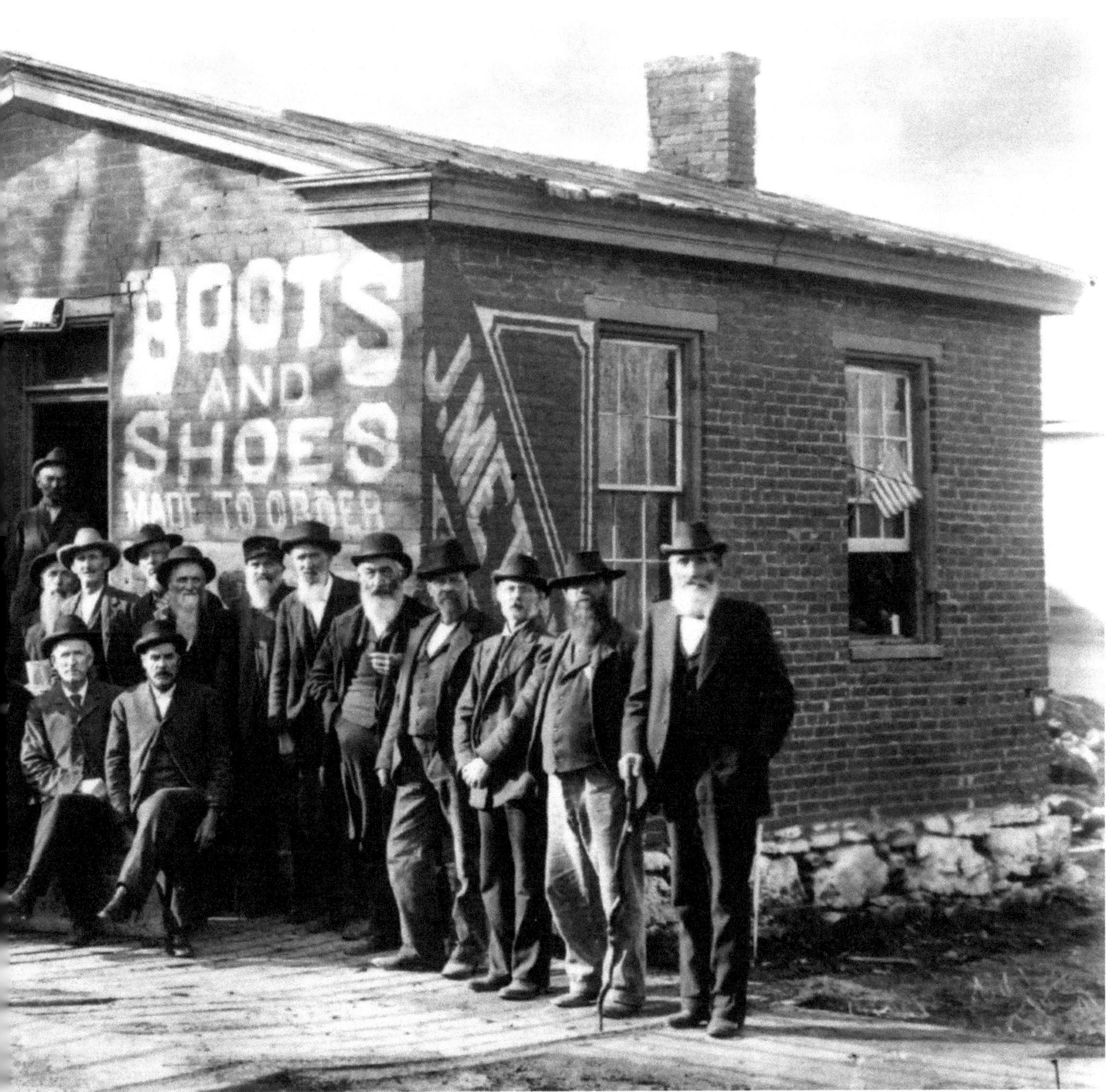
BOOTS
AND
SHOES
MADE TO ORDER

This is believed to be a photo of Jesse James in 1870 during an inactive period in the James Gang's career. After Frank, Jesse had joined Quantrill in 1864 and learned quickly the skills he would use as a bandit. The crossed pistols were one of his trademark looks and may have derived from his days with Quantrill when riders put extra pistols crossways in their shirts for quick access.

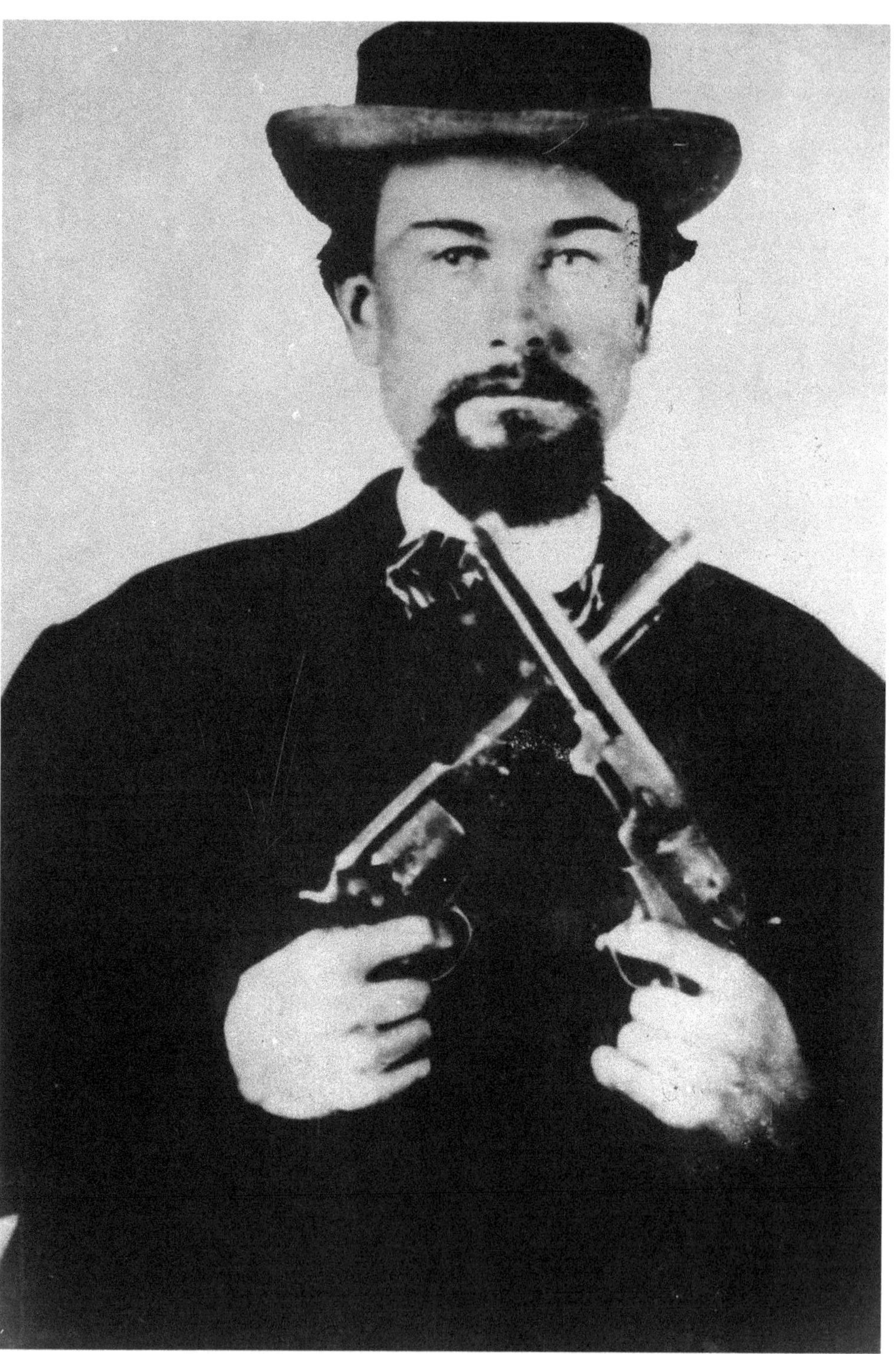

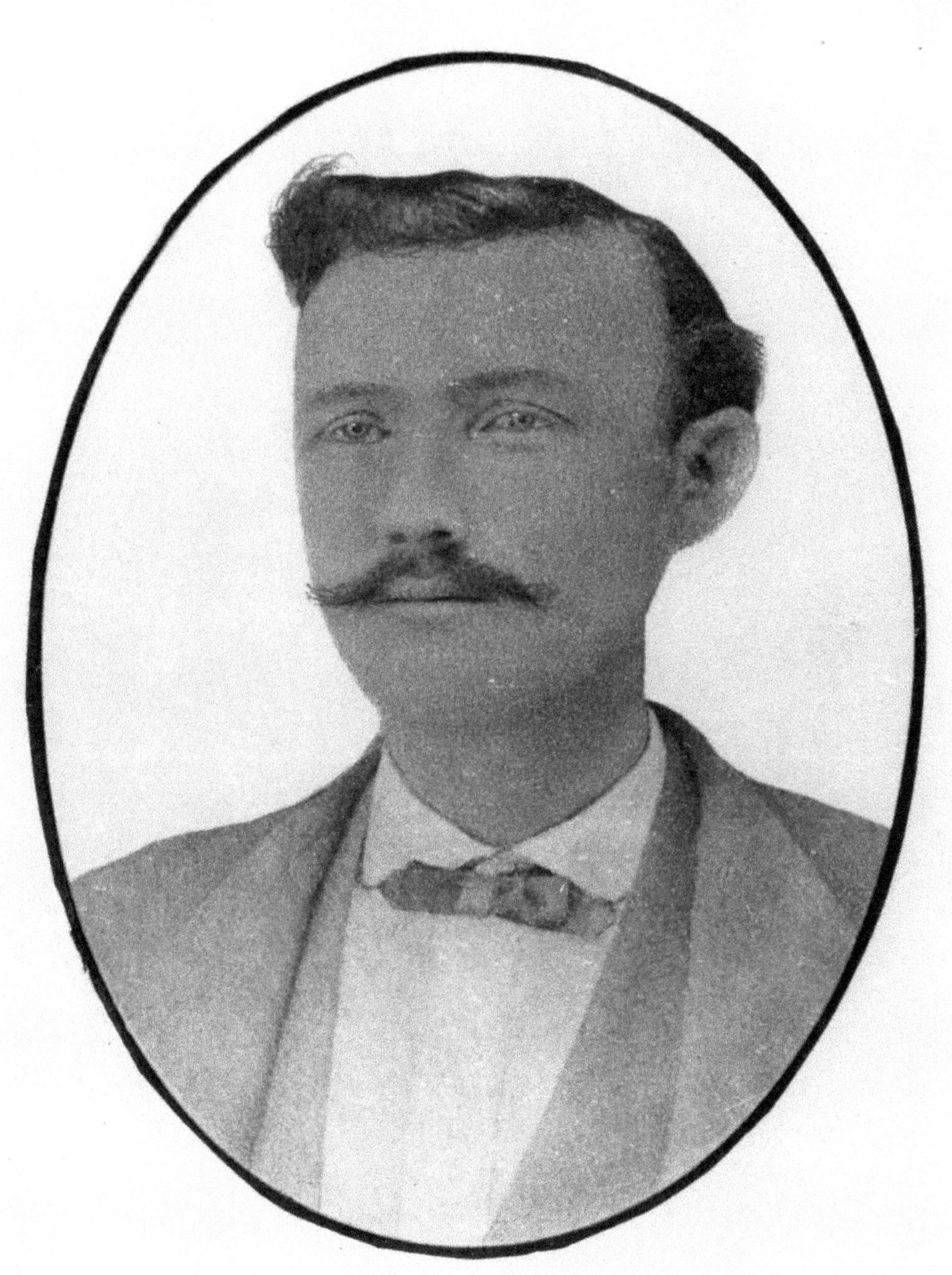

Billy Thompson (seen here in 1872), Ben Thompson's younger brother and likewise a gunfighter, was possessed of poor judgment and frequently needed his brother and friends like Bat Masterson to bail him out of his many jams.

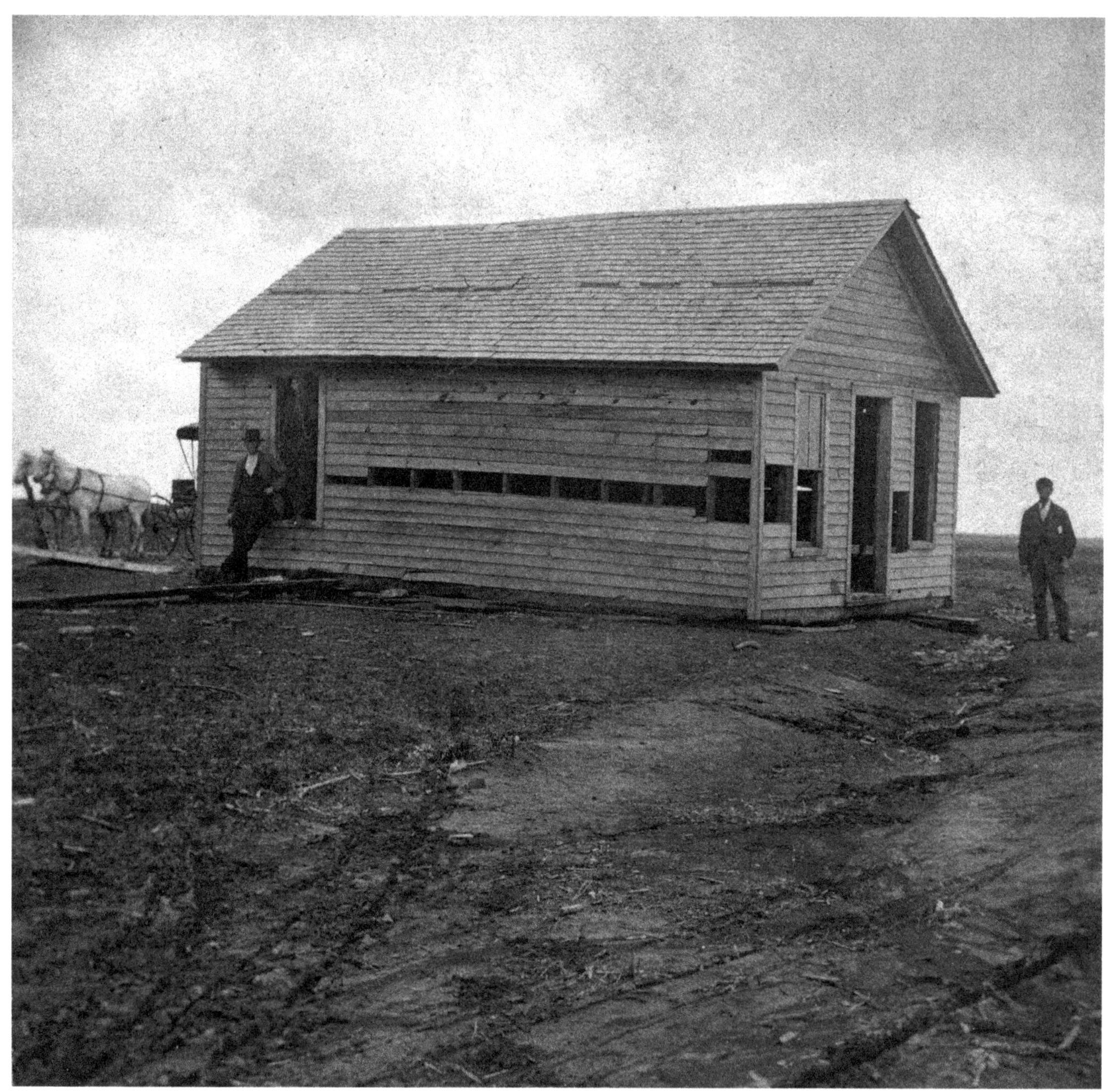

This is the scene at the Bender farm near Cherryvale, Kansas, in 1873. The remote farm was a way station for travelers in the area, but when several people were reported missing after visiting the farm, an investigation was launched.

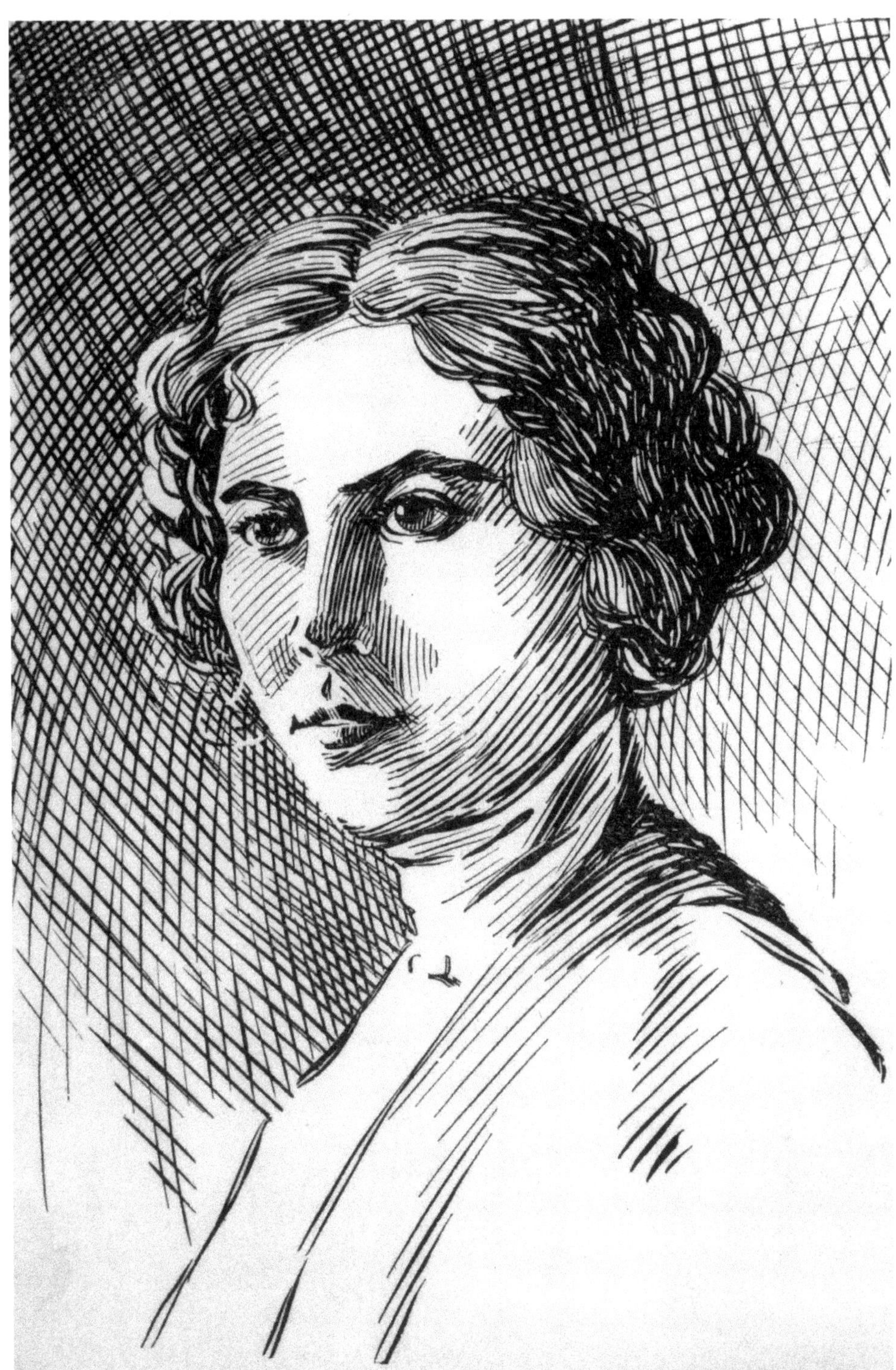

Kate Bender lived at the remote farm near Cherryvale with her father and advertised her services in the area as a clairvoyant with mystical healing powers. She distracted her victims with her beauty and charm while her family members delivered the death blow.

John Bender brought his wife, daughter, and son to the remote area of Kansas to carry out their heinous crimes. As victims sat with their back to a canvas sheet, distracted by daughter Kate, Bender would swing a heavy hammer down on the heads of the unfortunate travelers and pound the skull to a pulp.

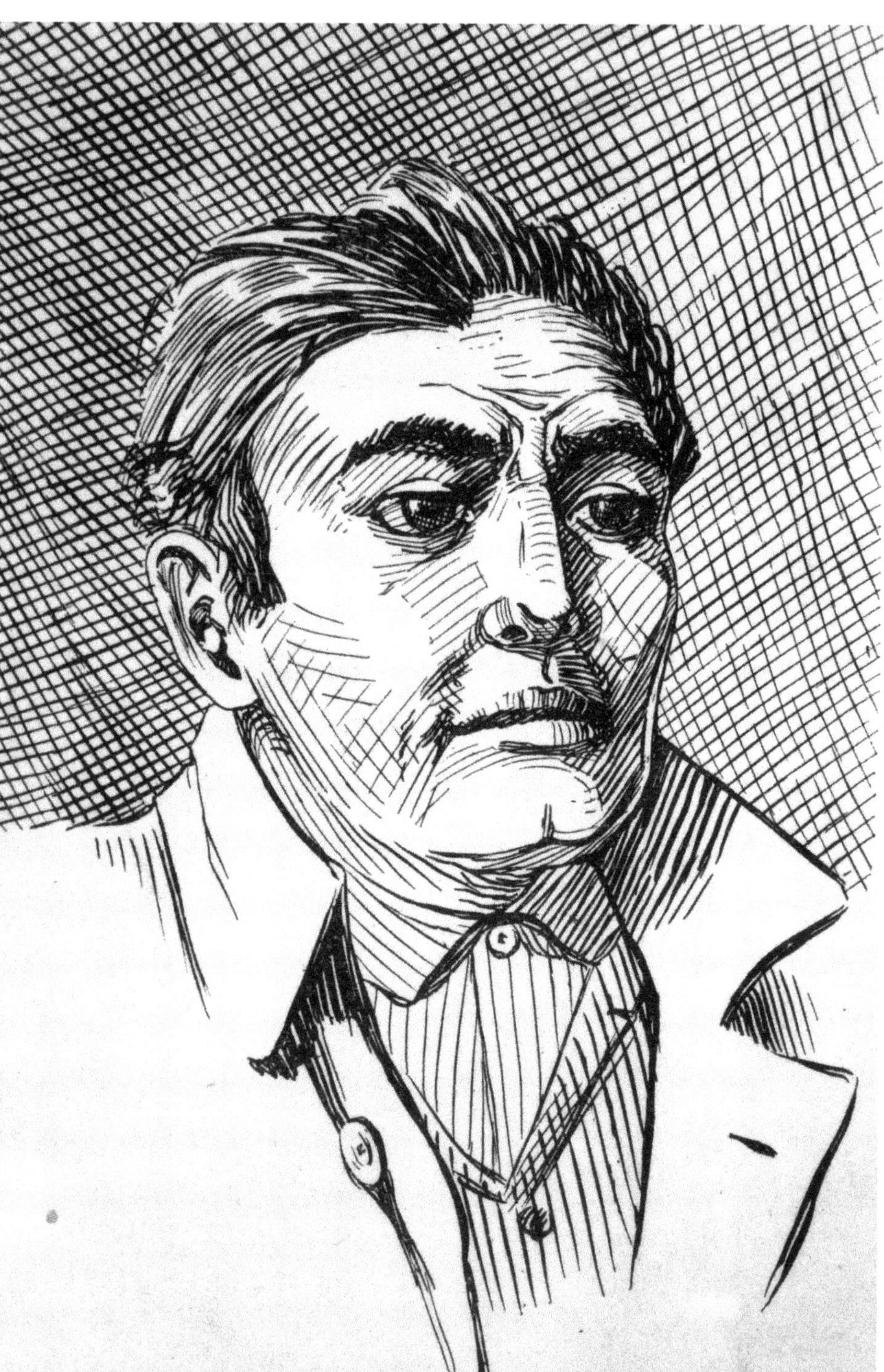

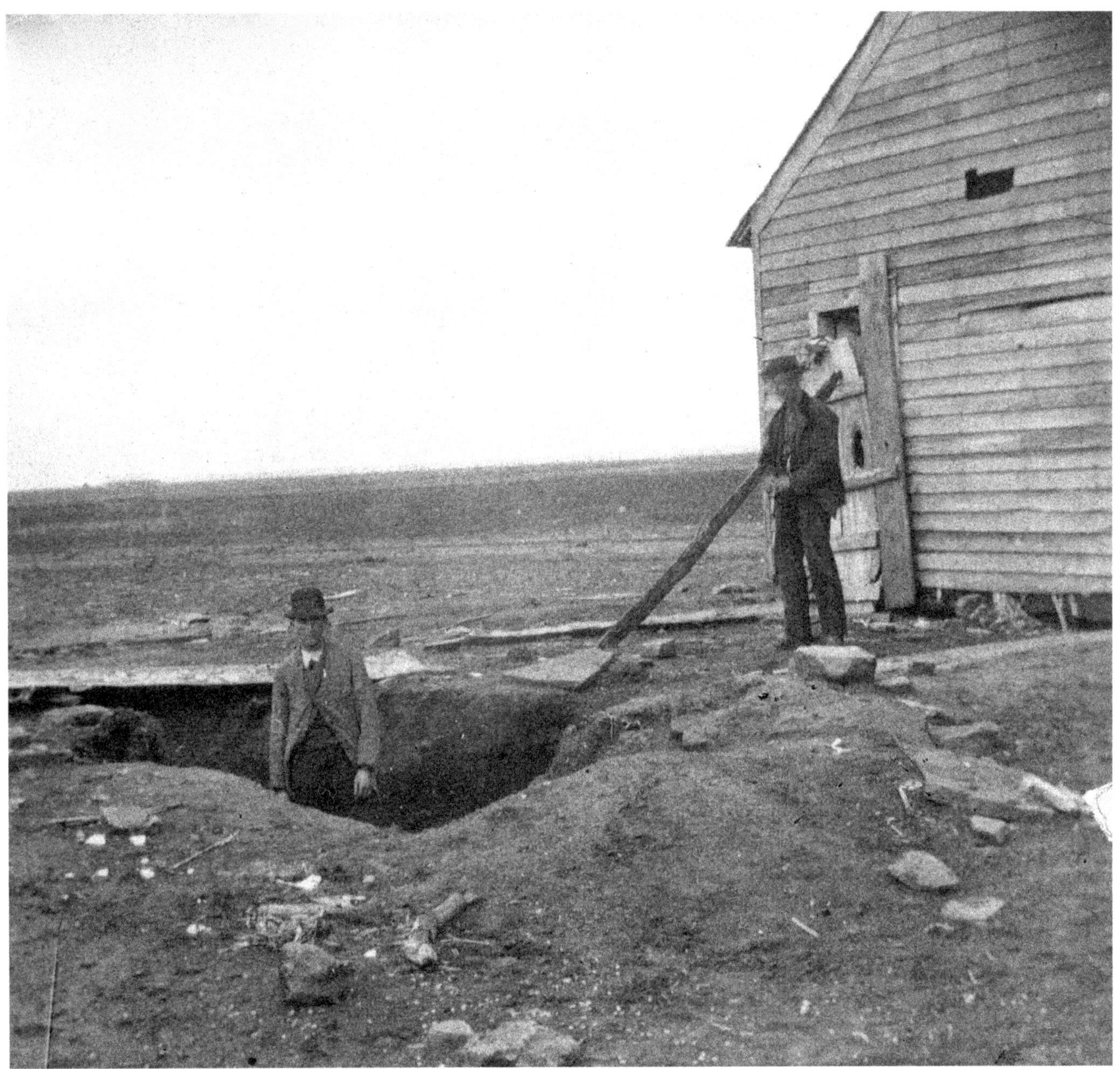

Because of the frequent traffic along the road past the Bender farm, a trapdoor was built in the floor of the house, through which bodies were dropped into a pit underneath. Then under cover of darkness, family members retrieved the bodies, slit the throat to ensure death, and took them out to be buried. In this view, the pit area is being excavated. Authorities would find a large amount of congealed blood.

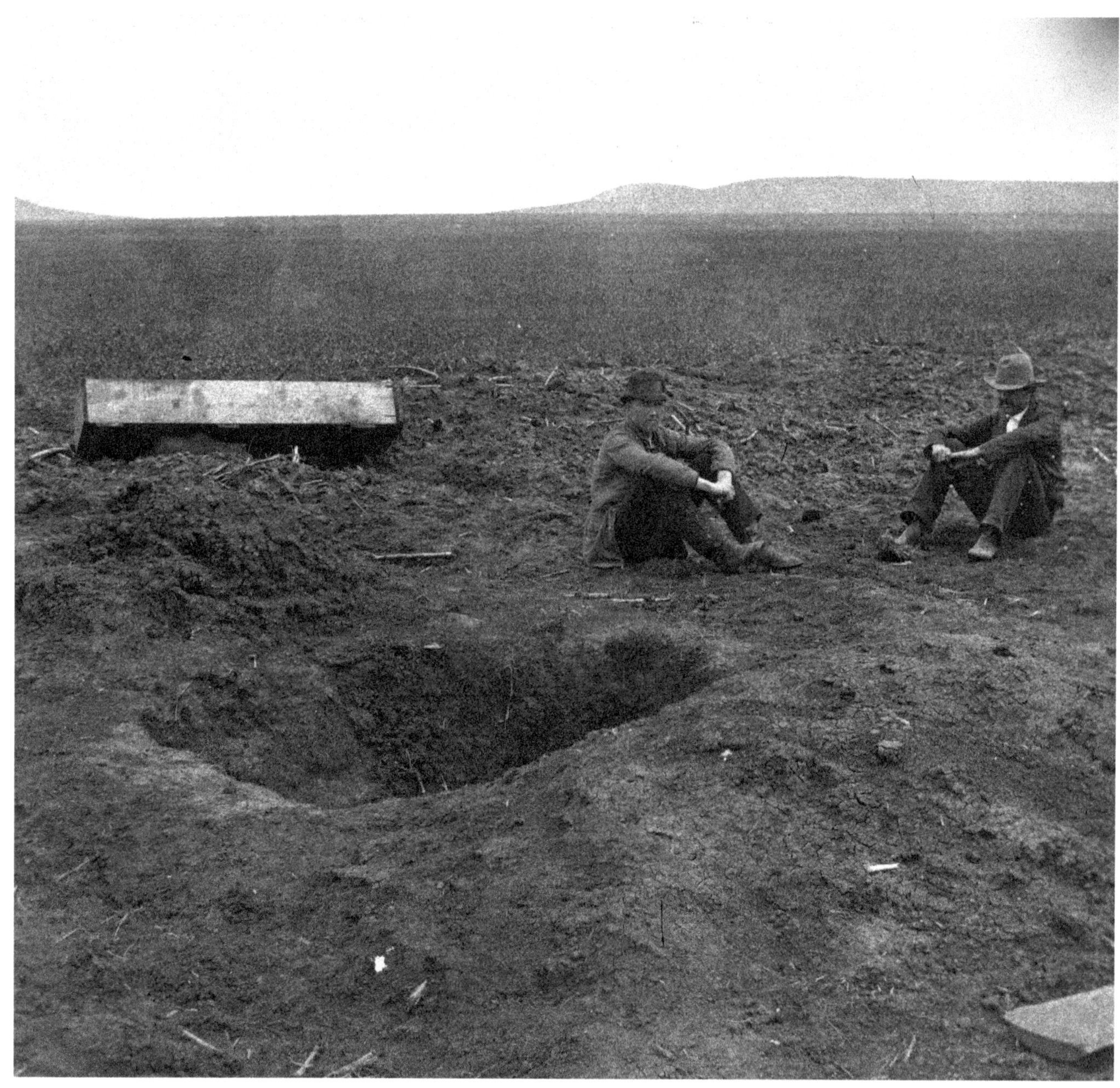

Investigators excavated the area around the Bender house and discovered the remains of 11 people. Two of the discoveries were little girls, who appeared to have died horrible deaths—one of them a baby who died of suffocation when her mutilated father was thrown on top of her in their grave.

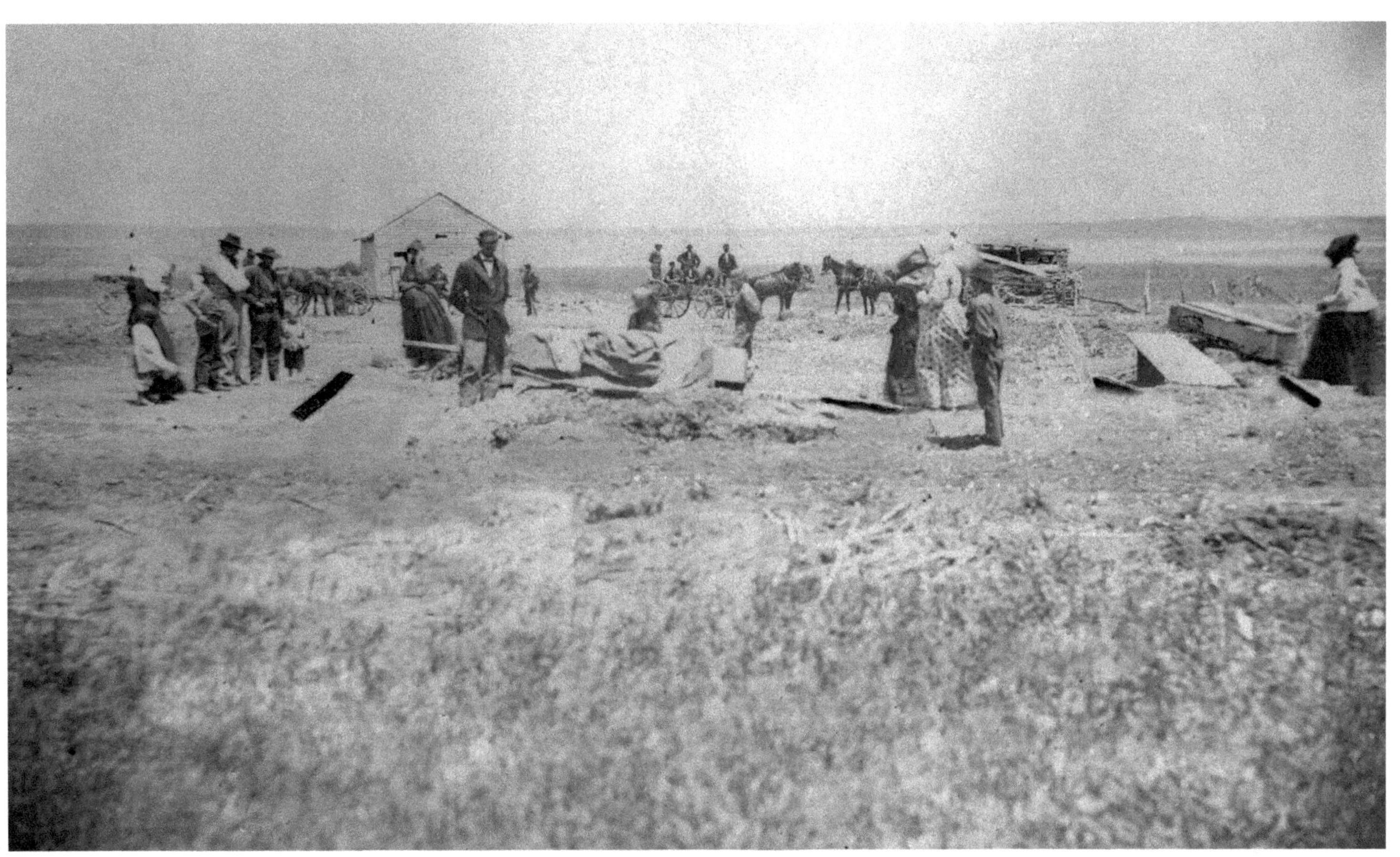

A view of the grave excavations at the Bender farm in Kansas. The Benders fled immediately when they came under suspicion and left all their possessions behind. They were never heard from again. It was generally assumed they made their escape, but some documentary evidence remains which suggests that vigilantes quickly caught them and killed them and never spoke of the tragedy again.

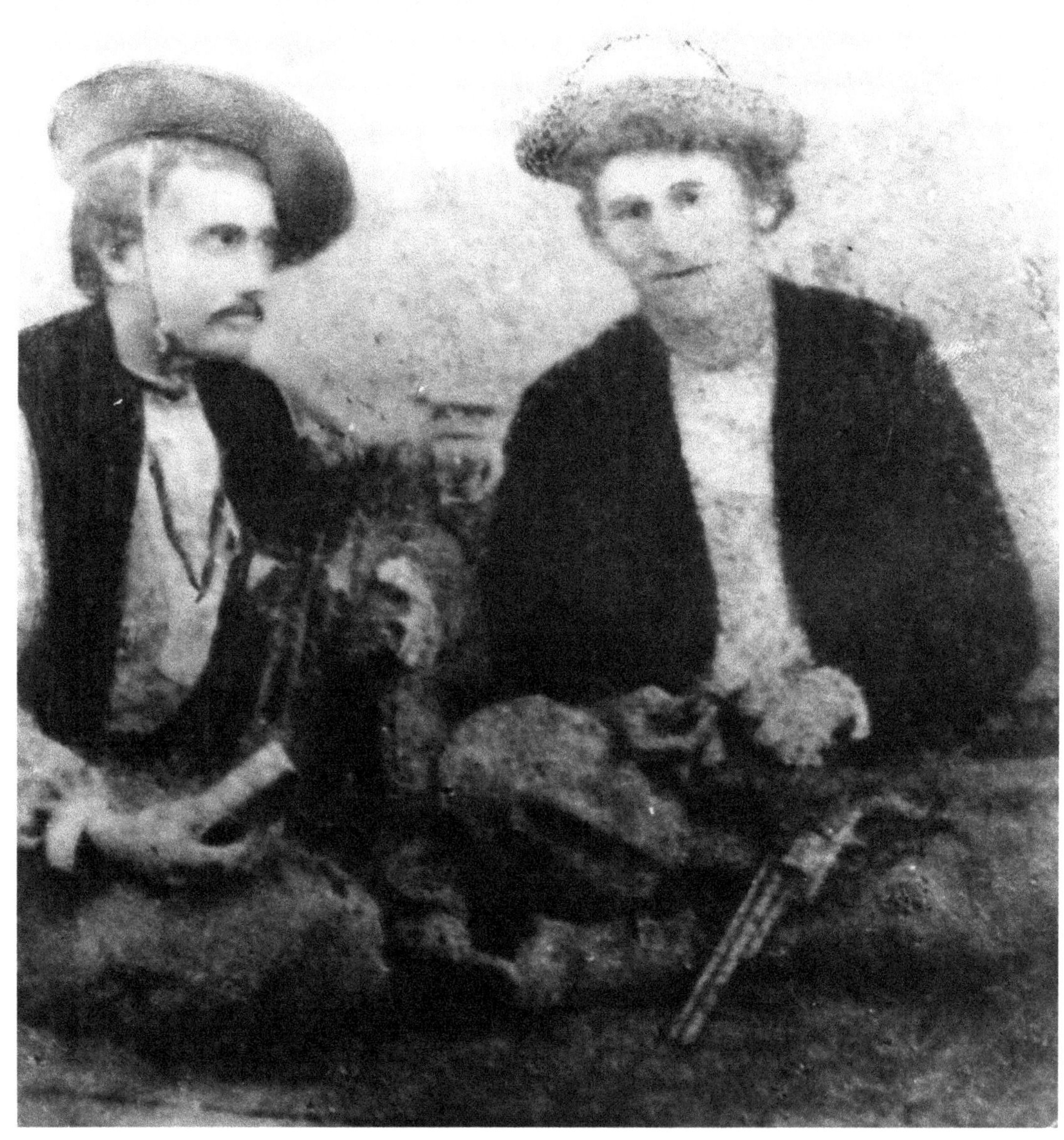

Gunman King Fisher (at left, in 1873) fit the mold of the sociopath one often finds in western tales. Orphaned young and raised by cowboys in south Texas, he was blessed with superior gunfighting skills and had no qualms about killing anyone who offended him, especially when it came to his flamboyant clothing. After dodging a prison sentence in 1876, he turned lawman and used his skills for law and order.

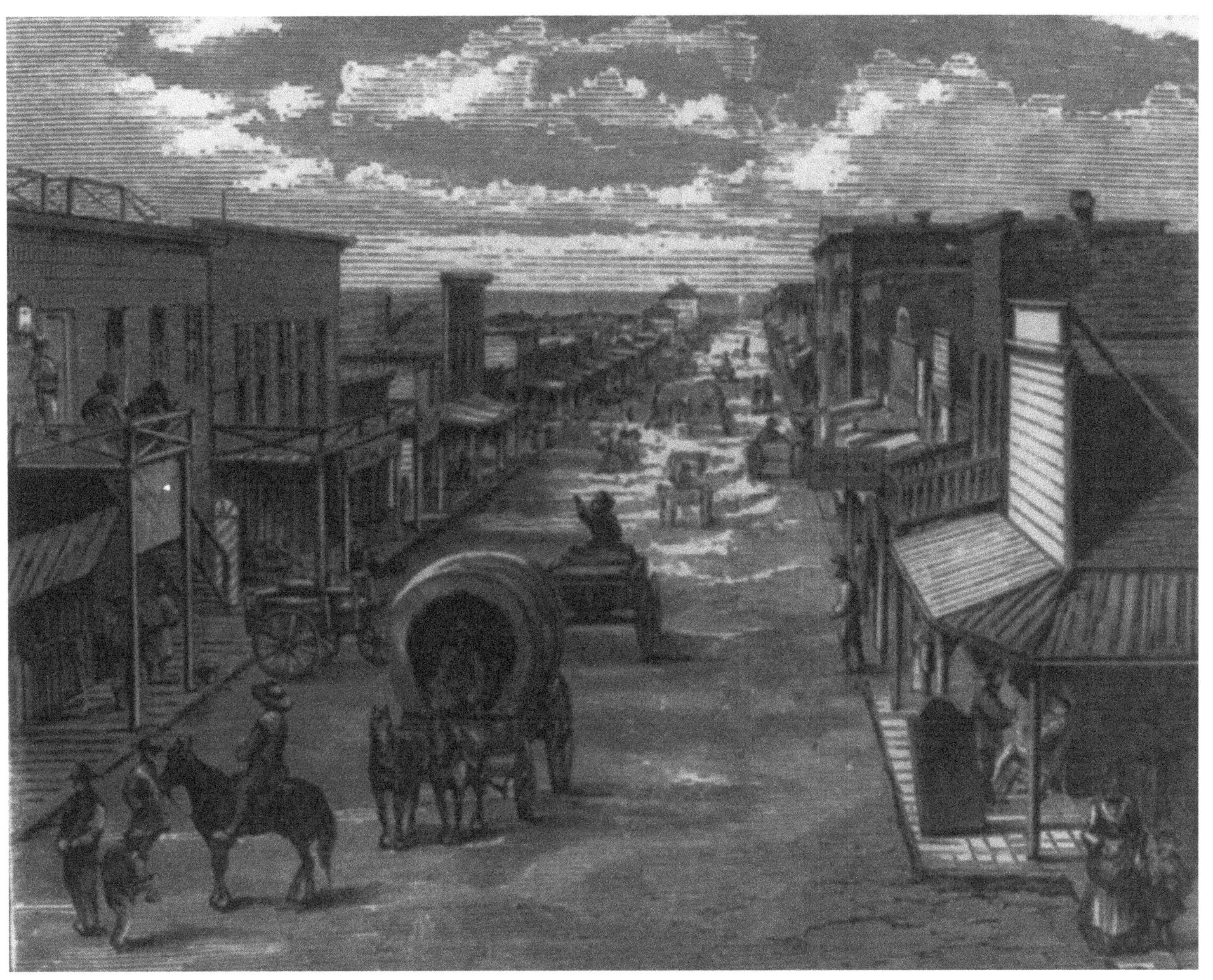

Wichita was established in 1870 as a stop on the Chisholm Trail, which brought cattle from Texas to the railroads in Kansas, but when a railhead was built there a few years later, it became one of the wildest cow towns in Kansas. This is the scene in 1874, about the time lawman Wyatt Earp arrived to help tame it.

Dapper Luke Short is high on the list of cold-blooded killers in the Old West. He was primarily a gunfighter and gambling operator who refused to let anyone come between him and maximum profit. He settled many debts with a revolver and was known as a quick draw who shot first. He befriended Wyatt Earp in Dodge City and partnered with him there and in Tombstone in the gambling business.

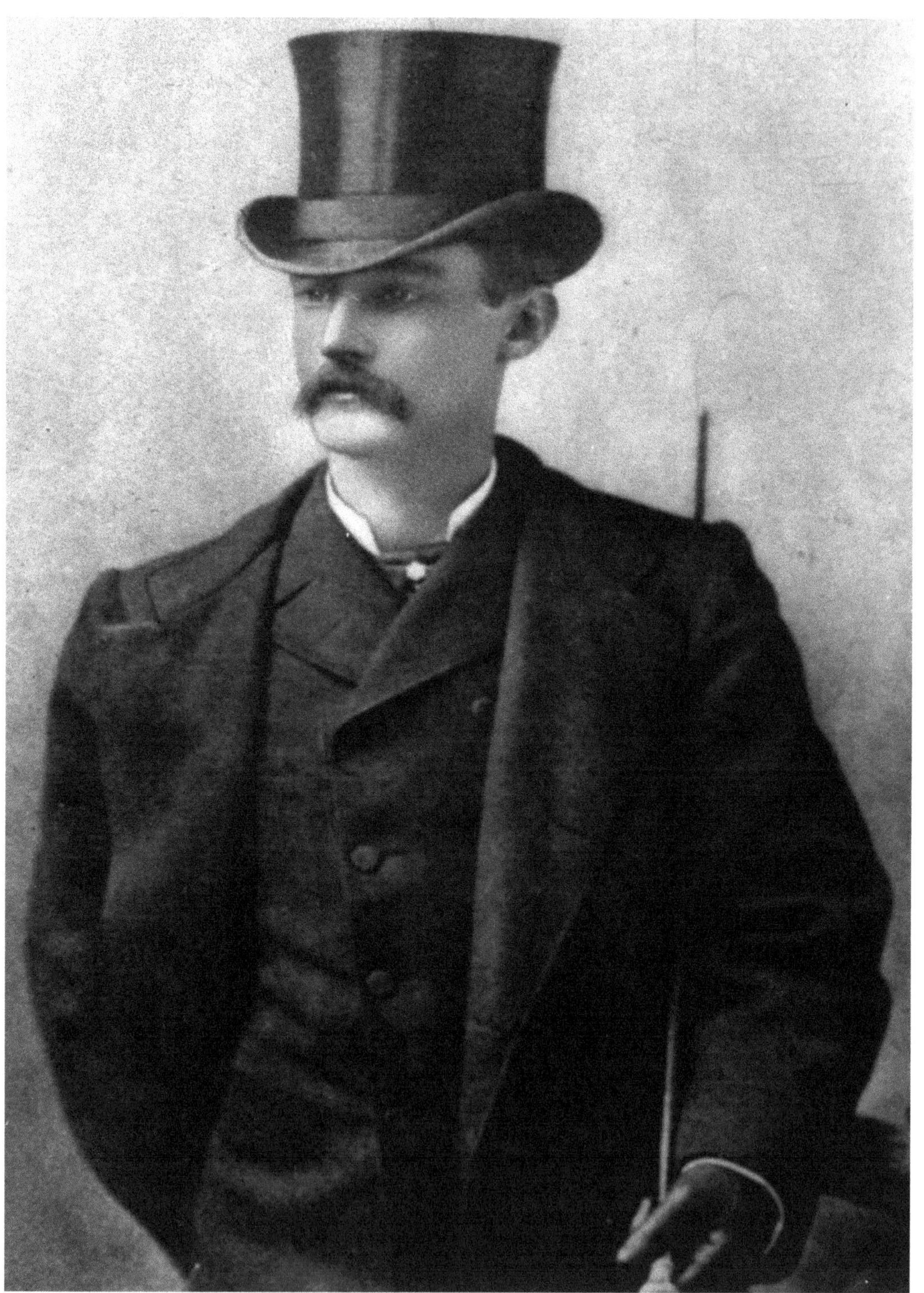

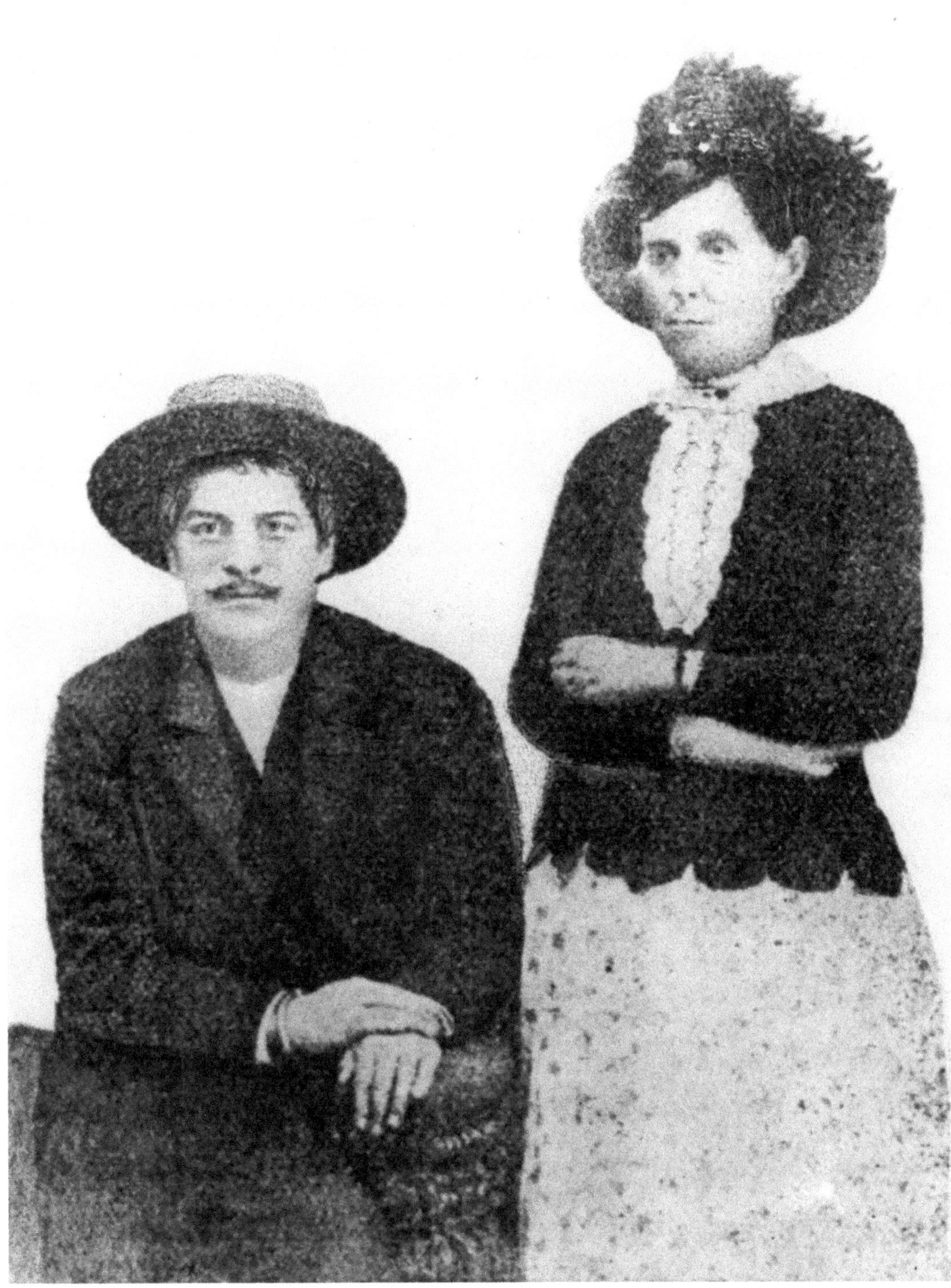

Though Belle Starr is today generally regarded with sympathy, crime historian Jay Robert Nash is of the stated opinion that she was "nothing more than a petty horse thief, an ugly harridan who used her gunfighter husbands to shoot down individuals she disliked."

The outlaw Younger brothers pose with their sister for a family photograph sometime in the 1870s. Clockwise, Henrietta, Cole, Jim, and Bob.

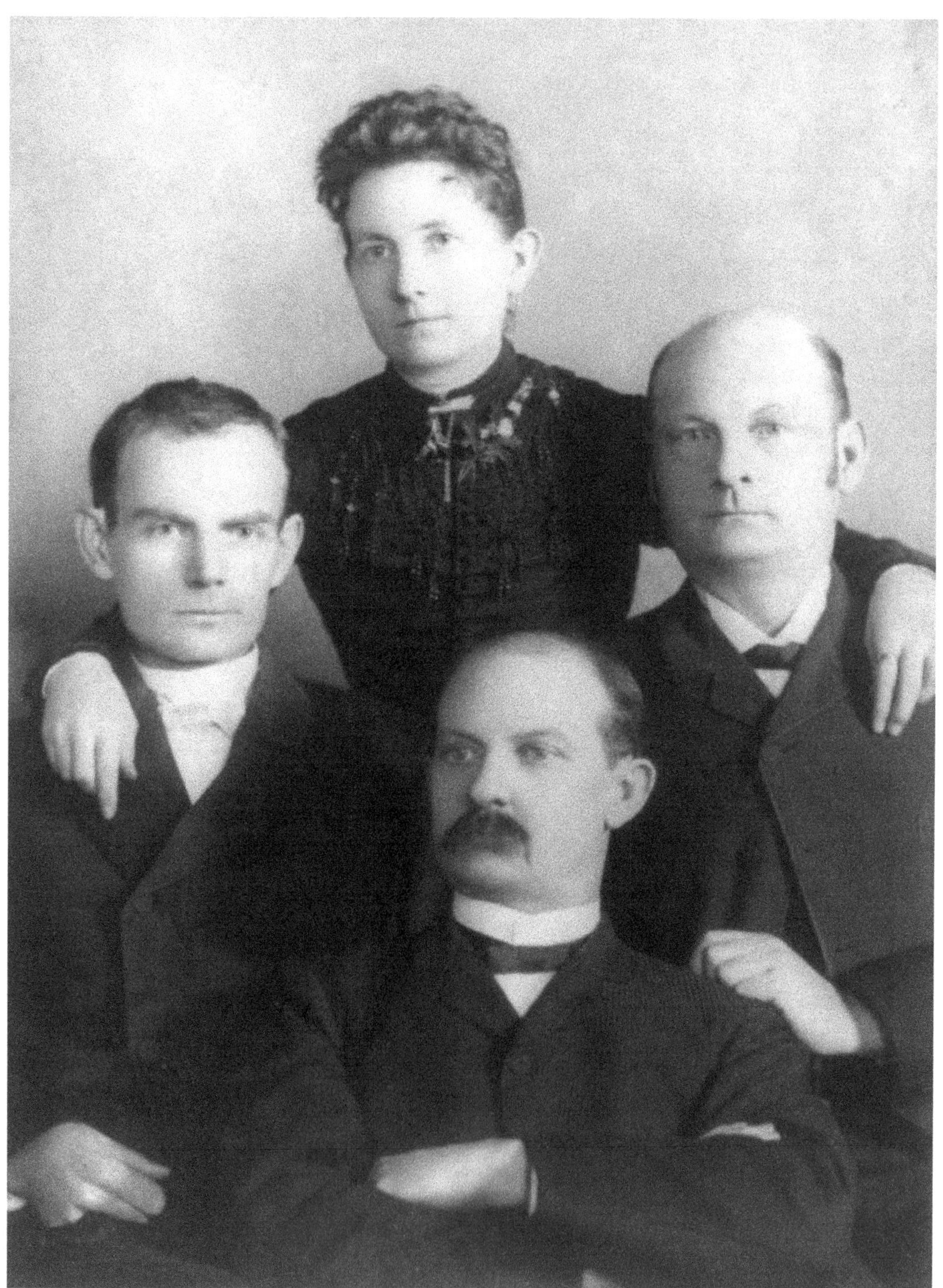

FIVE HUNDRED DOLLARS

REWARD!

WELLS, FARGO & CO.

WILL PAY

FIVE HUNDRED DOLLARS,

For the arrest and conviction of the robber who stopped the Quincy Stage and demanded the Treasury Box, on Tuesday afternoon, August 17th, near the old Live Yankee Ranch, about 17 miles above Oroville. By order of

J. J. VALENTINE, Gen'l Supt.

Oroville, August 18, 1875.

RIDEOUT, SMITH & CO., Agents.

In the summer of 1875, Colonel A. W. von Schmidt and his friends were traveling in a northern California stagecoach when a bandit forced it to stop. Typically, robbing stages was easy money, but this time the colonel slipped out of the coach with his own pistol and surprised the bandit. Although the robber got away, the colonel received a $1,200 watch from Wells Fargo for his efforts.

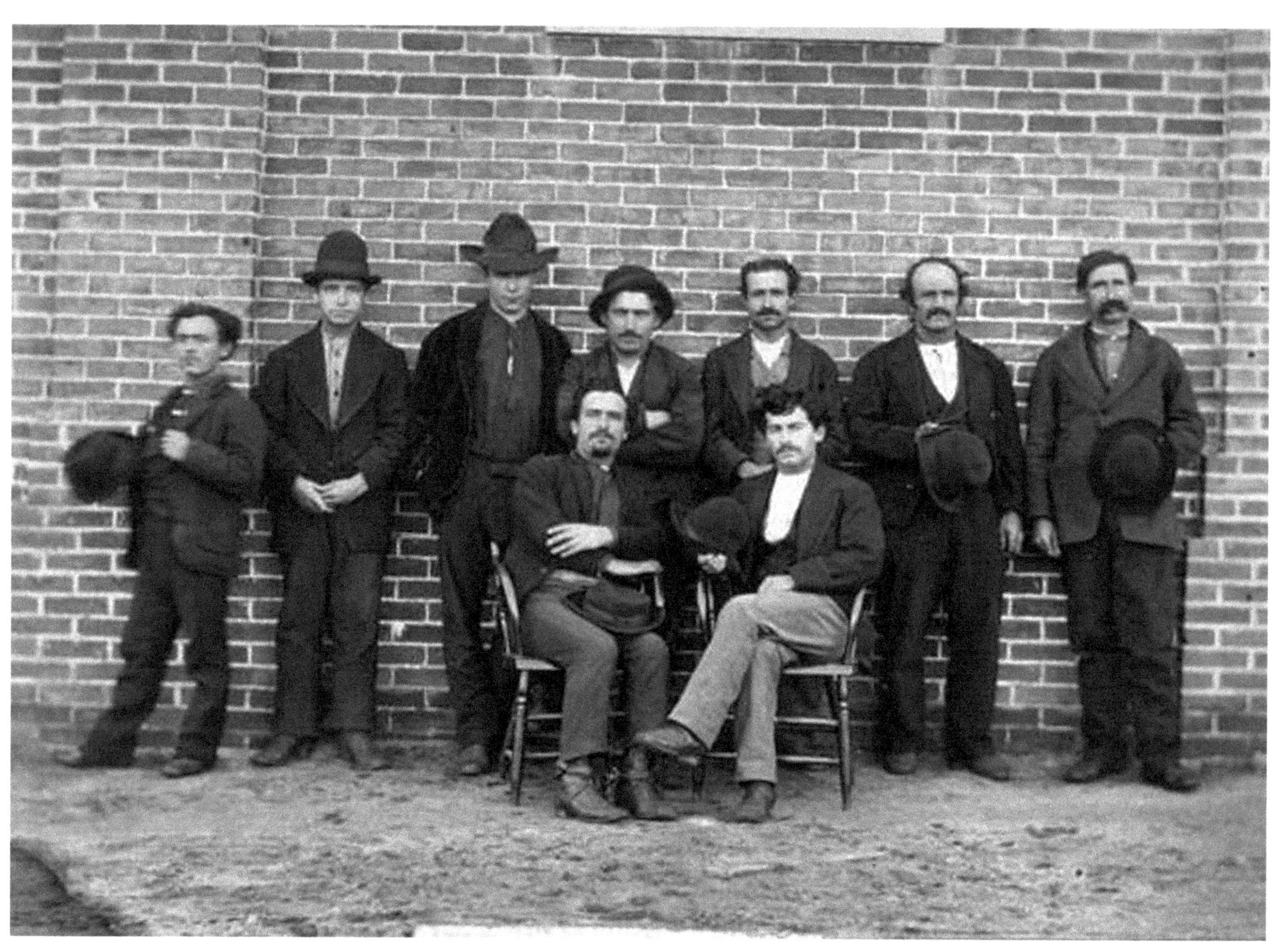

In a celebrated case in Denver in 1875, Filomeno Gallotti (at far-left) and his associates, known as the Italian Banditti, were tried for the gruesome murders of four fellow Italians. The trial revealed an intricate web of criminal activity led by Gallotti, but because of a loophole in Colorado's young legal system, he escaped the hangman and received a life sentence instead.

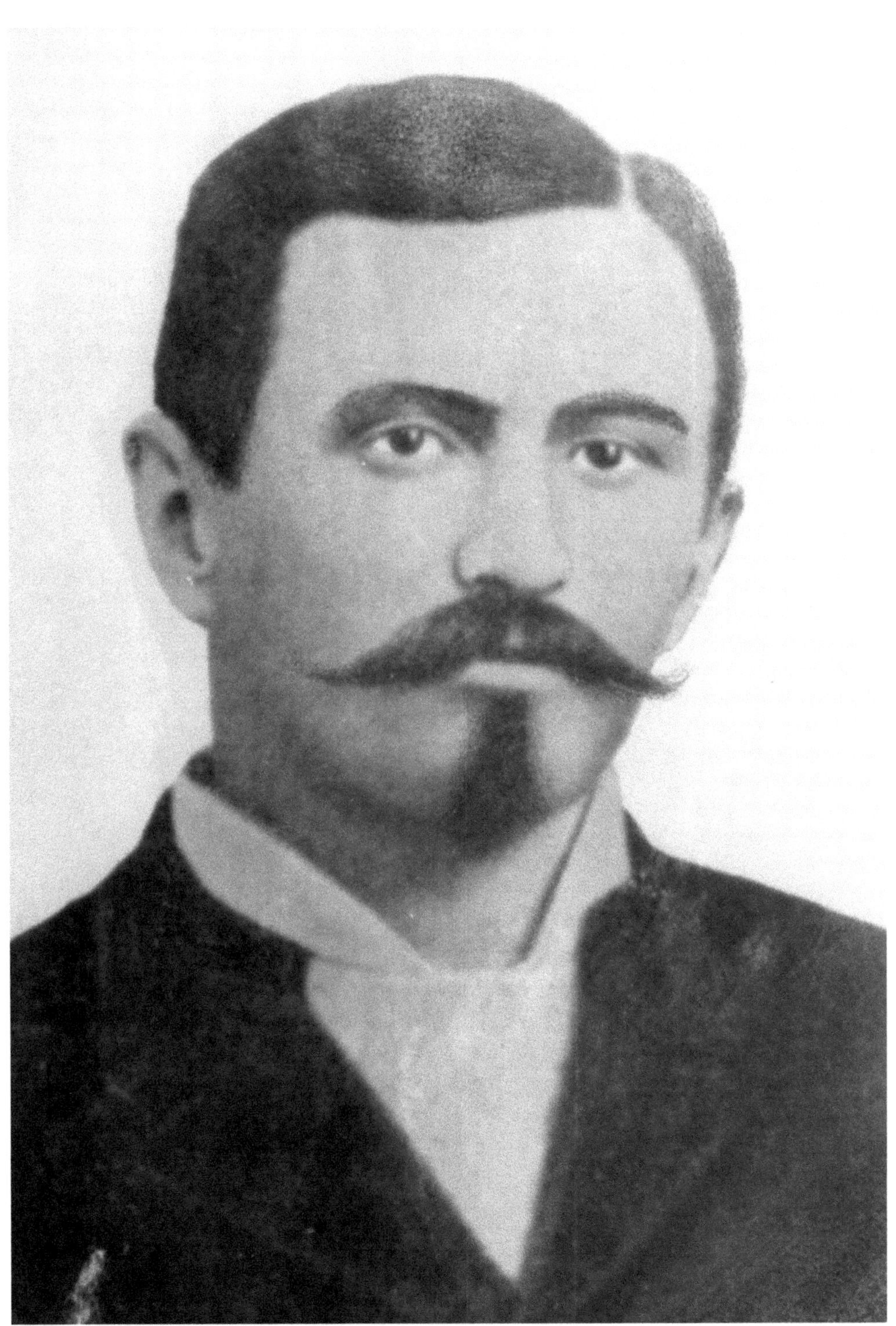

Western chronicler Charlie Siringo describes former lawman Jim McIntire as a "bad-man cowboy of the old school. . . . He had shot and killed several men before he came to the Texas Panhandle in the middle seventies. [He] was of a nervous disposition. When angry, his slender frame shook like a leaf and his black eyes sparkled with rage. . . . [He] finally became a dope fiend in El Paso, Texas, where he died a human wreck."

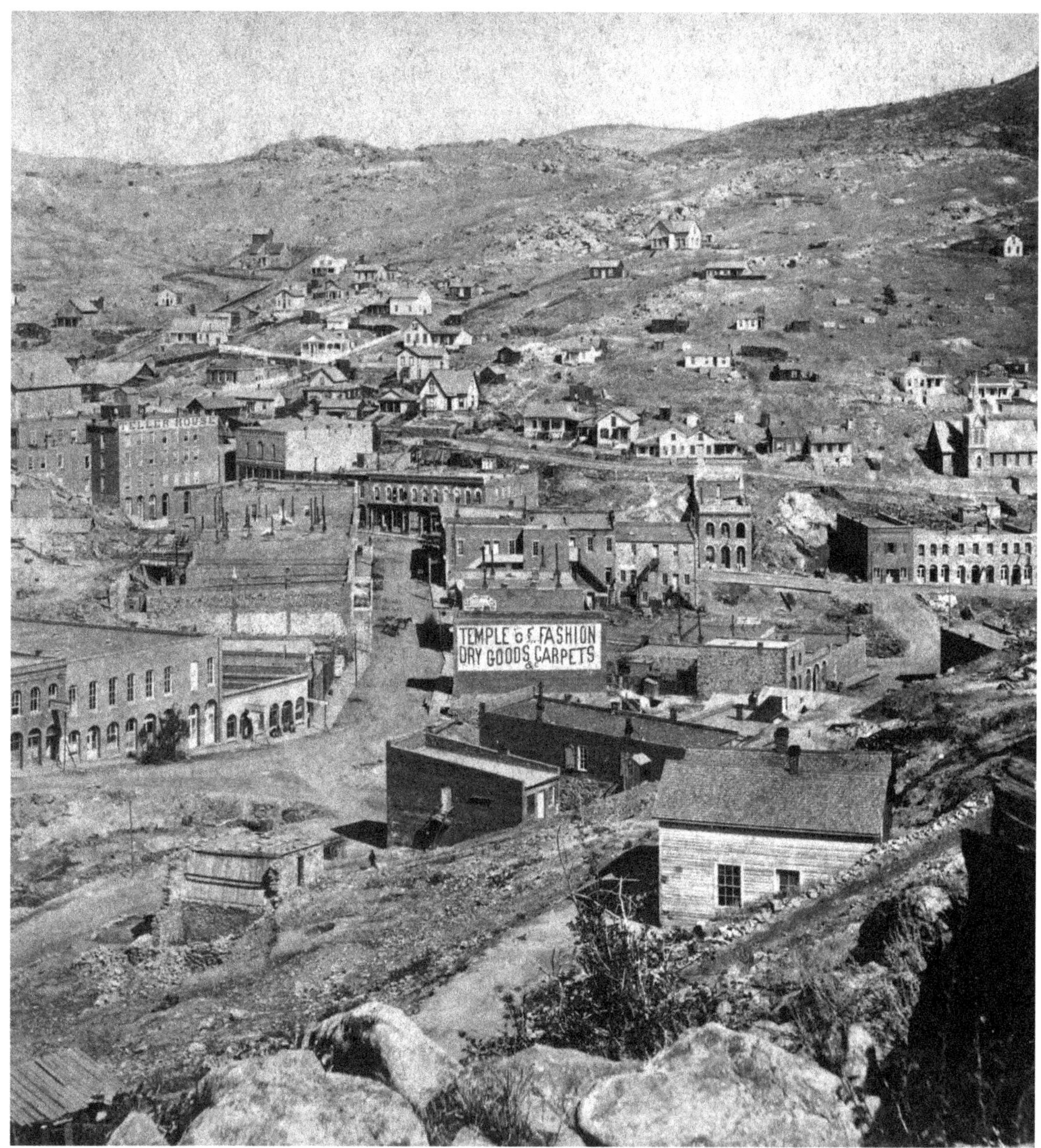

This is the view of Central City, Colorado, as it might have been seen by the numerous outlaws inhabiting the mountains around it. Central City chronicler Christine Bancroft recalled, "They made it a practice to hold up a lonely horseman, rob the stagecoach, or make forays on isolated mine buildings ready to make a large shipment."

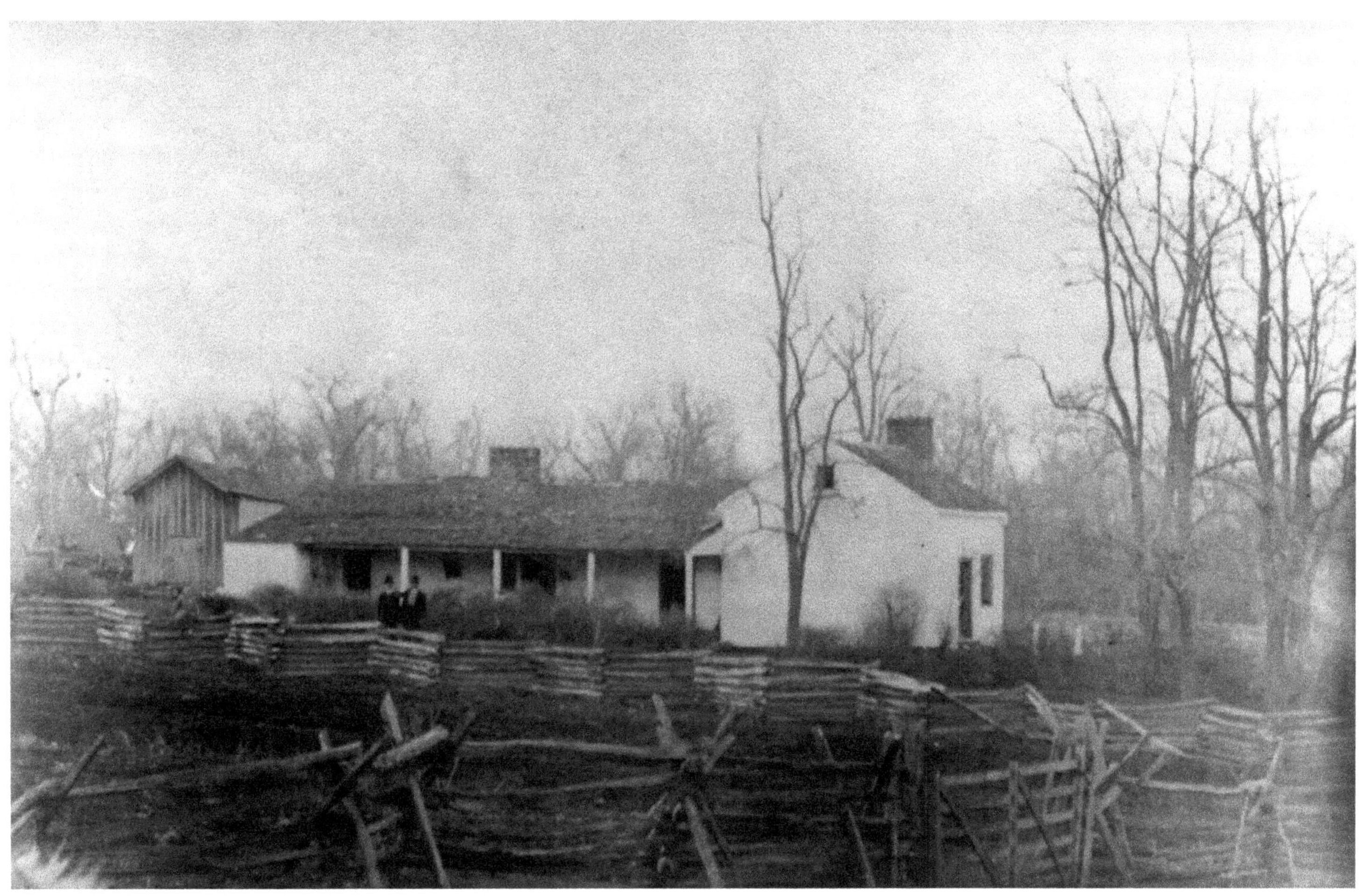

The James farm in Kearney, Missouri, about 1875. That year the Pinkerton Agency hurled a bomb into a bedroom window. Frank and Jesse were not there, but the bomb blew off their mother's arm and mangled their 8-year-old brother, who died in severe pain. Despite all the violence dealt by the Jameses themselves, the sympathy generated by this act went a long way to making them folk heroes.

This photo of Jesse James is believed to have been made in 1876 just before the Northfield, Minnesota, raid. Now in their tenth year of robbery, the James Gang was flush with success and confidently rode toward Northfield's fat bank intent on taking back the money its carpetbagging president had looted from the South.

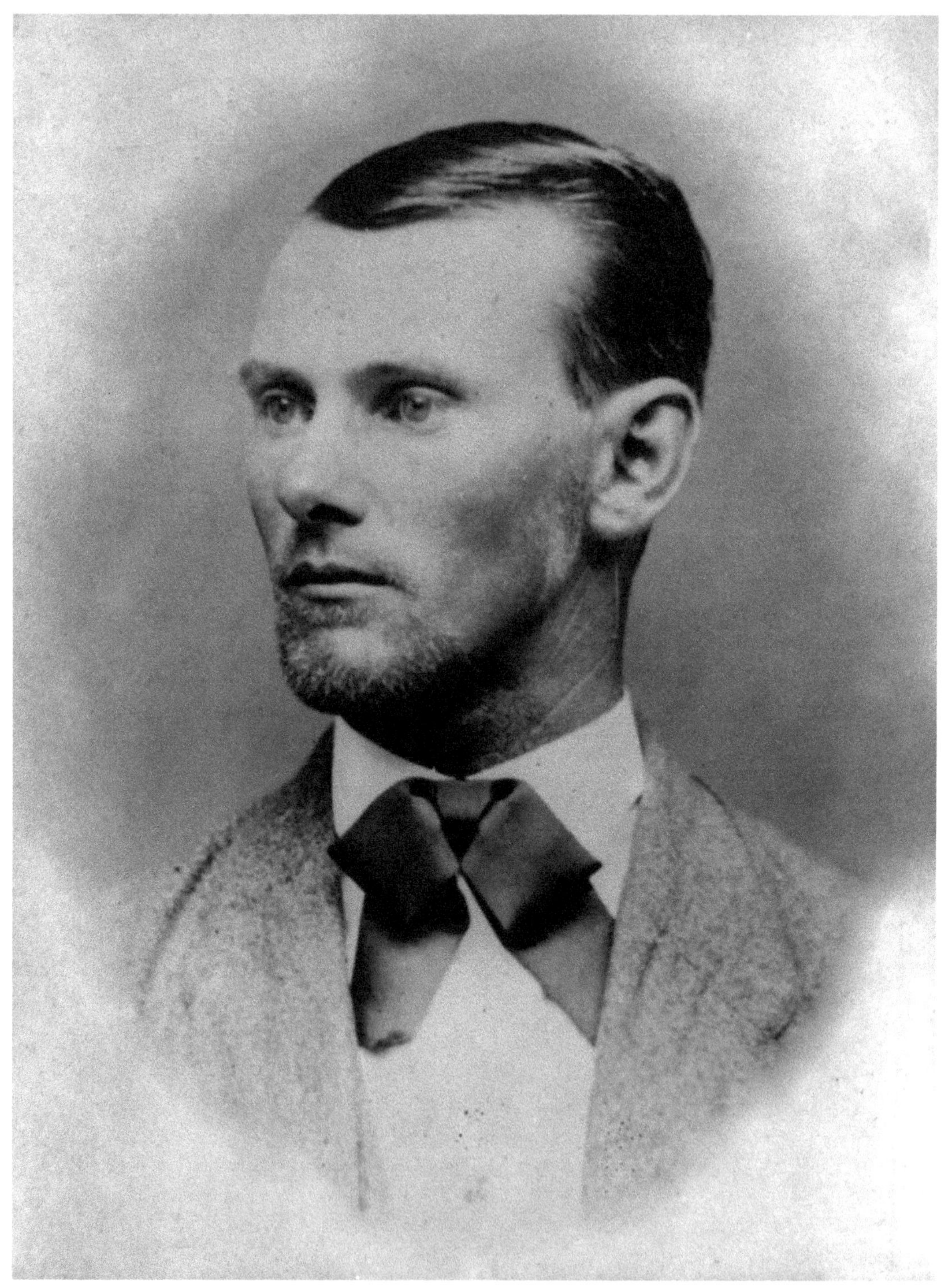

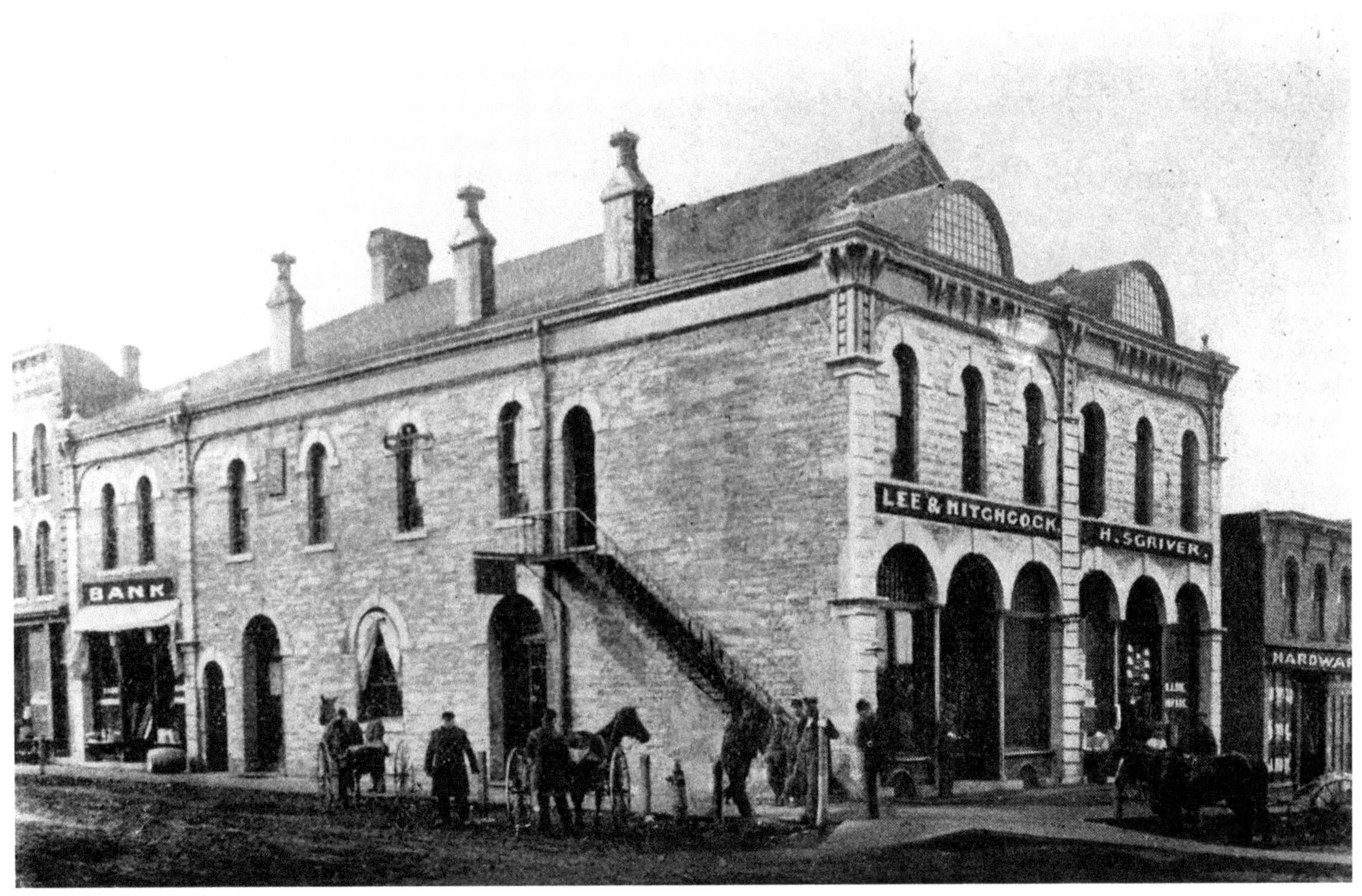

The First National Bank of Northfield, as it appeared the day the James-Younger gang rode in to rob it. Eight bandits rode into town; five stood guard and three entered the bank. But when a bank employee was killed for refusing to open the vault, citizens armed themselves and began firing at the bandits. Ultimately, the Jameses escaped, the Youngers were imprisoned, and three robbers and two citizens were killed. The notorious James-Younger gang was no more.

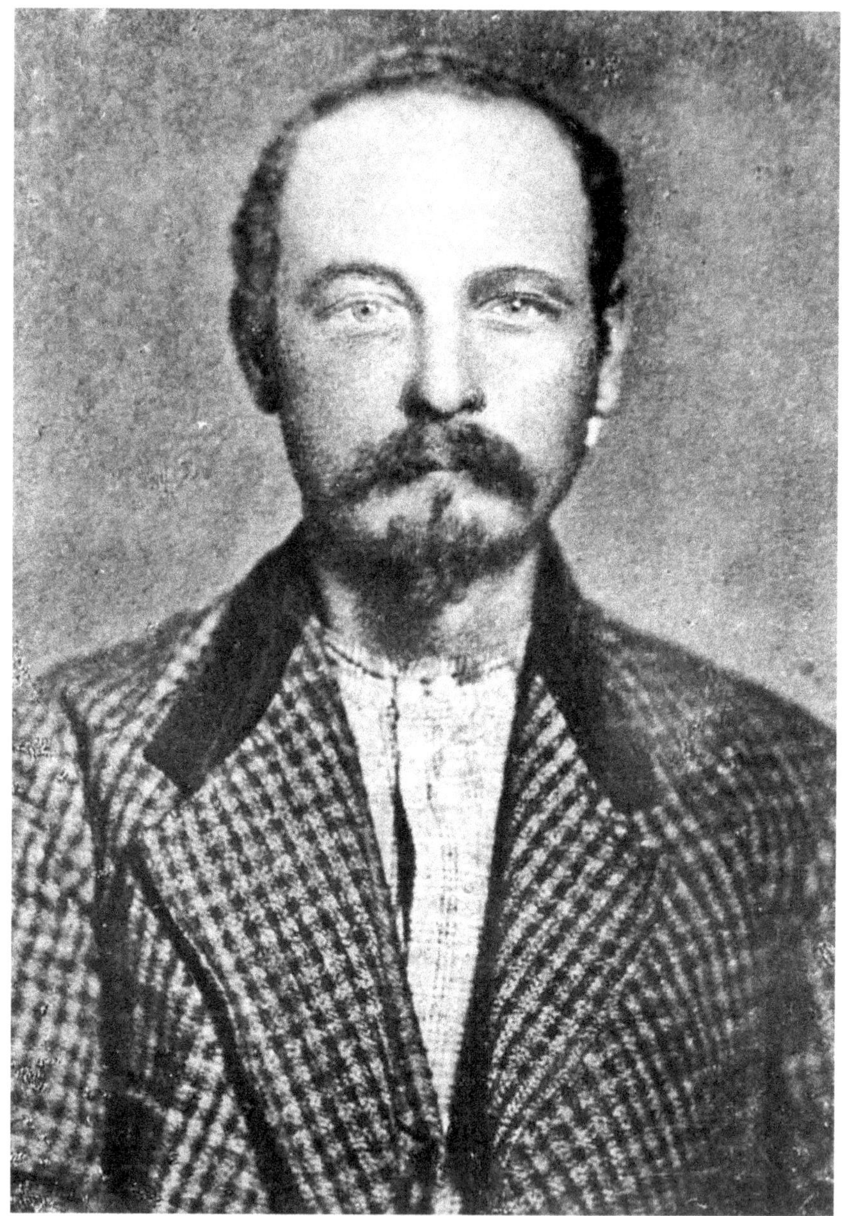

Cole was the oldest of the four outlaw Younger brothers and was a member of Quantrill's Raiders, during which time legend says he pursued a liaison with 16-year-old Myra Maybelle Shirley (a.k.a. Belle Starr). Immediately after the Civil War, he joined the James brothers in their raiding activities in Missouri for nearly ten years until he was captured fleeing the botched Northfield, Minnesota, raid. Seen here is his mug shot.

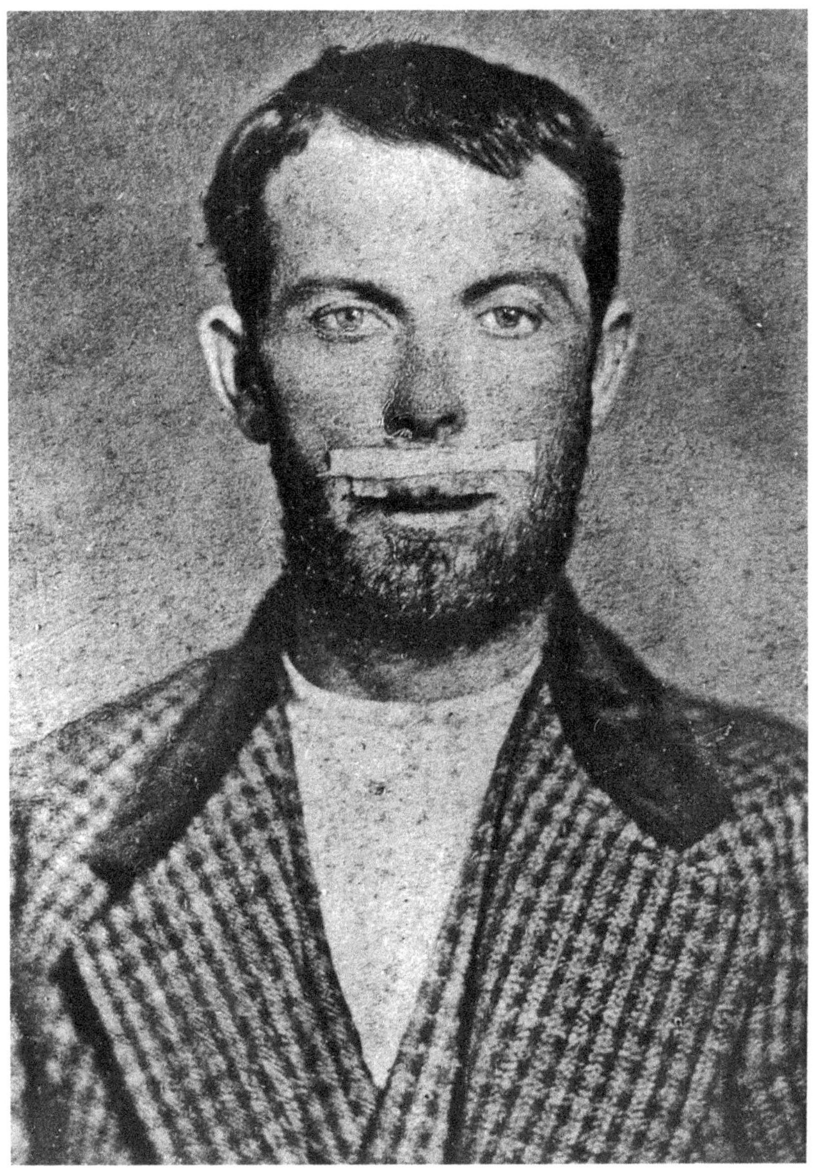

Jim Younger was only a part-time member of the James-Younger gang in the 1870s and generally tried to earn a living legitimately, but he agreed to take part in the Northfield raid just the same. He was badly wounded and captured during the firefight and sentenced to Minnesota's Stillwater prison. Paroled after 25 years, he committed suicide upon learning that his terms prohibited him from marrying his fiancée.

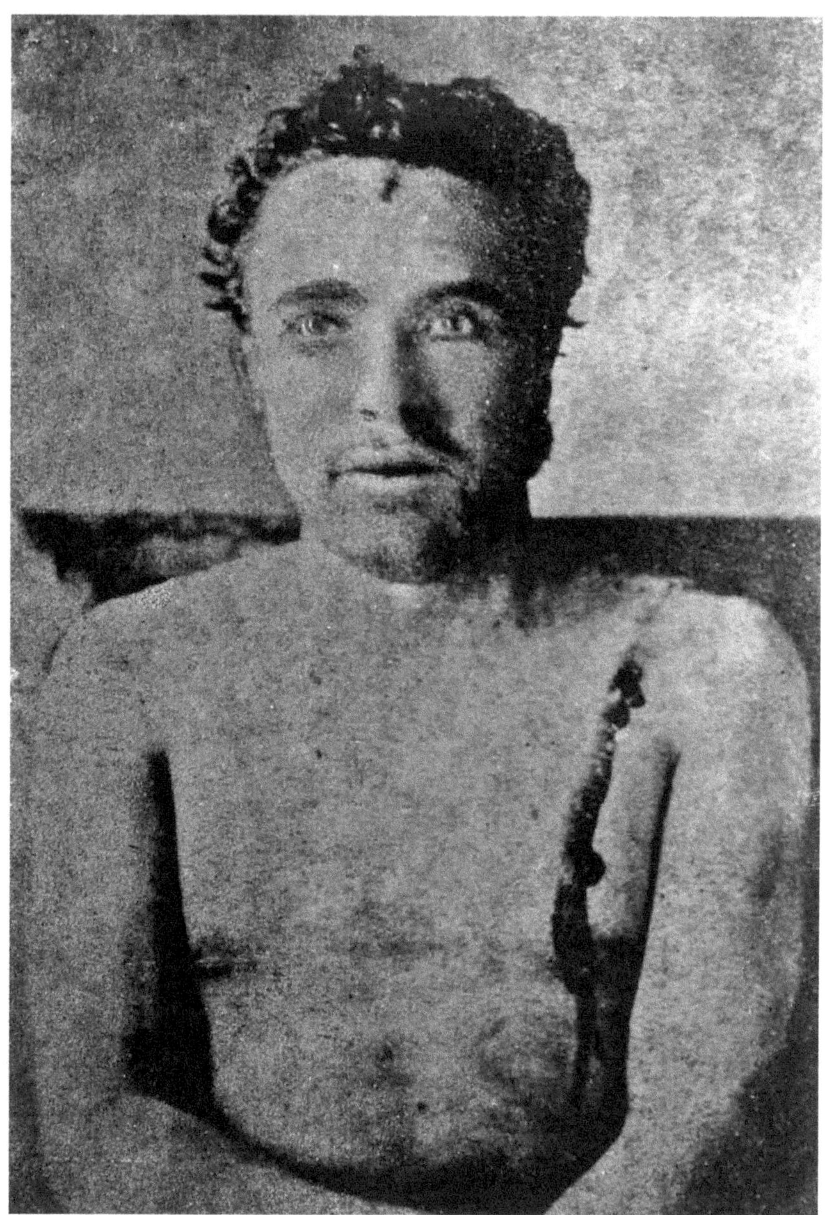

Clell Miller learned to accept violence at an early age having begun riding with Bloody Bill Anderson's Confederate guerrillas in Missouri at 14. Subsequently, he became part of the James Gang and led more than a dozen bank and train robberies in the 1870s. In 1876, he was felled by a townsman's bullet as the James-Younger Gang made its escape from the ill-starred Northfield, Minnesota, raid.

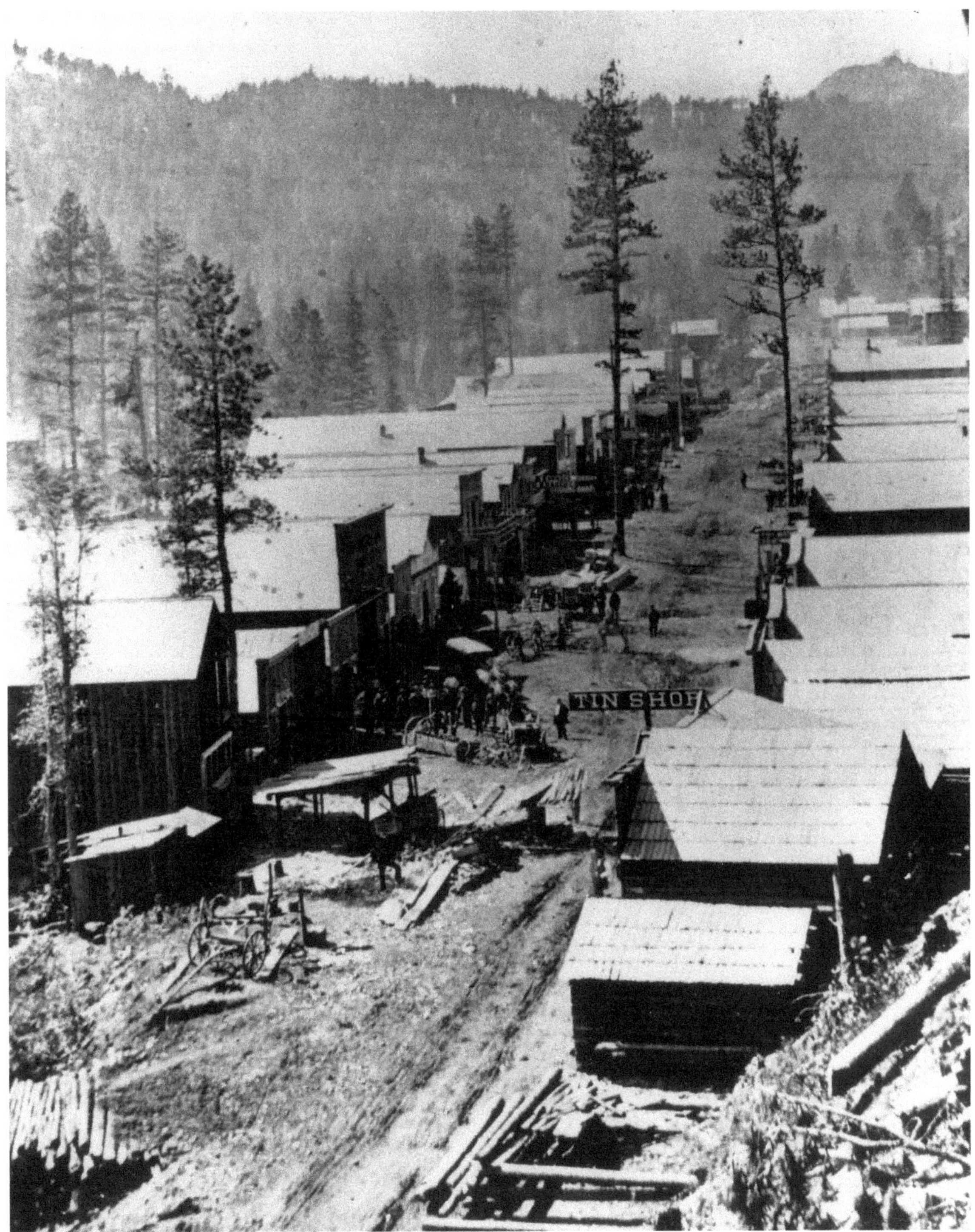

Gold fever struck the Black Hills of South Dakota in the mid-1870s, and in 1876 Deadwood became a raucous boom town. Because it was actually on Sioux land, there was no provision for government and the small settlement seen here had four saloons, six stores selling whiskey, a dancehall with eight dancers from Cheyenne, and a whole lot of trouble.

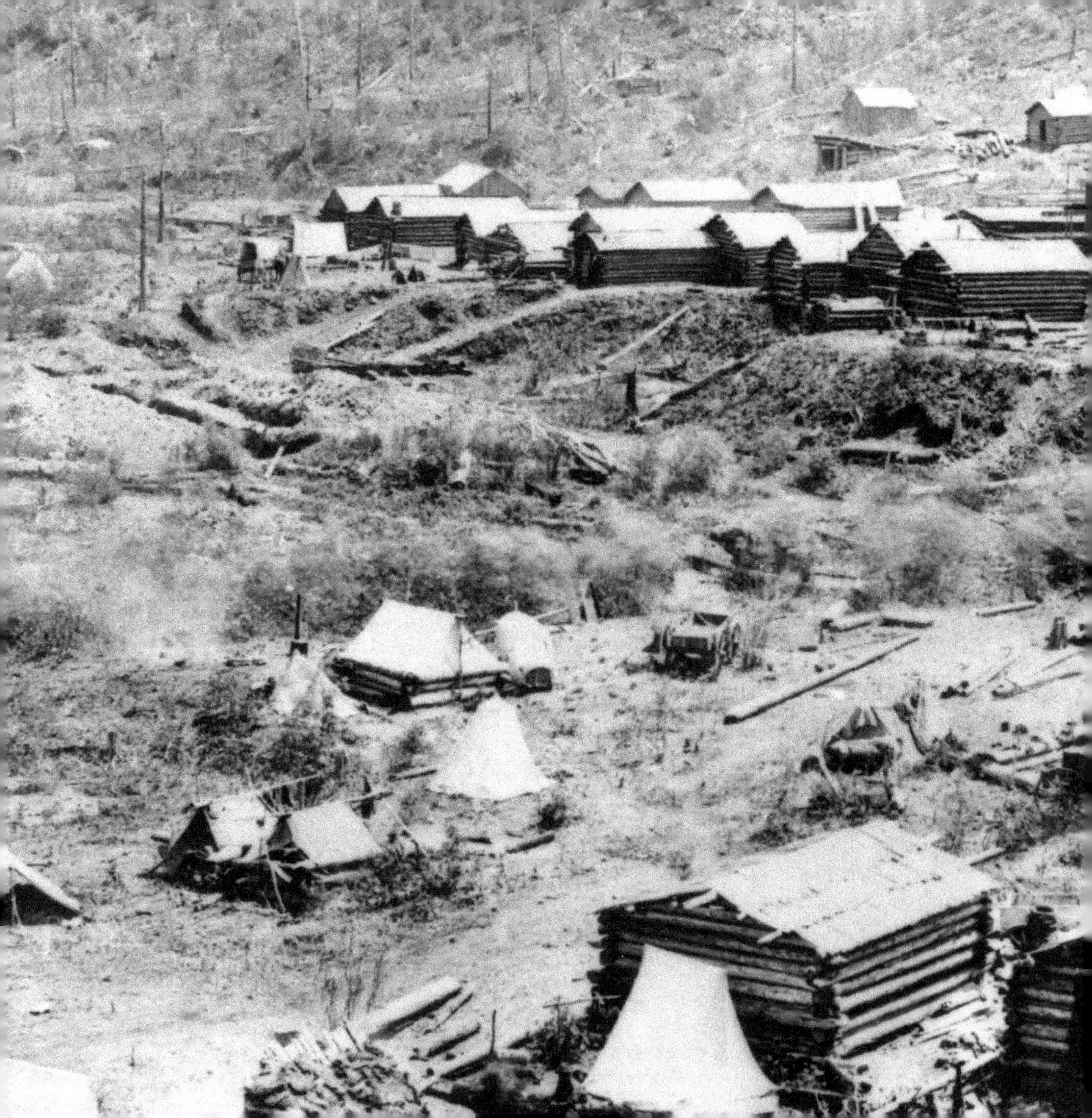

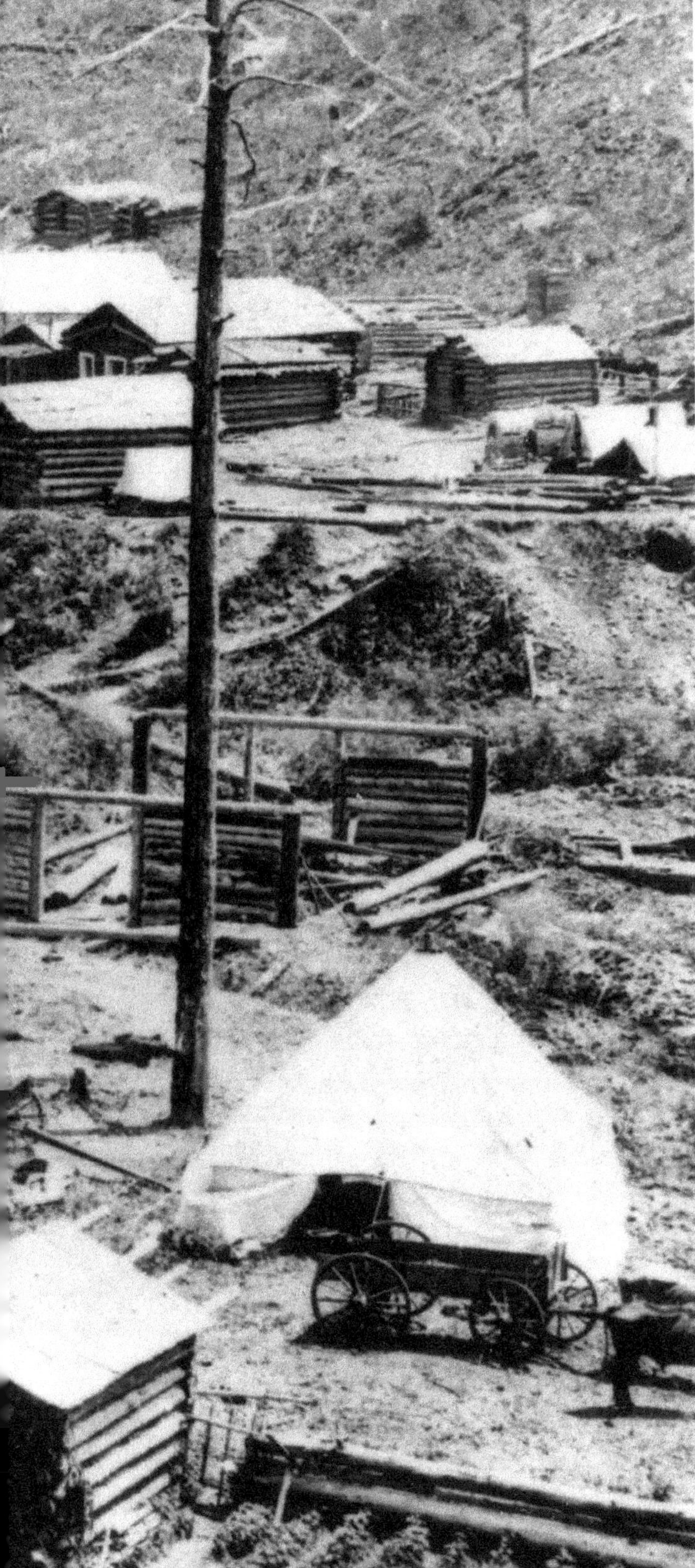

Deadwood continued to boom throughout 1876, and lawlessness became an acute problem. An observer from Denver opined that the town was "tenanted with all probability by the vilest specimens of human nature on God's earth" and "so many better men tempted by them and their agents and co-conspirators have perished."

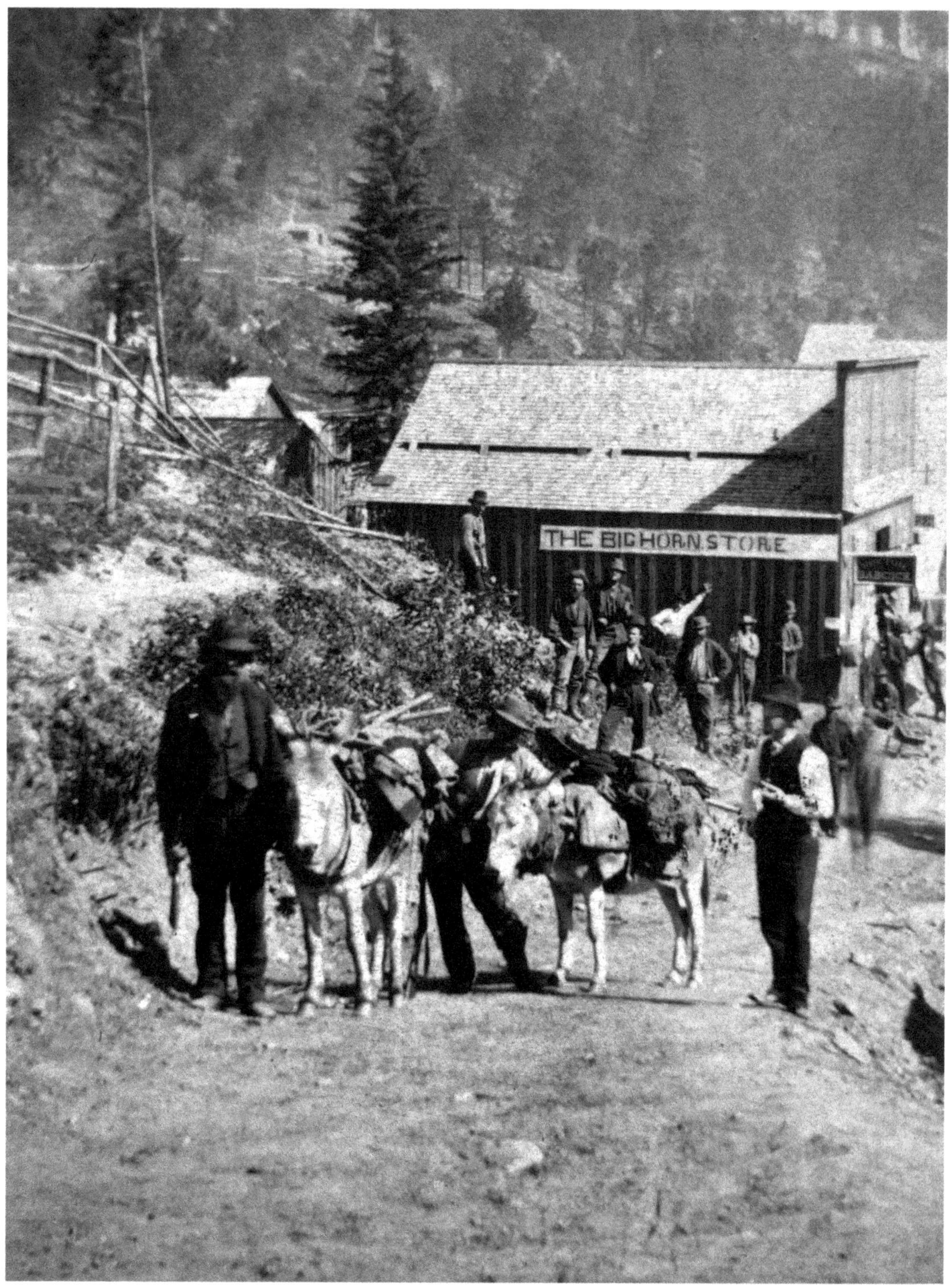

This view of Deadwood, South Dakota, was recorded from the south road into the city in 1876. Following the murder of Wild Bill Hickok that year, town organizers placed a star on the chest of Seth Bullock and ordered the new sheriff to clean up the town. He did so, quickly and efficiently and without loss of life. Despite its violent beginning, Deadwood was scarcely known for outlawry afterward.

I'm Not Afraid to Die like a Man Fighting, but I Would Not Like to Be Killed like a Dog Unarmed

(1876–1885)

While the nation celebrated its centennial in 1876, another event that year signaled the end of an era in outlawry in the West. In the fall, the James-Younger gang rode into the town of Northfield, Minnesota, after a decade of robbing banks and trains on the fringes of civilized society in the West. They had proved adept at their trade, extracting substantial amounts of wealth from their prey as well as being impossible to apprehend or prosecute. At Northfield, however, they were wiped out in an afternoon with only Frank and Jesse James escaping, then going into self-imposed retirement for several years. This event, though pivotal for the James-Younger gang, did nothing to dampen the enthusiasm of outlaws generally.

During this period, train robberies increased dramatically as the railroads extended their octopus reach across the country to places like Deadwood and the rich mining areas of New Mexico and Arizona, while the use of stagecoaches (and robbing stagecoaches) declined in equal measure. Towns now began to form along the tracks, for the potential of wealth the railroads made possible, and the old patterns of settlement were repeated. The histories of many of the West's towns are strikingly similar because of the similar ways they came into being.

A trend in this period was the development of "rings" of men in various territories, who conspired to control their regions through a consortium of lawyers, politicians, law enforcement, and businessmen and divide the spoils among themselves. At times, these cabals were challenged by other groups, each side enlisting the aid of outlaws and gunmen as extralegal enforcers of their will. Many of these hired guns committed murder, thievery, arson, and other crimes under the aegis of their employer, but were generally considered dispensable when the gunman attracted too much attention. The stories of Billy the Kid in the Lincoln County War and the Earp-Clanton feud in the Arizona War are typical examples of this phenomenon.

The territorial rings owed their existence, at least in part, to the sparse legal systems in the areas in which they operated, as well as poorly trained law enforcement and confusing overlaps in jurisdiction; for example, a county sheriff might oppose a town marshal, but neither had authority over the other. These weaknesses were exploited by outlaws.

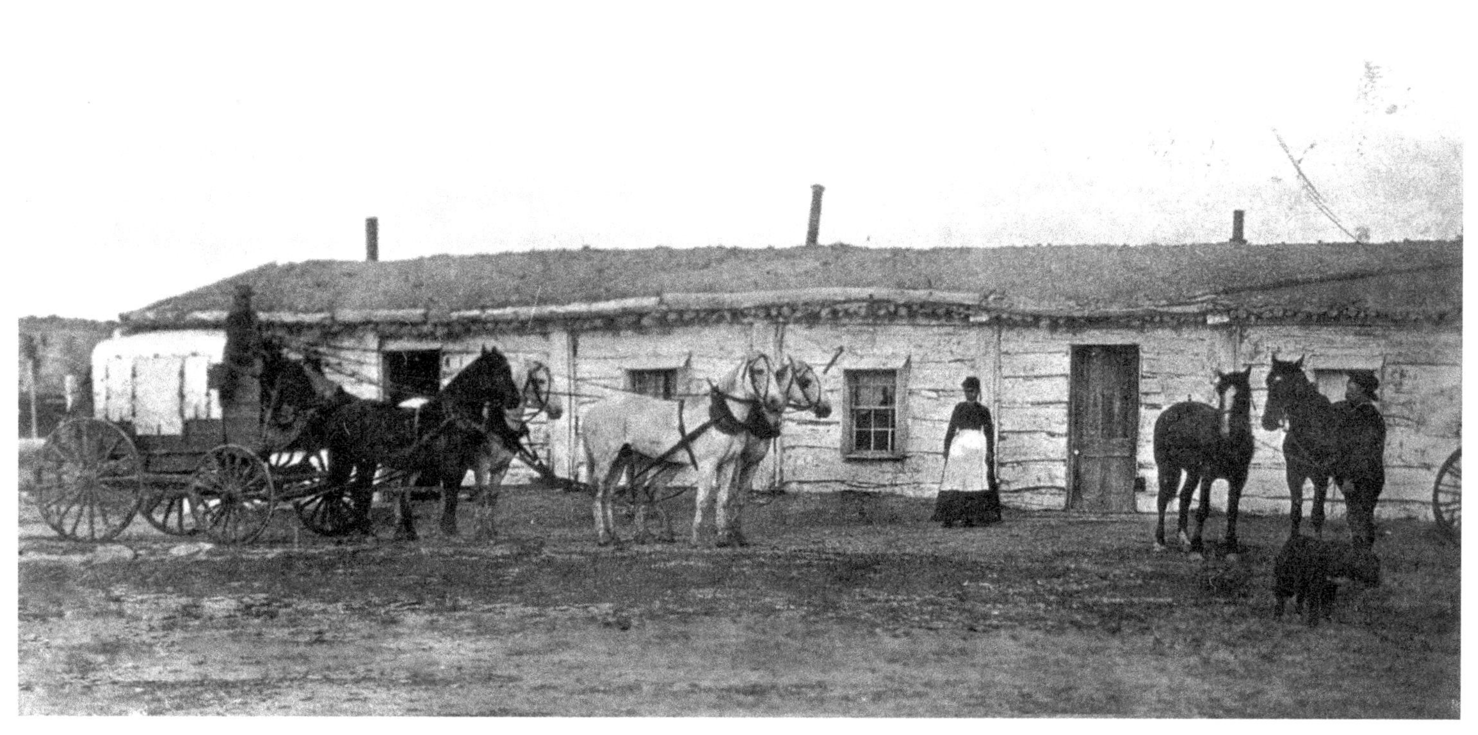

Robbers' Roost Station was a way point on the Cheyenne to Deadwood stagecoach route. It was a place of apprehension for northbound travelers and a respite for those southbound. The route north was filled with winding narrow roads and plenty of cover for the highwaymen who lent their name to the place.

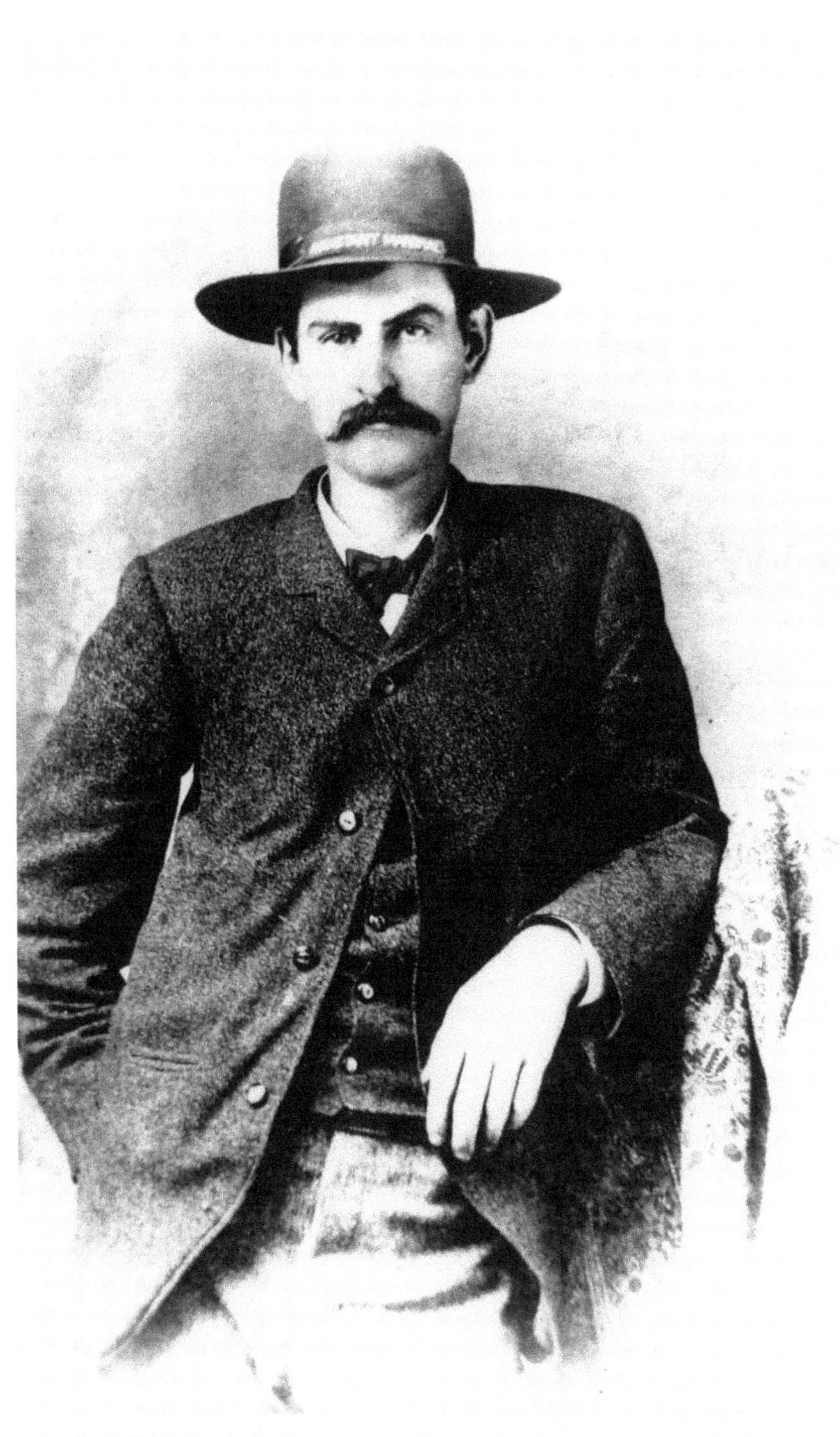

"Mysterious" Dave Mather had a rather peculiar career as an outlaw. He began his crooked ways as a common cattle rustler and card sharp, but he had a way about him that endeared him to lawmen. He wound up serving as a deputy in several towns, including Dodge City, where he worked for both Wyatt Earp and Bill Tilghman. Mather was no straight arrow, however, and always abused his authority.

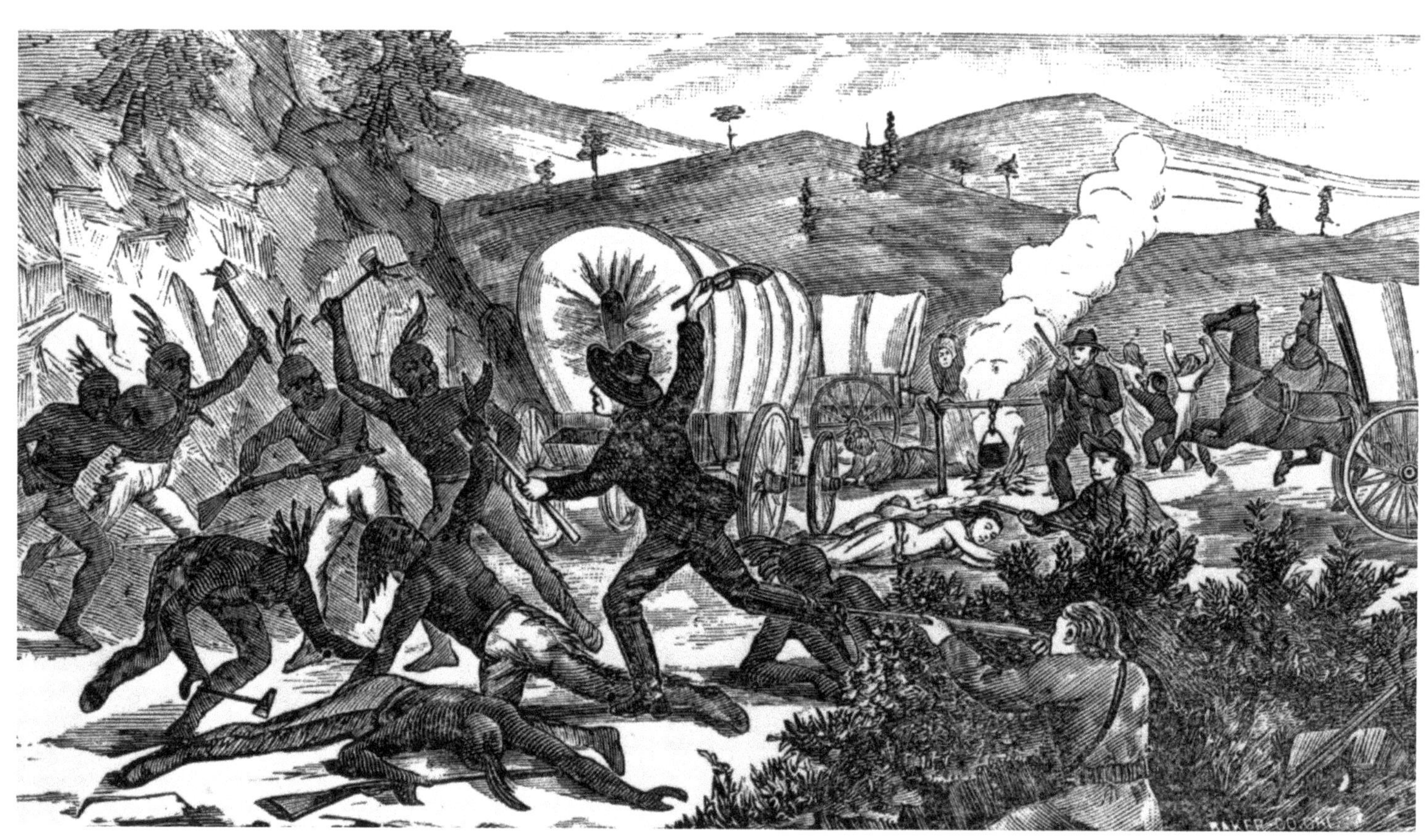

Sociopaths were present, but most outlaws in the Old West were not without some human decency. This illustration depicts a tale about Billy the Kid in which the Kid and a friend were on the outlaw trail and witnessed a party of 16 Apaches attack a family of settlers. The Kid fought with a Winchester, then a pistol, and finally an axe to save the family, killing 8 of the attackers.

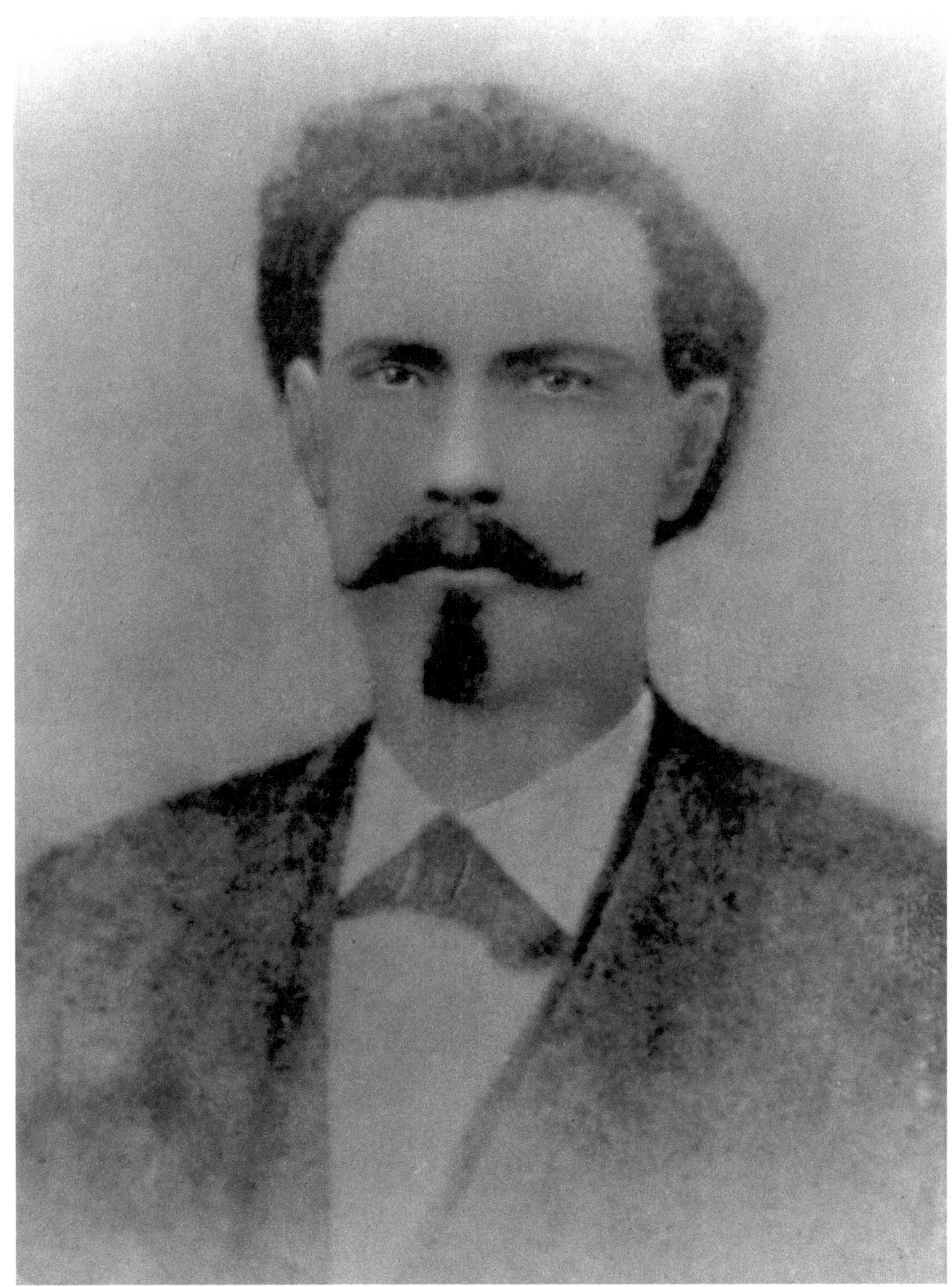

John Wesley Hardin has long been the prototype for the murderous sociopaths that existed in the Old West, but Bill Longley was at least as cold-blooded and ruthless as Hardin. Longley began killing at 17 and over a ten-year period claimed he killed 32 men, most of them black or Hispanic. He was executed in 1878.

Sam Bass (standing, at left) poses with his gang during his successful but short career of stagecoach and train robberies. After making a lucky strike on a Union Pacific train in Nebraska in 1877, which netted his gang $60,000 from the railroad and $1,300 from the passengers, Bass terrorized the Dallas area for about a year. He died at the hands of Texas Rangers on his 27th birthday in 1878.

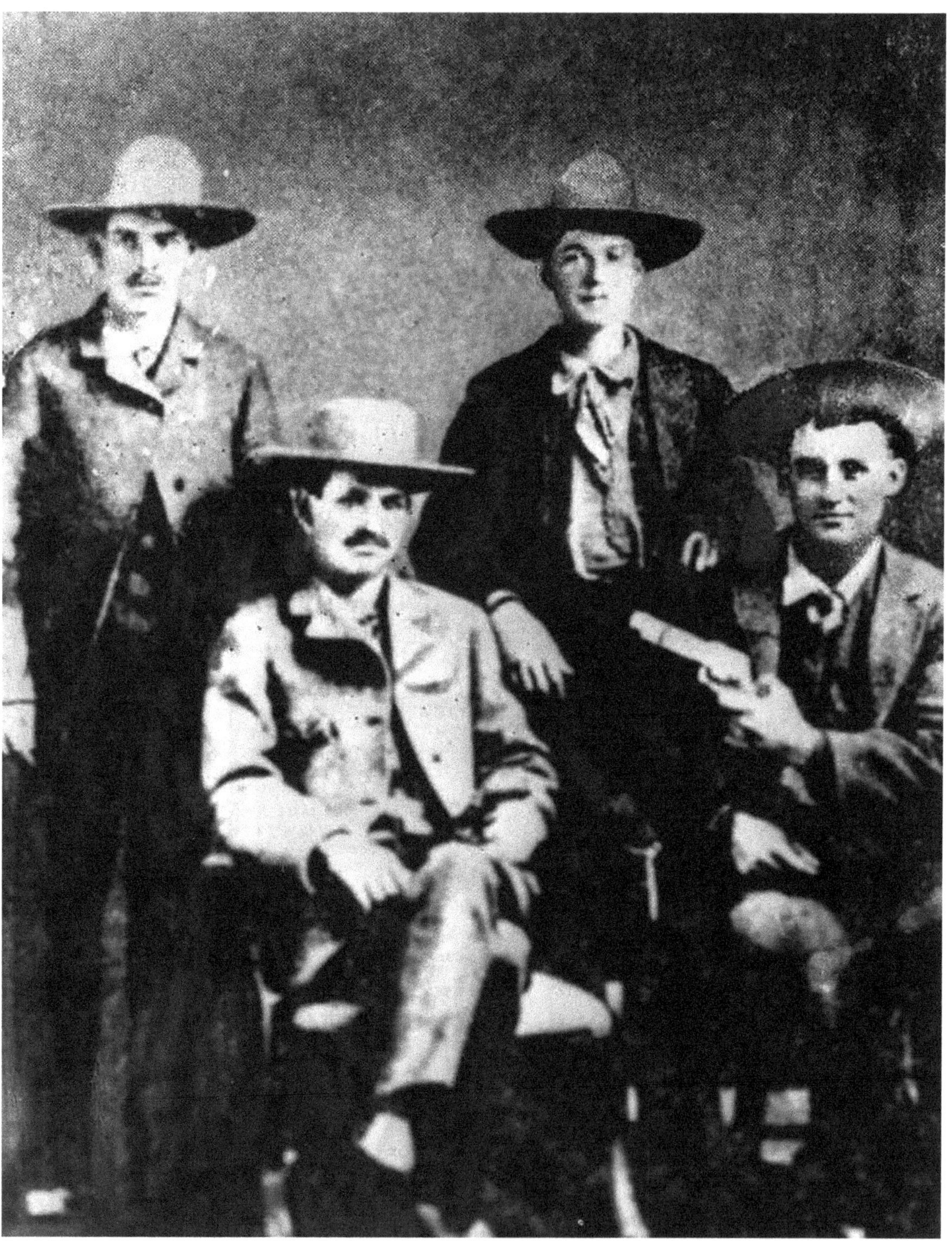

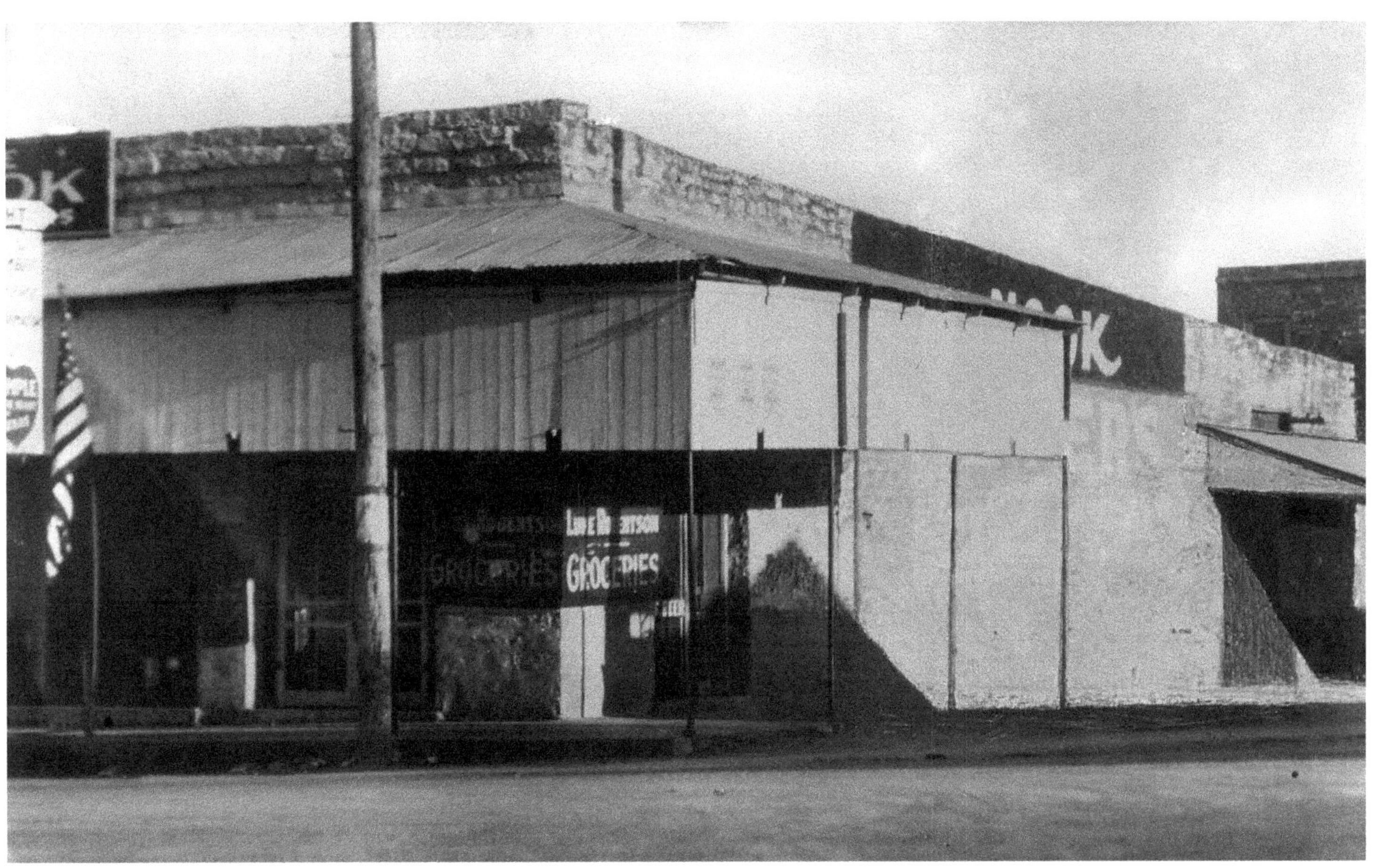

Kopperal's General Store, Round Rock, Texas, scene of the shoot-out which led to the demise of the Sam Bass gang in 1878. Bass and two others were in town to case a bank when they stepped inside the store for tobacco. After being tipped off by a treacherous member of the gang, lawmen were ready to ambush them; nonetheless, a deputy was killed as they fled the store.

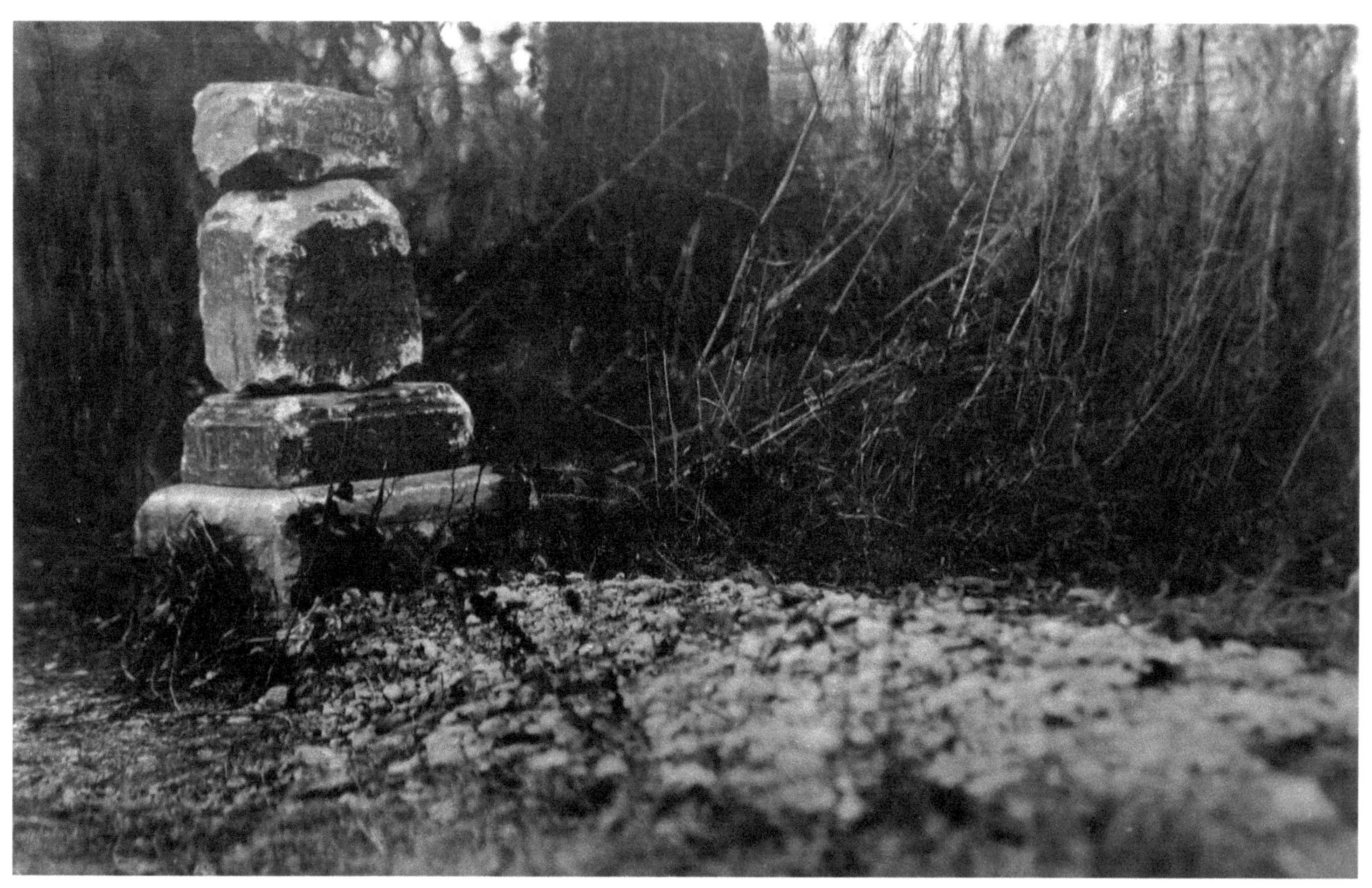

Though Texas Rangers planned to exhibit the body of outlaw Sam Bass at the state capitol, they could not find enough ice for the trip from Round Rock to Austin, so Bass was buried in the city's cemetery. The original grave is seen here, with the inscription, "A brave man reposes in death here. Why was he not true?" After a hundred years of vandalization it was replaced with a new marker.

FRONTIER TIMES 11

Complete Version of the Sam Bass Song

Frontier Times has received a number of requests from subscribers, asking for the song, "Sam Bass." Recently we found this song in the Dallas Semi-Weekly Farm News. It is believed to be the complete and correct version. Thirty years ago this old song was heard around every hearthstone and beside every campfire on the range. Many of our older readers remember the tune:

Sam Bass was born in Indiana,
It was his native home;
And at the age of seventeen
Young Sam began to roam.

He first came out to Texas,
A cowboy for to be;
A kinder hearted fellow
You hardly ever see.

Sam used to deal in race stock,
One called "the Denton Mare,"
He matched her in the scrub races
And took her to the fair.

Sam always coined the money
And spent it mighty free;
He always drank good liquor
Wherever he might be.

Sam Bass had four companions,
Four bold and daring lads,
Jim Murphy, Jackson, Underwood,
Joel Collins and "Old Dad."

Four bolder, reckless cowboys
The Wild West never knew;
They whipped the Texas rangers
And chased the boys in blue.

Sam left the old Joel Collins ranch
In the merry month of May,
With a herd of Texas cattle
The Black Hills for to see.

They sold out at Kansas City
And then got on a spree.
A tougher lot of cowboys
You seldom ever see.

They started back to Texas
And robbed the U. P. train,
Then split up into couples
And started out again.

Joel Collins and his partner-
Were overtaken soon,
And with all their hard-earned money
They had to meet their doom.

Sam Bass got back to Texas
All "right side up with care,"
He rode right into Denton,
His old friends met him there.

Sam's life was short in Texas—
Three robberies he did do,
He robbed the Longview passenger—
The mail and express, too.

Sam had another comrade,
Called "Arkansaw' for short,
He was killed by a Texas ranger
Who thought it was great sport.

Jim Murphy was arrested,
And then released on bail.
He jumped his bond at Tyler
And hit the Terrell trail.

But Major Jones had posted Jim,
And that was all a stall—
It was a plan to capture Sam
Before the coming fall.

Sam met his fate at Round Rock
July the twenty-first,
They filled poor Sam with bullets
And emptied out his purse.

Now Sam is a decaying corpse.
Down in the Round Rock clay,
While Jackson's on the border
A-trying to get away.

Jim Murphy borrowed Sam's good
money
And did not want to pay,
So he set out the game to win
By giving Sam away.

He sold poor Sam and also Barnes,
And left their friends to mourn.
Jim Murphy will a roasting get
When Gabriel toots his horn.

Some think he'll go to heaven,
For none can surely tell,
But if I'm right in my surmise
No doubt he'll go—the other way.

Though not as universally loved as Billy the Kid would be, Sam Bass found a place in the hearts of Texans who at times considered him as something of a Robin Hood figure, perhaps because few bemoaned the losses of the widely despised railroads. He was memorialized in stories and songs such as this one.

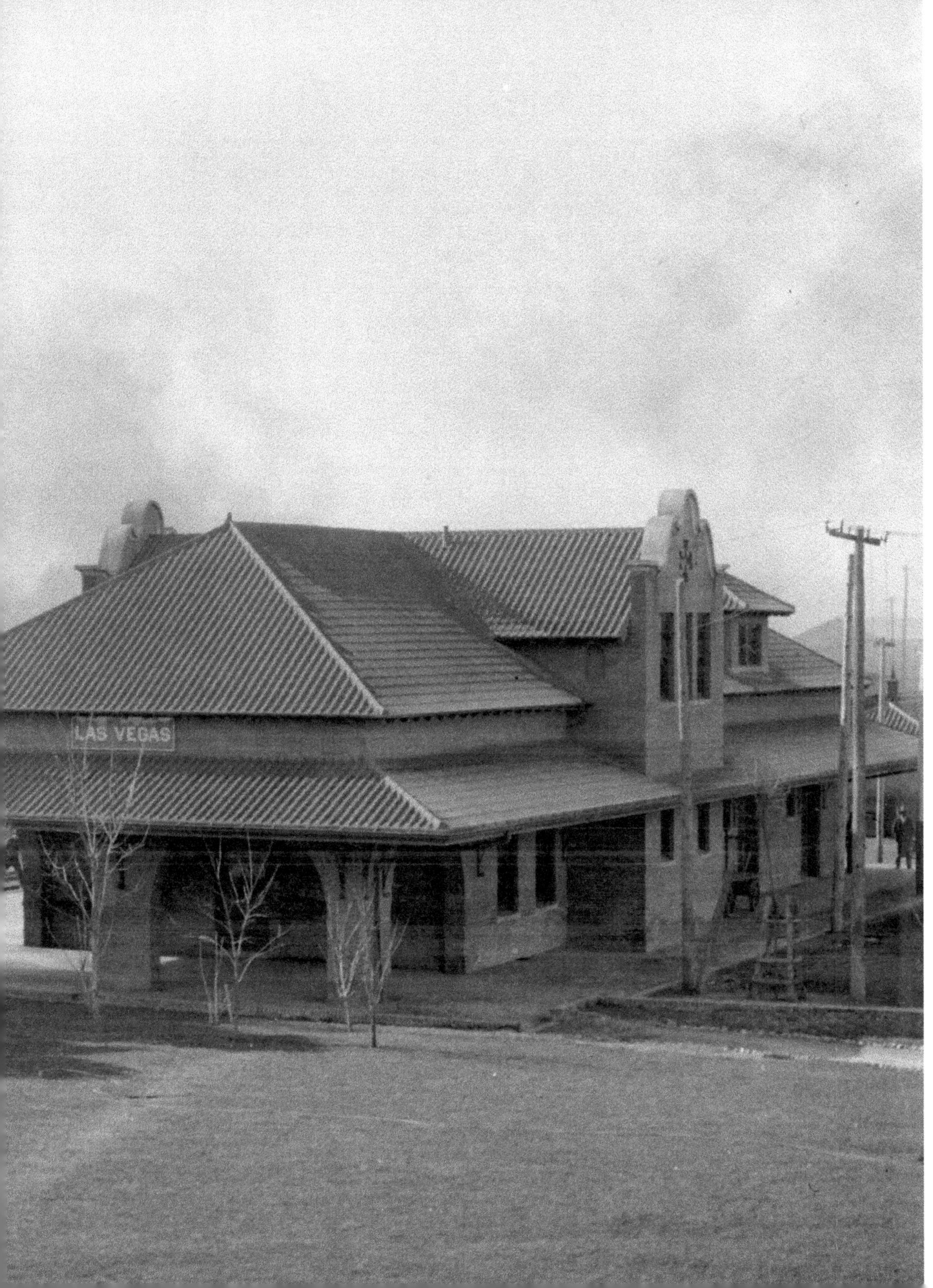

Though photographed much later, this view of the Atchison, Topeka and Santa Fe Railroad depot in Las Vegas, New Mexico, is symbolic of the arrival of the first train there in 1879. Railroads always made a profound impact on new towns, but the list of rogues these rails brought reads like an encyclopedia of badmen, including Doc Holliday, Billy the Kid, and Bob Ford.

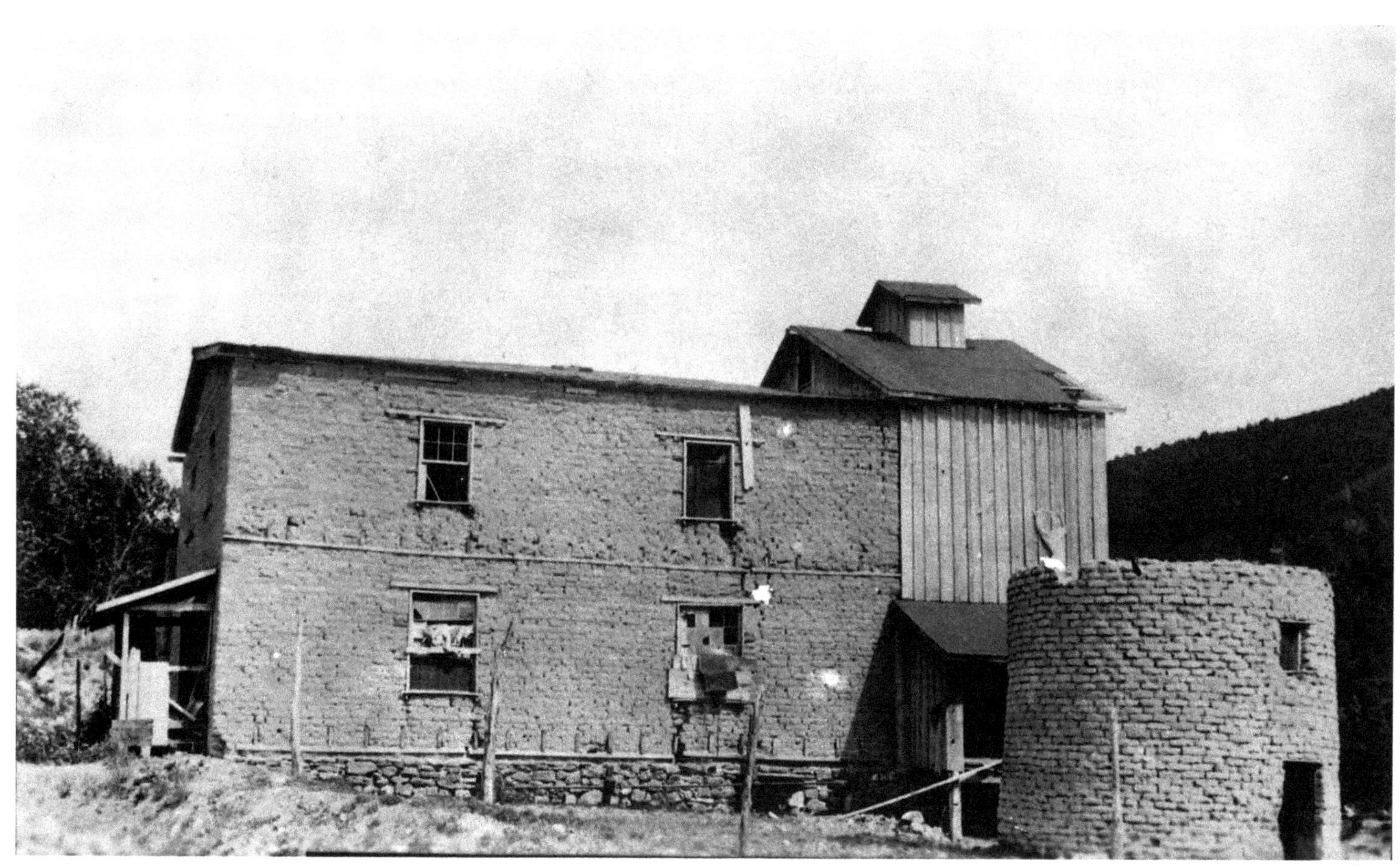

The Lincoln County War was essentially a trade war which erupted into violence between two factions in New Mexico in the 1870s. Billy the Kid was part of the Regulators in the employ of John Tunstall and when Tunstall was murdered, they hunted down his killers. One pitched battle was at Blazer's Mill (seen here) in which one of their opponents fought off 14 Regulators, including the Kid, who was knocked out cold.

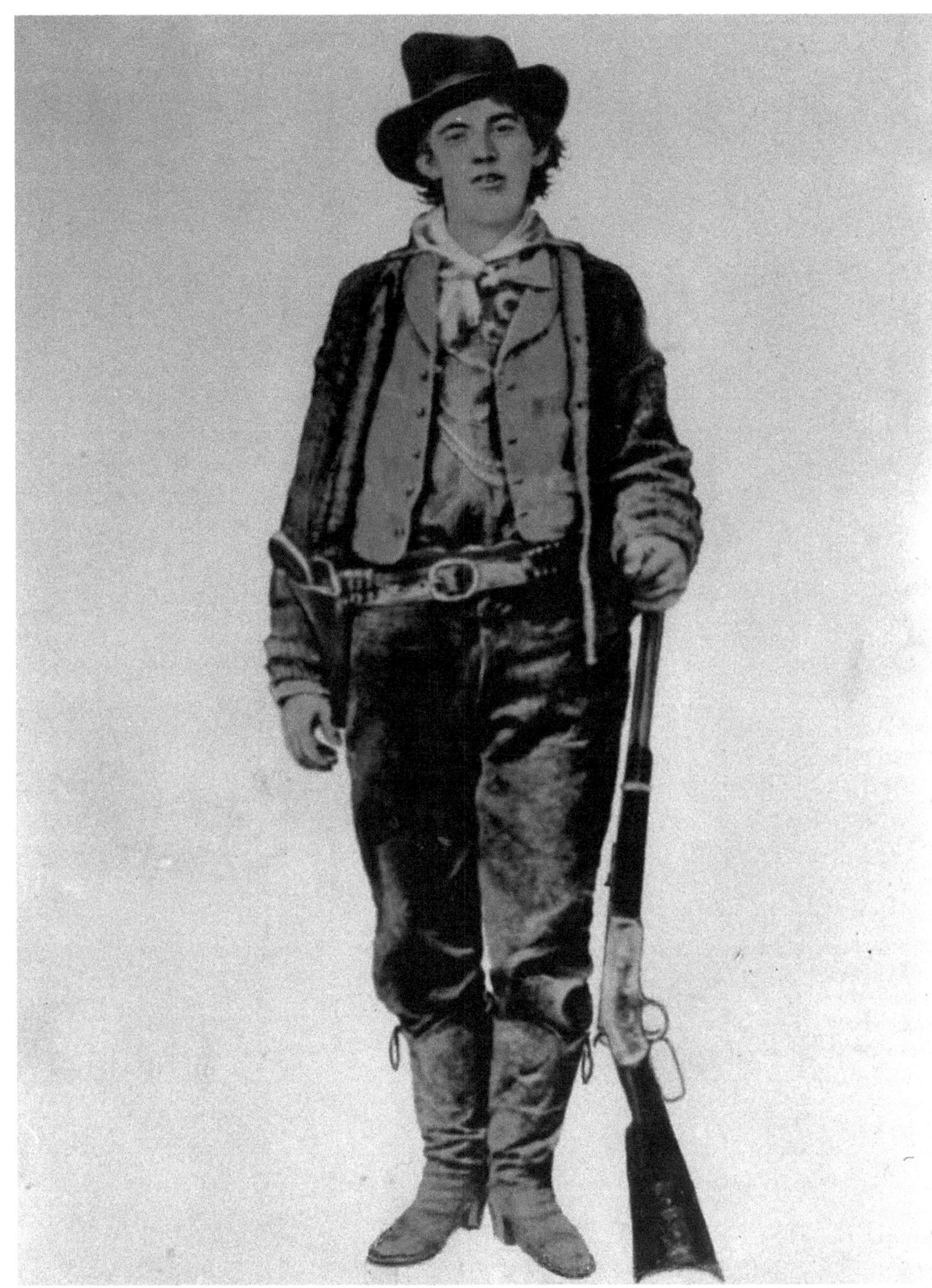

One of the most mythologized characters in American history, East Coast–born Billy the Kid (a.k.a. William H. Bonney) became a legend during New Mexico's Lincoln County War in the late 1870s. Despite his reputation as a quick-draw killer of 20 men (the Kid likely killed only four), his youth, affable nature, and a sensational post-mortem biography by Sheriff Pat Garrett secured him a beloved place in American folklore. The Kid once said, "I'm not afraid to die like a man fighting, but I would not like to die like a dog unarmed."

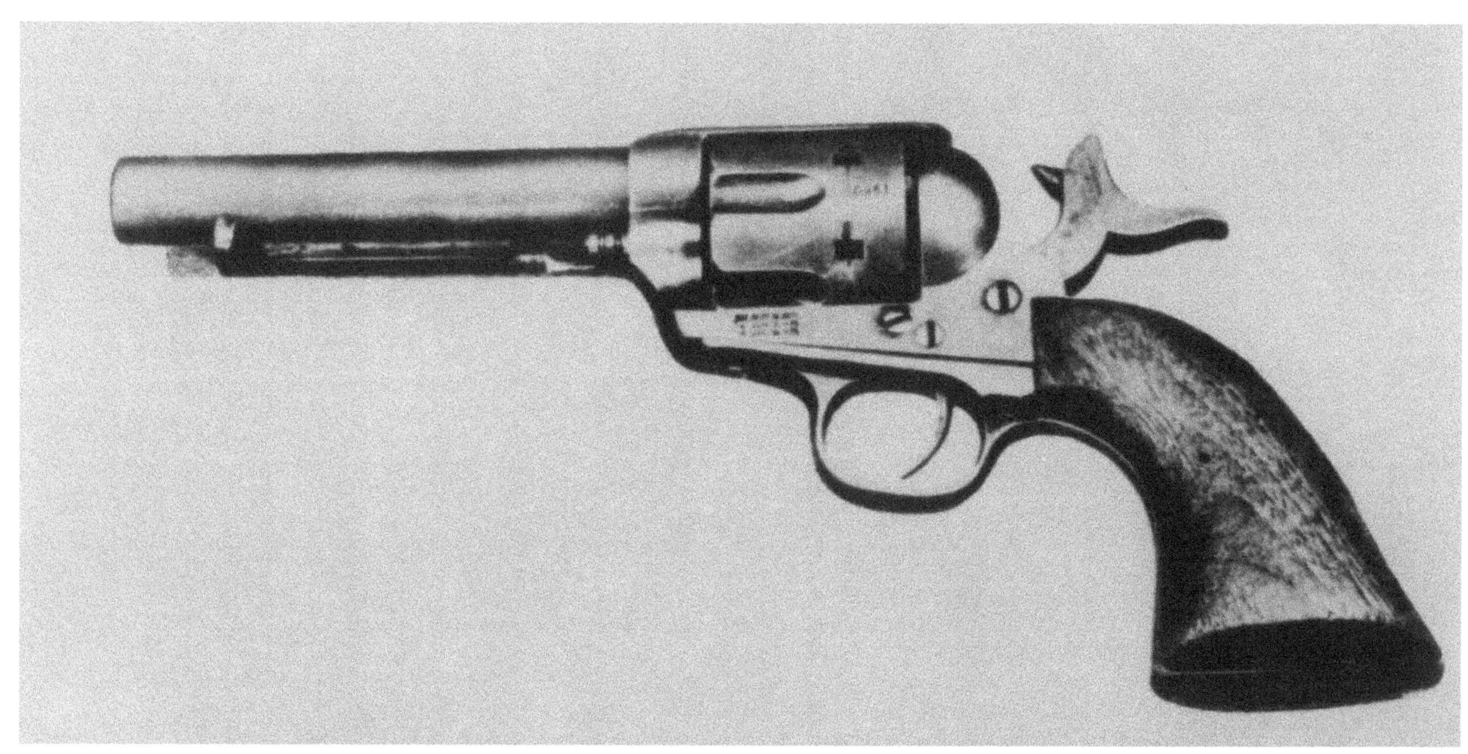

Seen here is the single-action Colt .44 revolver, which was taken from Billy the Kid when he was arrested by Pat Garrett for the murder of Sheriff William Brady in 1880. The photograph was taken to disprove theories that the Kid was a blood-thirsty killer addicted to fast shooting, double-action revolvers.

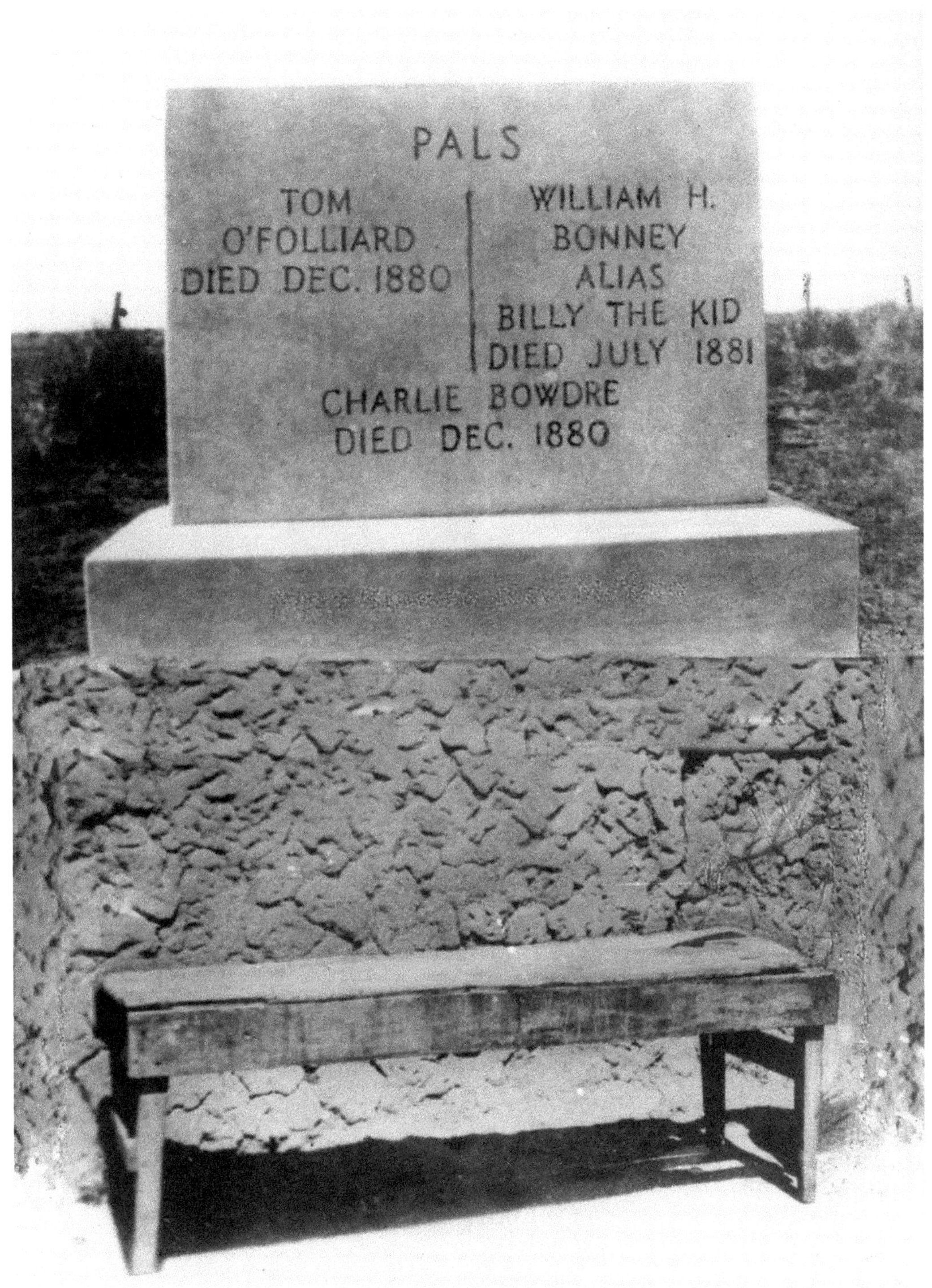

After the murder of Sheriff Brady, Billy the Kid and others were hunted down by Pat Garrett's posse in New Mexico. They gunned down the Kid's good friends, Tom O'Folliard and Charlie Bowdre, before the Kid's arrest and conviction for murder. Billy then escaped from jail after receiving a hanging sentence and was tracked down and killed by Garrett in 1881. The three are buried together at Fort Sumner.

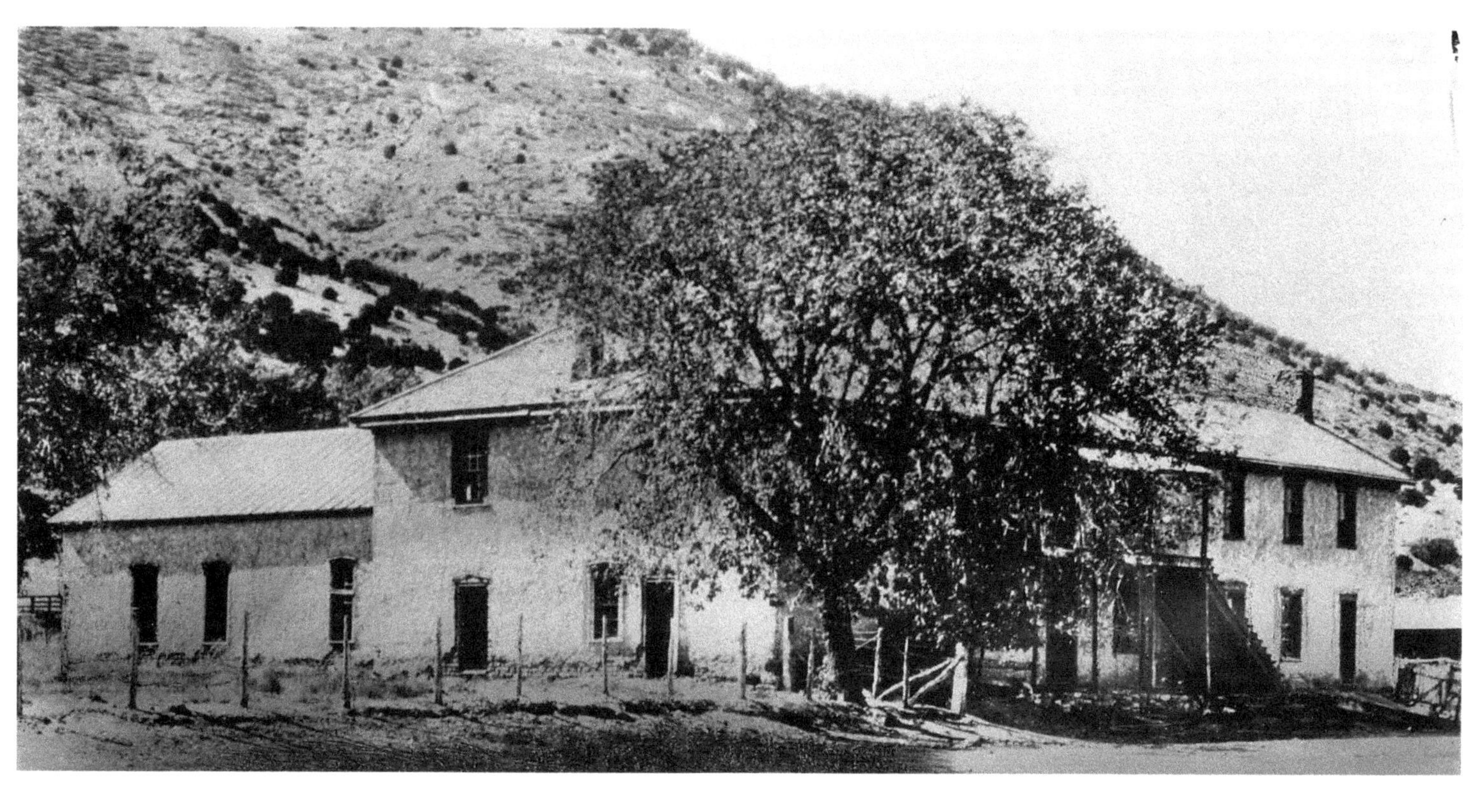

About two weeks before Billy the Kid's scheduled execution in 1881, he broke out of this county jail in Lincoln, New Mexico. Historians have not decided how exactly the escape went down, but many believe he had inside help obtaining a weapon. However it happened, the two deputies guarding him were definitely murdered. The Kid made his escape on a stolen horse.

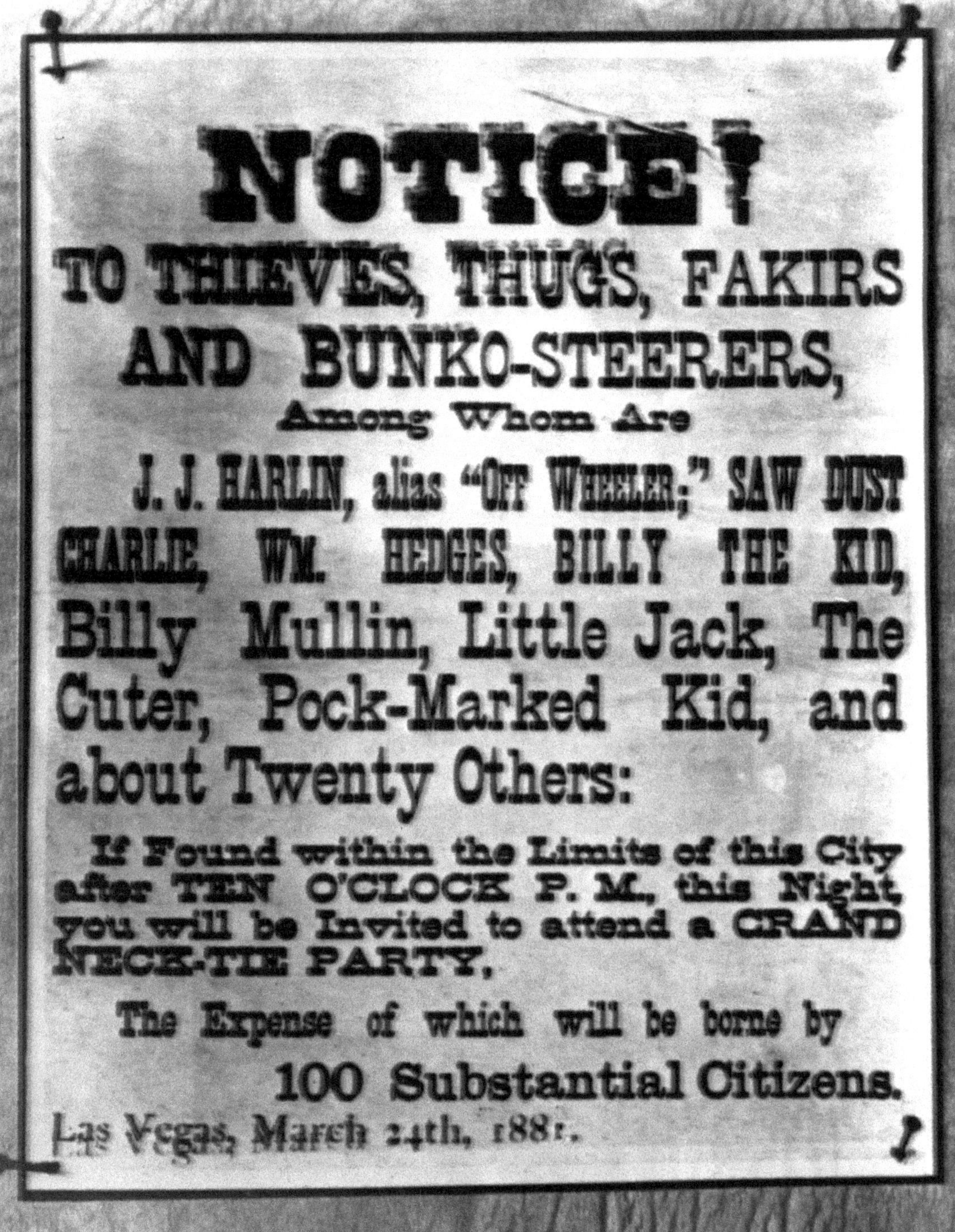

After Pat Garrett reported he had killed Billy the Kid in 1881, several people in New Mexico doubted his story. Two of Garrett's own deputies at the scene said it was not the Kid's body, and the coroner's report was suspect as well. This poster is often cited as fueling those beliefs. It was posted in 1882—six months after he was supposed to have been killed.

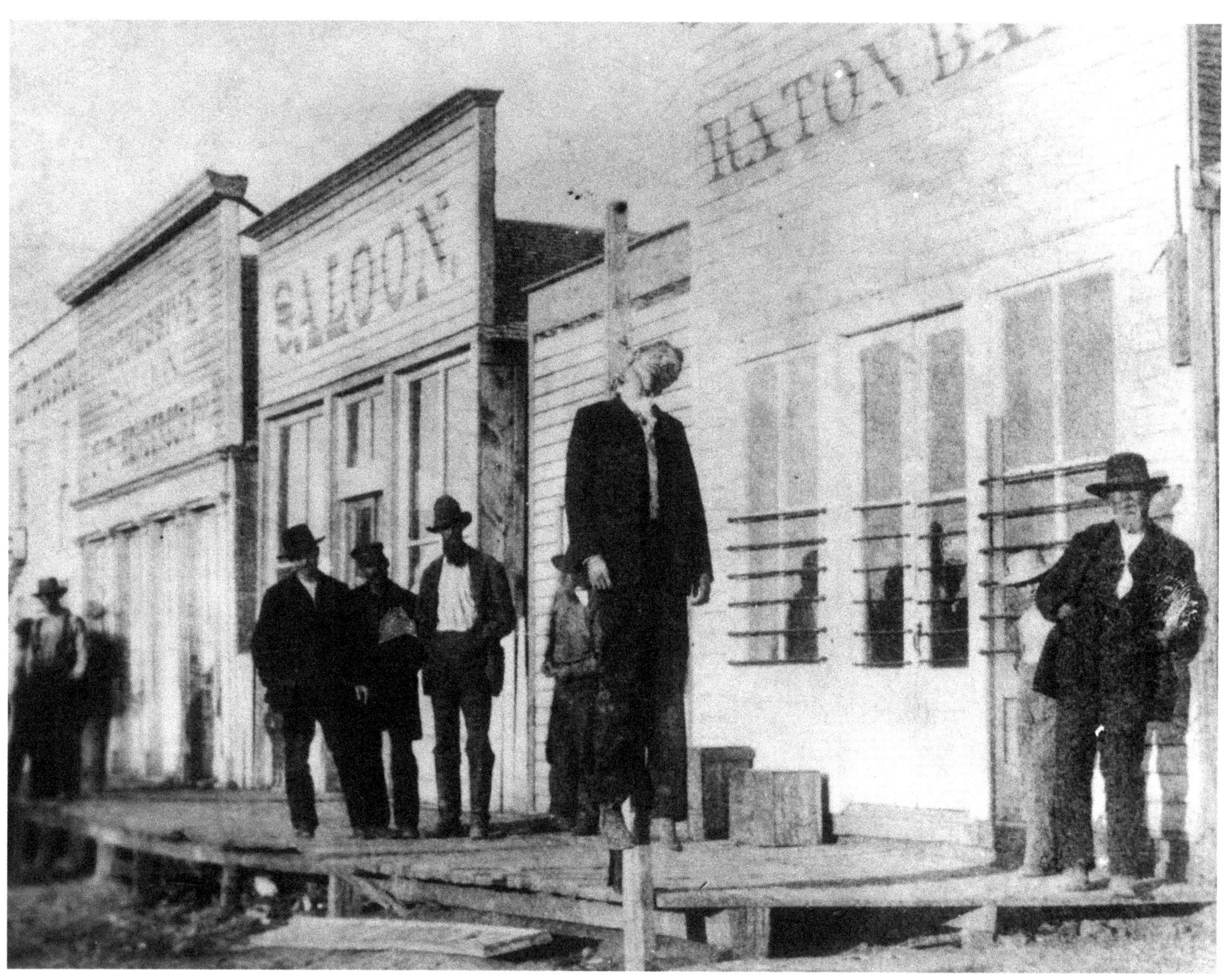

In another part of New Mexico another Kid met his end, in 1882. Gus Mentzer, sometimes known as the Billy the Kid of Kansas, had recently relocated from Dodge City to Raton, where he and his associates attempted to control the town. After repeated acts of violence and a threat on the life of the sheriff, a large mob strung up Gus (seen here) and four others.

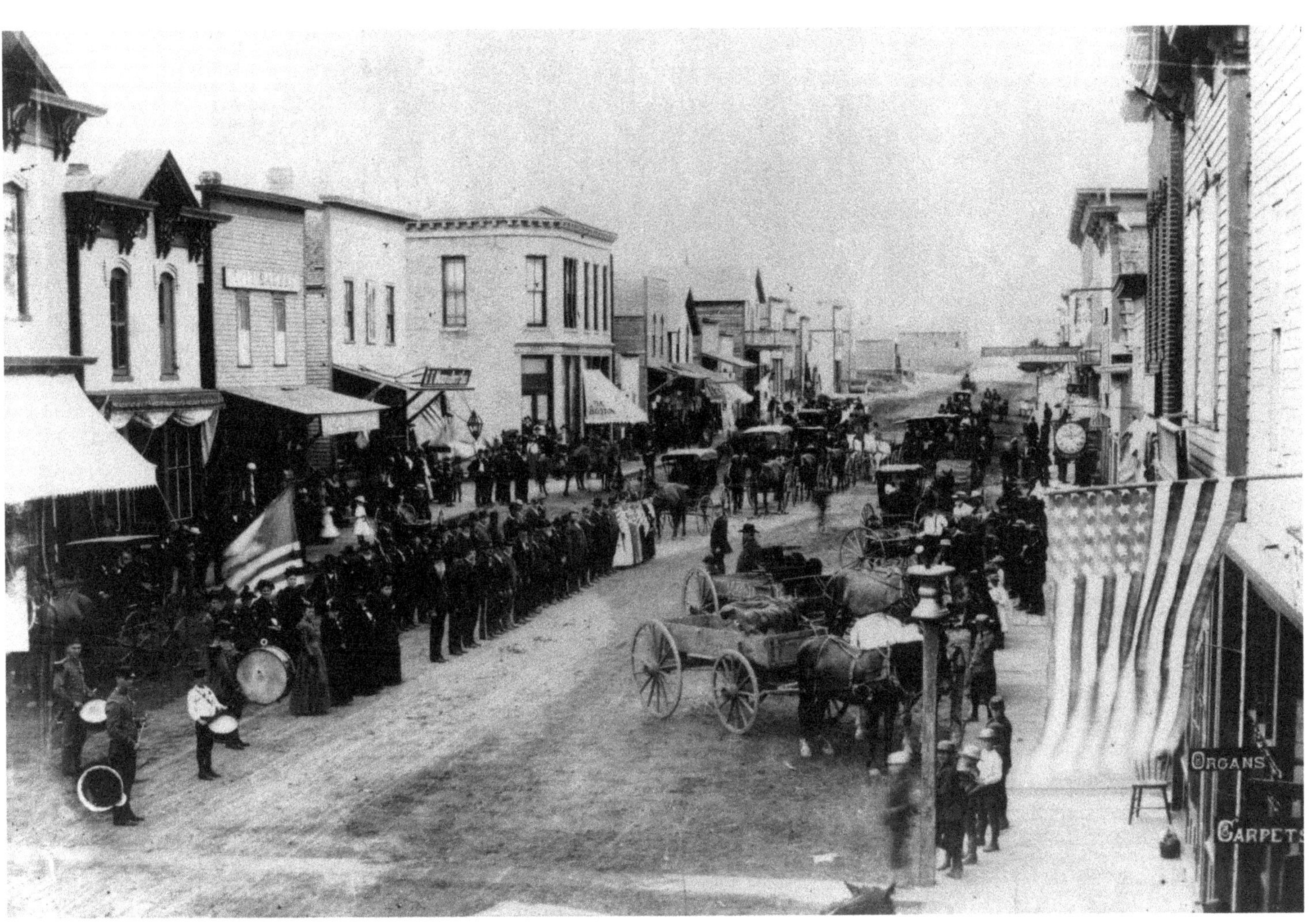

Ortonville, Minnesota (seen here in 1880), was a busy town on the border with Dakota Territory and carried on a brisk trade with the Sioux. Despite this, the town did not attract the usual criminal element, so local law enforcement was inexperienced when Joe Johnson and Jack Nolan of Doc Middleton's Nebraska gang arrived. The desperadoes were prevented from causing trouble, but still managed to shoot it out with a posse and easily escape.

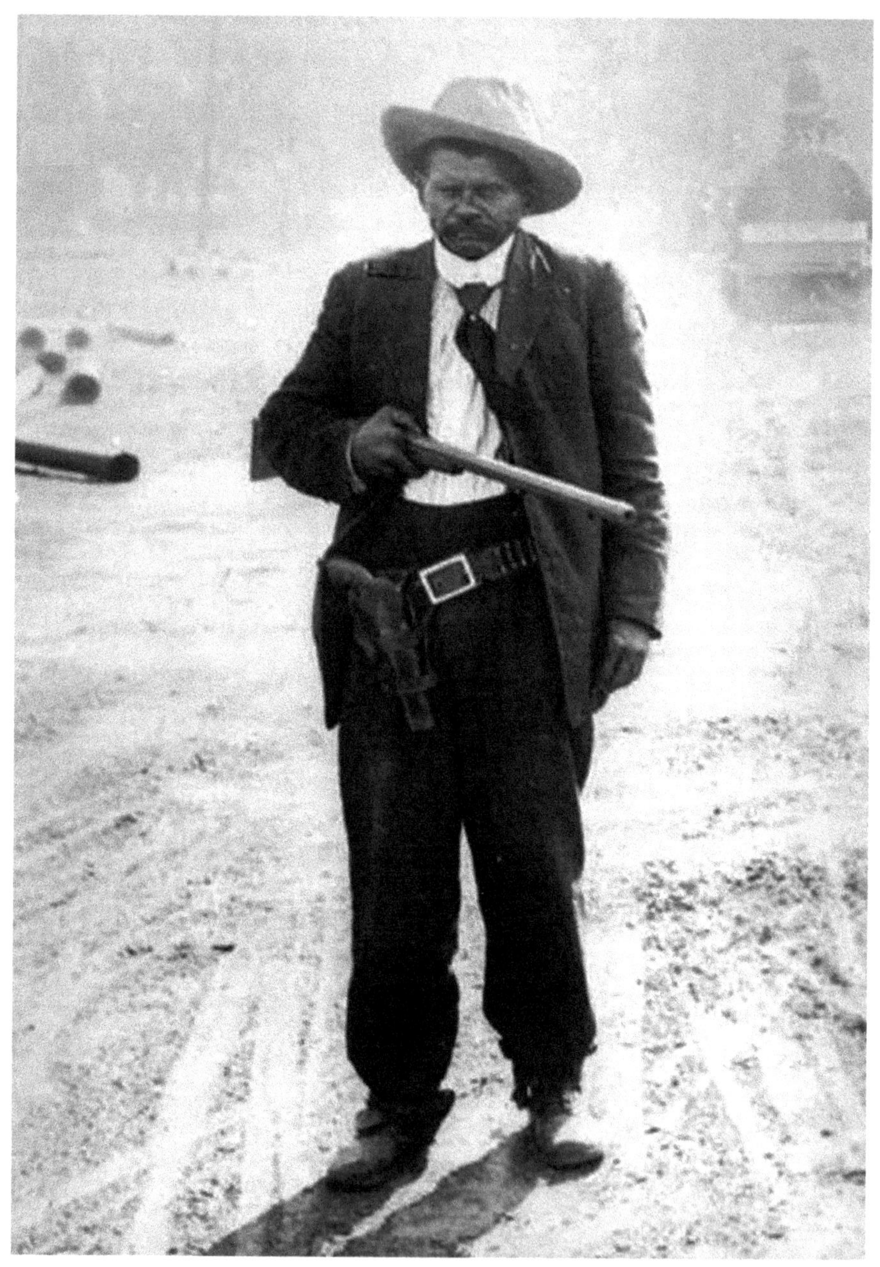

Benjamin Hodges was a black Mexican cowboy from Texas who came to Dodge City on a cattle trail in the 1880s and never left, making a career for himself as a con artist. Historian C. Robert Haywood wrote of him, "Generally treated as an audacious buffoon who gulled the greenhorns and other easy marks, the white cattlemen kept him on as a kind of western-style court jester."

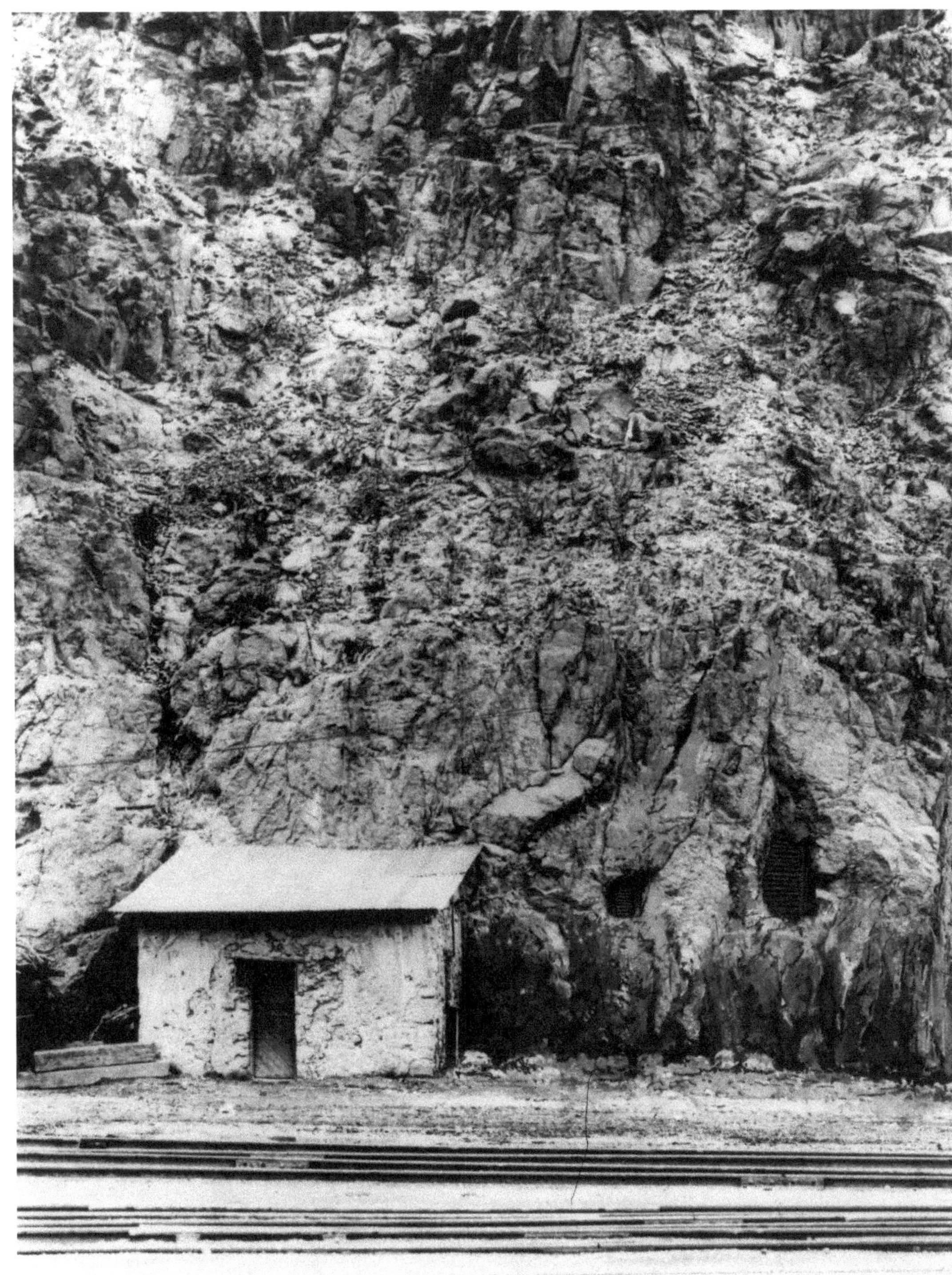

This humble stone jail was built in Clifton, Arizona, in 1878 by the owners of the copper mines in the area. Ironically, Margarito Barela, the man they hired to blast holes in the rock for the cells, celebrated too vigorously upon its completion and became the jail's first prisoner.

Breaking nearly every stereotype, gentlemanly Black Bart (née Charles Boles) was more akin to the Pink Panther's jewel thief than the West's bloodthirsty sociopaths. Bart robbed 29 stagecoaches of their Wells Fargo strongboxes over a period of eight years beginning in 1875. No one was harmed in his robberies, because he used wooden "guns" to steal the money and then invested it in small companies in San Francisco.

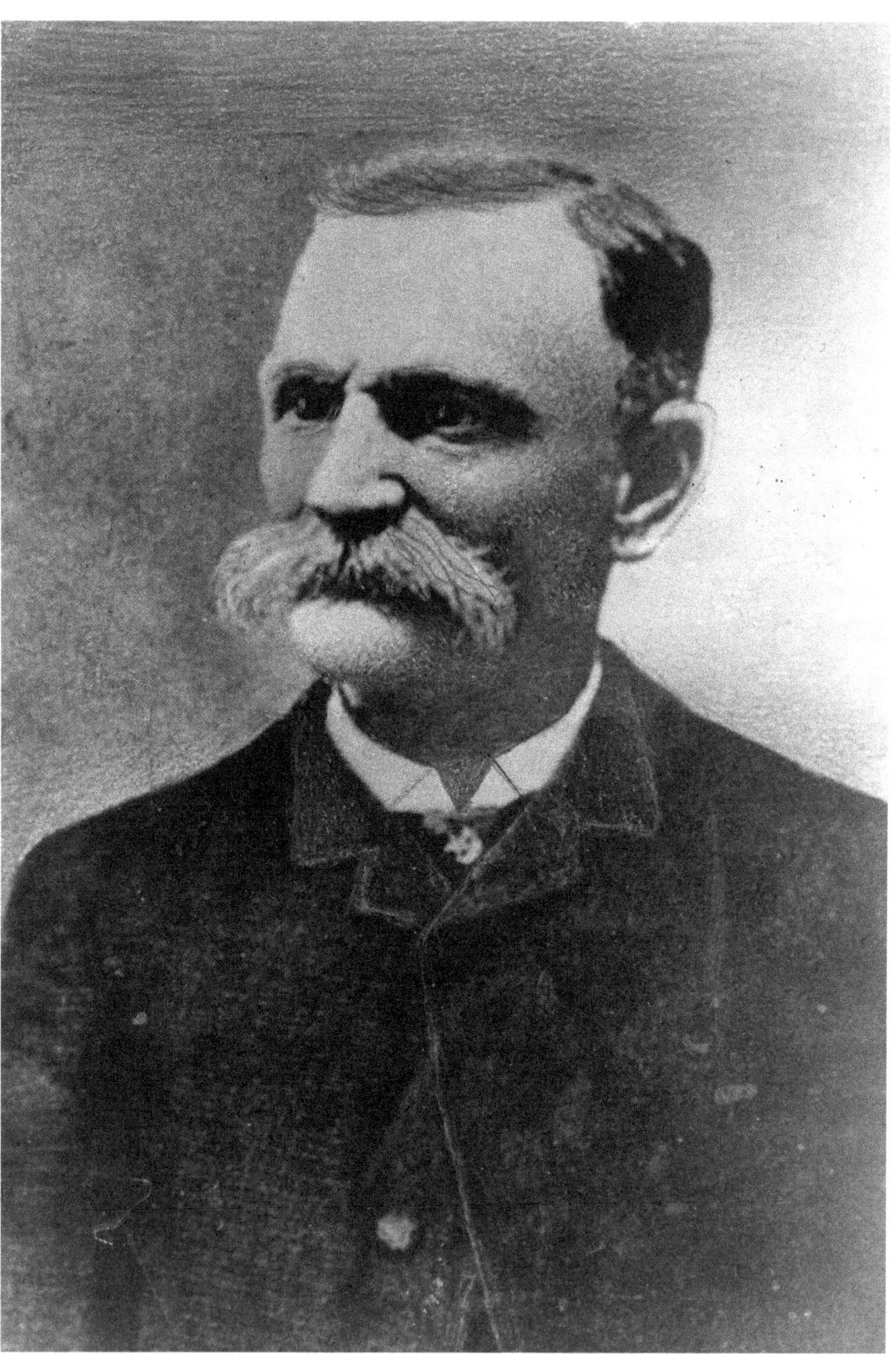

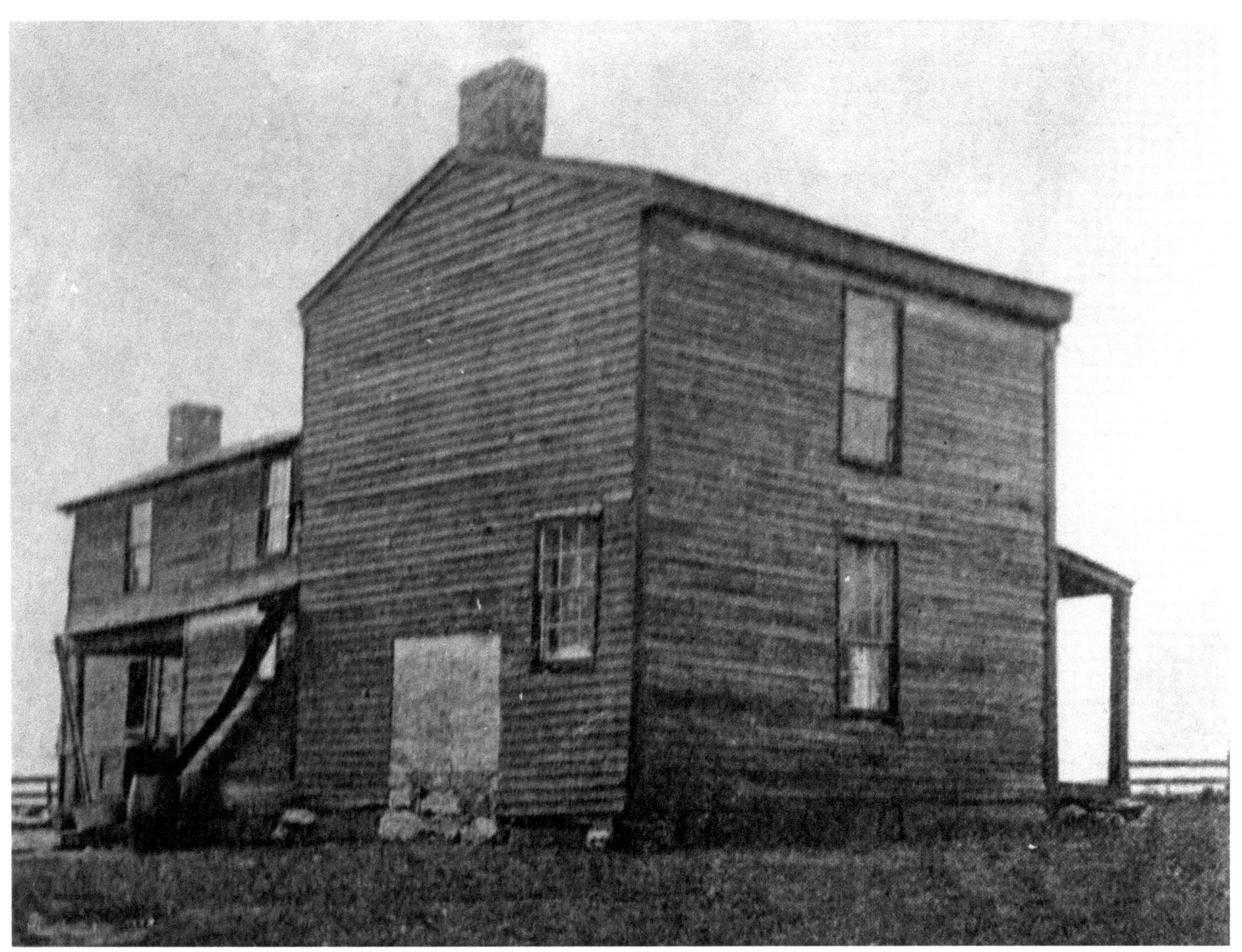

This farmhouse, long identified as the residence of brothers Charles and Robert Ford, was probably photographed in 1882. The Ford brothers often stayed at the home of their widowed sister, Martha Bolton (the Jameses were also known to consort there), and historians now suggest that this house may have been hers.

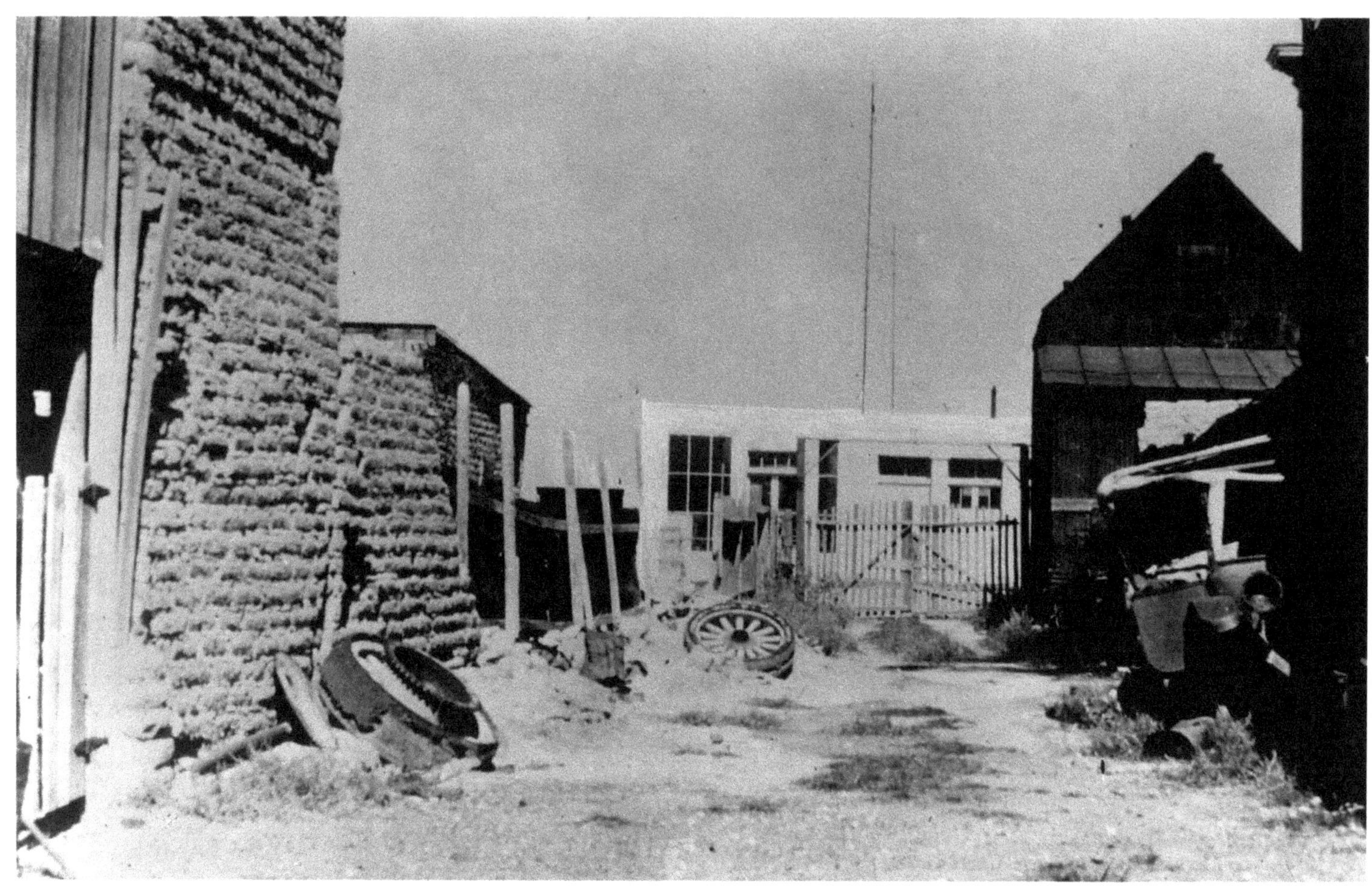

This is the site of the gunfight at the O.K. Corral in Tombstone, Arizona. The gunfight took place near this empty lot a few doors down from the corral. Rival factions squared off in the street—Doc Holliday and Virgil, Wyatt, and Morgan Earp against Ike and Billy Clanton and Frank and Tom McLowery. Eight men drew arms, three died, three were wounded, and two walked away.

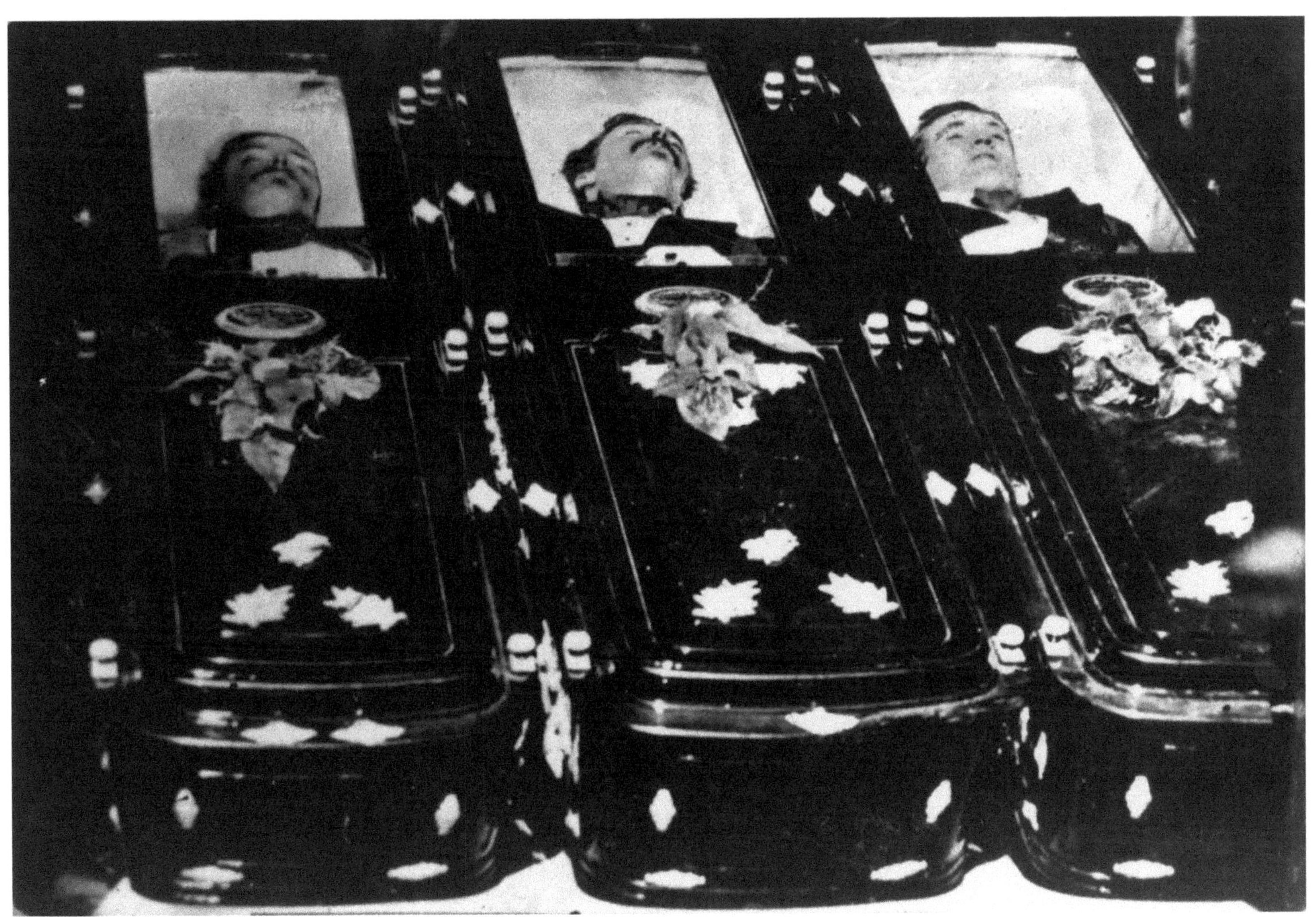

The gunfight at Tombstone in 1881 has become the American archetype for good versus evil. However, historical revision has suggested that the Earp brothers and friend Doc Holliday were not exactly lily-white as enforcers of the law and that the shoot-out with the Clanton-McLowery gang was really a settling of a blood feud between the two parties. The bodies of Tom and Frank McLowery and Billy Clanton are seen here in their extravagant coffins.

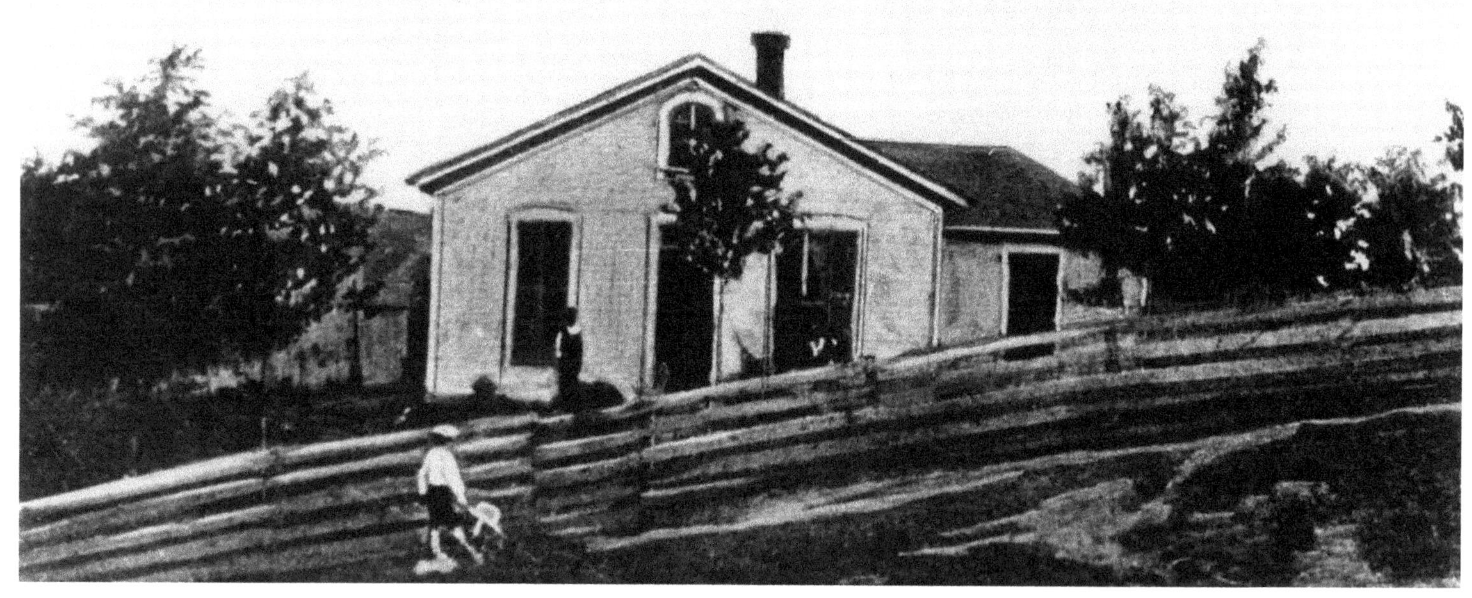

Following the botched Northfield robbery, the James Gang dissolved and the brothers removed to the Nashville area for about four years. Restless, Jesse moved back to northwest Missouri and rented this house at 1318 Lafayette Street in St. Joseph for himself and his wife and two children in 1881. He also invited two new members of his gang to live there—Bob and Charles Ford.

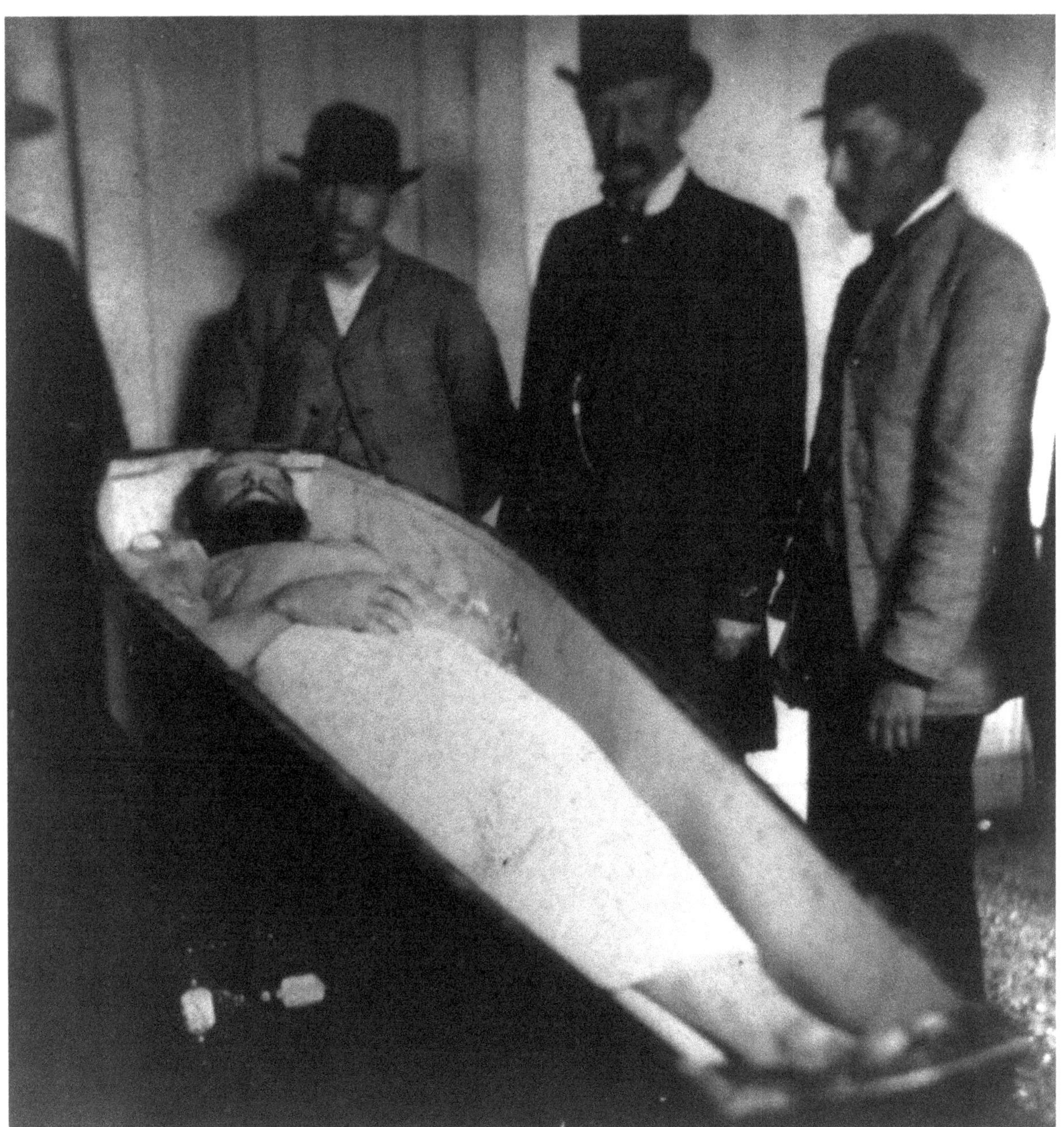

By 1882, Jesse James had lost his old trusted gang and became increasingly paranoid around his new one. On the morning of April 3, 1882, the Fords sat in the drawing room of the house in St. Joseph with James. When Jesse rose to adjust a picture on the wall, Bob Ford drew his pistol and shot James behind the right ear, killing him instantly. Here he lies in repose before burial at the family farm.

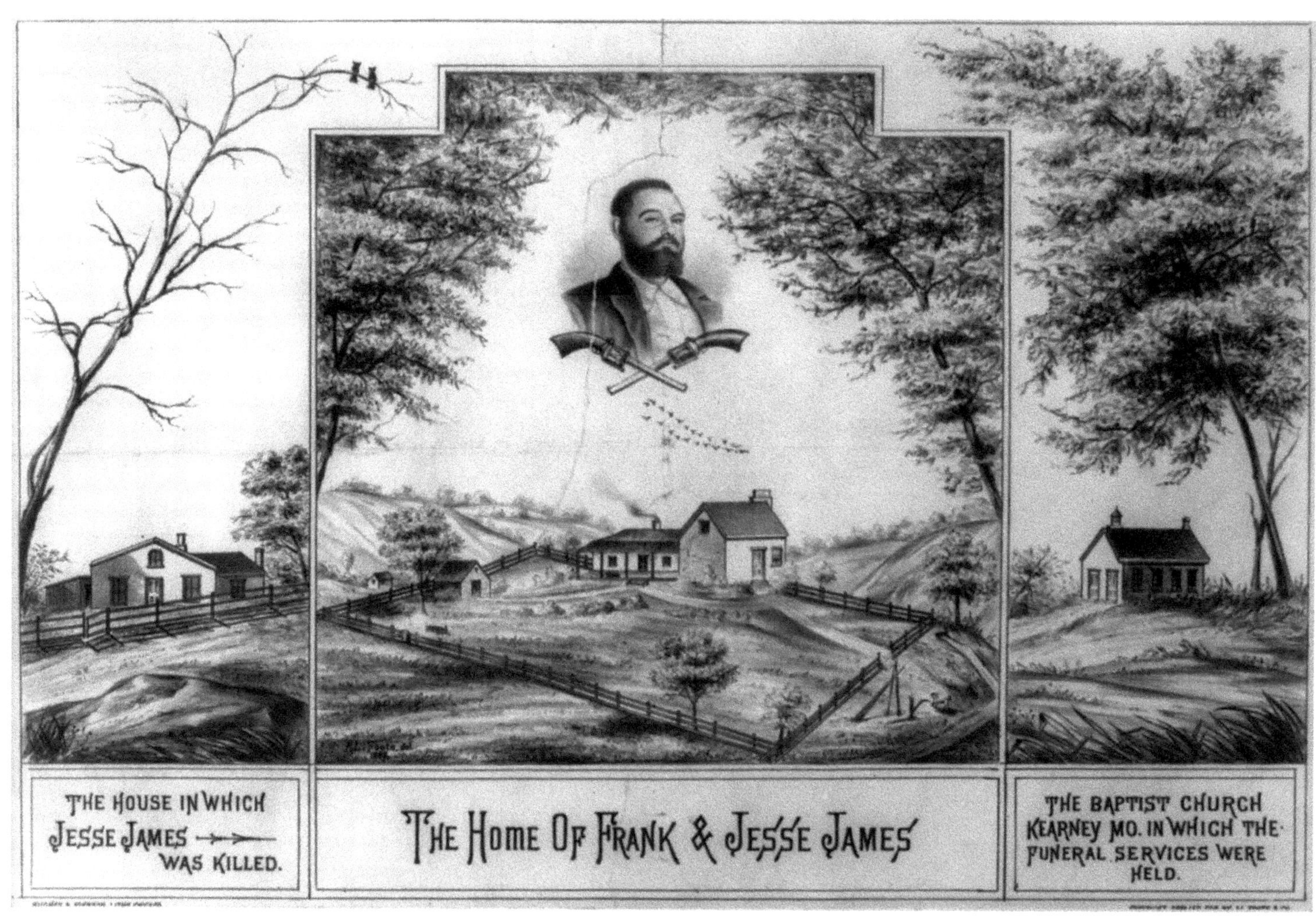

This lithograph, made soon after the assassination of Jesse James, exemplifies the veneration the public had for him by that time. After Jesse's death, the St. Joseph home became a tourist attraction and at the end of his life Frank James charged a quarter to tour the James Farm. The home and farm still stand.

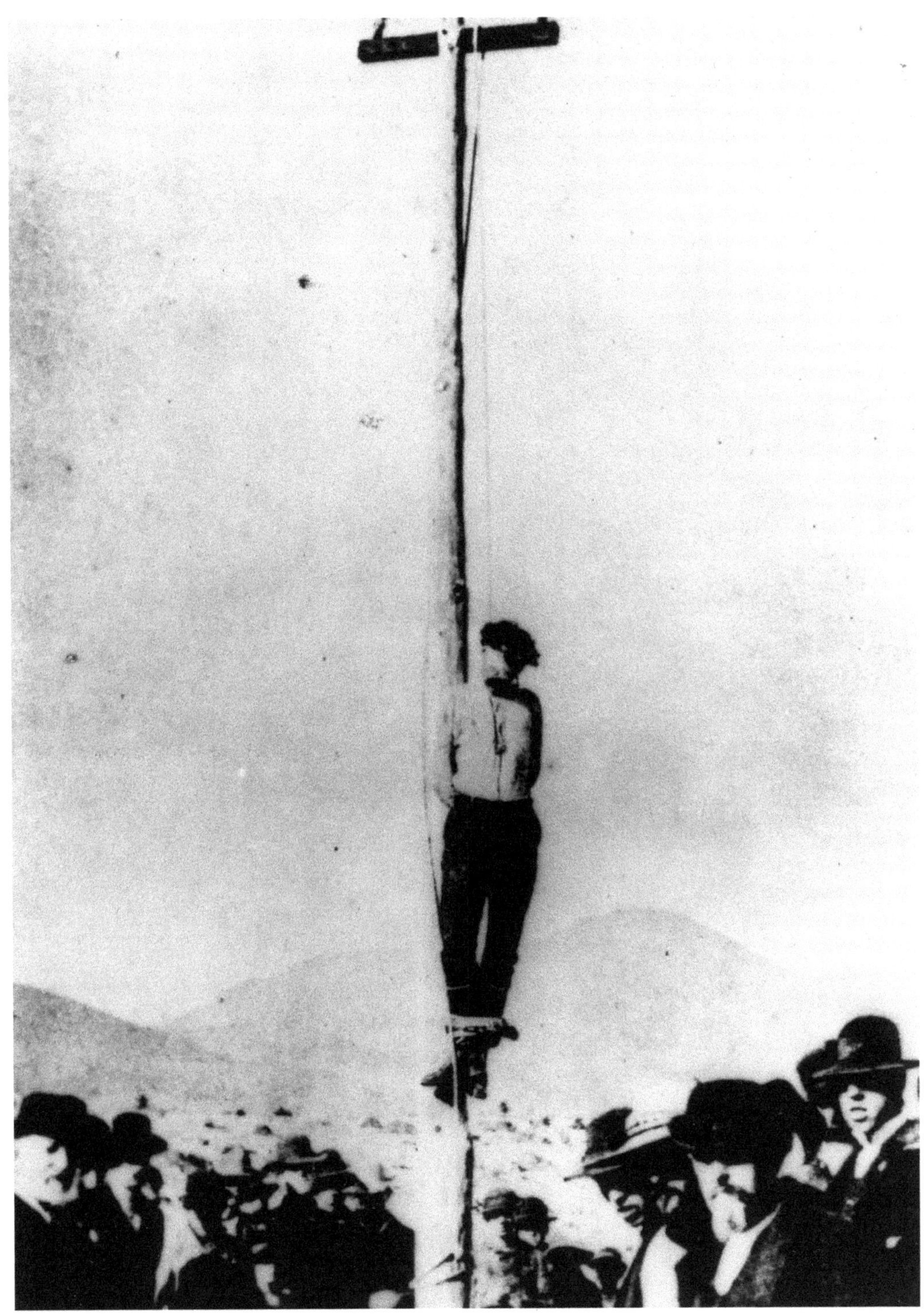

In December 1883, five desperadoes robbed the Goldwater-Casteneda store in Bisbee, Arizona. Despite complete cooperation, they turned murderous, killing five people and wounding several others. All five bandits received a death sentence, but the ringleader, John Heith, who did not participate in the actual robbery and who was implicated later, got life. Enraged at this verdict, Bisbee vigilantes locked the sheriff in the jail and strung Heith up to the nearest telegraph pole.

After a bloodthirsty youth, gunman King Fisher became a lawman in Uvalde County, Texas. While in Austin in 1884, he encountered the notorious Ben Thompson and the two traveled together for a time swapping gunfight stories until their past caught up with them in San Antonio. The two were ambushed and killed by men out for Thompson, the 30-year-old Fisher riddled with 13 bullets to the head and chest.

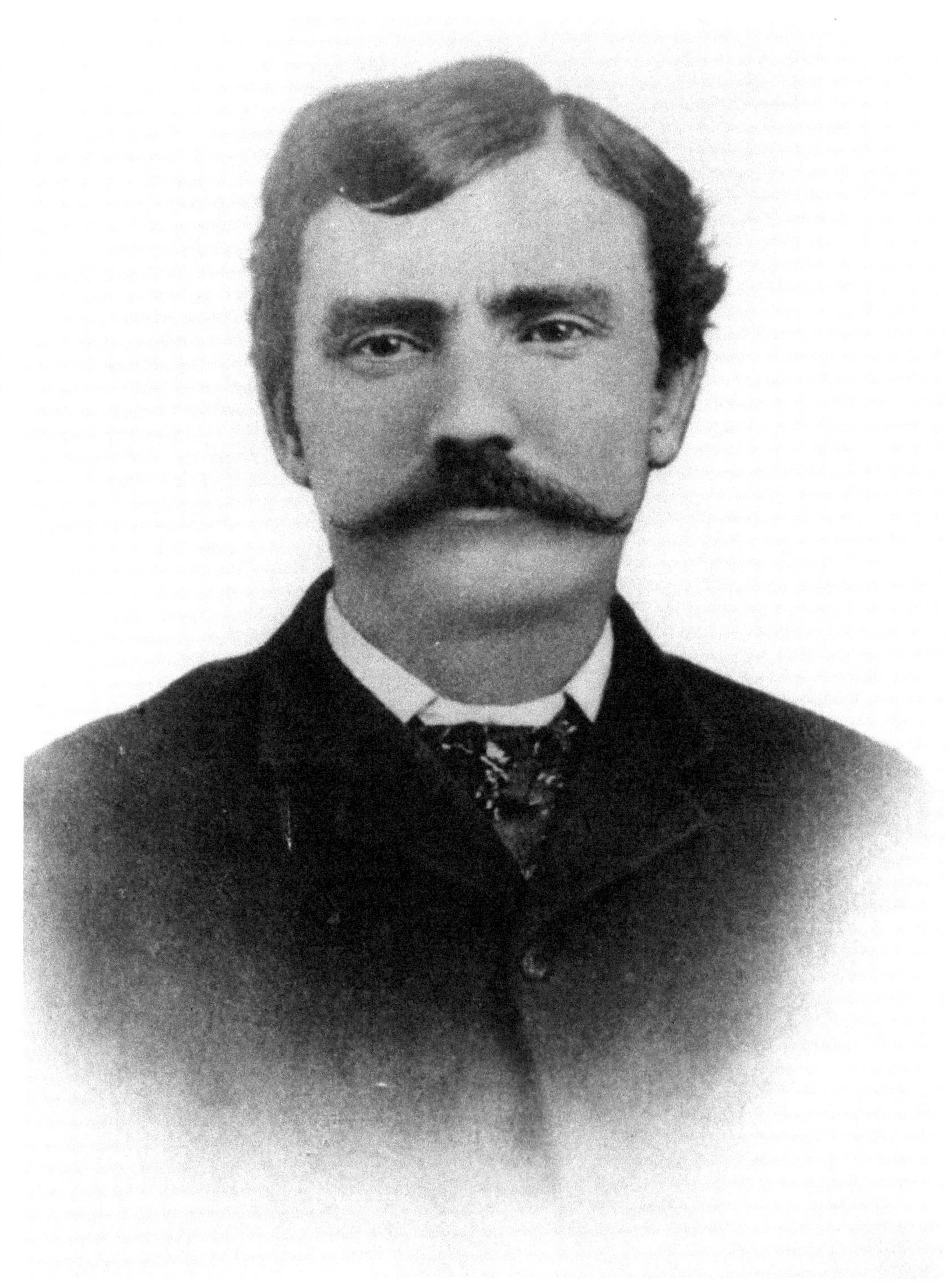

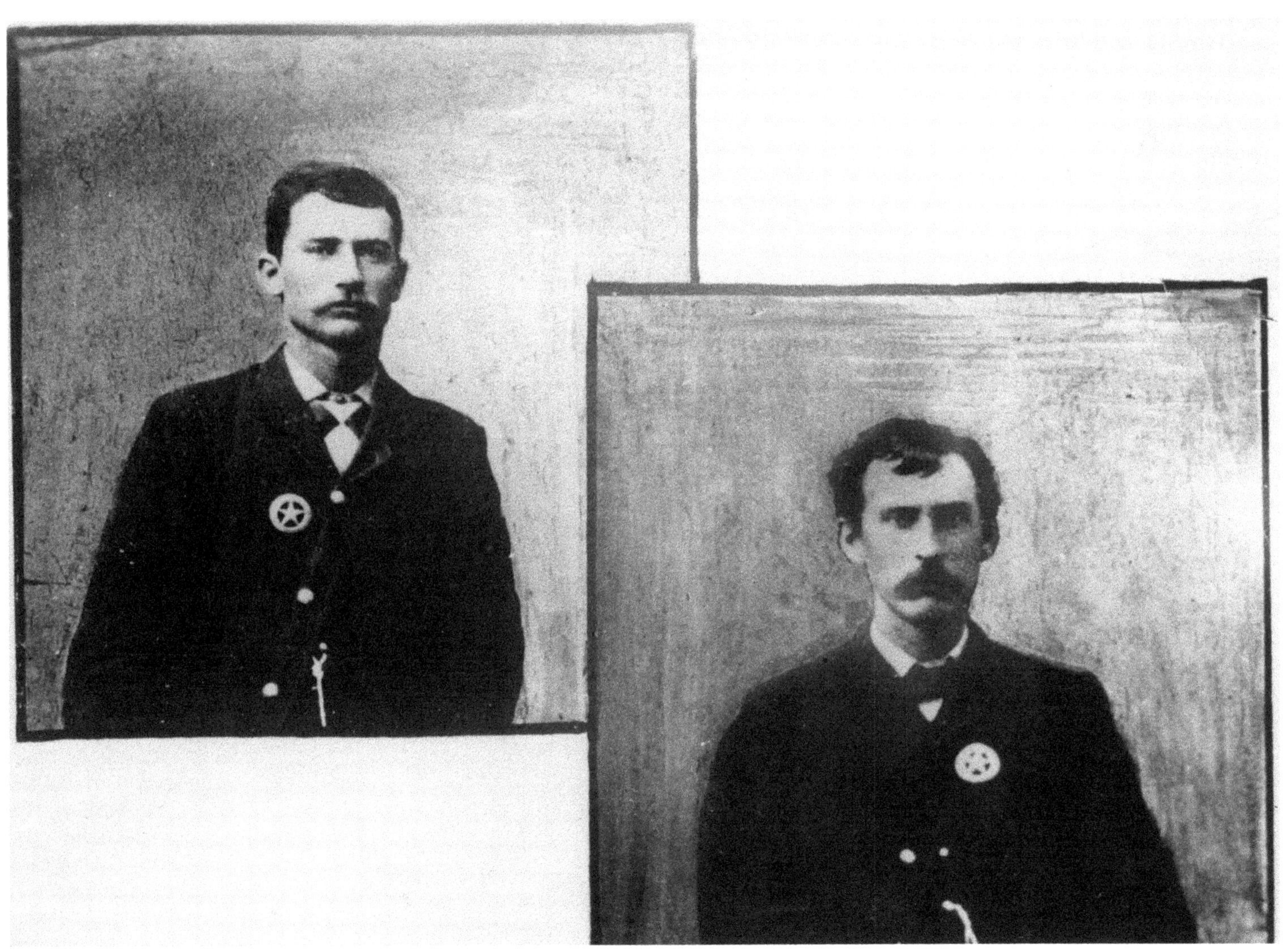

This souvenir card depicts Henry Newton Brown (left) and Ben Wheeler (right) around 1884. Brown was once a Regulator alongside Billy the Kid in the Lincoln County War and had come to Caldwell, Kansas, where he served as city marshal. They were effective law enforcers, but both had gunslinging in their pasts and were easily tempted by the prospect of easy money.

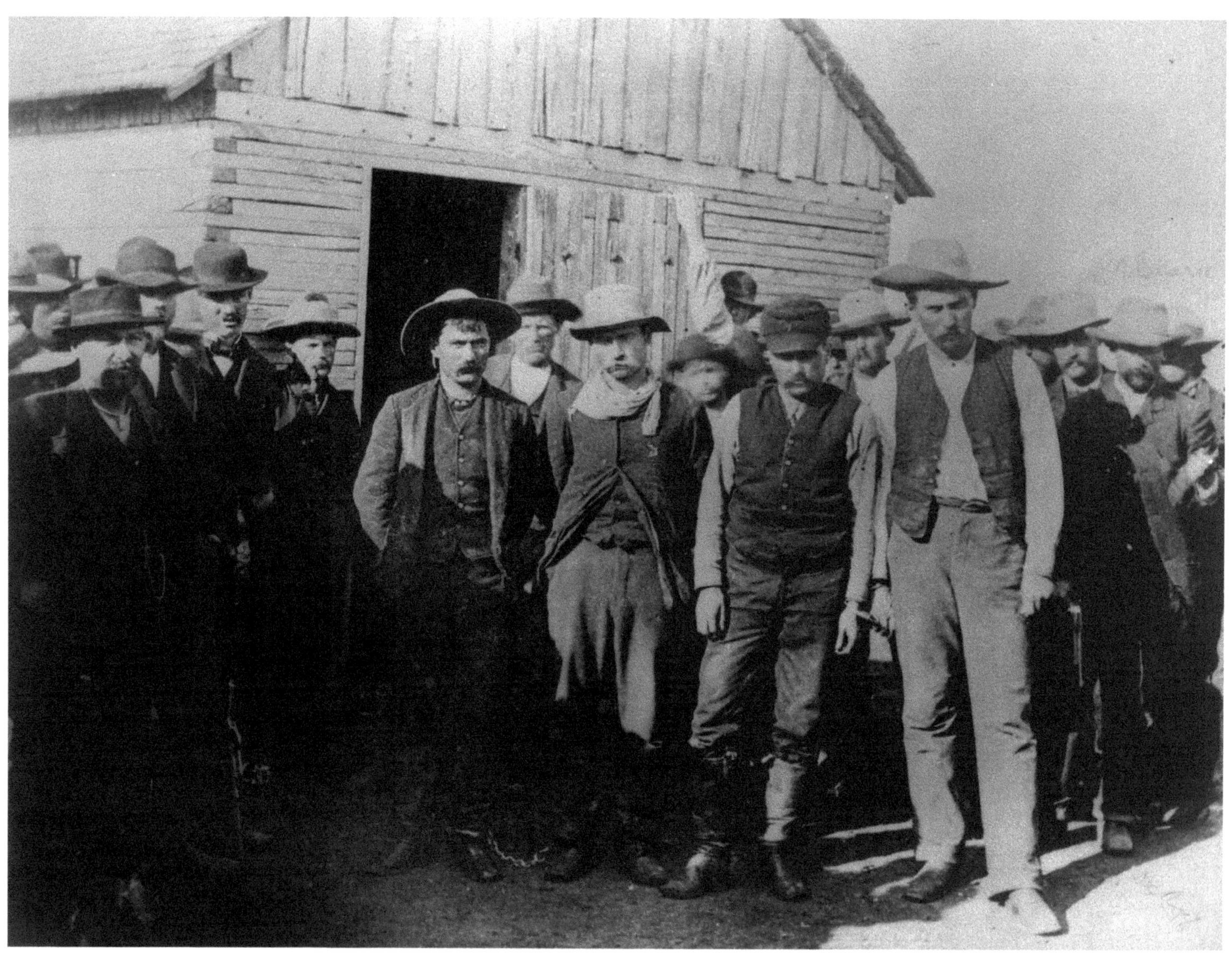

John Wesley, Henry Newton Brown, Billy Smith, and Ben Wheeler (in shackles) were foiled in their attempts to rob the bank in Medicine Lodge, Kansas, in 1884. Hours after this photograph was taken they made a run for it when a vigilante mob came for them—Brown was killed by the posse and the other three hanged.

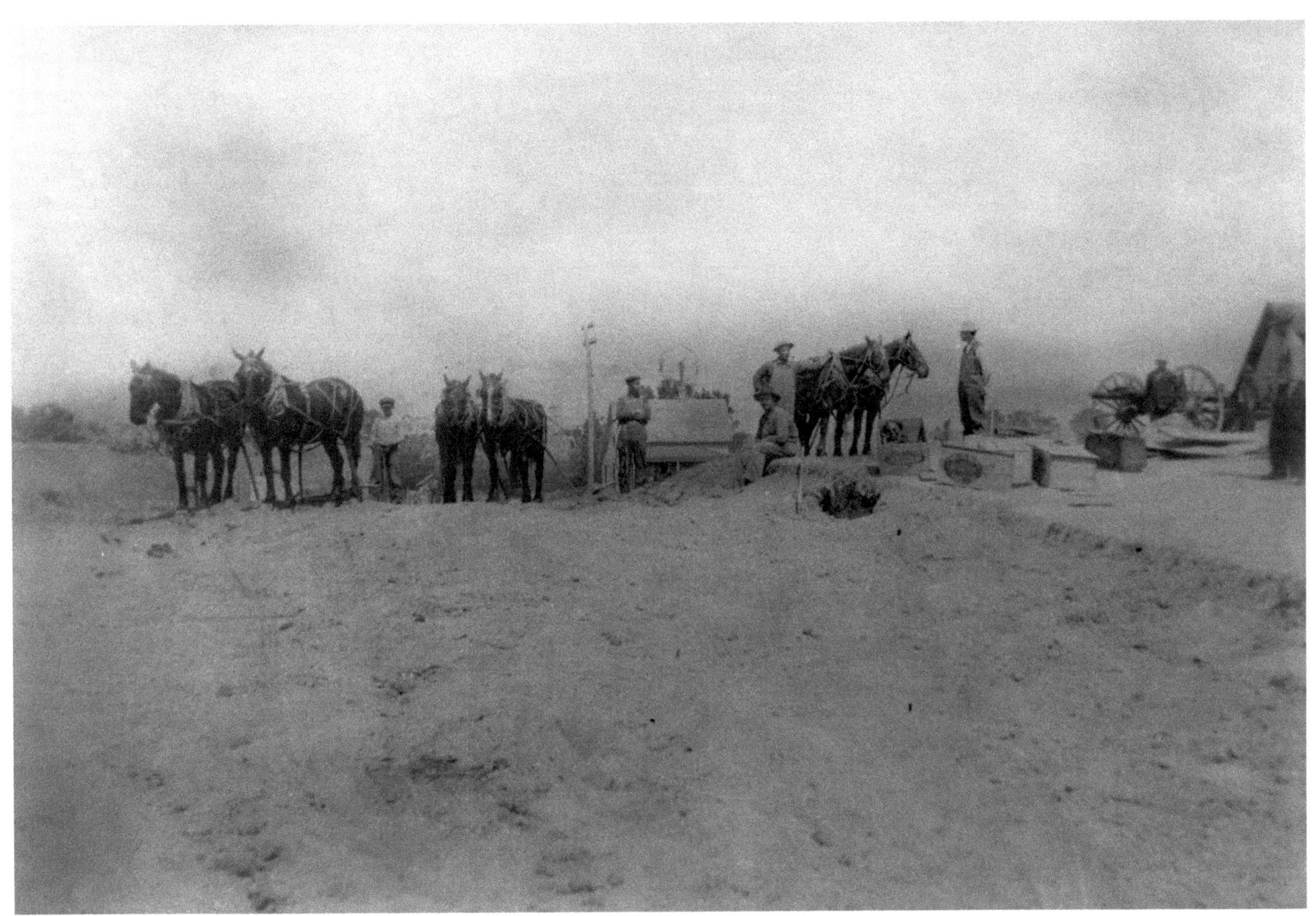

In the 1860s, Wild Bill Hickok, then the marshal of Hays, Kansas, selected a hilltop outside town to bury the many men killed in shoot-outs and drunken brawls in the wild cow town. Most were buried with their boots and other effects, so locals came to call it Boot Hill. Eventually, "Boot Hill" became a generic term for many such places in the West. Here it is being excavated in 1884 and permanent markers put in place.

Following Spread: The 1880s brought three railroads to the drowsy border town of El Paso, Texas, which began to boom as an entrepôt for trade with Mexico. Town organizers kept the place open to vice to encourage growth, but it became sinful beyond their imagination. One visitor reported, "If you bet, they get your watch and money. If you decline, they bring their six shooters down on you as a kind of moral persuader."

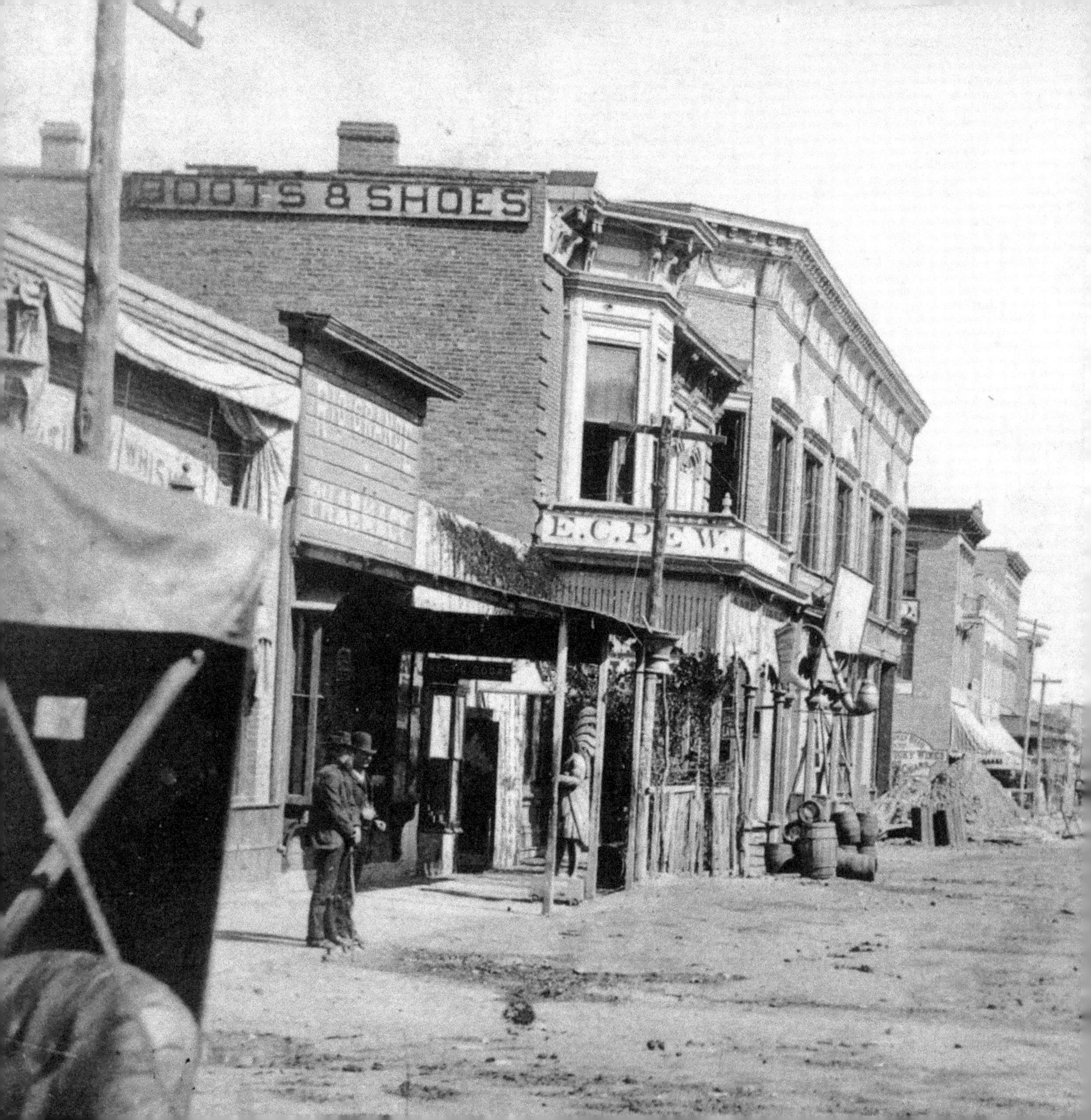
BOOTS & SHOES
E. C. PEW.

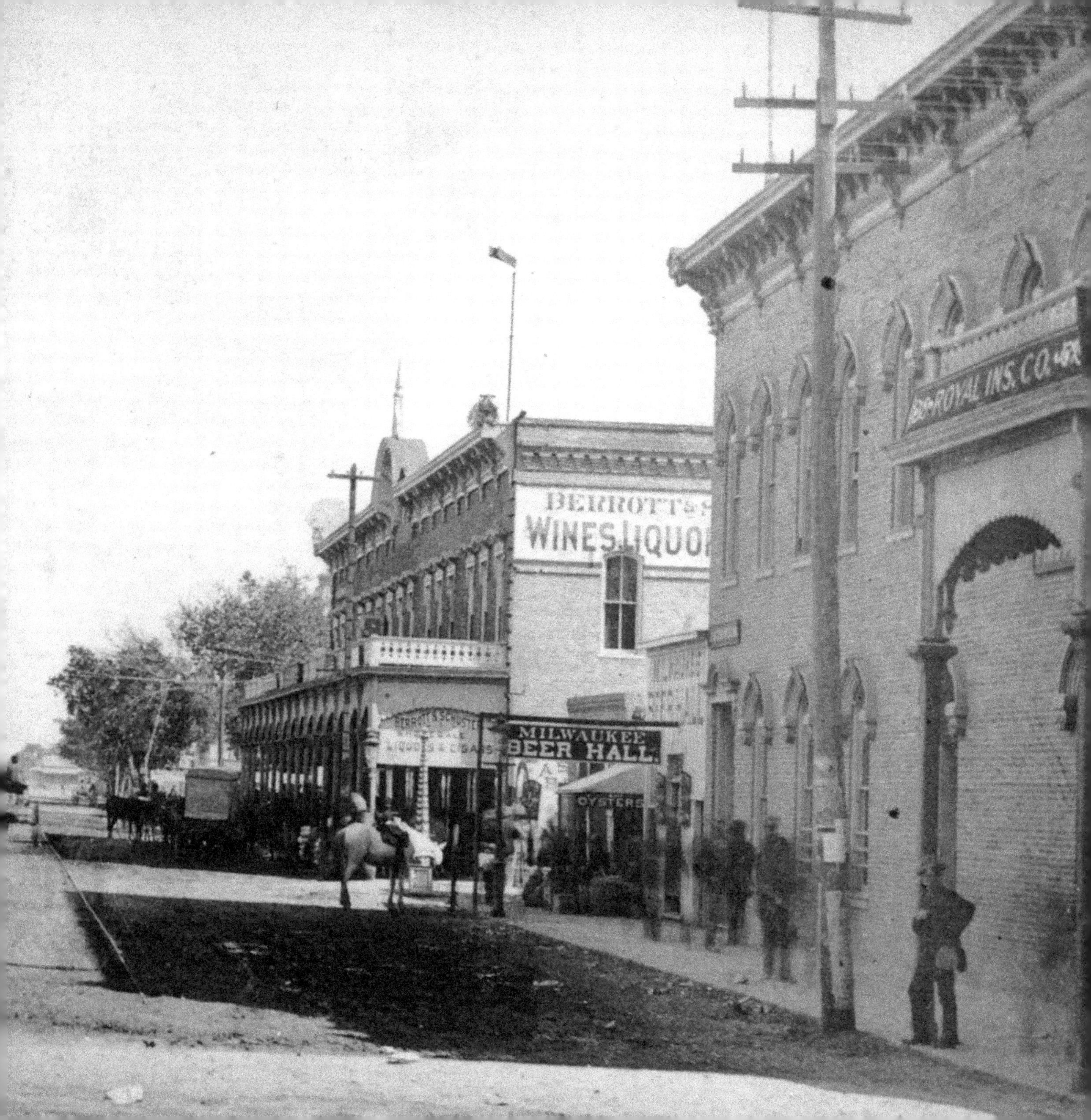
BERROTT & S
WINES LIQUOR
ROYAL INS. CO.
MILWAUKEE
BEER HALL.
OYSTERS

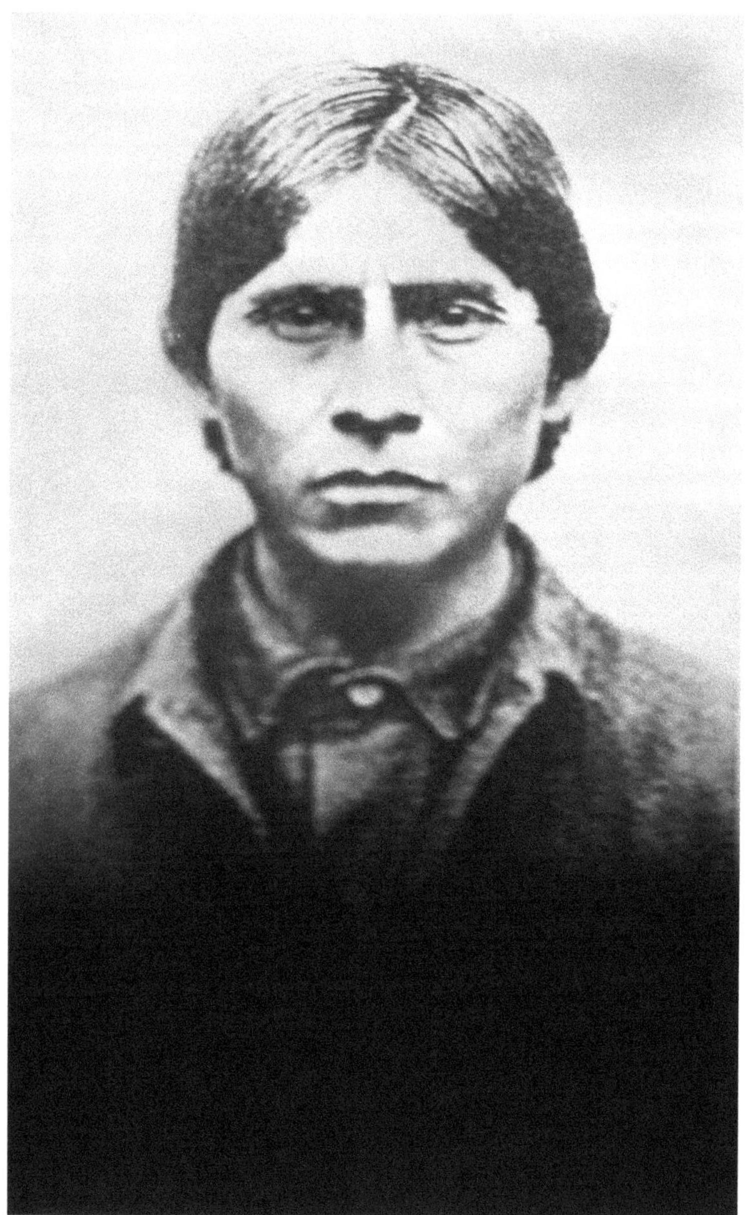

Onetime U.S. Cavalry scout Haskay-bay-nay-ntayl served time for desertion in the late 1880s. On his release he and two companions went on a crime spree in Arizona and eluded capture, which earned him the sobriquet "the Apache Kid." A Phoenix paper wrote, "The Kid has terrorized Arizona for five years and gives no signs that he is discouraged by the white man's bluff."

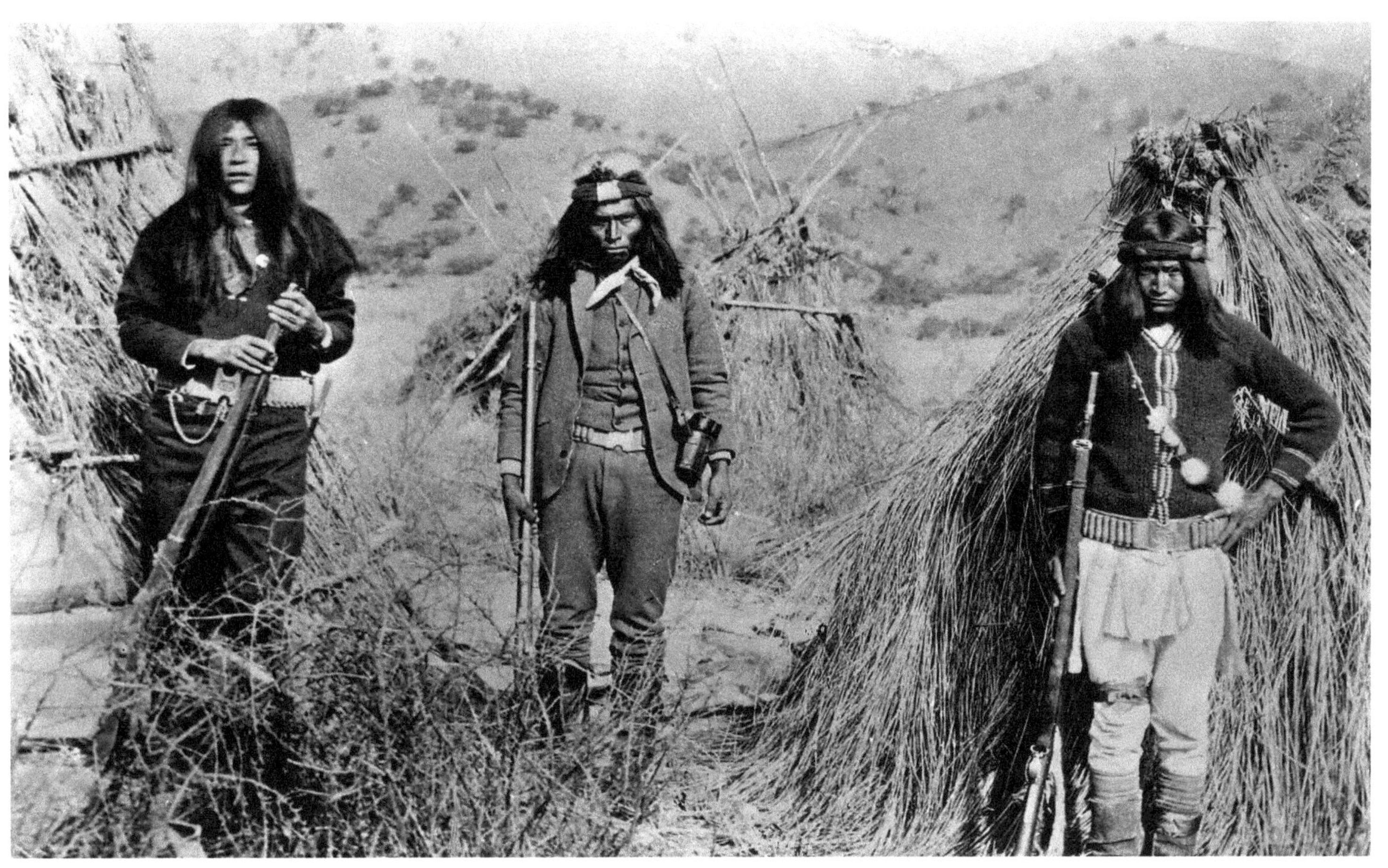

The Apache Kid typically worked as part of a three-man team, but he was known to have an encampment of at least a dozen associates on the Mexico side of the border with Arizona, which made raids throughout southern Arizona.

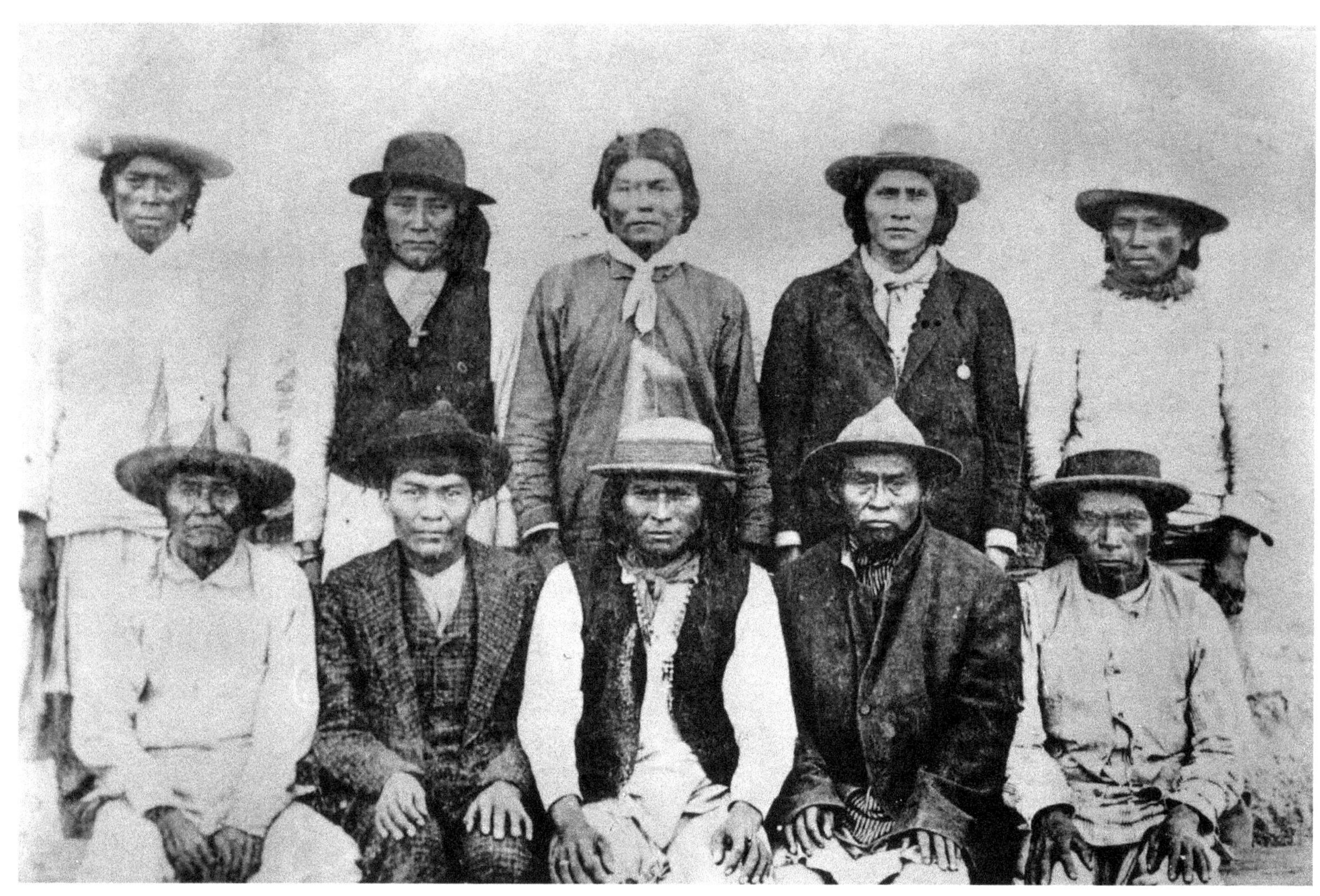

Several of the Apache Kid's associates were recaptured after their bloody escape during transportation to Yuma Prison, in which two of their guards were murdered and the Kid slipped away. Contemporary accounts held that the night before their execution, three of the five removed their traditional Apache sashes and strangled themselves while the remaining two met their fate on the gallows. The Kid is seen here standing, second from right.

We Never Sleep

(1886–1895)

The outlaws and their exploits were already slipping into the past by the time Hollywood got hold of them, and most of what modern Americans imagine of the Old West and its outlaws was molded by Hollywood westerns, which took their plots from dime novels and sensationalist newspapers of the era. By the mid-1880s, Billy the Kid and Jesse James were dead and the Gunfight at the O.K. Corral had been shot out; it was the popular media of succeeding years that was largely responsible for creating the mythological characters and events we know today. If Hollywood's role in creating the myth was paramount, it was preceded by that of writers like Owen Wister and Mark Twain, and the Wild West shows, most famously that of Buffalo Bill Cody, who brought the romantic West to the East and even to Europe.

This era saw the civilizers begin to encroach on the once wide open West and former cow towns and trading posts. Whistle-stops across the West, like Dallas, Houston, Denver, and Phoenix, became substantial cities. Because outlaws, highwaymen, and bandits typically avoided the larger towns and generally did not target ordinary citizens, they were pushed into areas of the West that remained remote.

At the same time, the civilizers began to concentrate on the outlaw problem and brought substantial resources to bear in apprehending them. Railroads offered copious amounts of cash and other rewards for capturing outlaws or for information leading to their arrest. They also began employing enhanced security measures like double safes and armed crewmen to ensure safe delivery of their cargoes. Law enforcement also began to coordinate their efforts across jurisdictions for the first time, employing the railroads and the telegraph for communication and quick organization of posses just minutes after an outlaw raid. The Pinkerton National Detective Agency was another factor, employing thousands of agents across the country to bring criminals to justice, sometimes in the employ of the federal government, other times for a wealthy client or corporation. Pinkerton's famous motto was "We never sleep."

All in all, it was becoming more difficult to be an outlaw. As parasitic beings, they relied on commerce and the movement of goods and people through regions of the West, but too much notoriety and too much civilization were now bringing too much heat.

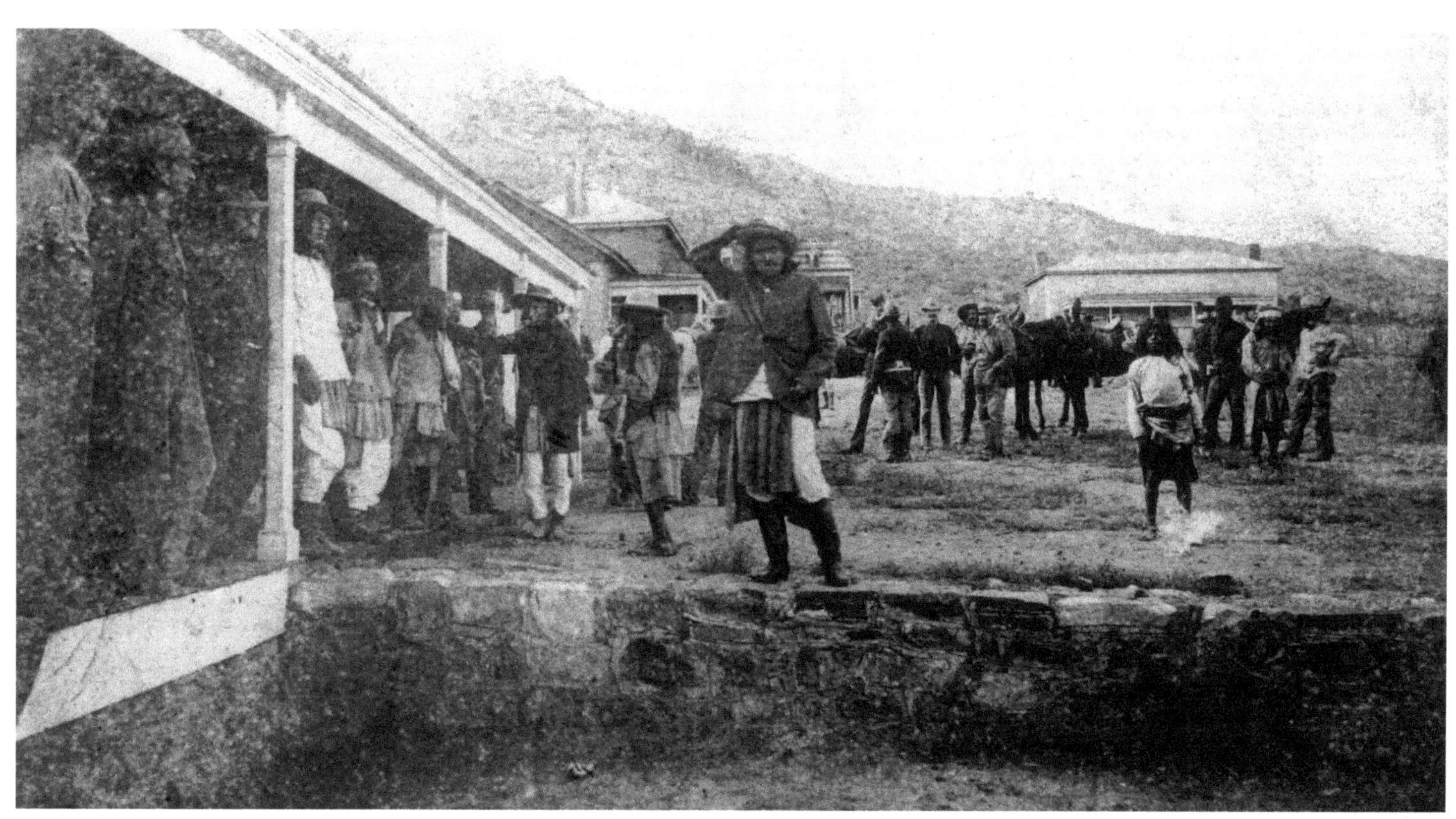

Apache leader Geronimo raided American and Mexican settlements in the Arizona-Sonora region much like Quantrill and Cleveland did during the Civil War. Although he was not technically an outlaw, the U.S. Army (and even some Apaches) viewed him as such because he and his band preferred raiding to life on the Apache reservation. He's seen here at Fort Bowie after his 1886 capture.

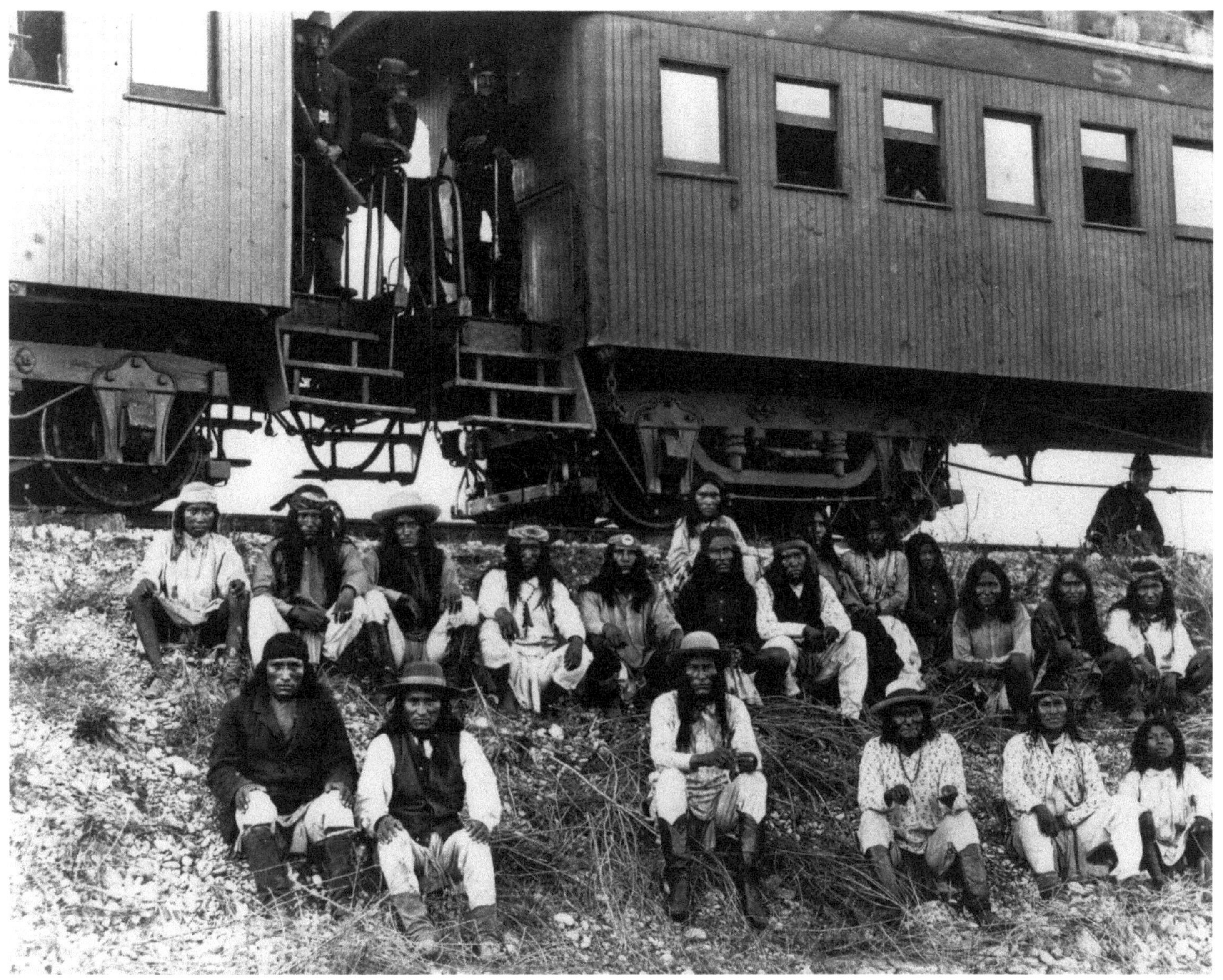

These Apache prisoners rest near Nueces, Texas, en route to the prison at Fort Pickens, Florida. The U.S. Cavalry spent most of 1886 chasing down Natchez (front, center) and Geronimo and his son (in matching spotted shirts, at left) after a decade of relentless Apache raids on Arizona settlements and trains.

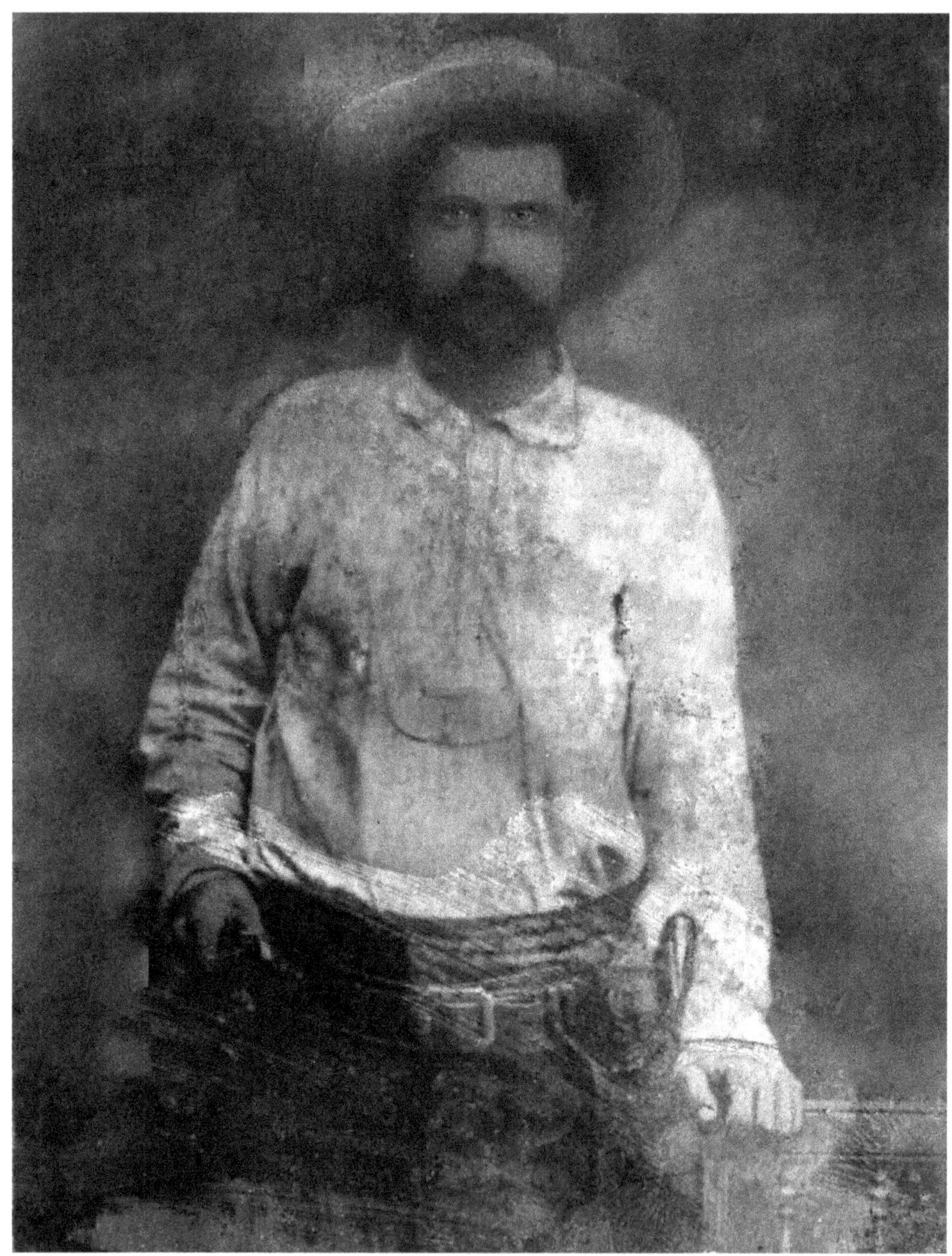

Brack Cornett hailed from south Texas and was a prominent member of a successful gang of train robbers in the region. After hitting lucrative trains at Cisco, McNeill, and Flatonia, they were ambushed by a posse at Floresville. Most of the gang were killed, but Cornett made a miraculous escape to Frio, Arizona, where Texas sheriff Alfred Allee caught up with him and killed him.

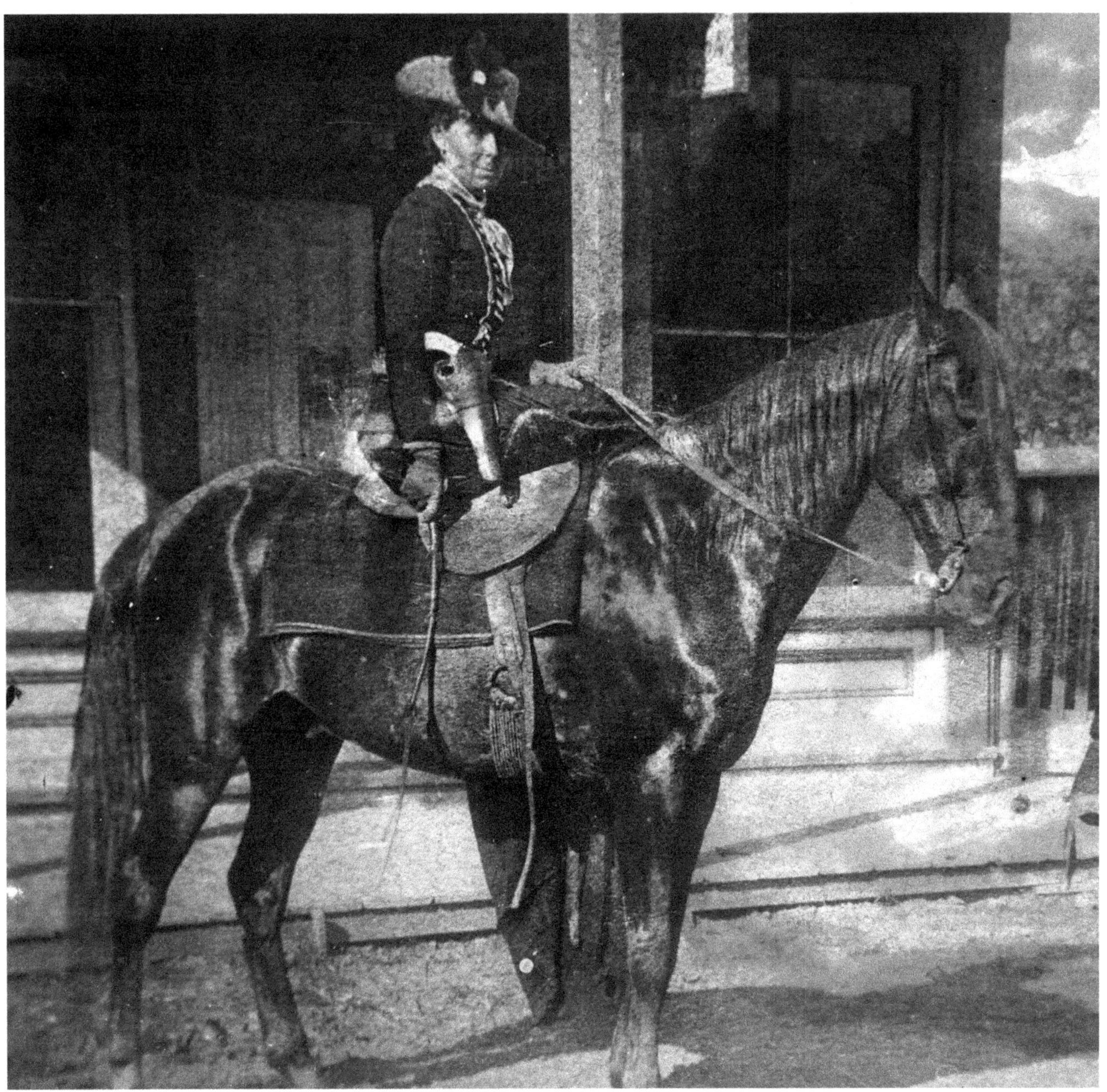

Belle Starr in Fort Smith after she was brought into court by Deputy Marshal Tyner Hughes on a robbery charge in 1886. Belle was caught off guard by Hughes and was quoted (perhaps apocryphally) as saying, "Hughes is a brave man and acted the gentleman in every particular, but I hardly believe he recognized his danger."

Early writers of Western fiction believed this 1886 photograph of Cherokee outlaw Blue Duck with Belle Starr proved their romantic involvement. Although it's certain Blue Duck was associated with the nefarious activities of Belle Starr's associates, many historians today believe this photo was simple publicity in support of Blue Duck's pending appeal of a murder conviction.

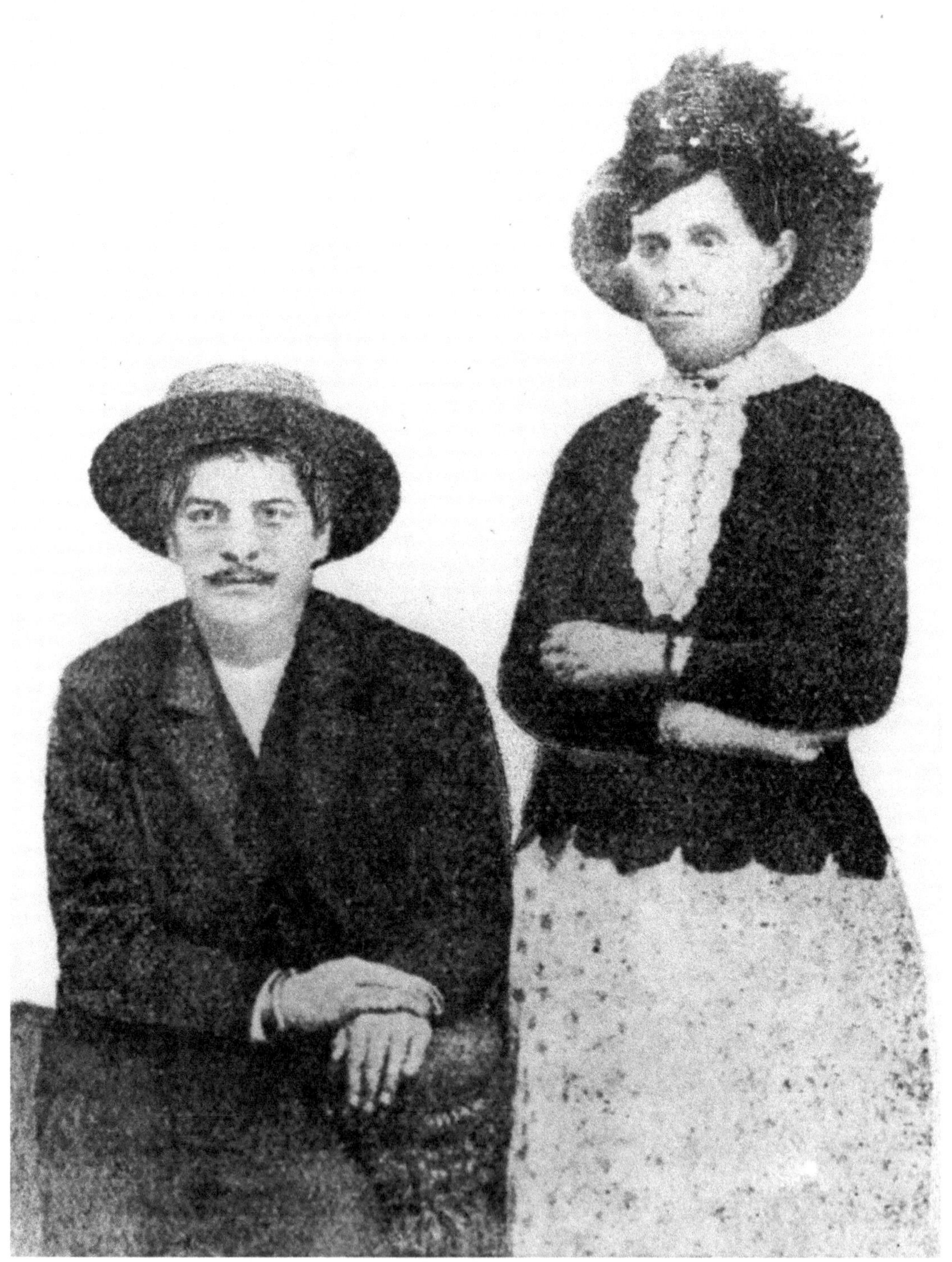

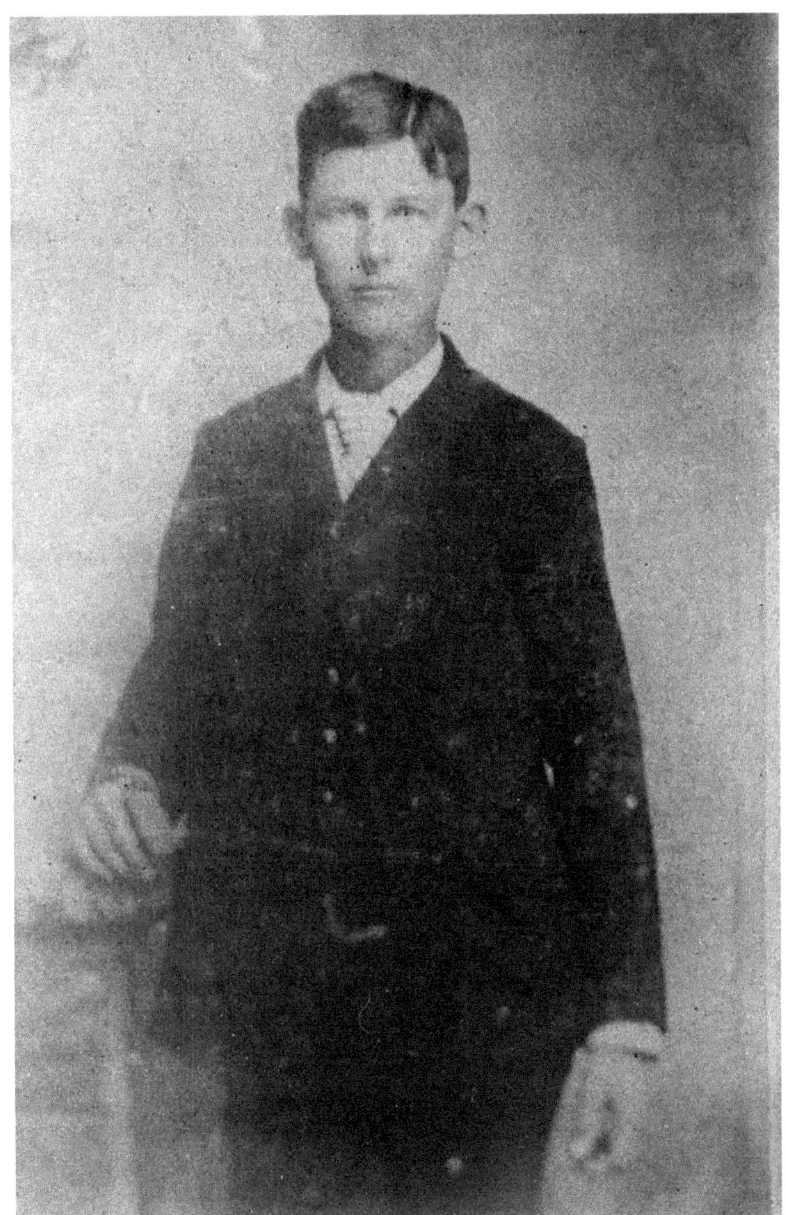

This view of a teenaged Emmett Dalton was recorded about the time he began to follow his idolized older brother Bob into a life of crime in northeastern Oklahoma. In reality, Emmett was possessed of a gentle spirit. As Marshal E. D. Nix remembered in his *Oklahombres* memoir, "Emmett Dalton was fearless and he loved excitement, but he lacked the bloodthirsty bravado of the successful bandit."

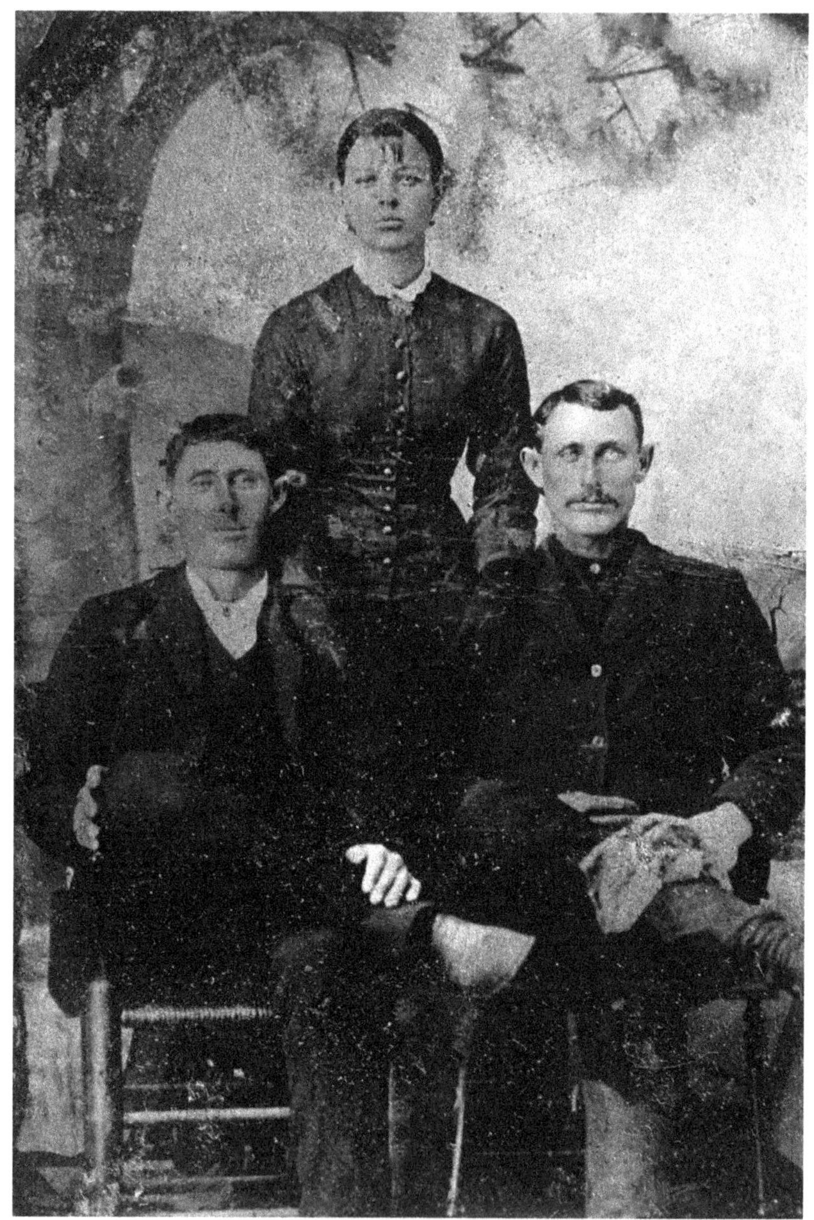

George D. Miller (left) began as a Texas Ranger in the 1880s and then appeared to settle down in Texas with his wife and children before inexplicably running off to Indian Territory, where he took up with outlaw "Red Buck" Weightman. The two committed a variety of crimes. After doing prison time, he went back to serving the law and died in the line of duty in 1923.

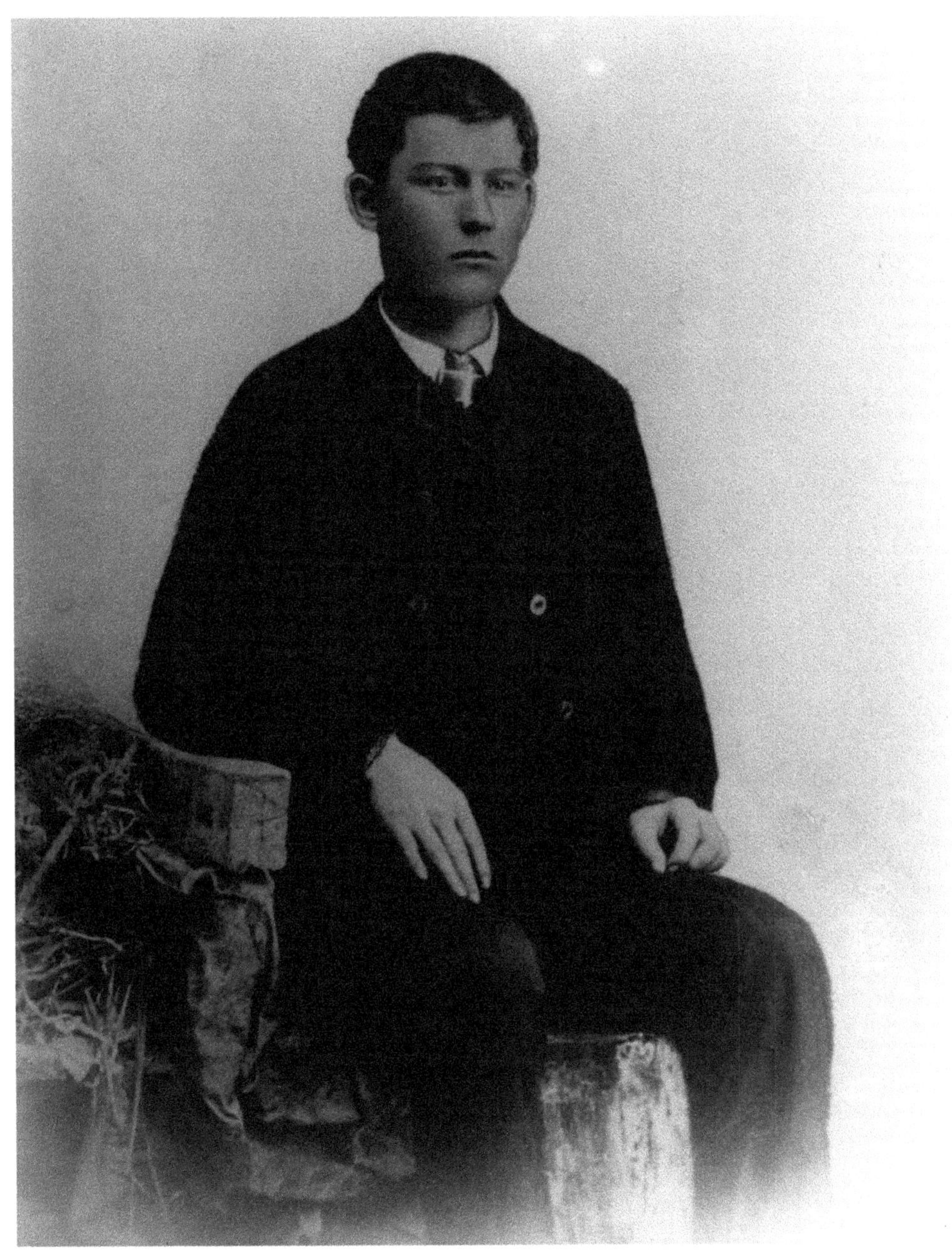

Unlike his counterparts Jesse James and Butch Cassidy, Bob Dalton was not as cunning as a leader of a criminal gang. That often made him more dangerous, because he preferred the more direct (and violent) approach to banditry. He's seen here in 1889, about the time he left employment as an Oklahoma lawman for a career in crime.

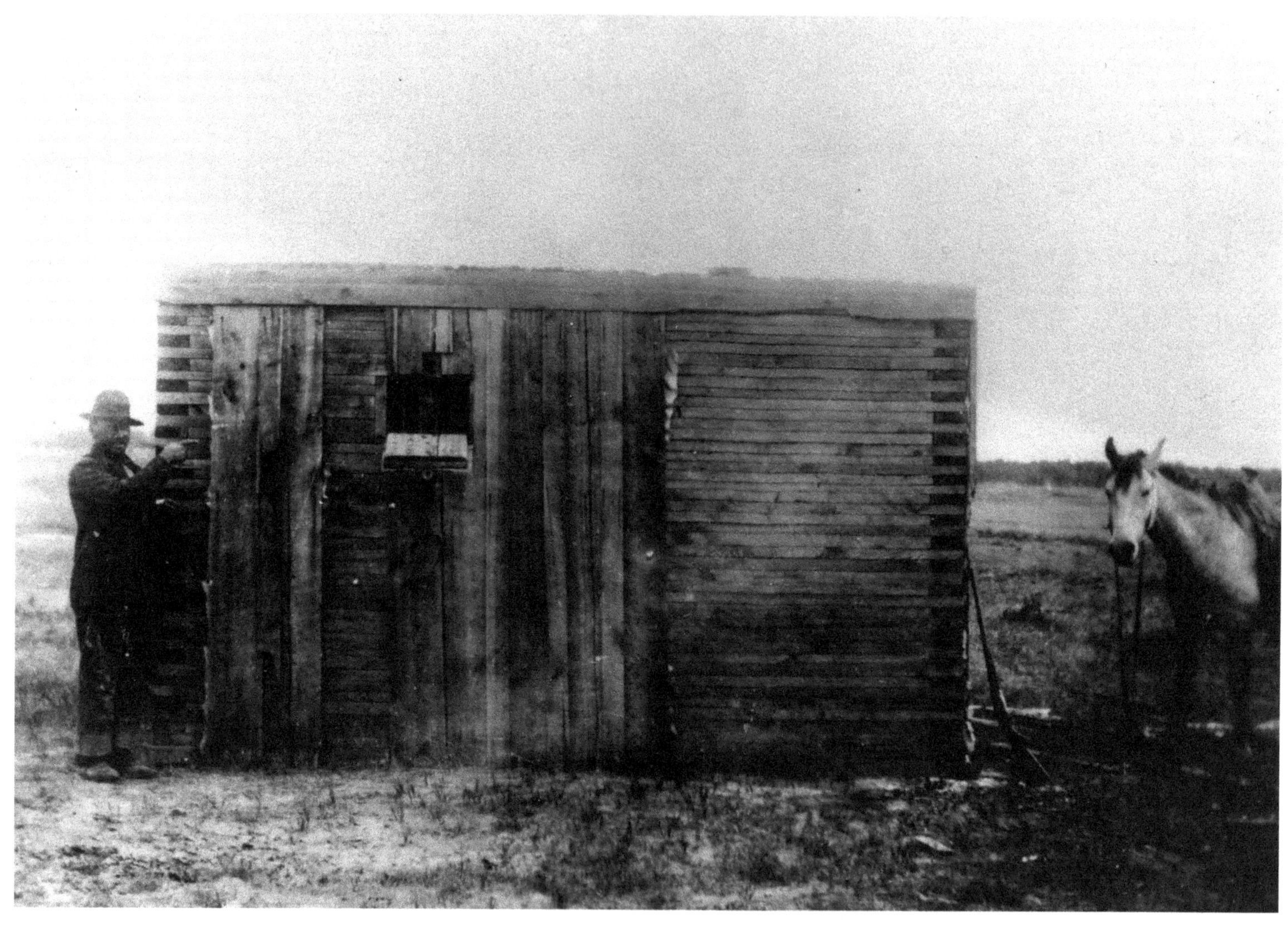

This old wooden jailhouse from Wyoming's territorial days (1868–1890) was photographed by noted naturalist C. Hart Merriam long after it was abandoned.

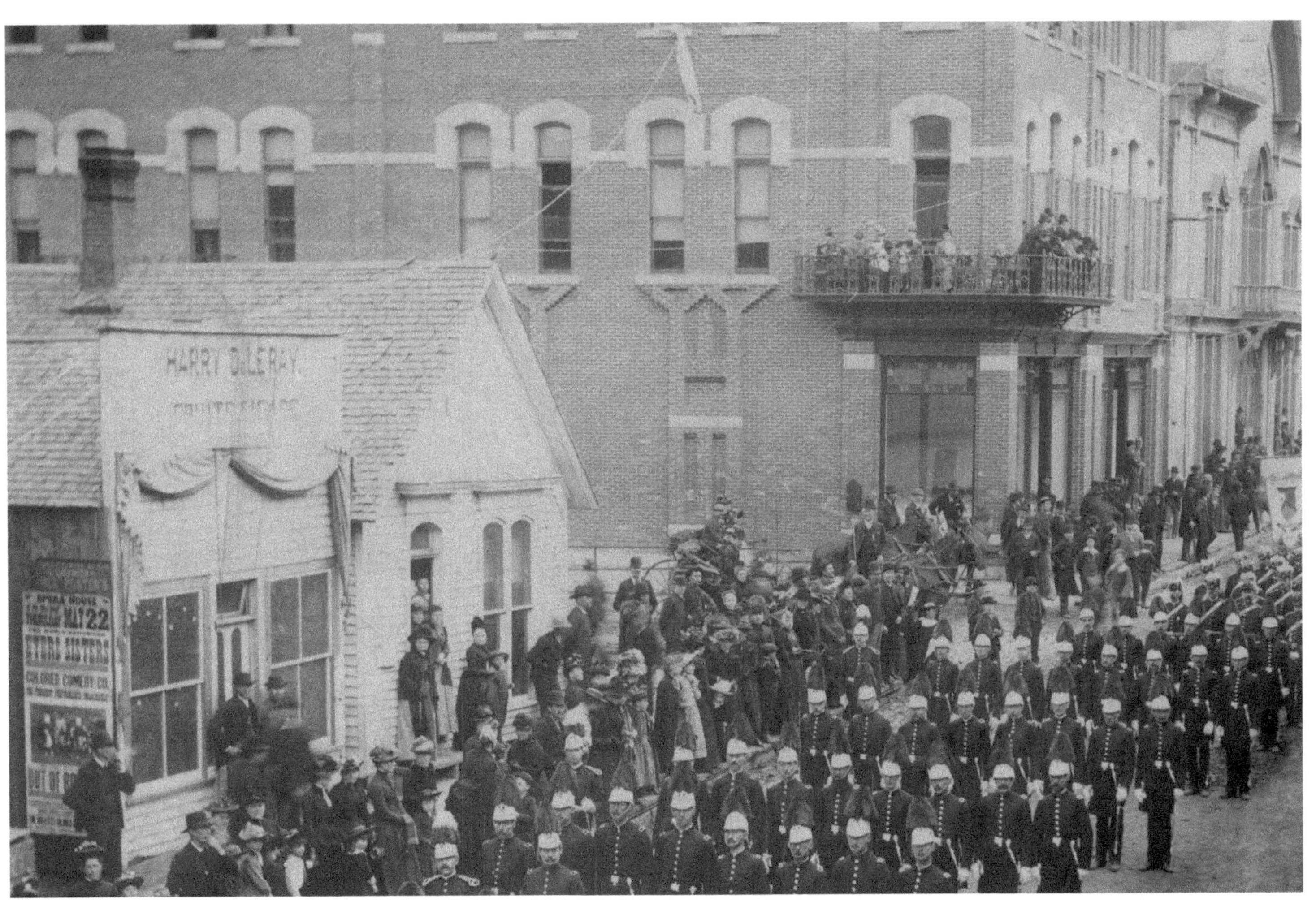

Deadwood, South Dakota, had already seen it wildest days as a mining boom town in the 1870s, when murder and mayhem were de rigueur. By the time these Odd Fellows paraded in 1890, the town had been ravaged by smallpox, fire, and gunmen like Jack McCall, who shot Wild Bill Hickok in the back of the head in 1876.

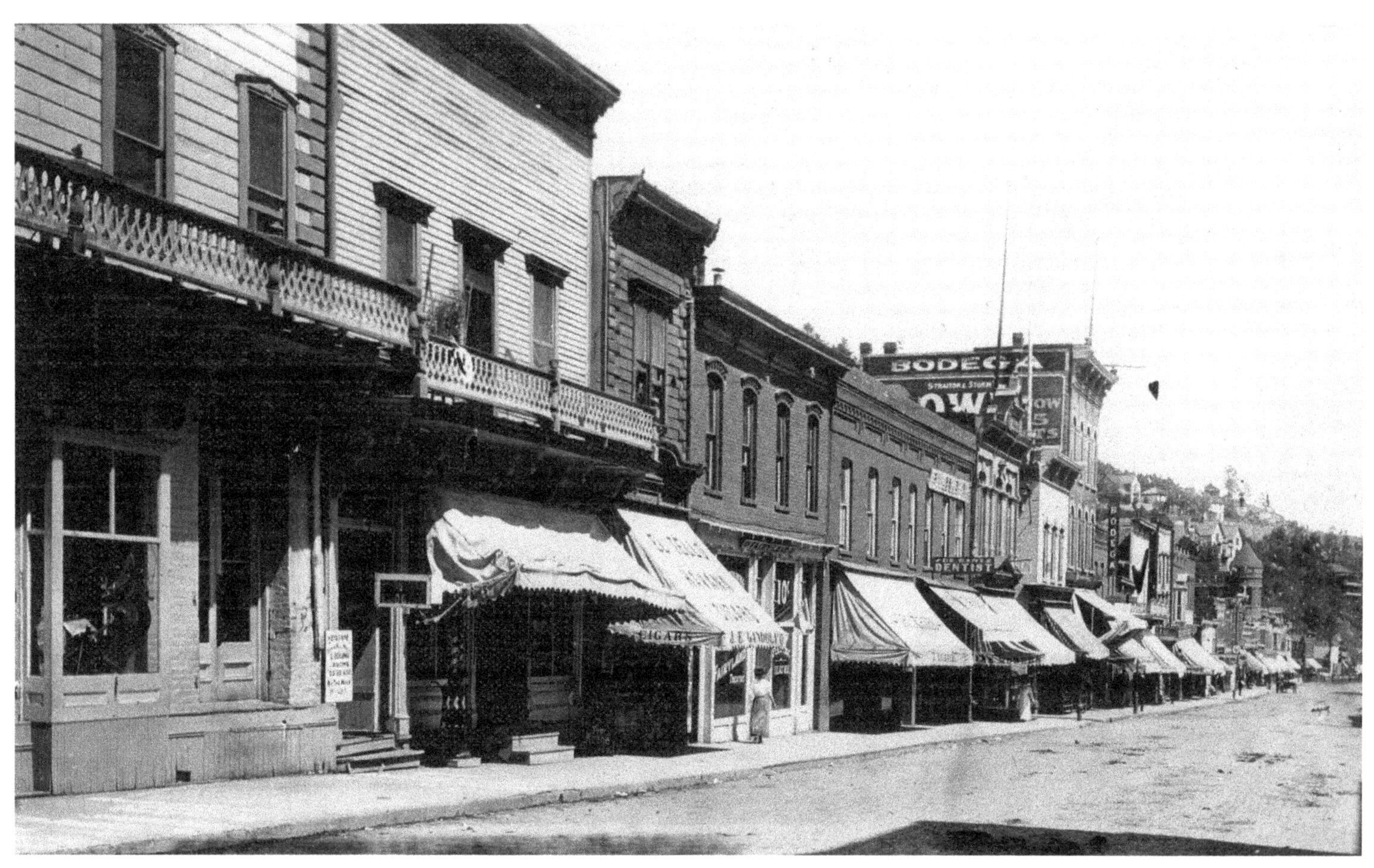

Unlike many of its western sisters, Deadwood showed remarkable resiliency, refusing to become yet another mining boom town turned ghost town. Successive booms of gold and diamonds were echoed as chemical processes using chlorine and cyanide enabled miners to recover even more gold in the 1890s, when this view of Main Street was recorded.

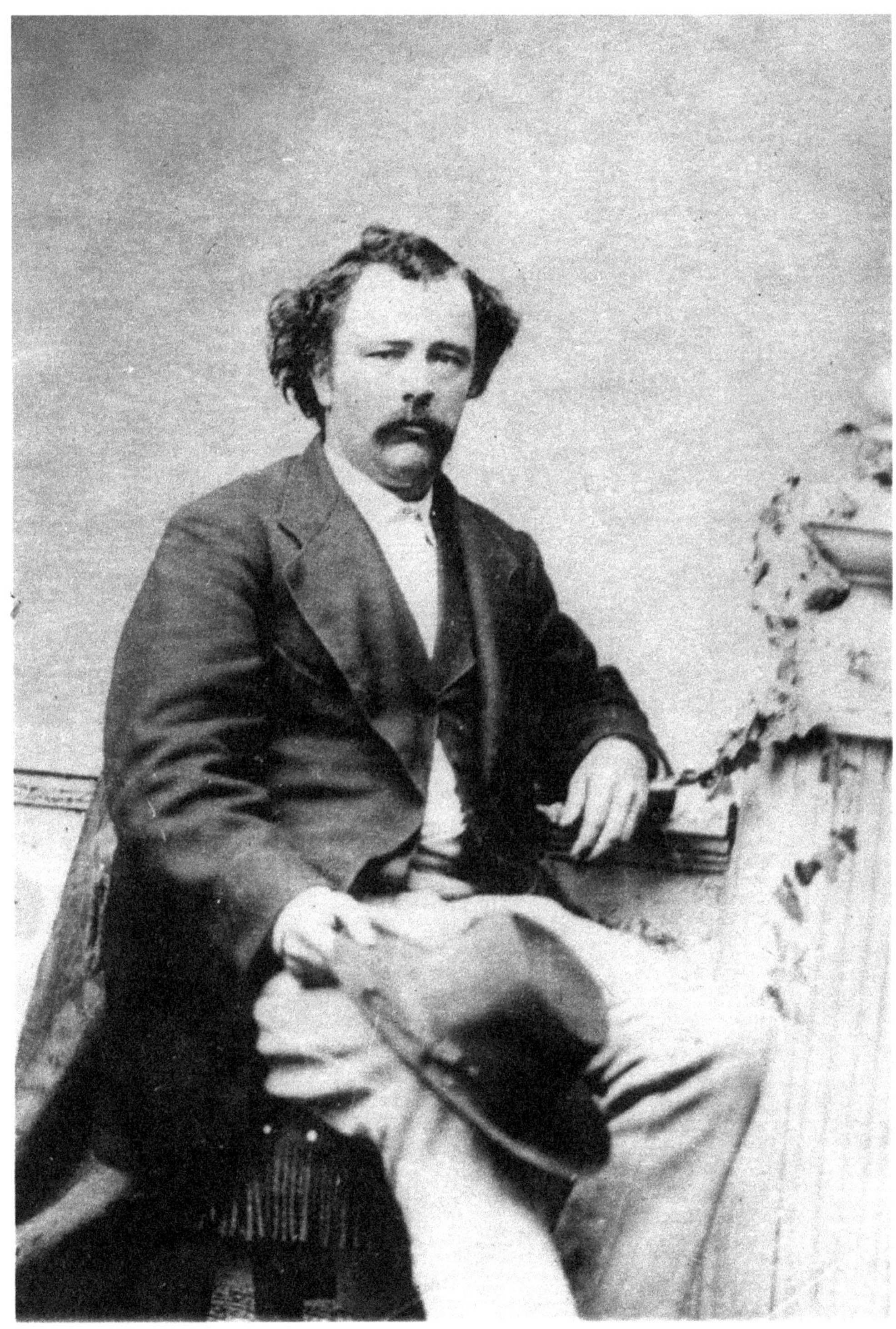

Texan Tom Ketchum got a rather late start at outlawry, having waited until he was almost 30 in the 1890s to start robbing trains and generally terrorizing the Texas Panhandle and New Mexico. Ketchum often worked with his brother Sam, but it wasn't until he matched up with Hole-in-the-Waller Kid Curry that he picked up the moniker "Black Jack" and showed himself to be quite ruthless.

This is the view down International Street in Nogales, the border between Arizona and Mexico in the 1890s. The border town was sometimes described as sleepy, but about this time the ruthless Christian Brothers from Indian Territory moved into southeastern Arizona and helped form the High Five Gang, which made the whole region their exclusive territory for robbing banks, trains, and post offices.

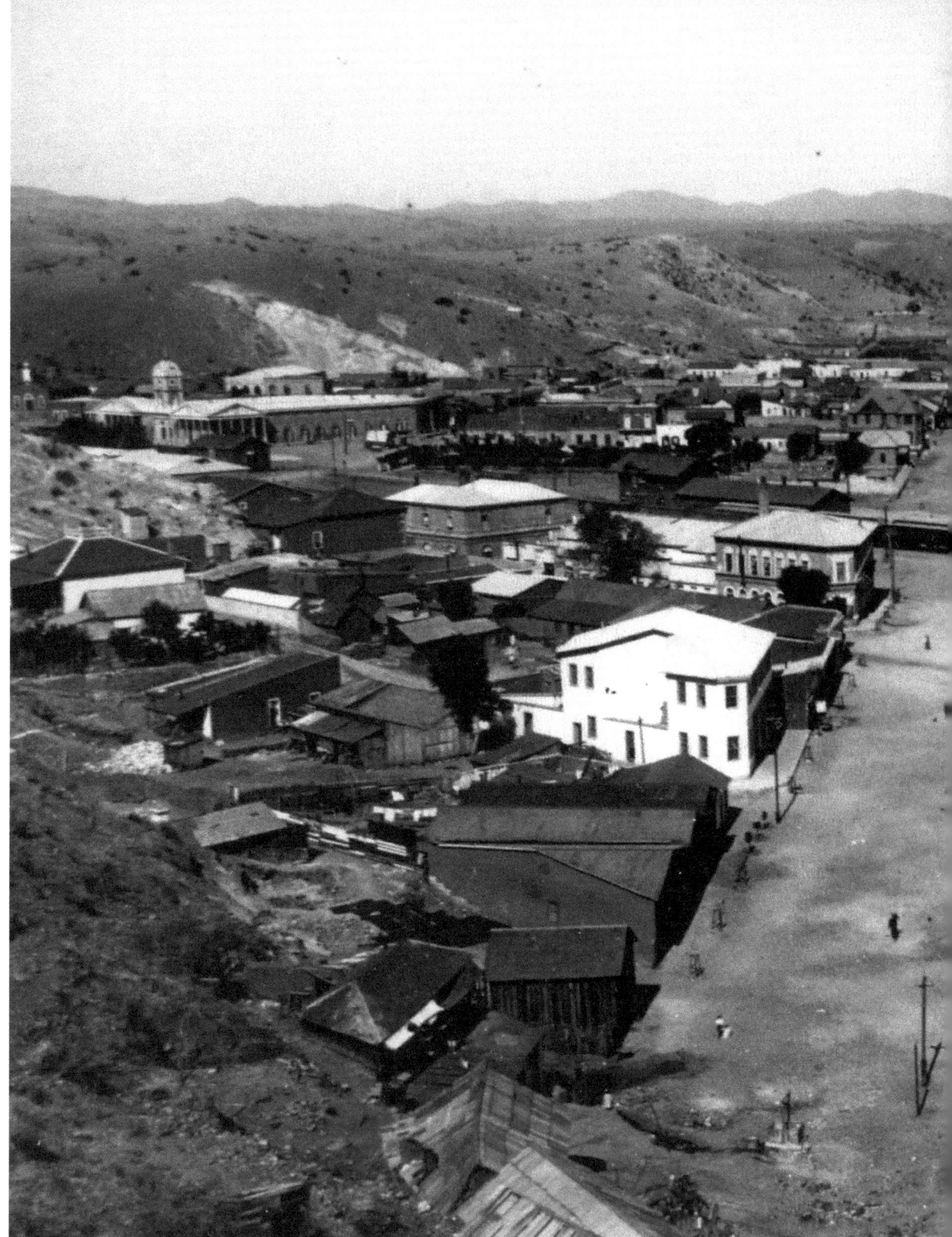

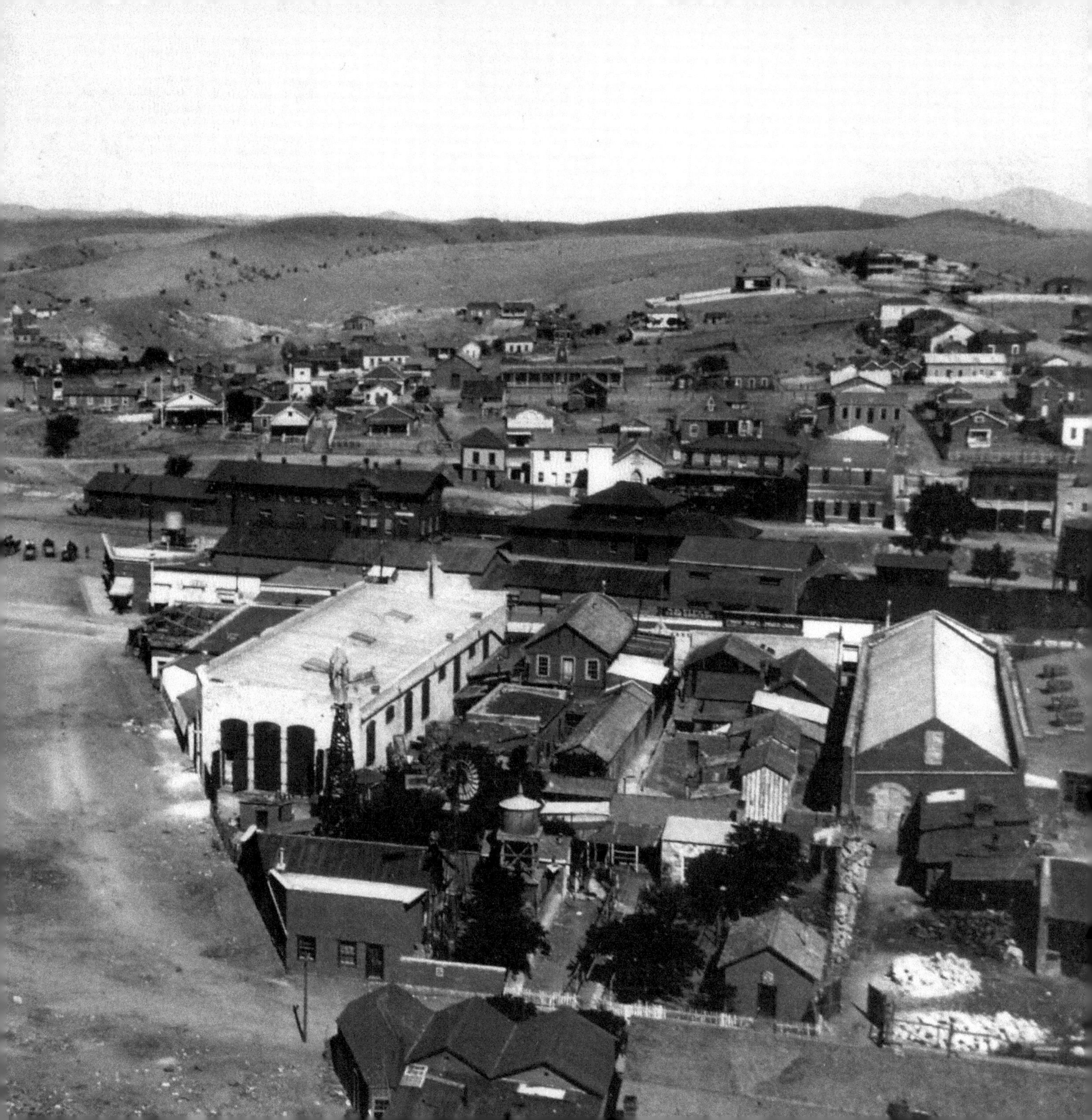

Texan James Riley became a specialist in horse thievery at the age of 14 and was sent to prison for life on a murder charge at 19. After a daring escape, he renamed himself Doc Middleton and resumed rustling and killing on the northern plains before serving another prison term in Wyoming.

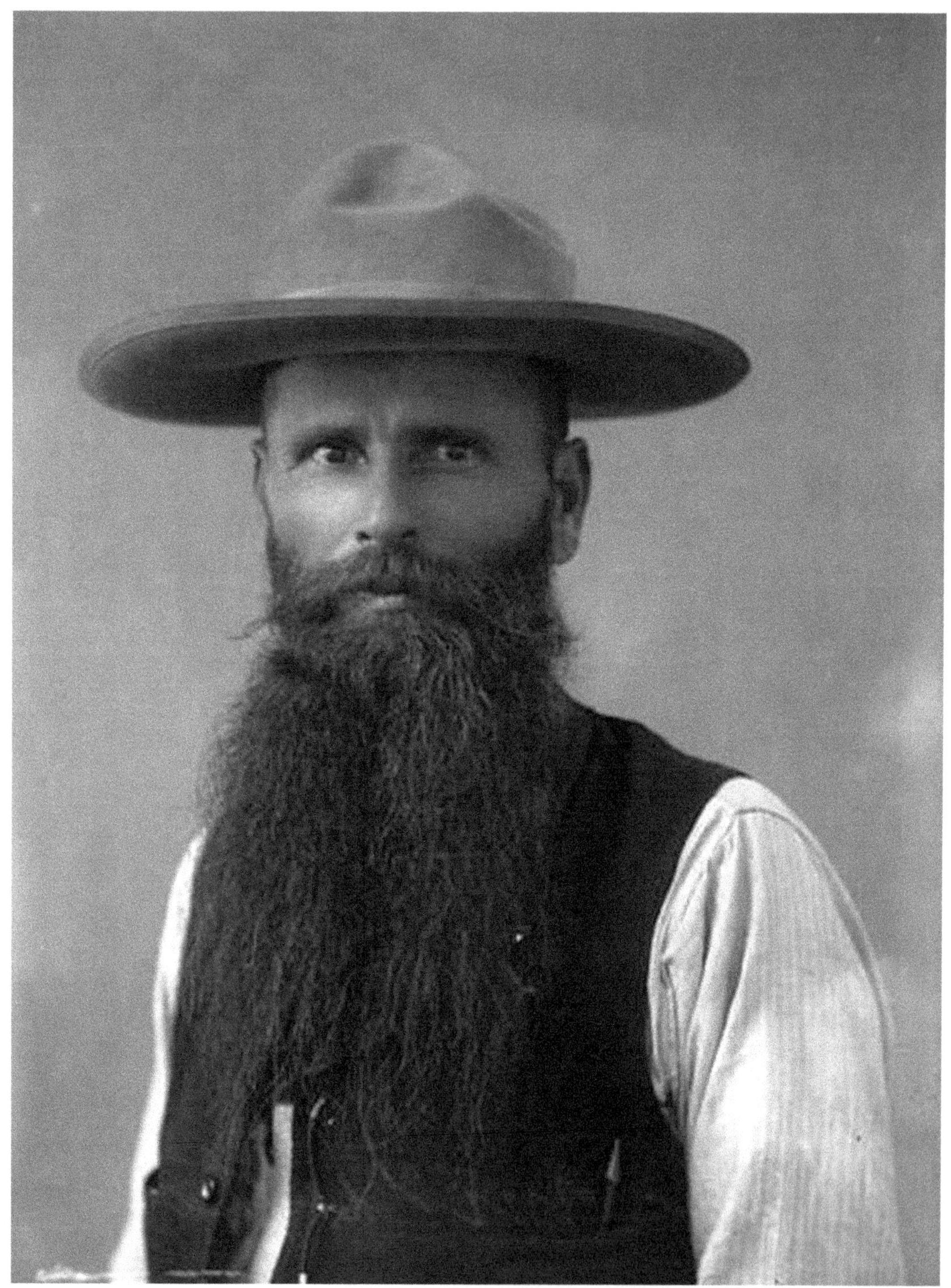

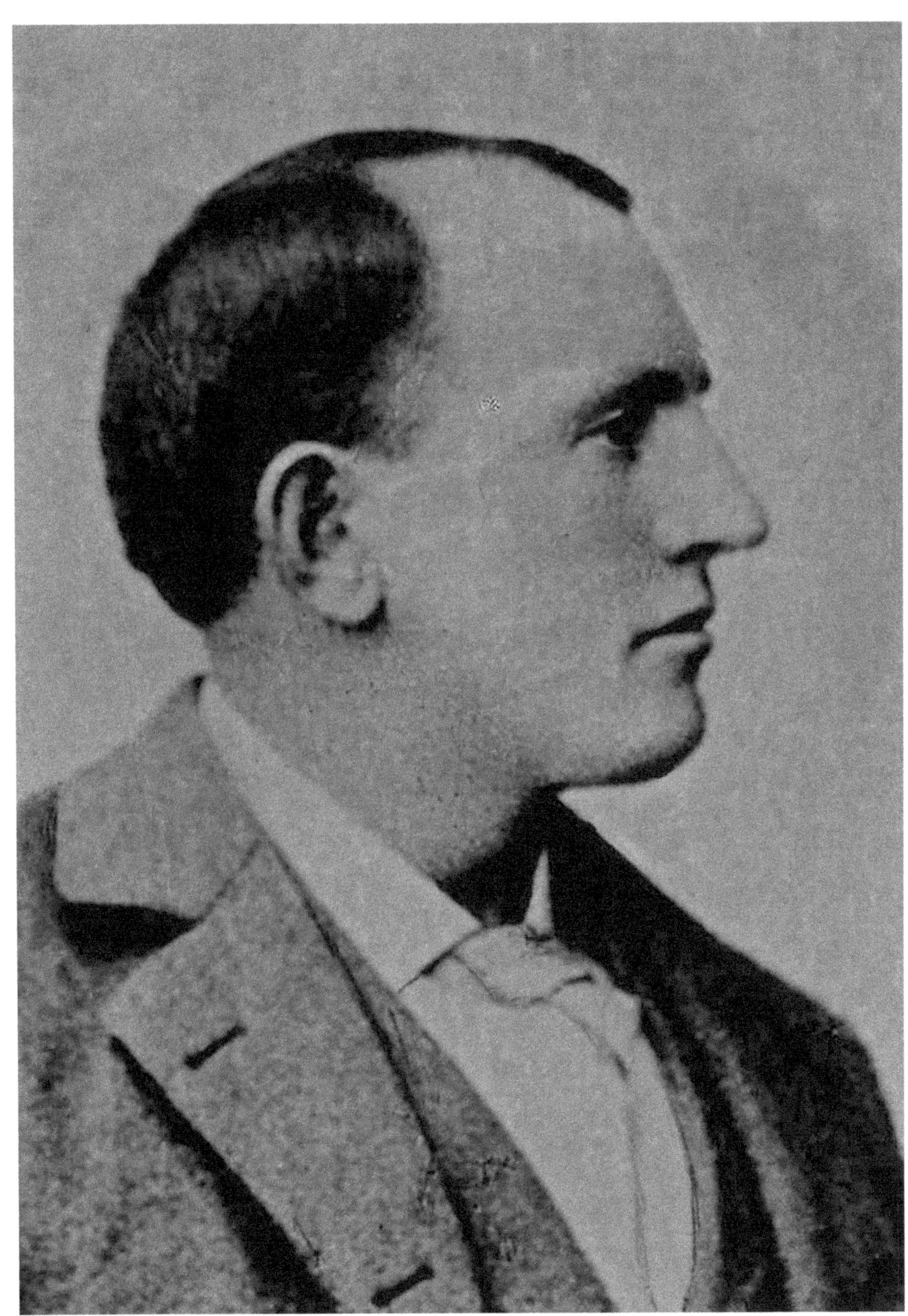

Tom Horn was an uncanny manhunter who waged war on the Apaches almost singlehandedly as an Army scout in the Indian Wars, becoming a Pinkerton detective and hired gun in Wyoming's Johnson County War in the 1890s. Often regarded today as a tragic hero, contemporary observers simply knew him as an unflinching killer. Or as he called himself before his execution for murder in 1903, "an exterminatin' son-of-a-bitch."

Hard-drinking Grat Dalton made a half-hearted attempt at being a lawman in Indian Territory before starting his life of crime. Around 1890 he joined his brothers and other associates like the Doolins in robbing banks and trains in the Southwest.

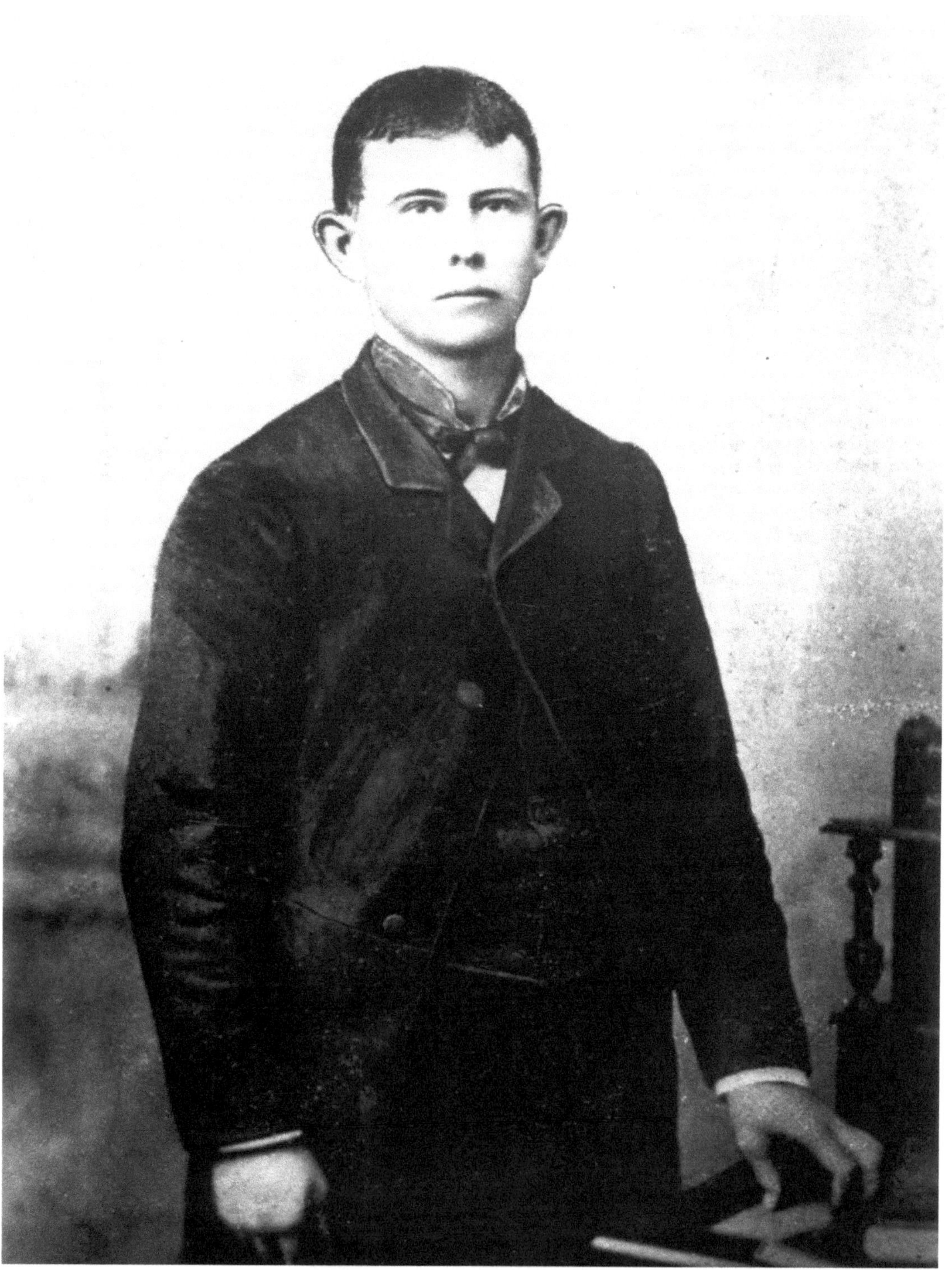

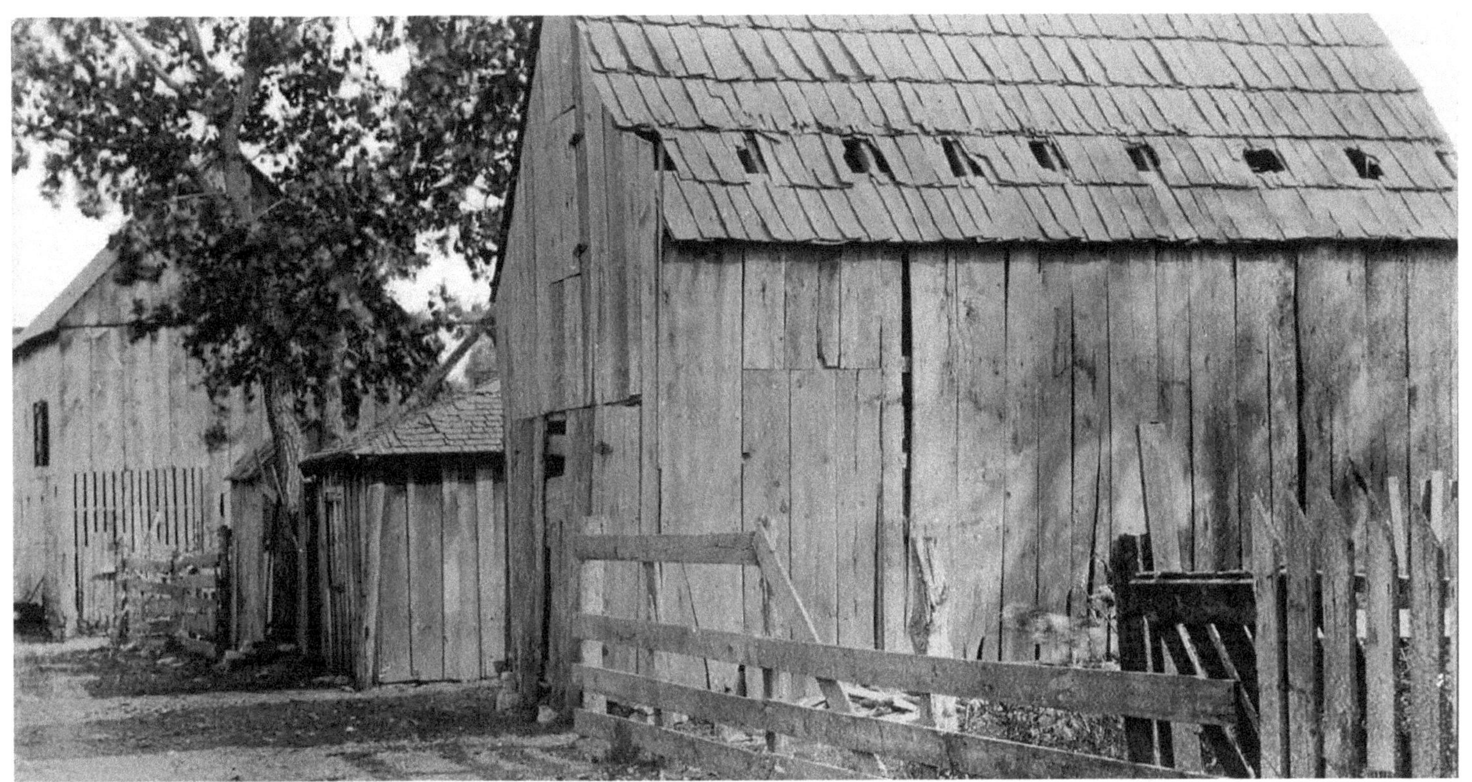

In 1892, Bob, Grat, and Emmett Dalton were joined by fellow gang members Dick Broadwell and Bill Powers in their attempt to rob two banks in Coffeyville, Kansas, at the same time and in broad daylight. Likely complacent because of their recent successes, the Daltons underestimated the townspeople and the fact that many would recognize them in their former hometown. Seen here is the fence where they tied their horses.

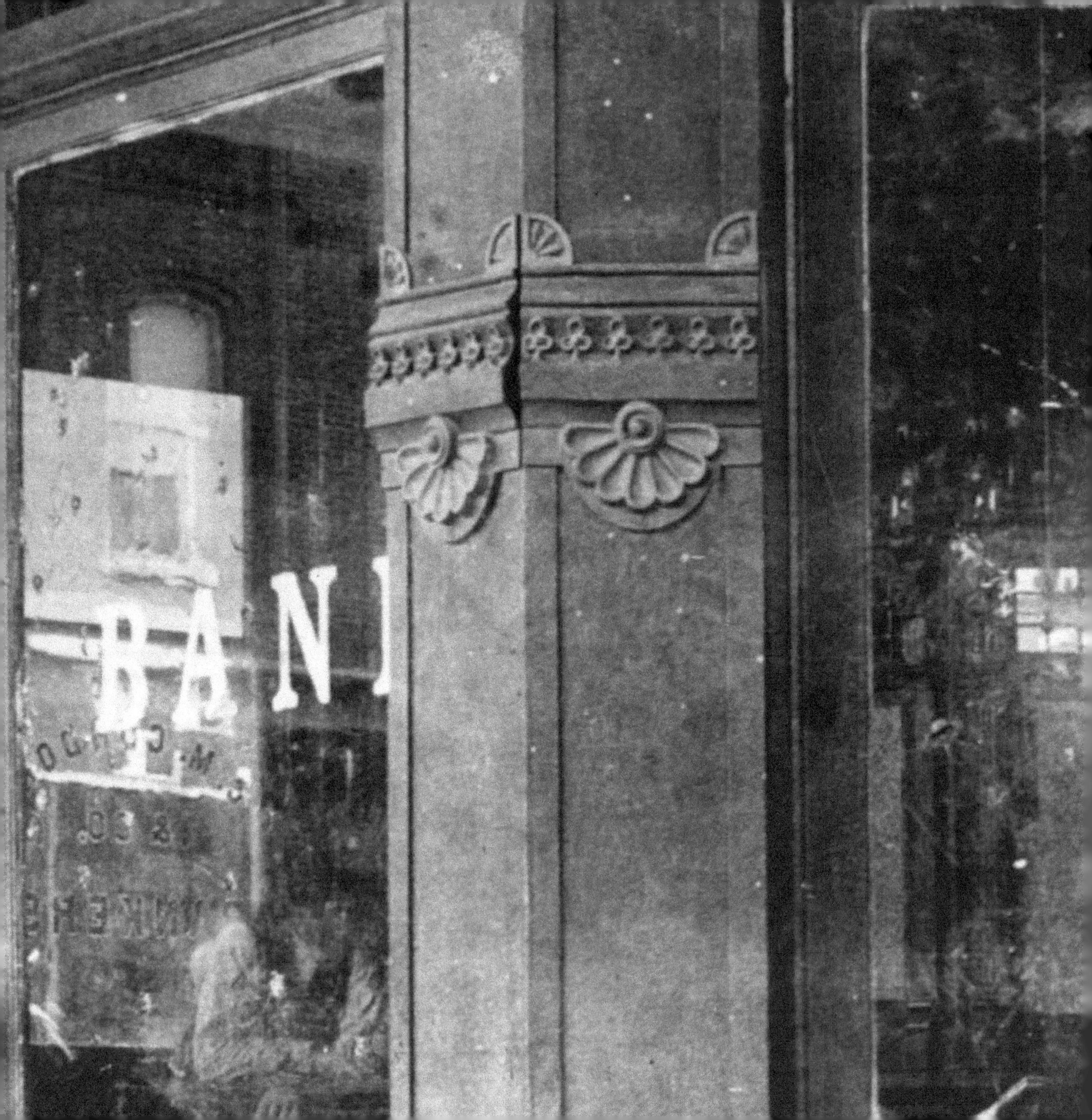
BAN

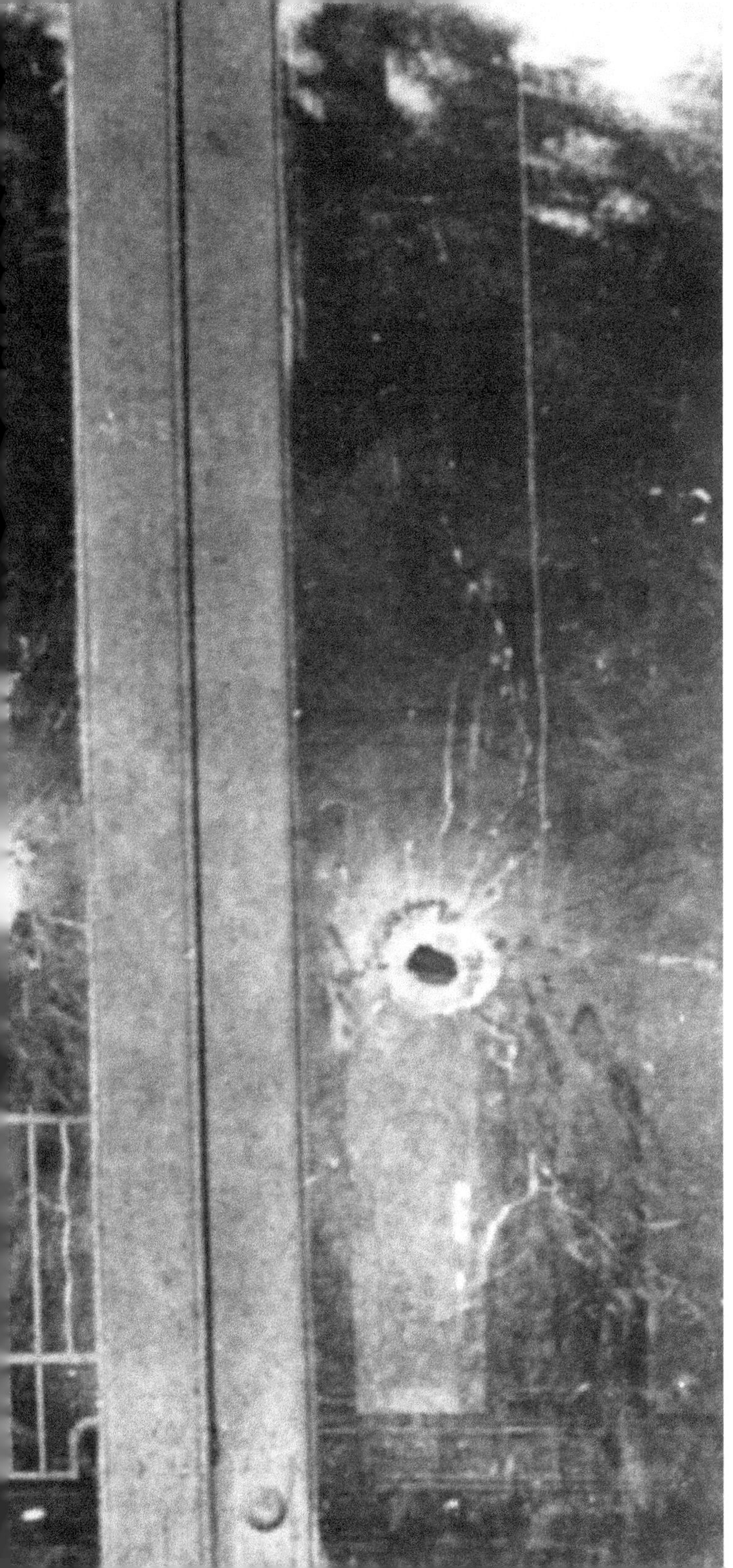

Because Coffeyville had begun to modernize, the hitching posts on the main street had been removed and the gang was forced to walk through town, whereupon they were easily recognized. Citizens quickly filed into a hardware store to arm themselves for a fight with the gang. Here is one of the bank windows, said to have sustained more than 300 bullets during the confrontation.

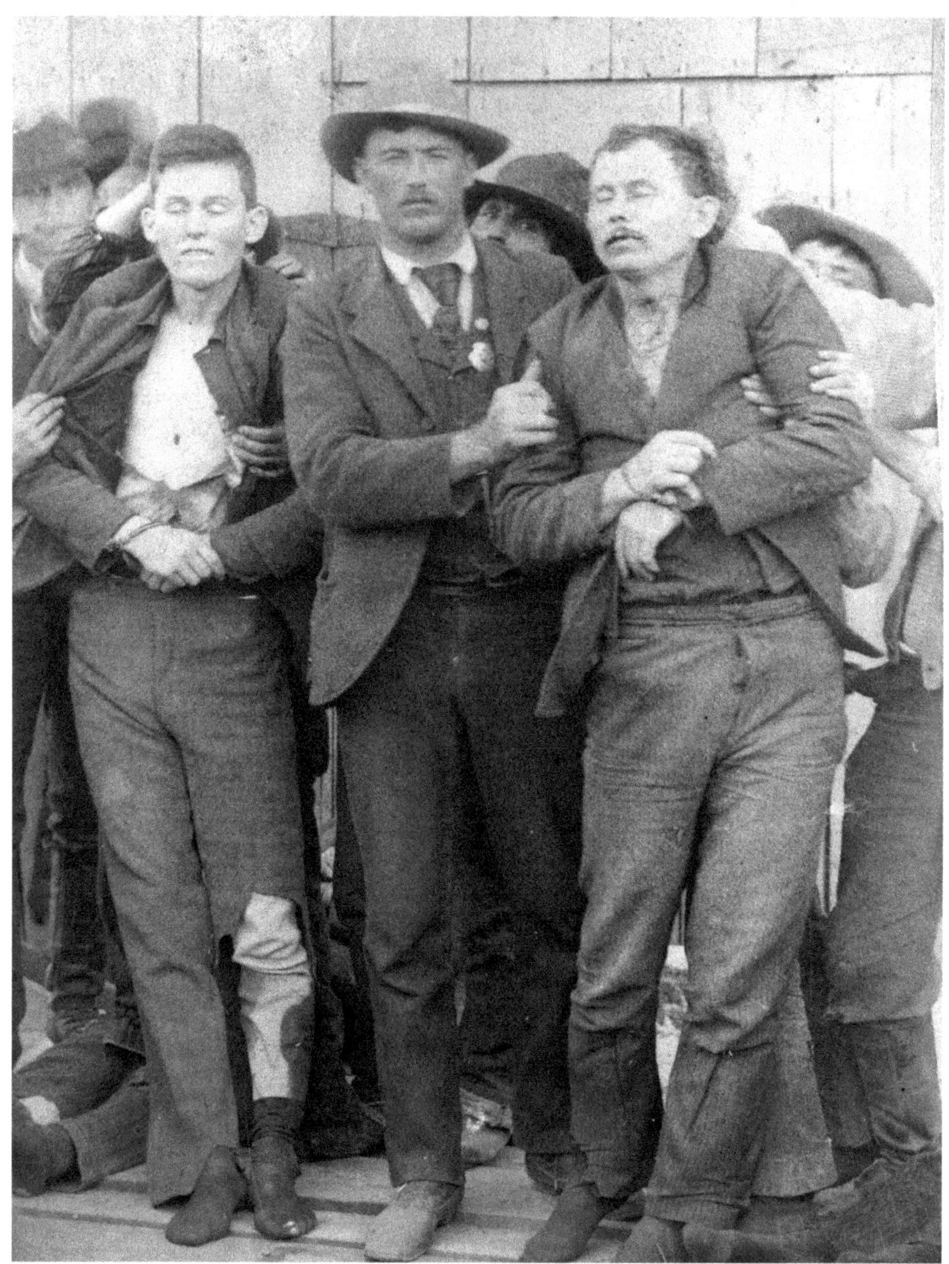

The wild ride of two of the Dalton boys, Bob (left) and Grat (right), ended in a bloody shoot-out with townsfolk in Coffeyville. Bob led part of the gang into the First National Bank and Grat led the others into the Condon Bank. As they tried to leave, they were met with a hail of bullets from the town's defenders.

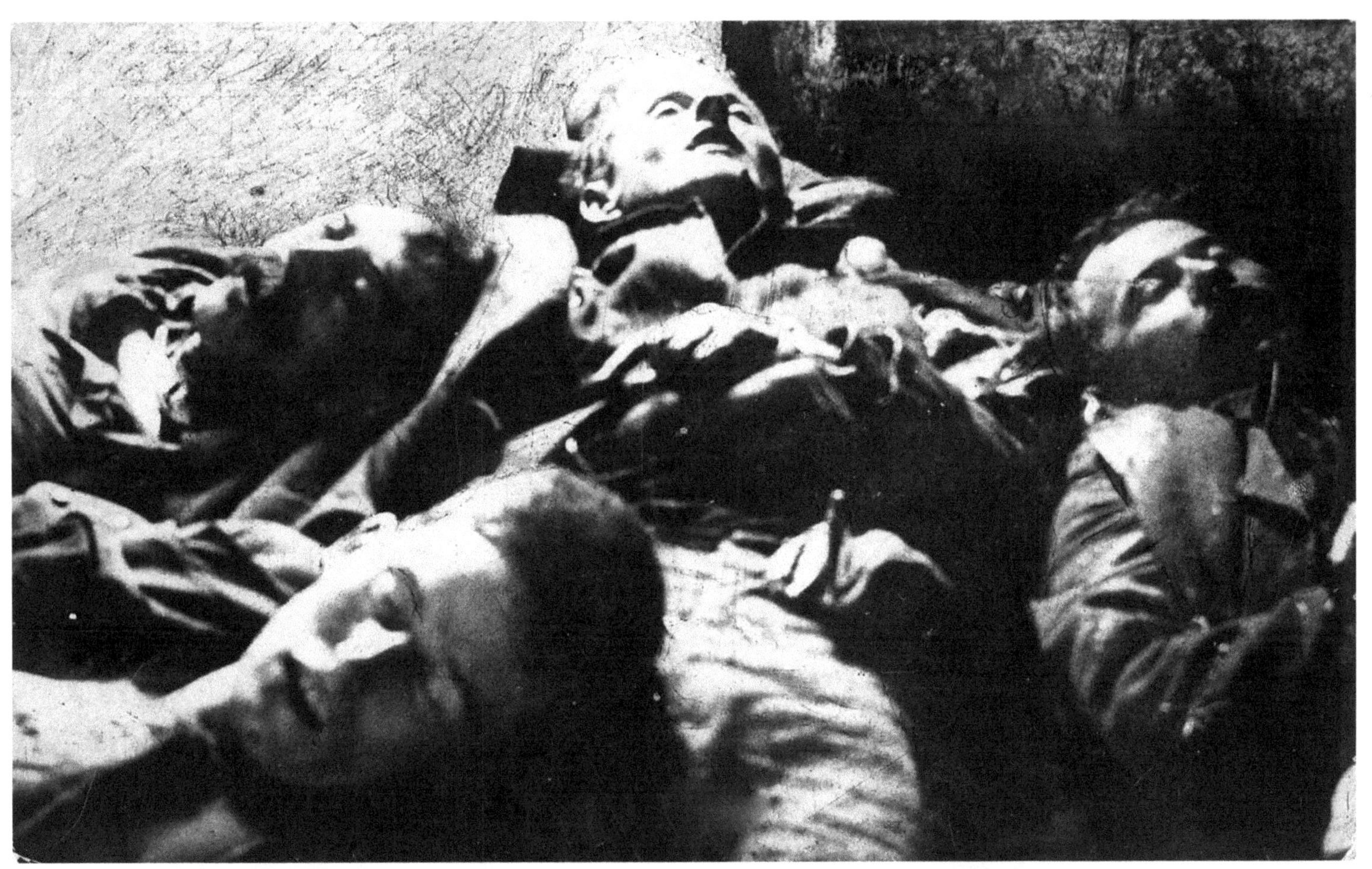

Powers was gunned down in the street and Broadwell was killed making a run for it. The Daltons held out in a barn for a few minutes, but Bob and Grat were killed and Emmett was gravely wounded with at least 20 holes in him. Unfortunately, the town lost its marshal and three other citizens as well. Once the bodies were collected, they were laid out in this livery stable.

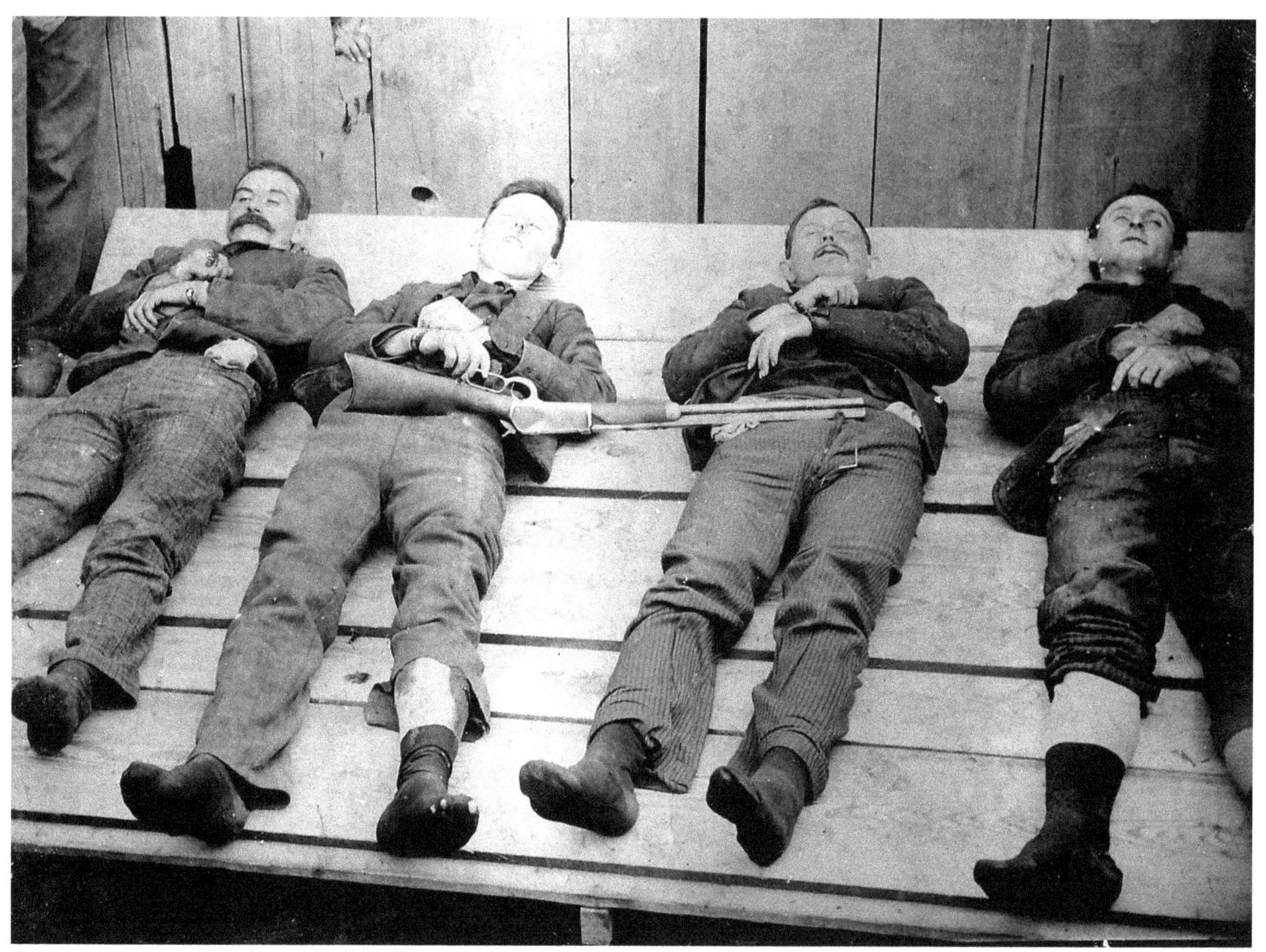

Hours after the Coffeyville shoot-out, trainloads of thrill seekers arrived to mock the dead outlaws (left to right: Bill Powers, Bob Dalton, Grat Dalton, Dick Broadwell). Opportunistic Kansans had already cut swatches of fabric from their clothing and tufts of hair from their horses to sell as souvenirs, and photographers had already begun mass-producing cards with photographs like this one.

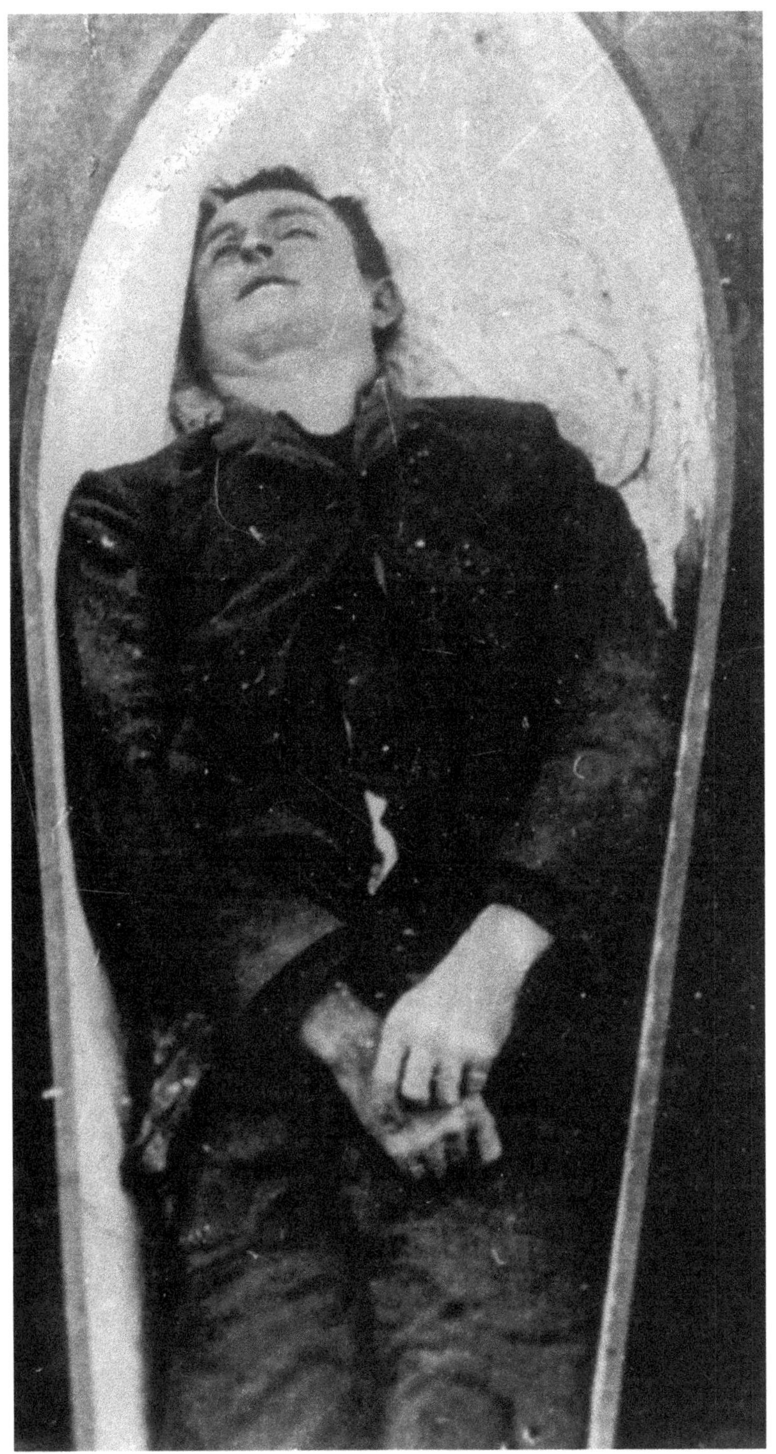

Dick Broadwell, sometimes called Texas Jack, began life as a member of a prominent Hutchinson, Kansas, family, but a series of adverse circumstances led to his involvement with the Dalton Gang. He proved to be bloody and adept at robbing banks and trains, but he met his end during the Coffeyville Raid, where he was riddled with bullets as he tried to escape the town on horseback.

After 23 lead slugs were extracted from him and he was well enough to stand trial for the Condon Bank robbery in Coffeyville, Emmett Dalton received a life sentence in Lansing State Prison. A model prisoner, his sentence was commuted after 14 years.

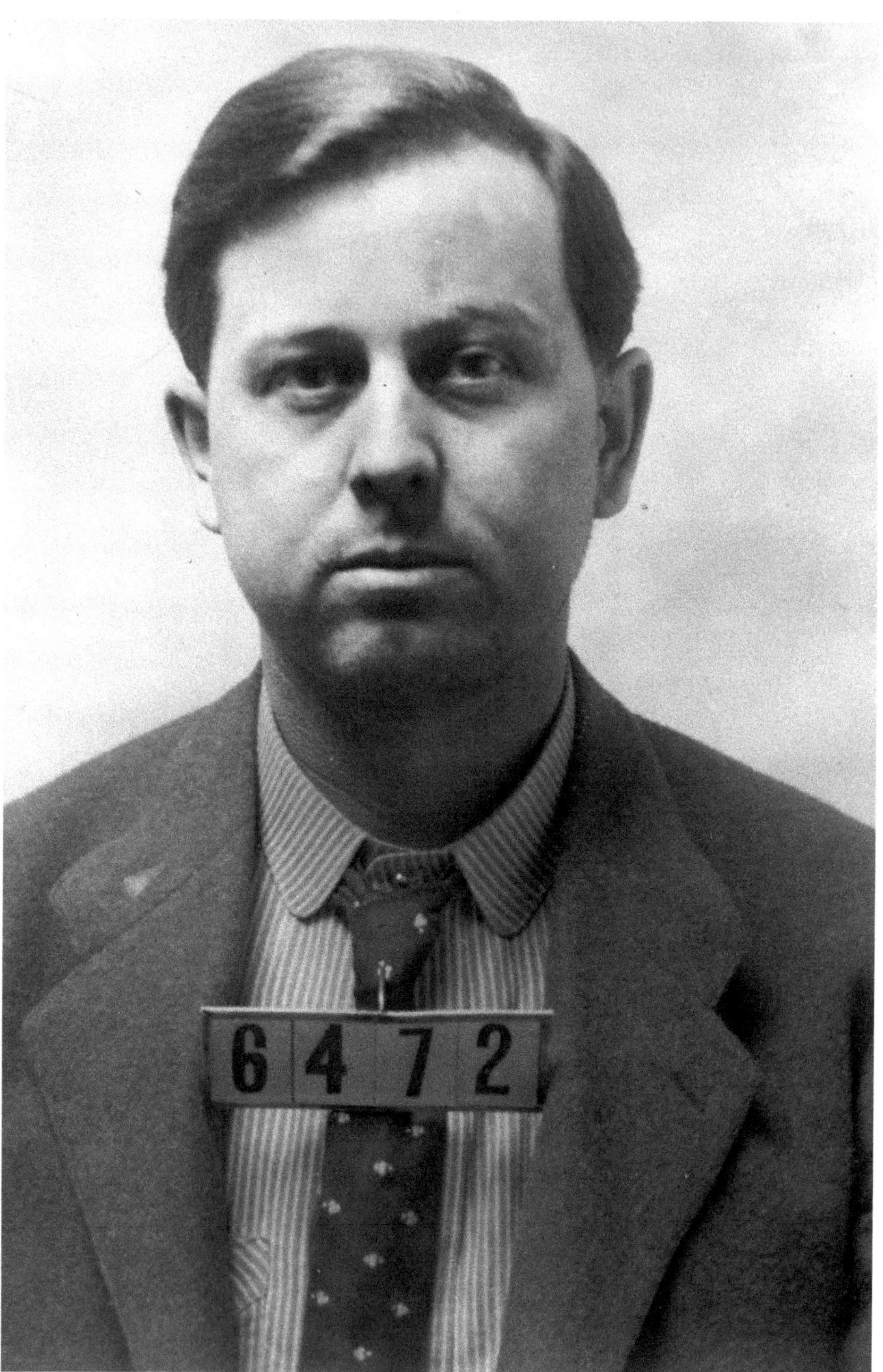

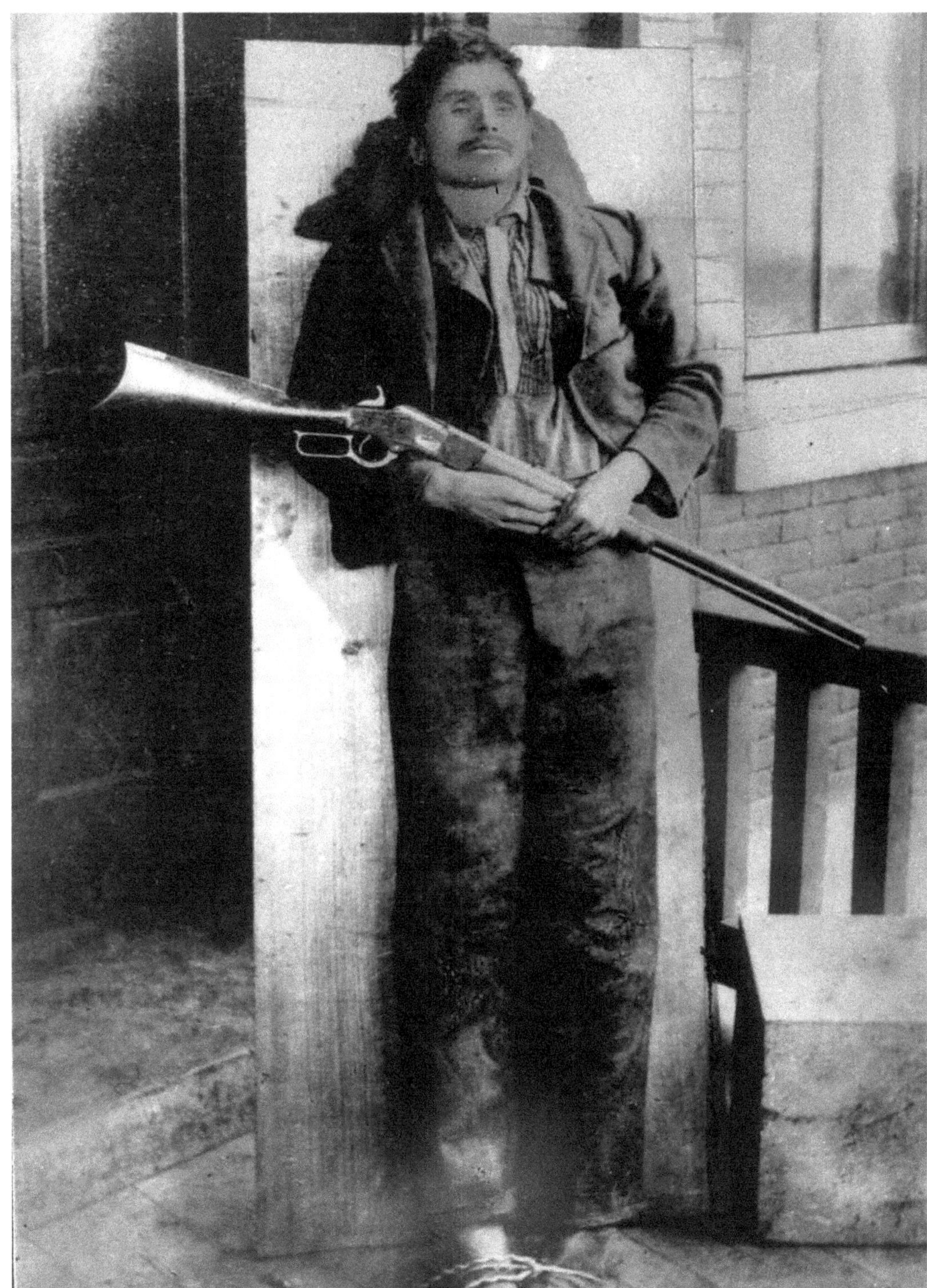

One of the more enduring controversies in Oklahoma history is the case of Cherokee outlaw Ned Christie, framed for the murder of Deputy Marshal David Maples in 1887. Christie went on the lam, evading authorities for five years before his death in a shoot-out in 1892. He was exonerated 30 years later.

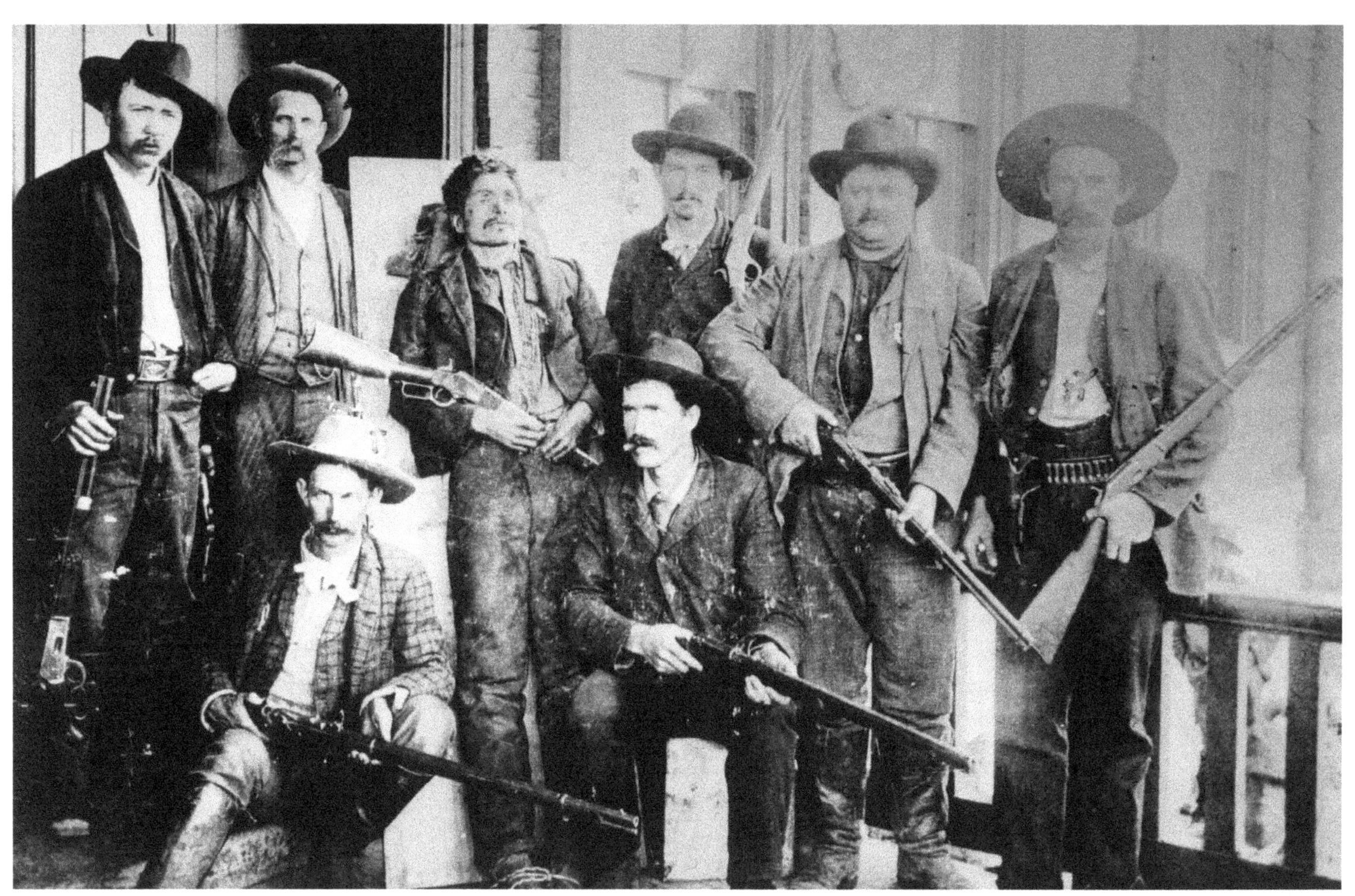

Deputy Marshal Paden Tolbert (standing, at left) led this posse which made the final assault on fugitive Ned Christie's hilltop fortress in the Cookson Hills. The lawmen used a cannon and dynamite during the two-day siege to blast Christie (dead, at center) out of his refuge. The outlaw was finally gunned down as he fled the burning cabin.

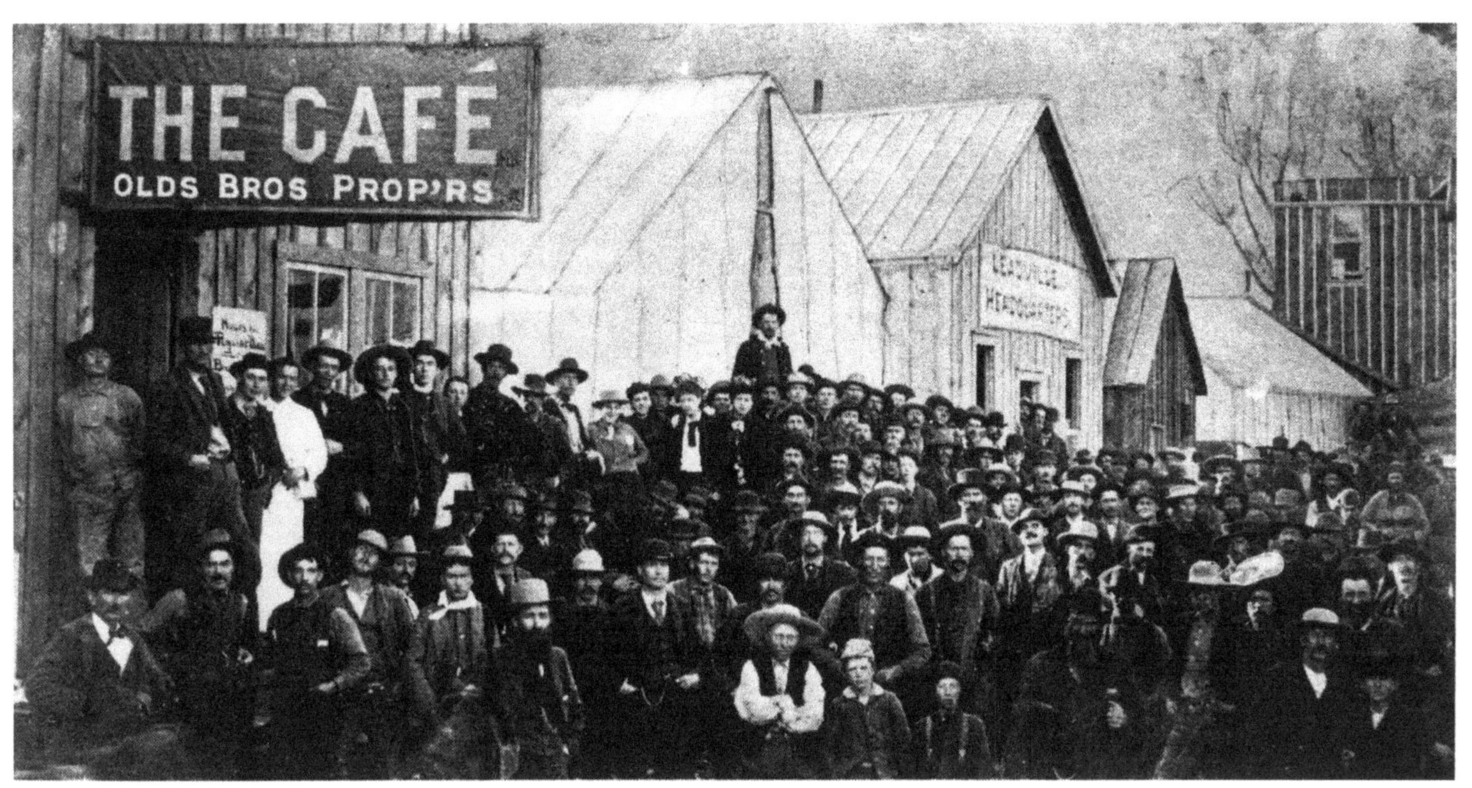

After his assassination of Jesse James, Bob Ford roamed the West in shame as "the dirty little coward," but after ten years, he found acceptance upon opening a dance hall in the southern Colorado boom town of Creede. Moments after lowlife Ed Kelley killed Ford in June 1892, this crowd formed to string him up in the street. Already in police custody, Kelley was safely escorted to jail.

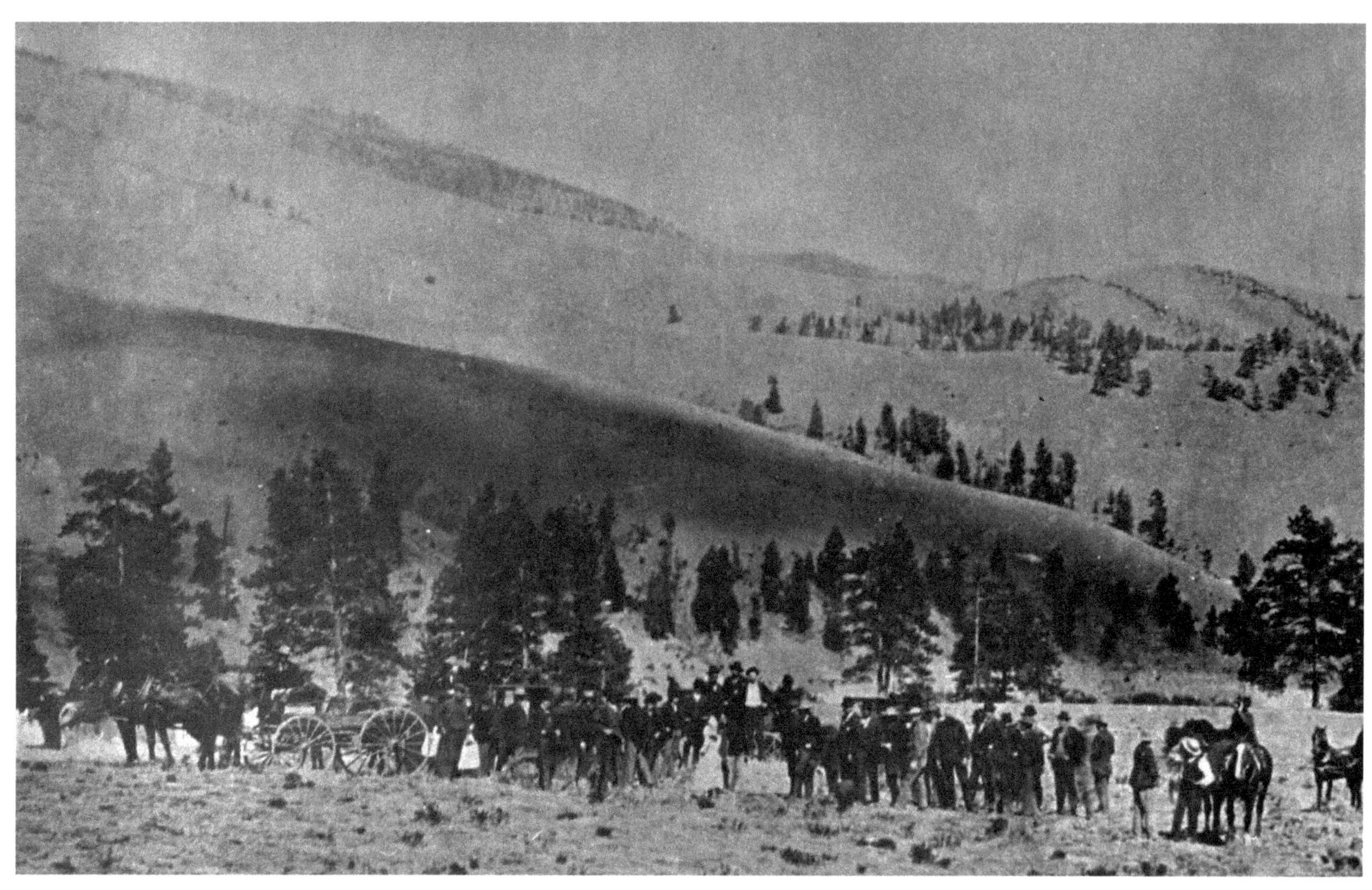

Though not necessarily loved in Creede, Bob Ford somewhat redeemed himself and about 50 people attended his funeral. The sermon was based on a rumored slip of paper found in Ford's possession, which read, "Charity covereth a multitude of sin." He was buried outside the cemetery with prostitutes and other undesirables, "where both abandoned burros feed / and coyotes call—for this is Creede."

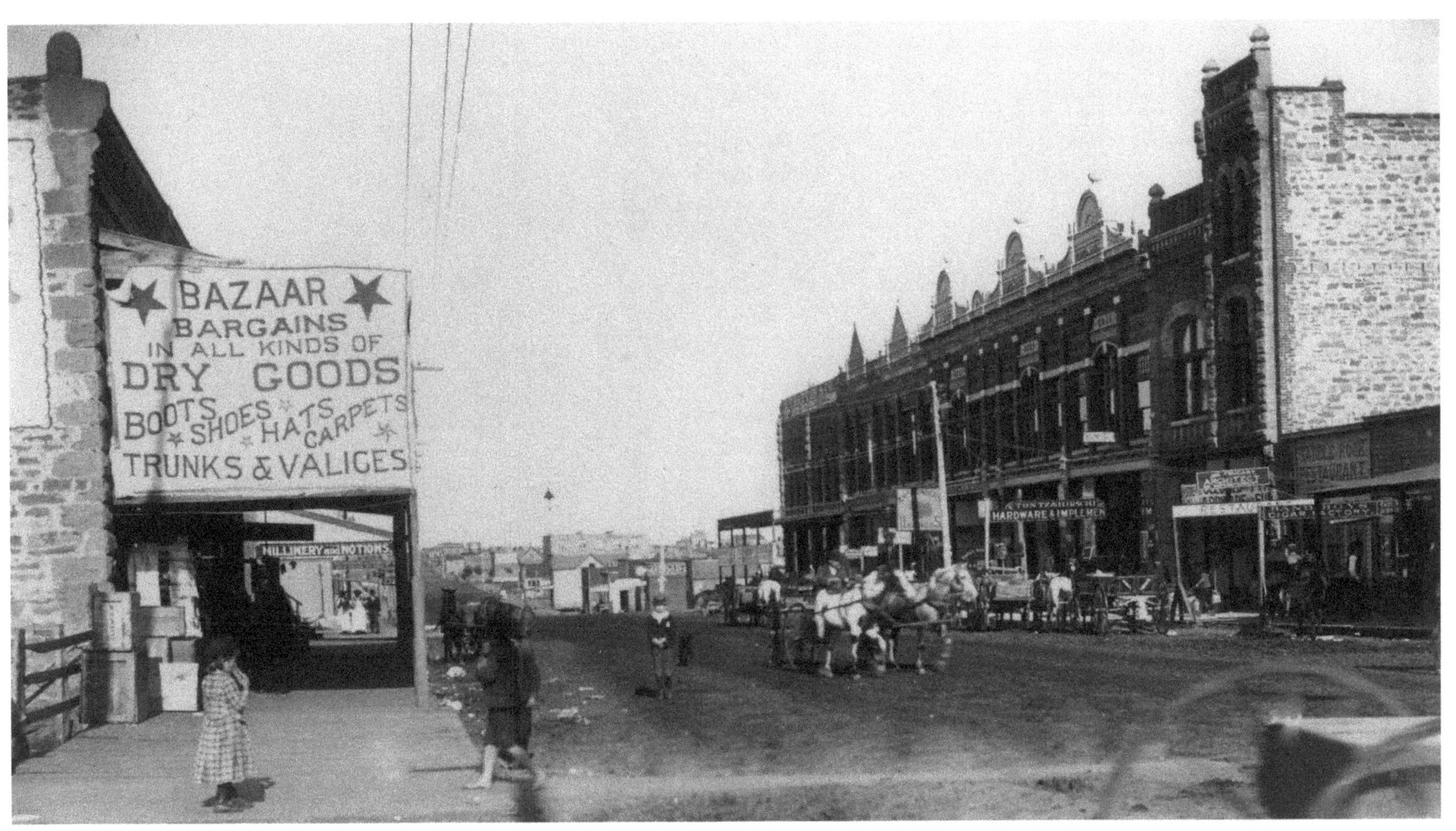

This is the scene along Harrison Avenue in Guthrie, Oklahoma, in 1893. Formed three years earlier, Oklahoma Territory continued to fall prey to roving gangs of bandits until Marshal E. D. Nix took office that year and assembled a formidable force of deputies to aggressively attack the criminal element rampaging the area.

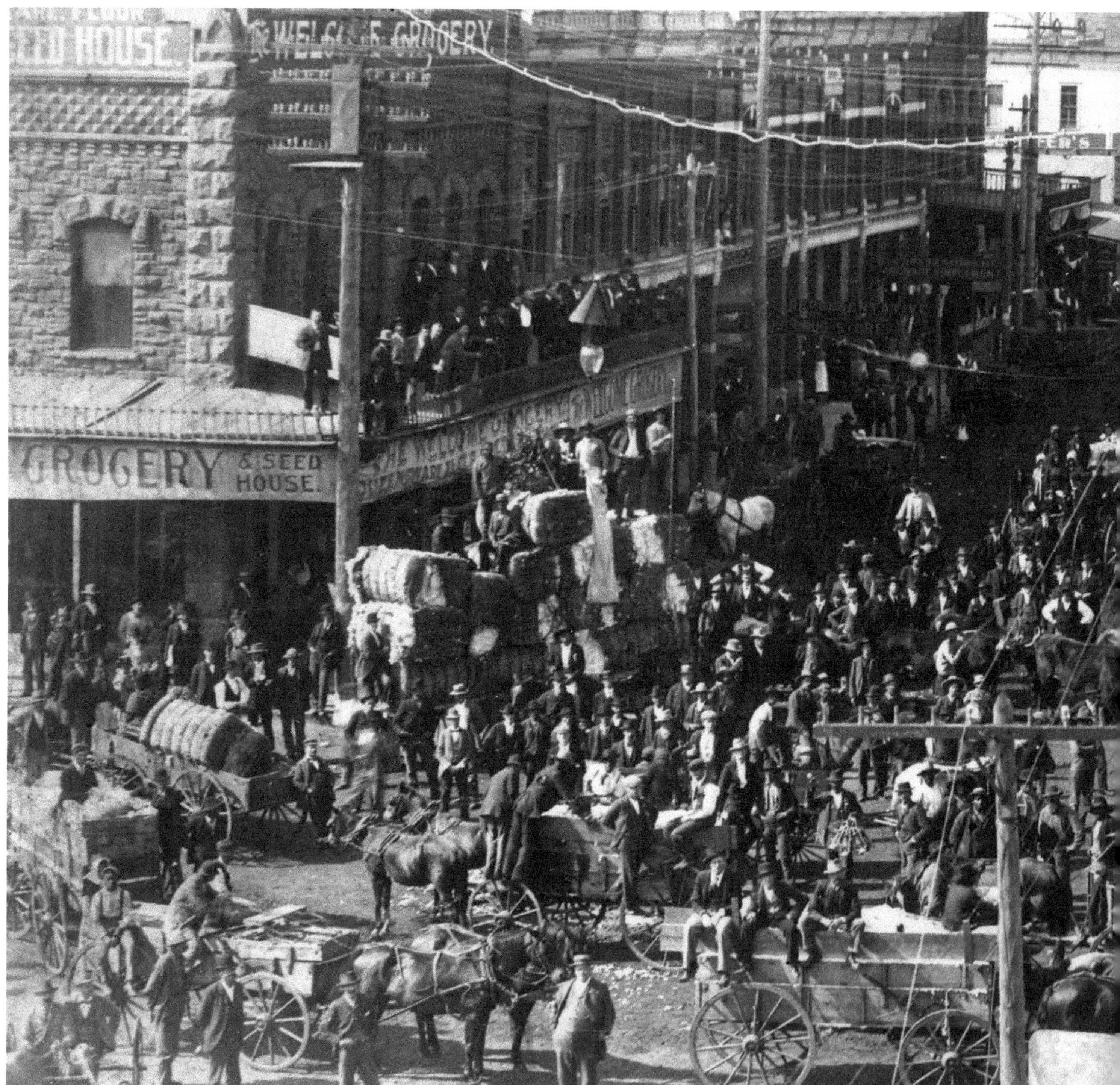
HOUSE.
GROCERY
GROCERY
& SEED
HOUSE.

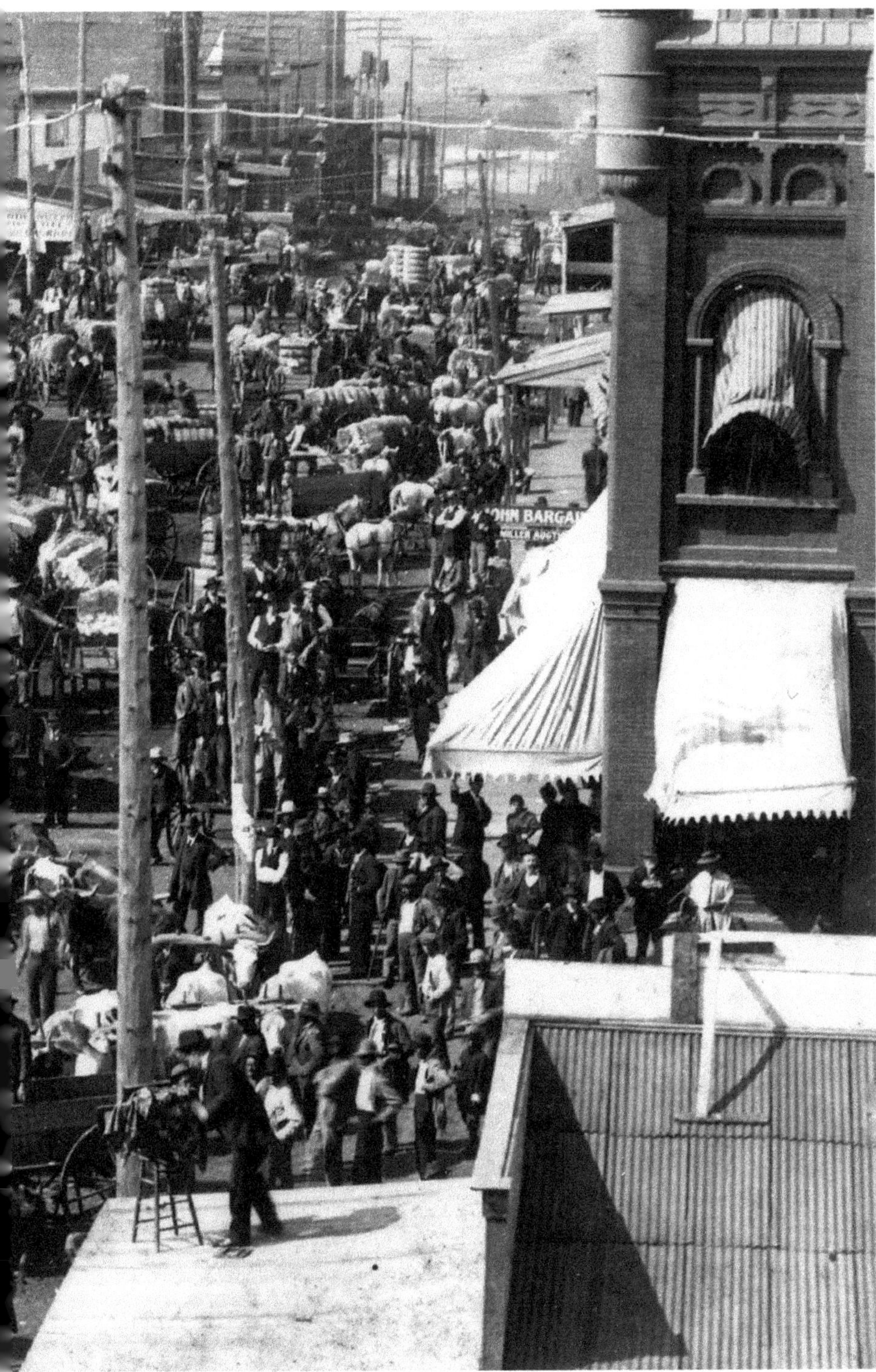

Because it was the territorial capital of Oklahoma, Guthrie was the base of operations for Marshal Nix. When his deputies neutralized their quarry, they generally brought them to Guthrie (alive or dead) for identification, to provide proof for the collection of their rewards. Crowds like this one rippled with excitement when the train brought in the deputies and their prey.

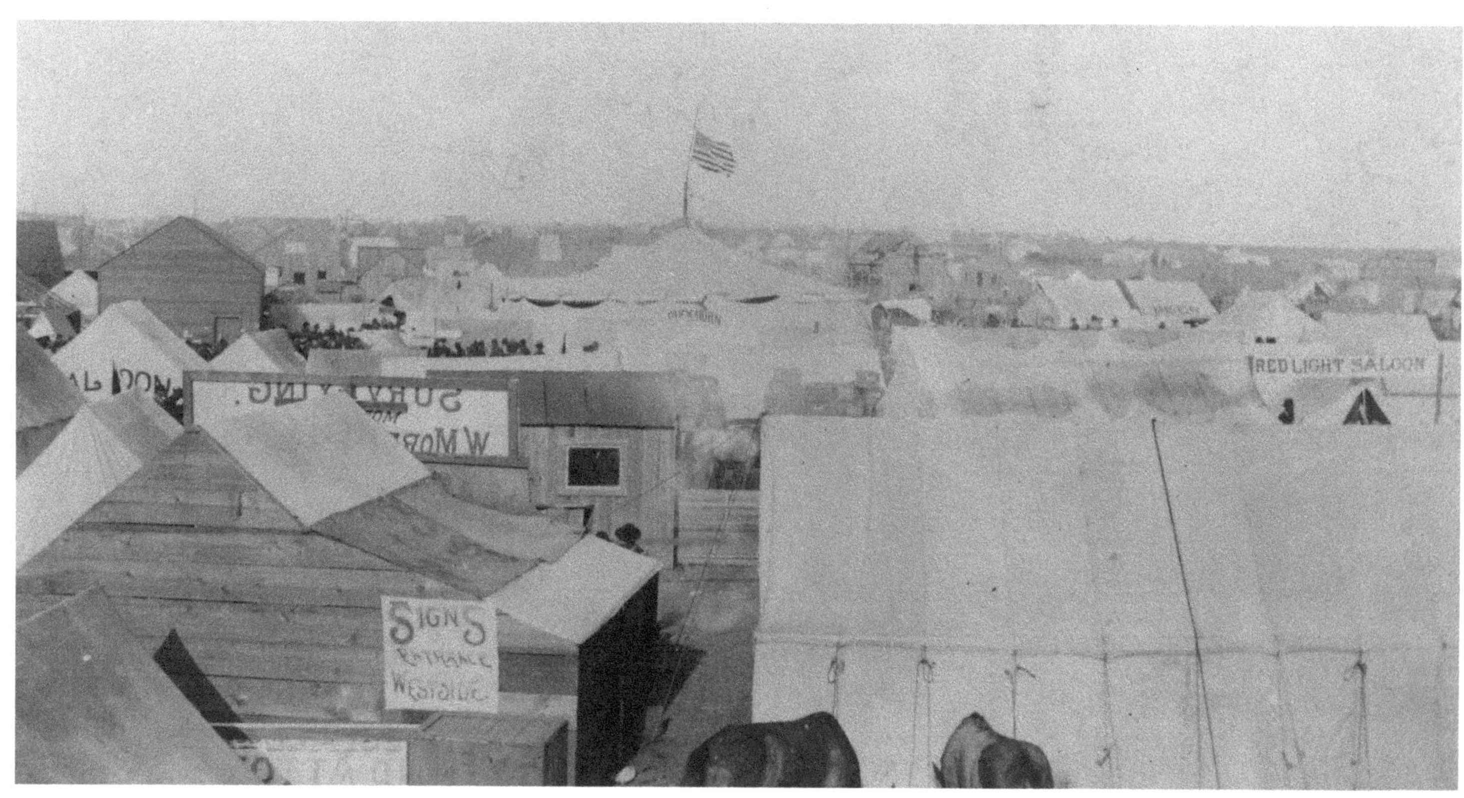

Perry, Oklahoma, rose to a city of 25,000 people overnight after the Cherokee Outlet opening in 1893, and its Hell's Half Acre soon had 110 saloons frequented by outlaws like the Doolins and Daltons based in nearby Ingalls. Marshal Nix made it a priority and dispatched two deputies to tame it.

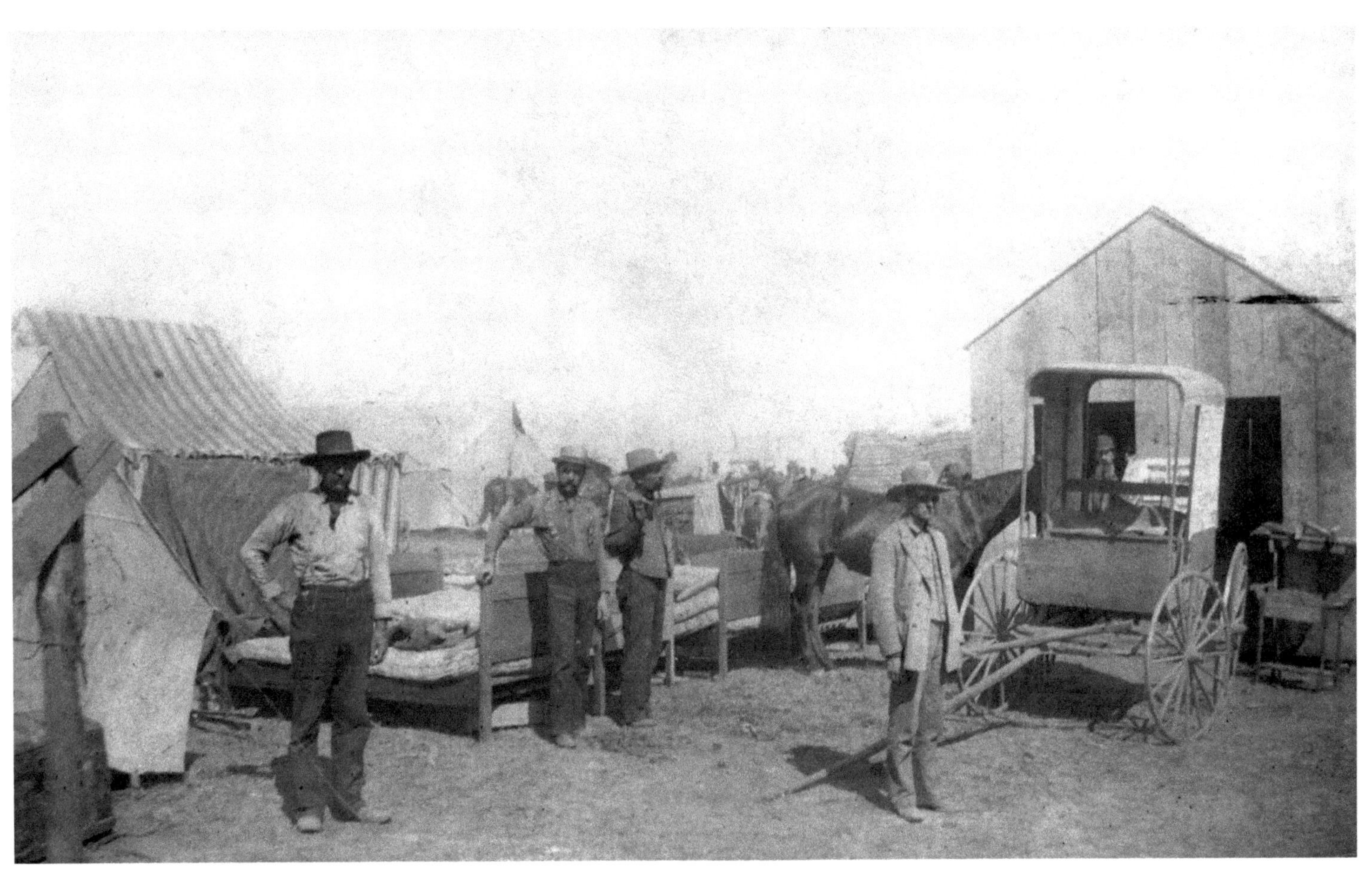

This is Calamity Avenue in Perry, Oklahoma, 1893. A contemporary observer wrote that the area was inhabited by "a class of shiftless men who have never done well and will never do well and . . . a set of gamblers, thugs, and blacklegs of every description."

Known bank robber Stephen A. Bowen may have been present during Henry Starr's first big bank robbery in Bentonville, Arkansas, in 1893. The gang netted more than $10,000.

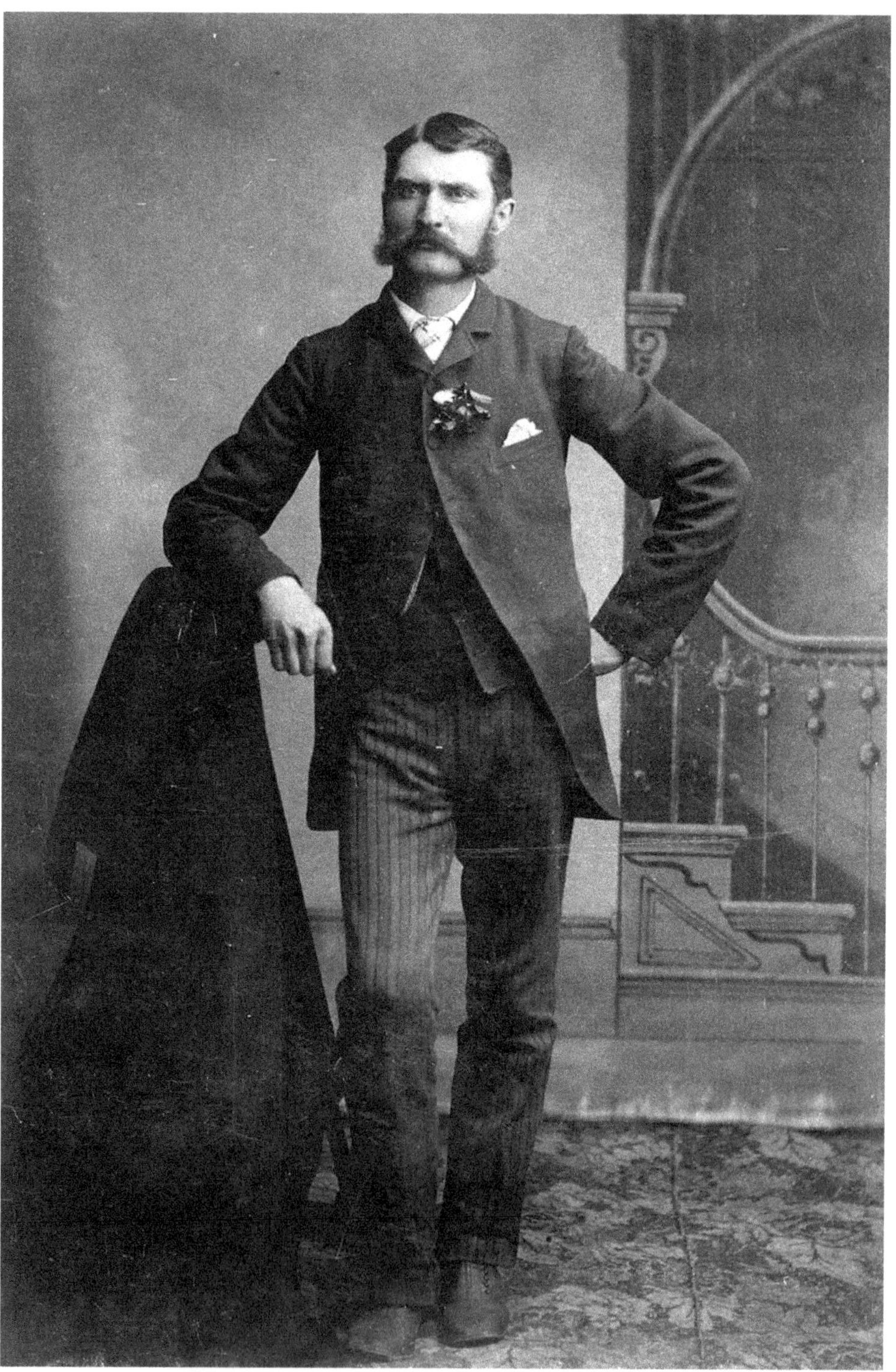

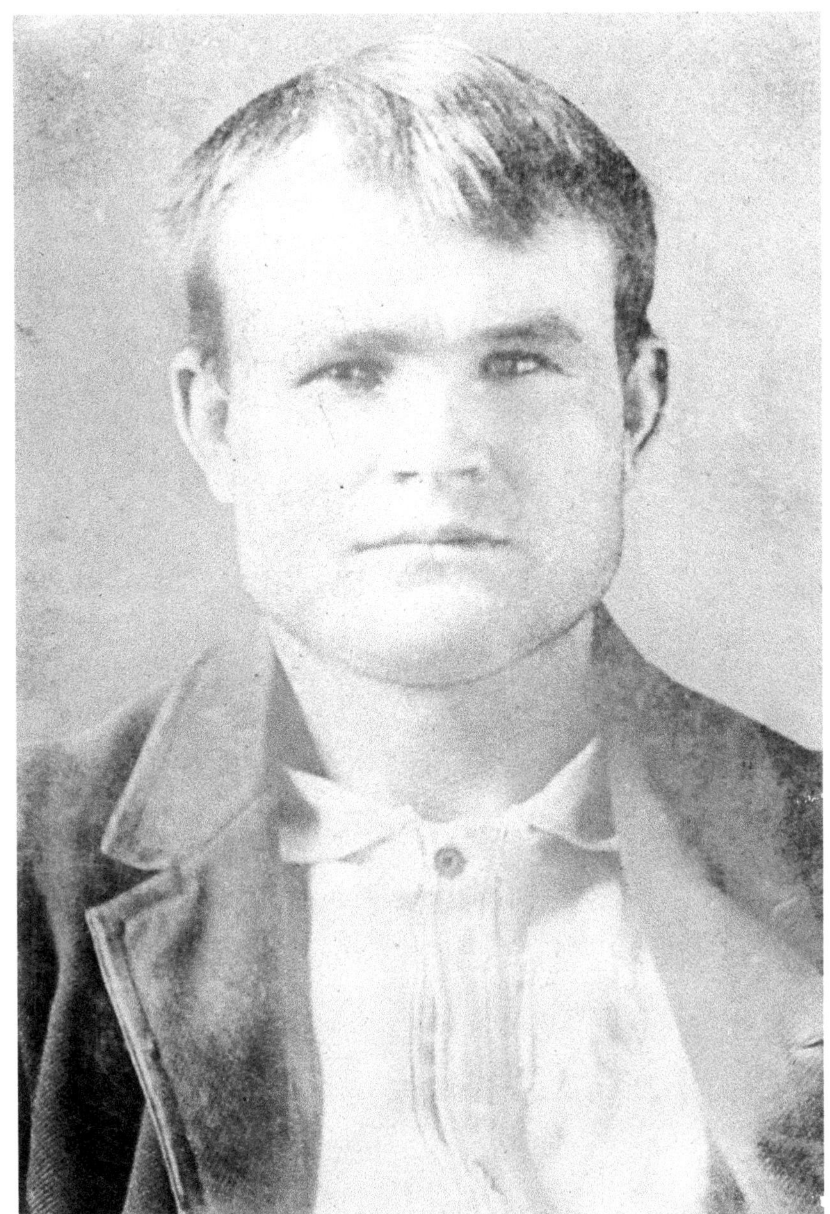

Undeniably one of the Old West's most intelligent outlaws, Robert Leroy Parker, a.k.a. Butch Cassidy, was born into a large Mormon family in Utah. He was the mastermind behind the exploits of the highly successful Hole-in-the-Wall Gang, which operated primarily in the mountain West preying primarily on corporate victims and was generally nonviolent. In addition to his superior planning skills, he was also adept at leadership and conflict resolution.

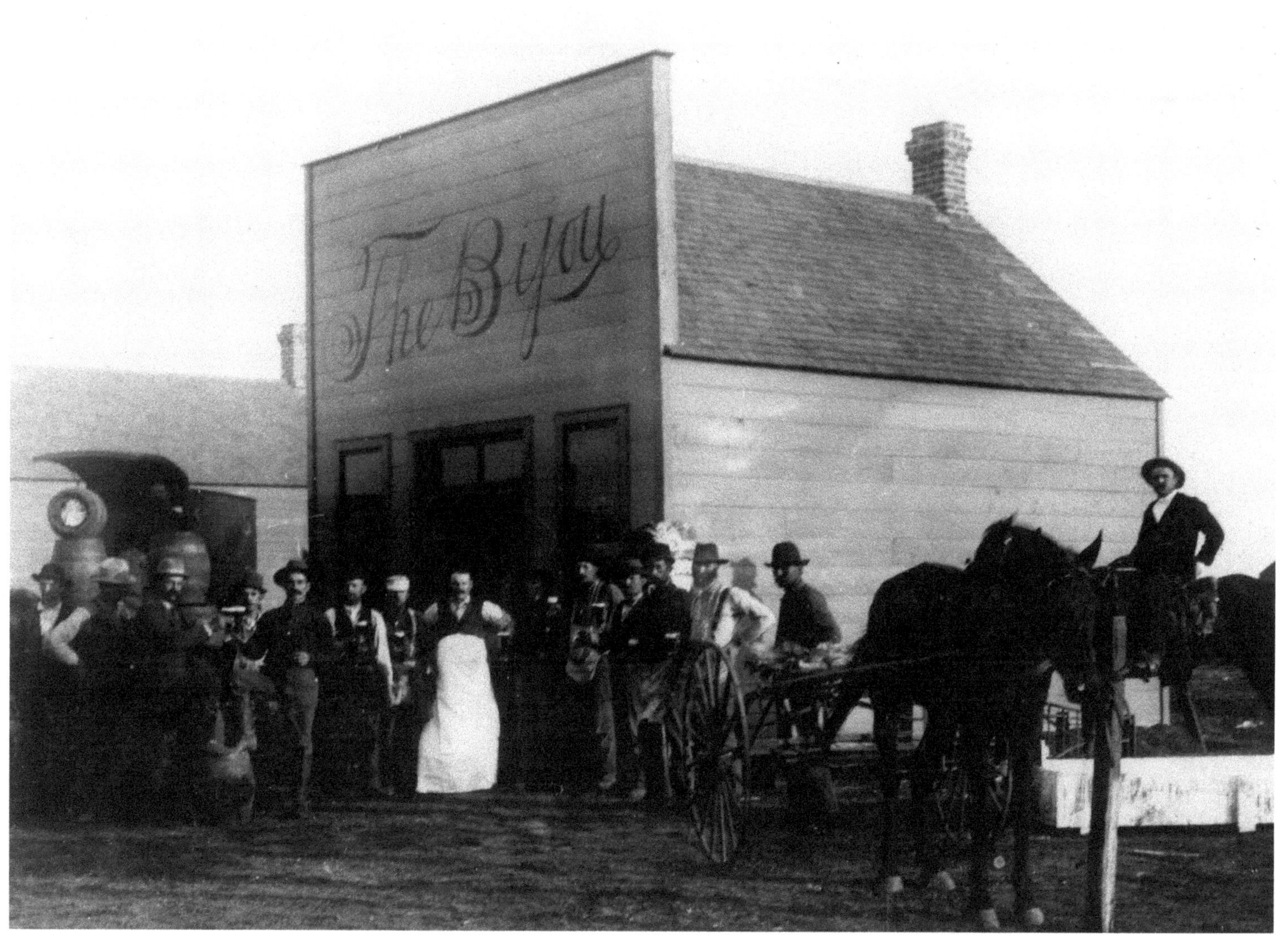

Kegs are being unloaded at Kelley's Bijou saloon in Round Pond, Oklahoma Territory, in 1894, a few months after the Cherokee Strip was opened by land run. United States Indian Police kept close tabs on places like this one because it was illegal to sell alcohol to the nearby Cheyenne and Arapaho tribes and many a rustler or horse thief in the area supplemented his income this way.

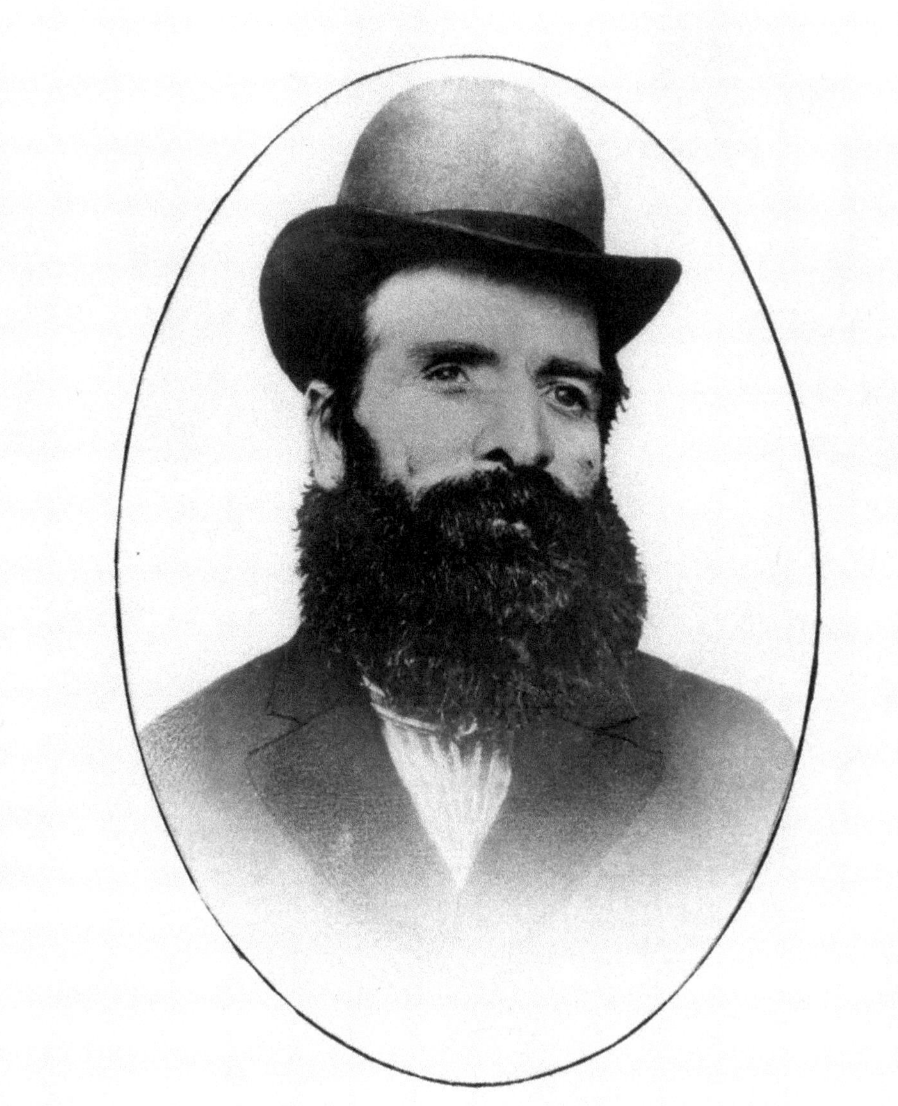

After a string of robberies on the Southern Pacific Railroad, fingers were pointed at California farmer Chris Evans and his business partner John Sontag. Evans adamantly denied any involvement in any train robbery, but he chose to make his stand with a gun rather than in the courts, killing and wounding several lawmen as a fugitive before his capture. Convicted of murder, he entered Folsom Prison in 1894.

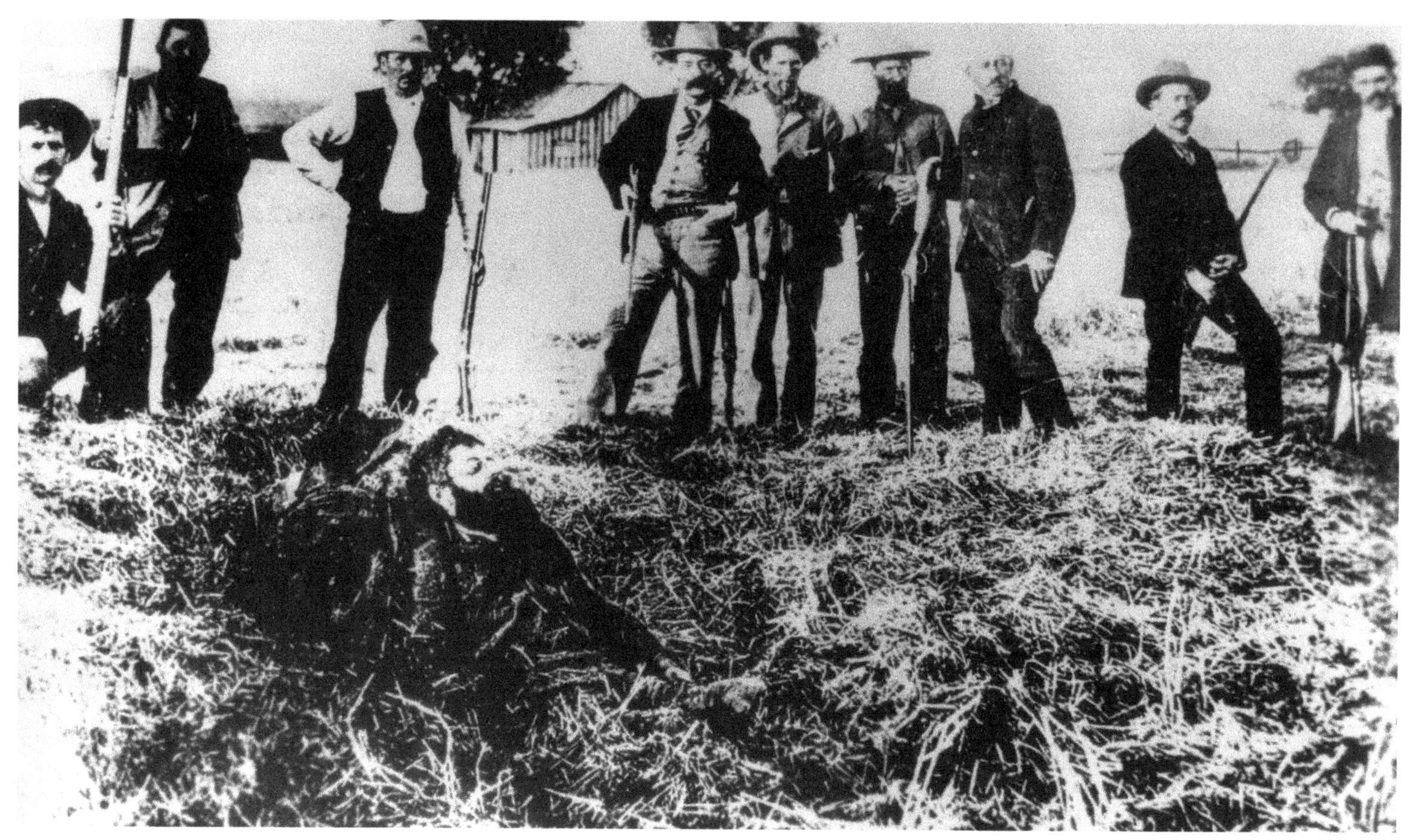

After Apache scouts trailed Evans and Sontag to a remote cabin near Visalia, California, a posse surrounded them and demanded their surrender. The desperate men chose to shoot their way out instead. Evans was wounded and captured, but Sontag suffered fatal wounds. Sontag lay dying in the grass for hours while the posse summoned a photographer to shoot photos like this one.

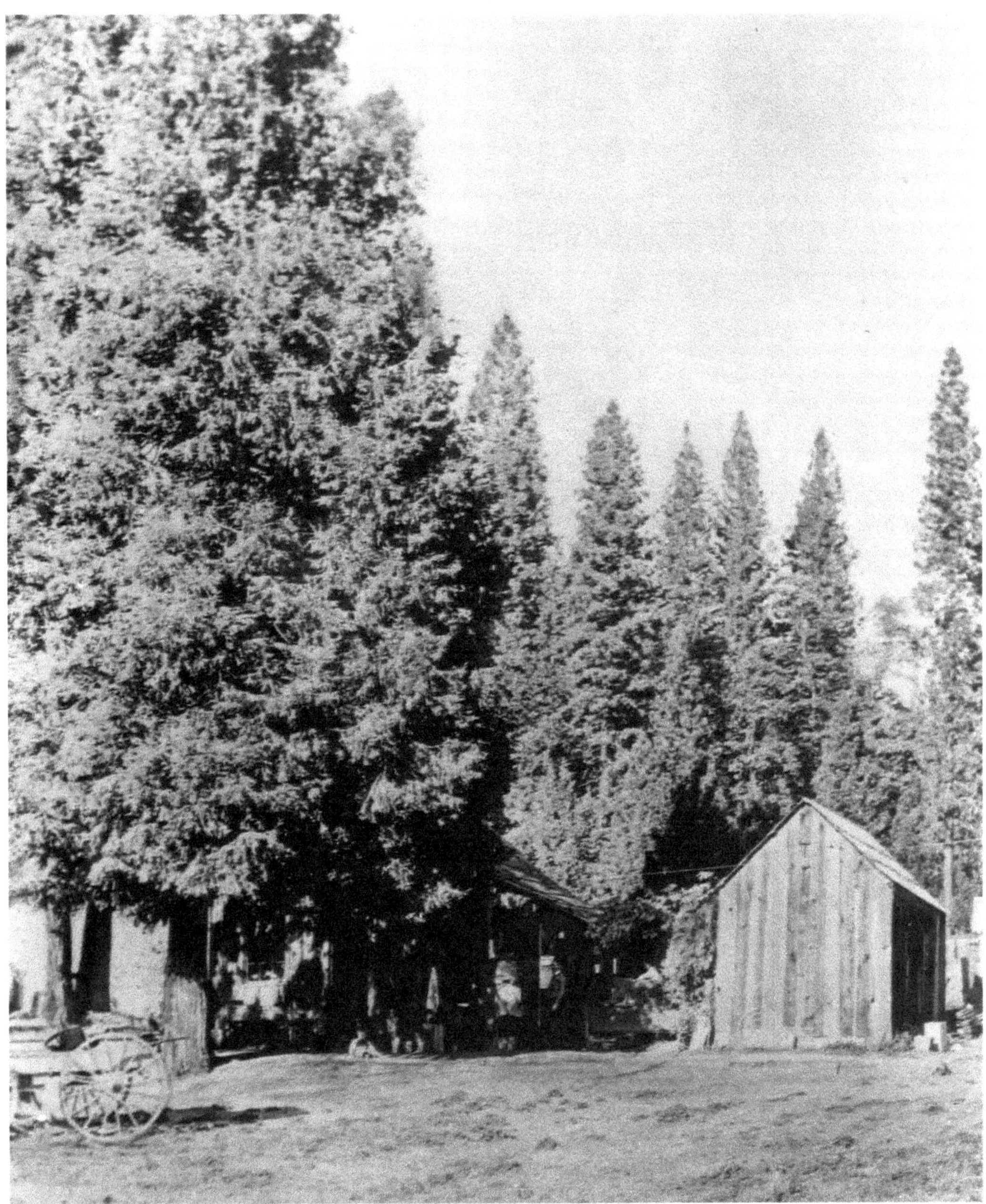

This is the homestead of Chris Evans near Visalia in the San Joaquin Valley. Evans and his wife had five children at the ranch, where they faced much adversity. His accusers cited this fact as motive for his crime, but his benefactors including the Hearst newspapers cited defense of home and hearth to be the reason for his bloody resistance.

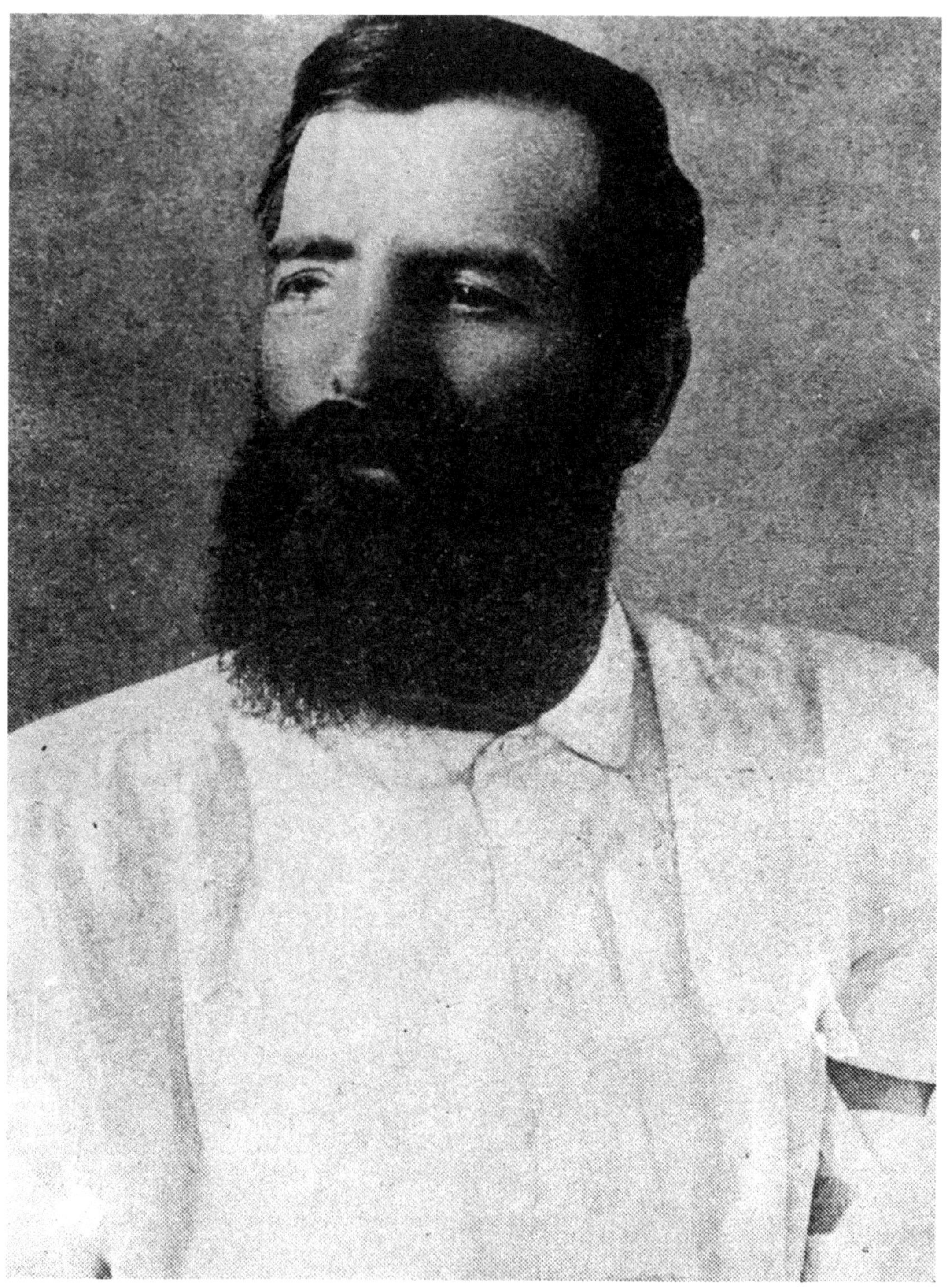

This photograph of Chris Evans depicts the soulful quality of the man. Evans used his prison term, 1894–1911, to better himself and even published a utopian novel, *Eurasia,* in 1900. Evans died in 1917, neither admitting to being a train robber nor explaining why he killed the men sent to arrest him.

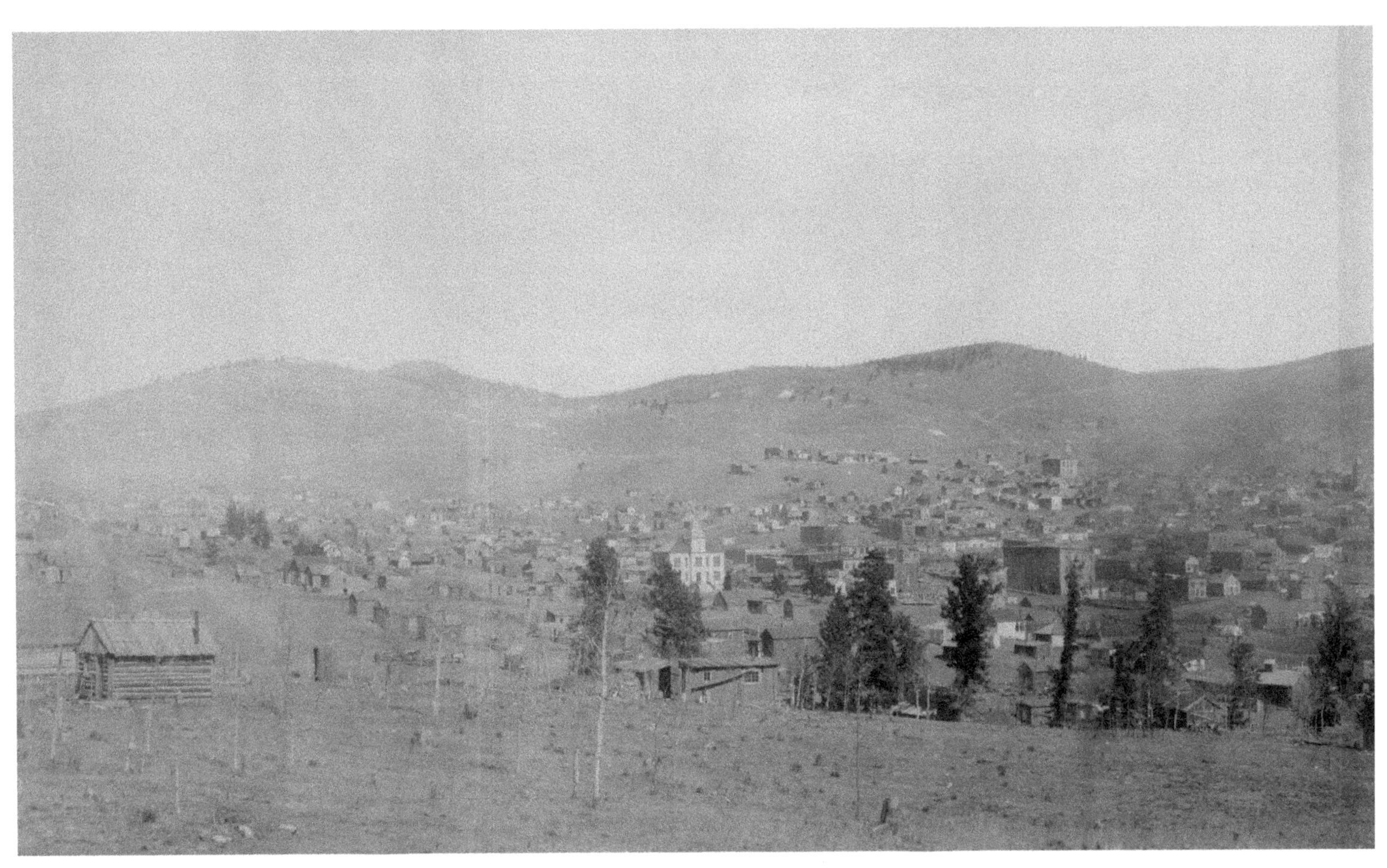

Cripple Creek's high valley at the base of Pike's Peak was the scene of Colorado's last big gold boom when a lode was struck in 1890. In 1894, Wild Bunch member Bob Lee was dispatched there to open a gambling joint and set up a hideout for the gang. He was captured there after robbing a train in Wyoming in 1899.

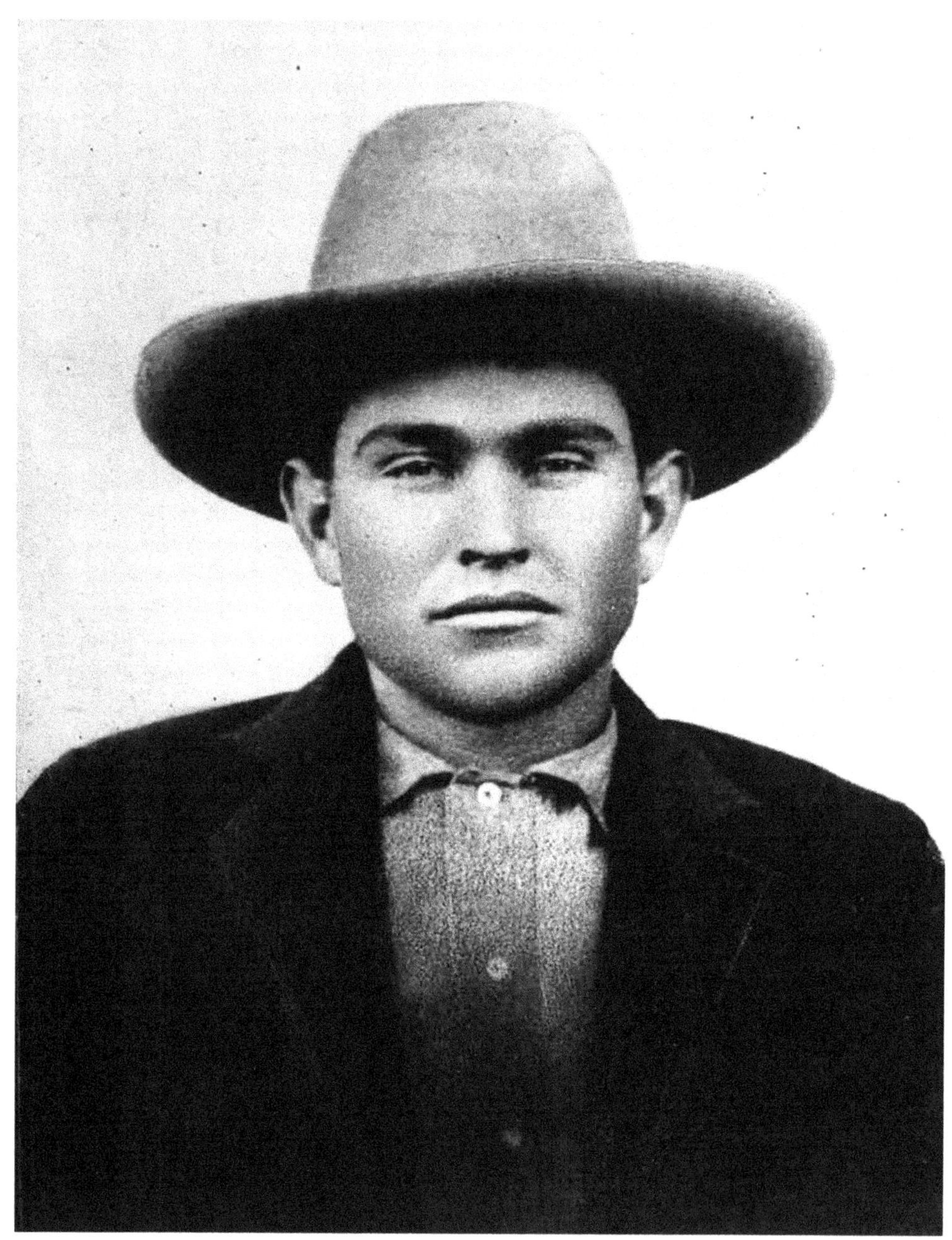

Bill Cook was the leader of a particularly vicious and prolific band of outlaws that struck real terror into the people of Indian Territory in the 1890s. Their hold-ups and robberies of everyone and every place had a strongly negative effect on the regional economy. Cook himself was not particularly violent, but others in his group were. He was captured in early 1895 and died in prison by 1900.

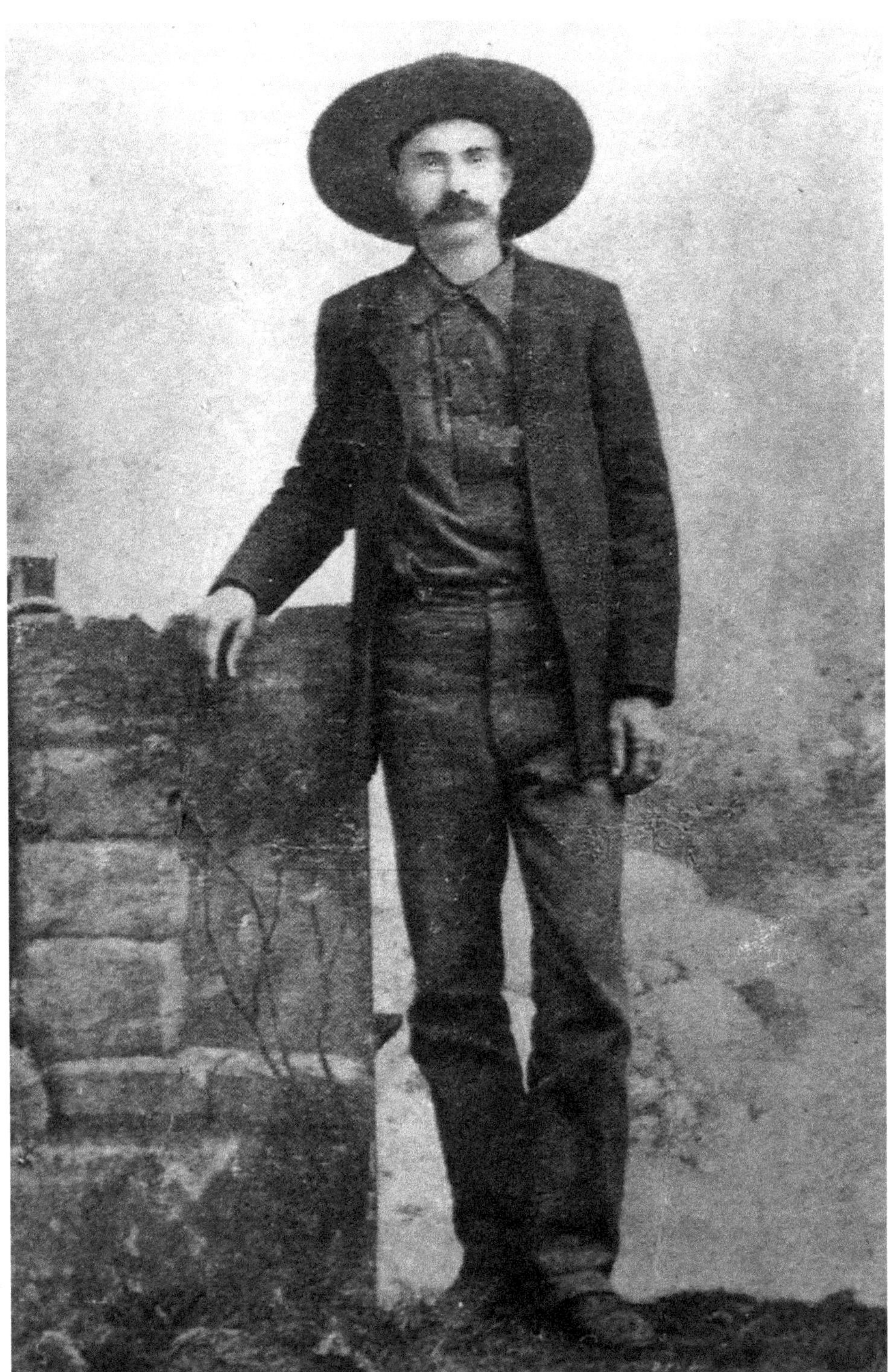

One of the dozen or so members of the Bill Cook gang was Thurman "Skeeter" Baldwin. He was known to have participated in a few of the gang's activities, but was not quite so violent as Cherokee Bill and a few others.

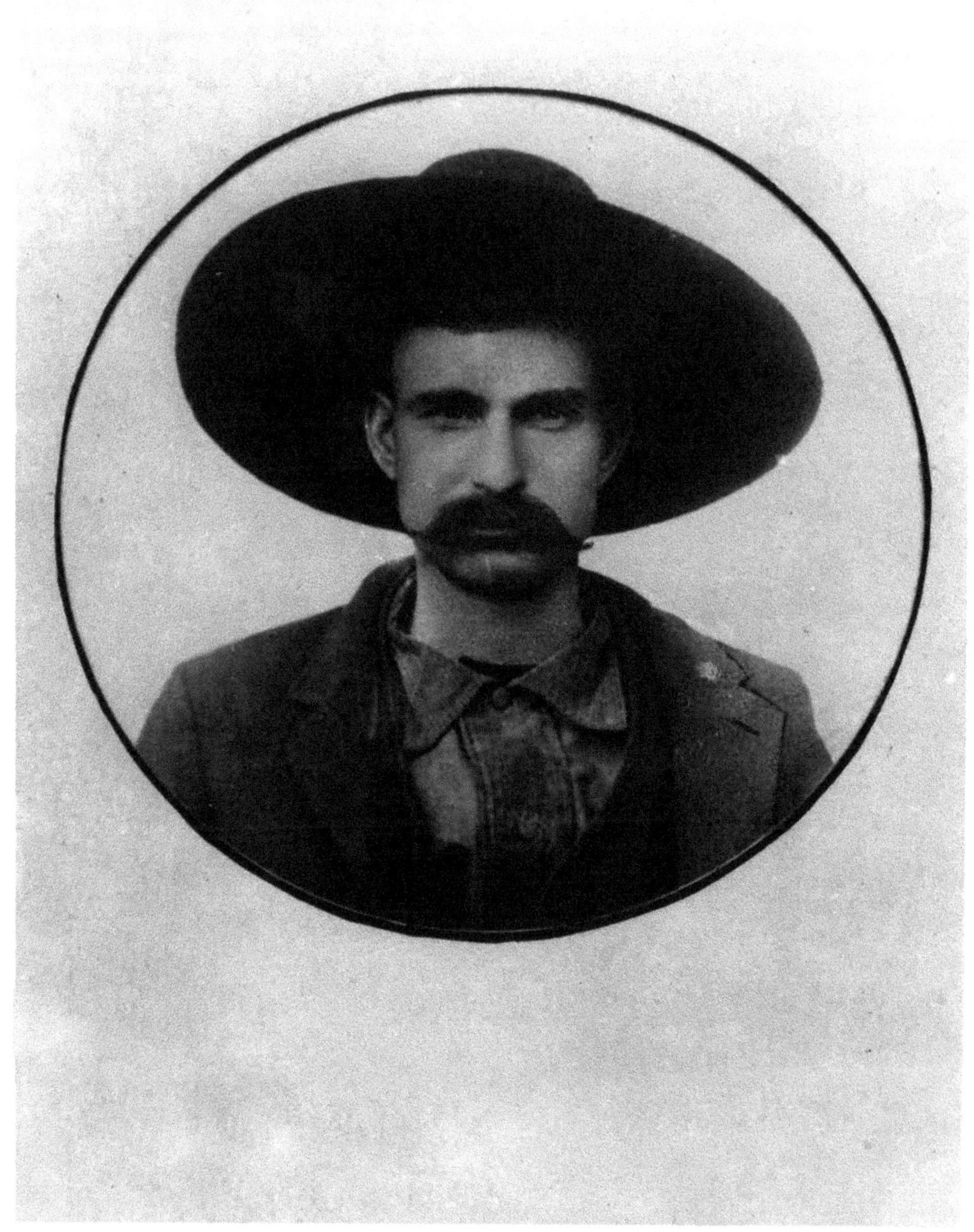

All the outlaws knew that if they pled guilty of train-robbing before a judge (saving the hassle and expense of a trial), they generally got a much lighter sentence. But Captain Bill McDonald of the Texas Rangers recalled an exception to the rule. When "Hangin' Judge" Isaac Parker decided to make an example of Thurman Baldwin and gave him 30 years, Baldwin exclaimed, "Well, this is a hell of a court to declare guilty in!"

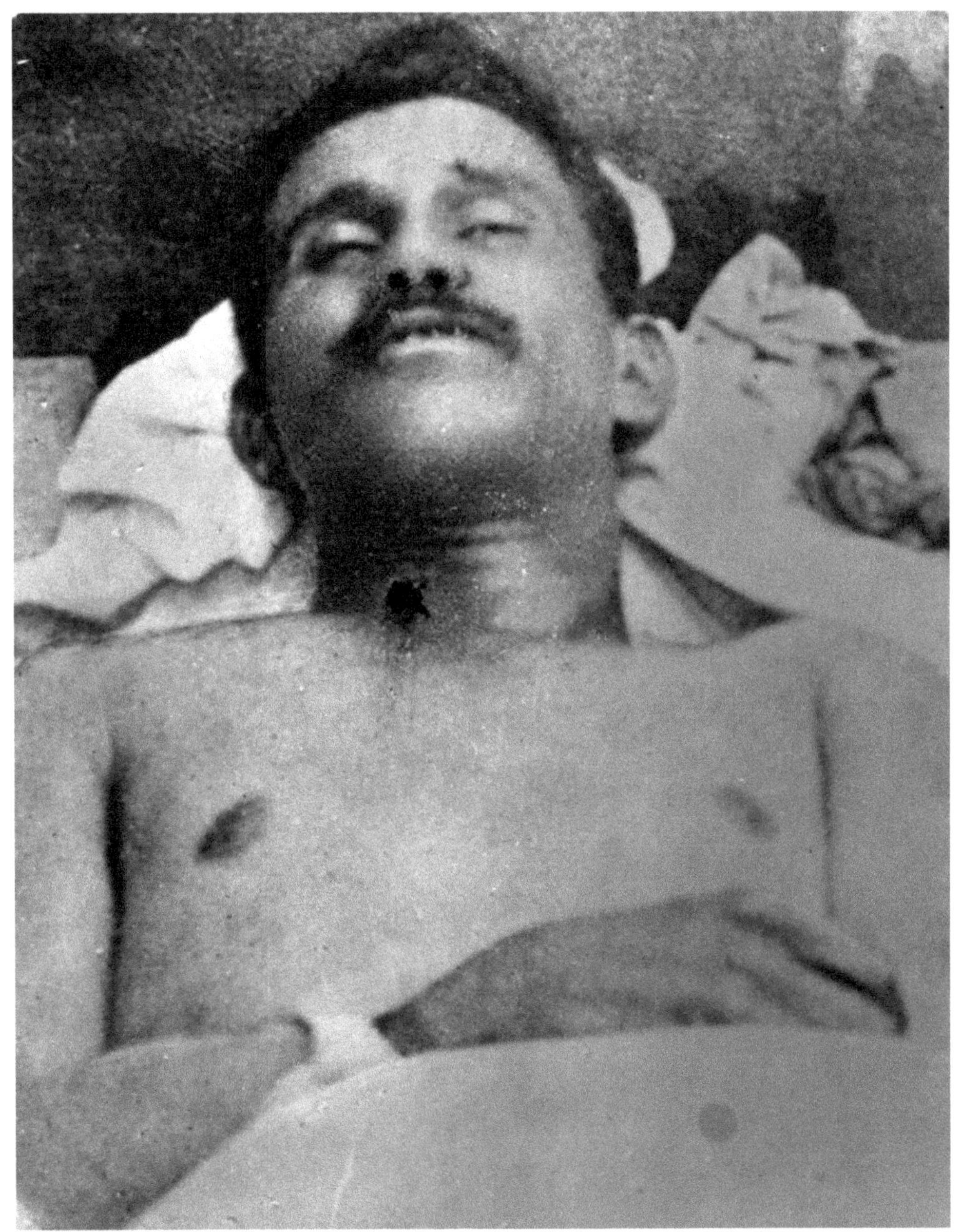

A lesser figure in the Bill Cook outfit in Indian Territory was Henry Munson. He had joined in the robbing of a Frisco train in July 1894, but he and several others were ambushed in a house outside Sapulpa a few weeks later. Munson and Lon Gordon were killed, but Cook escaped.

In 1894, Cherokee Bill (a.k.a. Crawford Goldsby) joined with the Cook Gang on a crime spree in Indian Territory, murdering, robbing, and killing all in their path. He was soon captured (seen here, at center) and after a year in prison received the death sentence from Fort Smith's "hangin' judge" Isaac Parker.

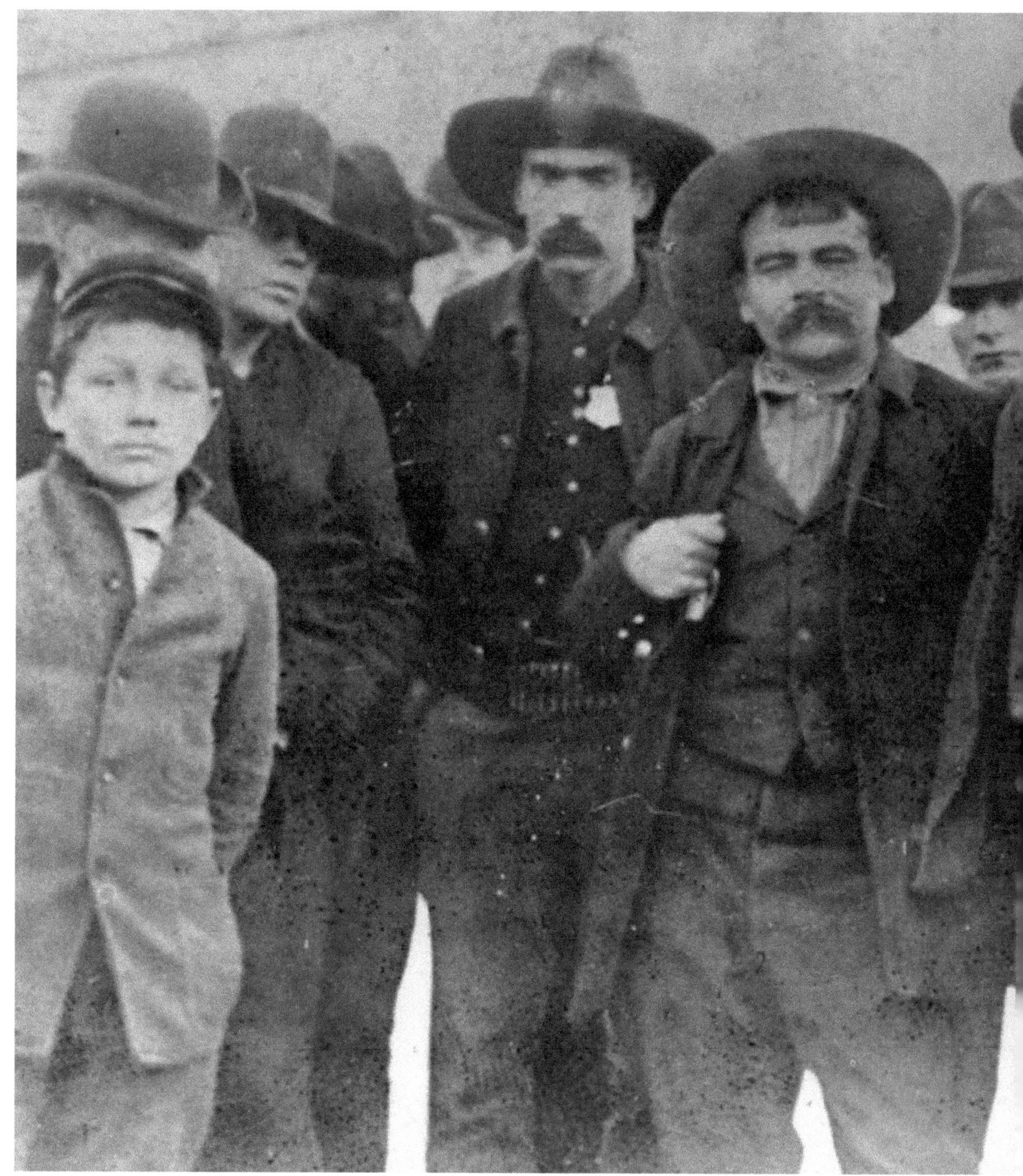

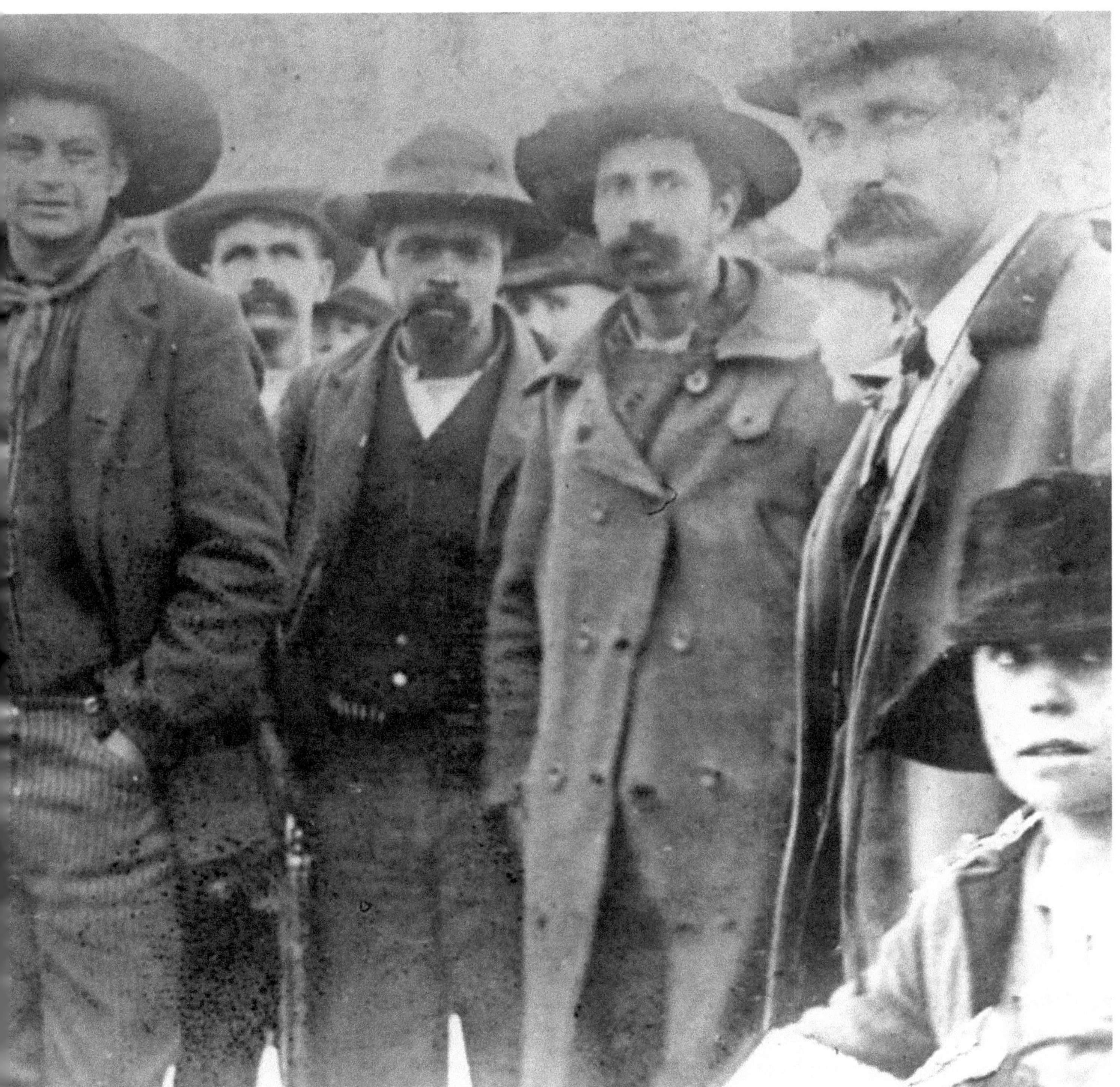

During his imprisonment pending trial, Cherokee Bill surprised his jailers and tried an escape. He shot jailer Lawrence Keating in the stomach and while Keating stumbled downstairs, Bill fatally shot him in the back. He did not escape and was executed by hanging. As the noose was put around his neck, he told the crowd, "Today is as good a day to die as any."

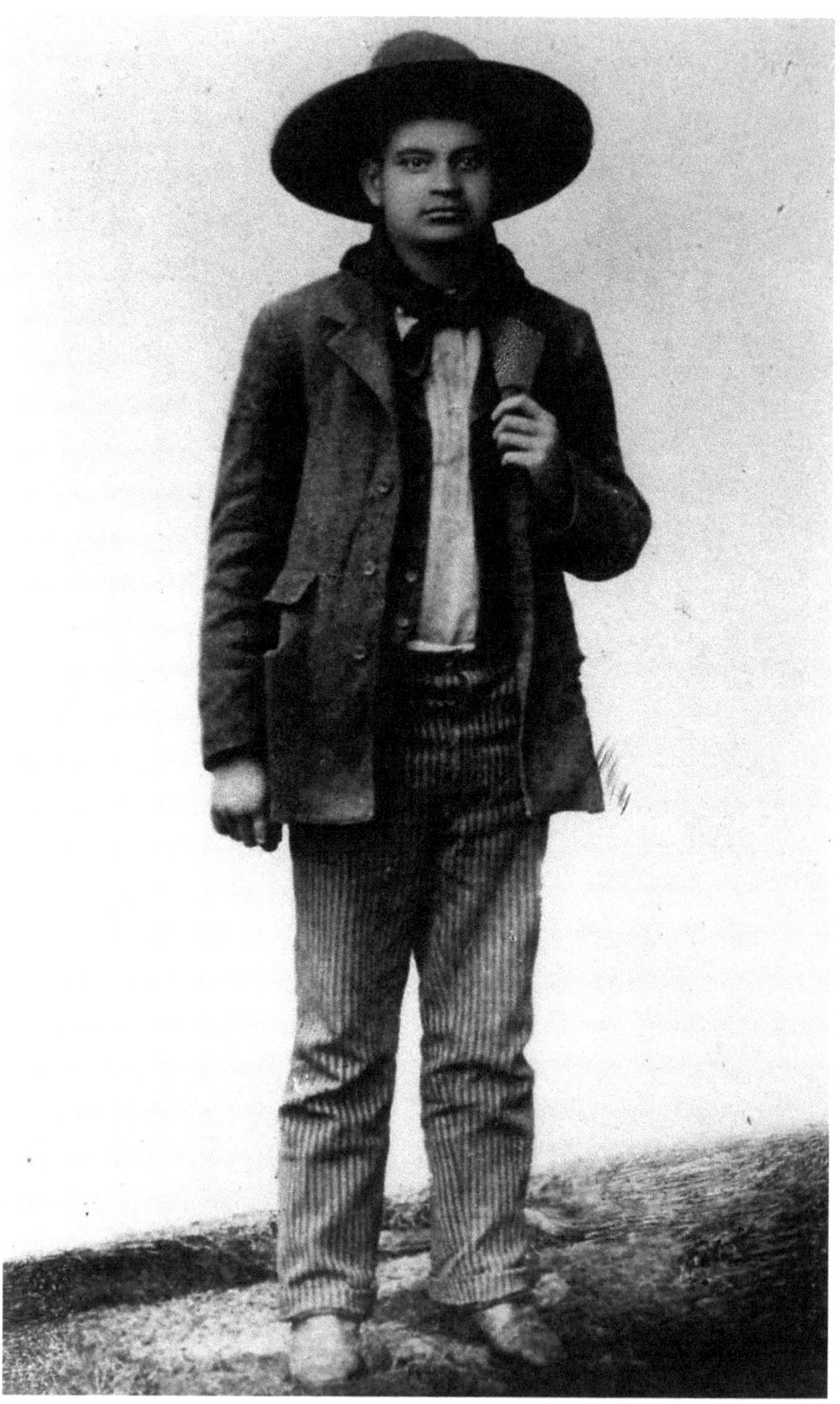

If He'd Just Pay Me What He's Paying Them to Keep Me from Robbing Him, I'd Quit Robbing Him

(1895–1935)

As the twentieth century approached, all the former territories of the West had matured into full member states of the Union with the exception of Arizona, New Mexico, Oklahoma, and Indian Territories. Outlaw trouble could still flare up anyplace at anytime, however.

Outlaws in the Old West typically were only active in their late teens and twenties and were generally dead or in prison by thirty. One interesting phenomenon in this era was that the new generation of outlaws had not known the world that motivated Jesse James and Billy the Kid and lacked the same motives and life experiences which led the earlier generation to lives of crime. They had no pretense of exacting ideological or political revenge and seemed to be motivated more by the adrenaline rush and the possibility of easy money.

Another development in the 1890s was the reemergence of well-organized gangs making coordinated attacks on trains, banks, and mine payrolls in some of the more remote parts of the West. Most notable of these was Butch Cassidy's Hole-in-the-Wall Gang (a.k.a. the Wild Bunch). Like Jesse James, Cassidy was a brilliant strategist and excelled at surrounding himself with competent men. He exhibited great leadership skills in building teams, instilling loyalty, and putting the right person in the right job. His men were also expert at not getting caught—until the fateful day in 1900 when they took a photograph together in Fort Worth, Texas. Prior to that, Pinkerton agents had no photographs of them and often did not know for whom they were looking. Within a few short years, the gang was rounded up and many of them went to prison or the gallows.

Whereas Cassidy and his gang represented a refinement of the old order of outlawry in the West, in Indian Territory (and later the state of Oklahoma) a new type of bandit appeared in the person of Henry Starr. Starr came from a long line of criminals in the Indian Territory and received his tutelage in banditry from the many nefarious types in the region. Starr was an innovator, though; he used new technologies like automatic weapons and the automobile to move quickly and strike several banks in one locale in rapid succession. His methods would become the model for the likes of Bonnie and Clyde and Pretty Boy Floyd in succeeding decades.

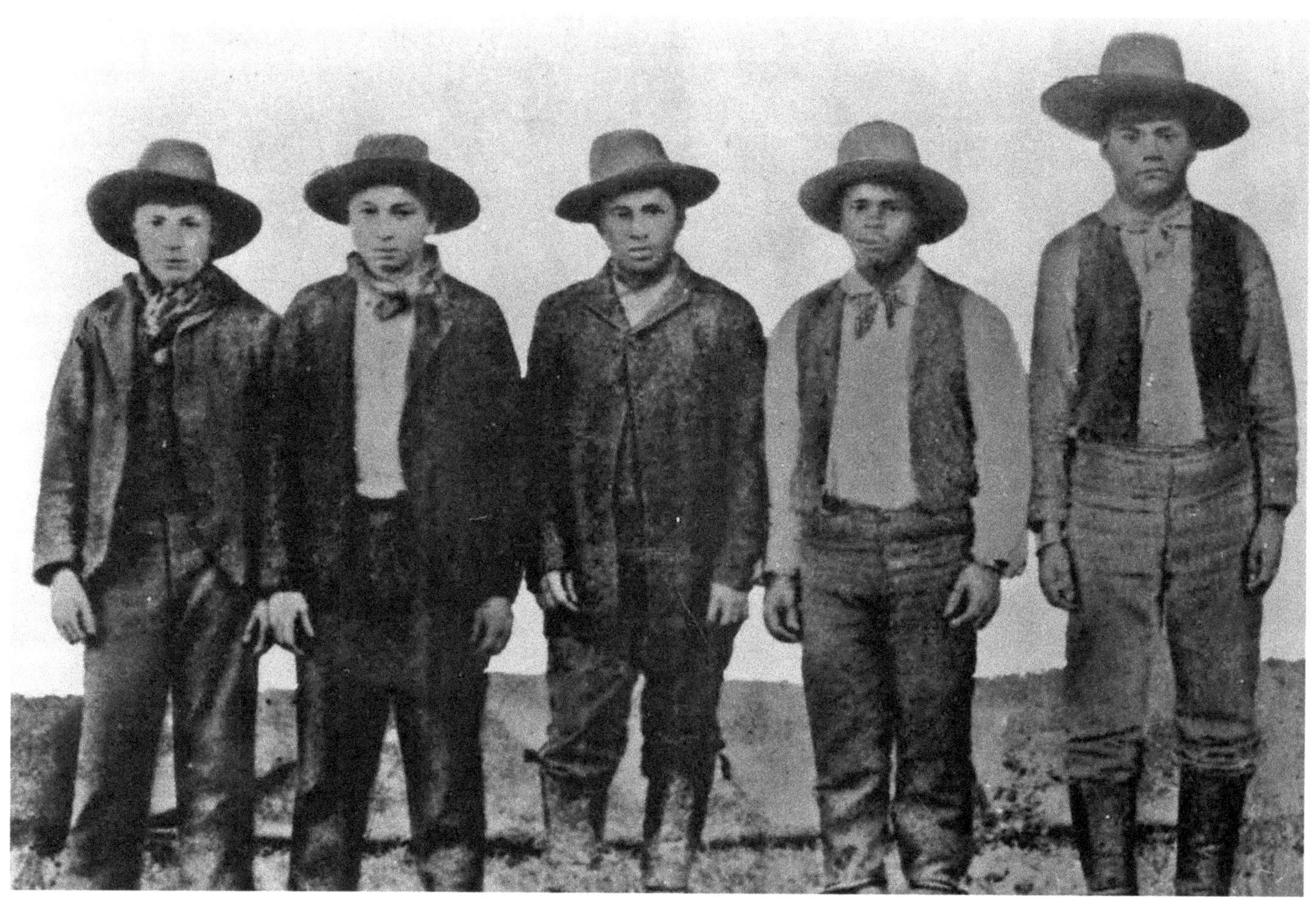

The Rufus Buck Gang embarked on a short-lived reign of terror in 1895 after the young group of mixed-blood Creeks and blacks joined forces to exact revenge on white intruders in the Creek Nation by way of murders and robberies. After killing an Okmulgee sheriff, they were apprehended by Creek Light Horse, tried, and hanged at the court in Fort Smith.

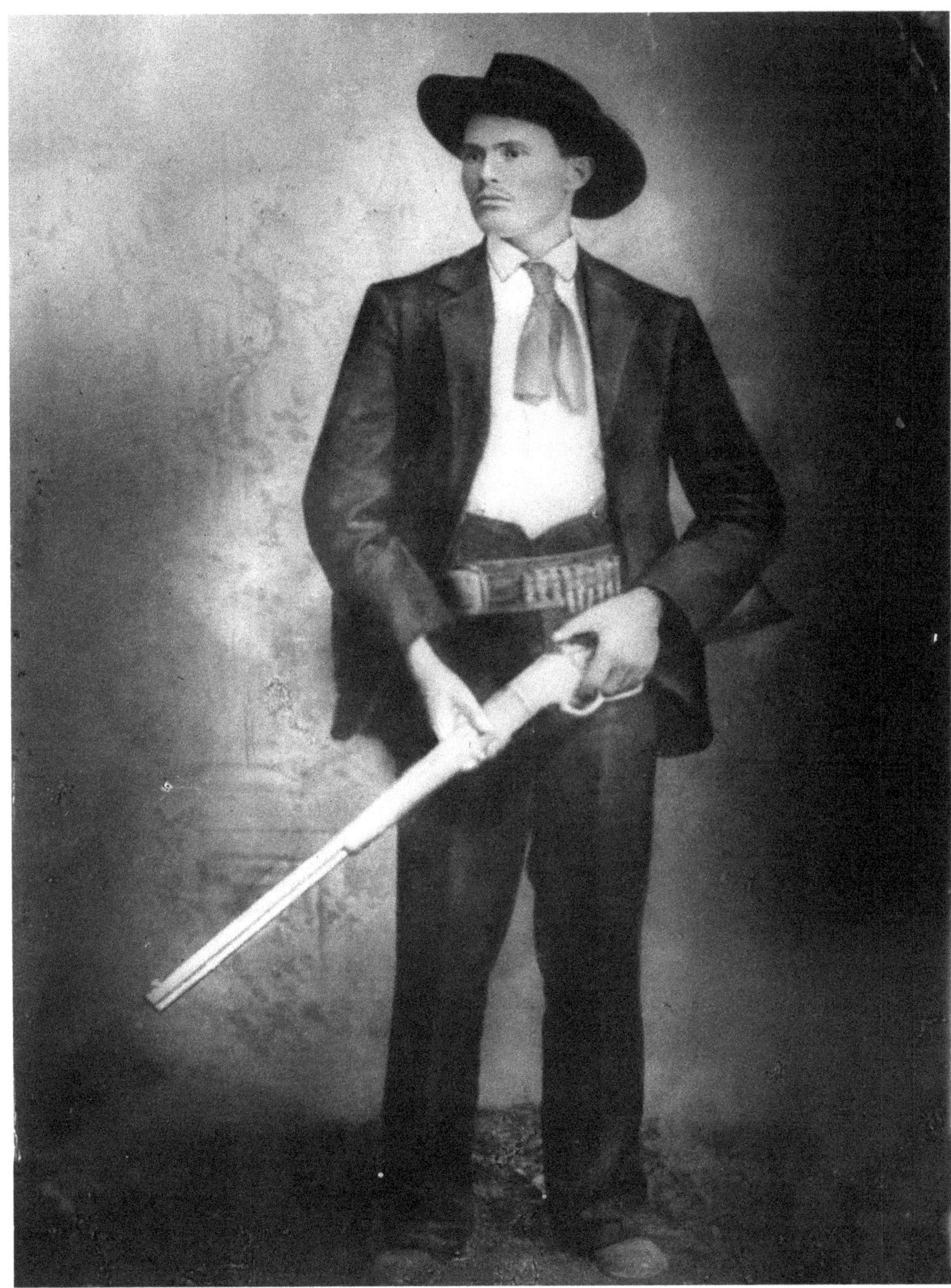

Though he got off to an inauspicious start after failing to open a safe, Bud Newman became a train-robbing specialist working with the Taylor gang in southwestern Texas in the late 1890s. He met his end after turning state's evidence and agreeing to track down his companion Bill Taylor. Taylor killed him from ambush.

Starstruck teenage wannabes Jennie "Little Britches" Metcalf (right) and "Cattle Annie" MacDougal (left) became enamored of the Doolin Gang, which operated for a time near their Oklahoma farms, and joined up as lookouts. When the gang dissolved, they turned to horse thievery and smuggling liquor and proved to be surprisingly tough and elusive when marshals came looking for them. They were soon caught, though, and served two years in prison.

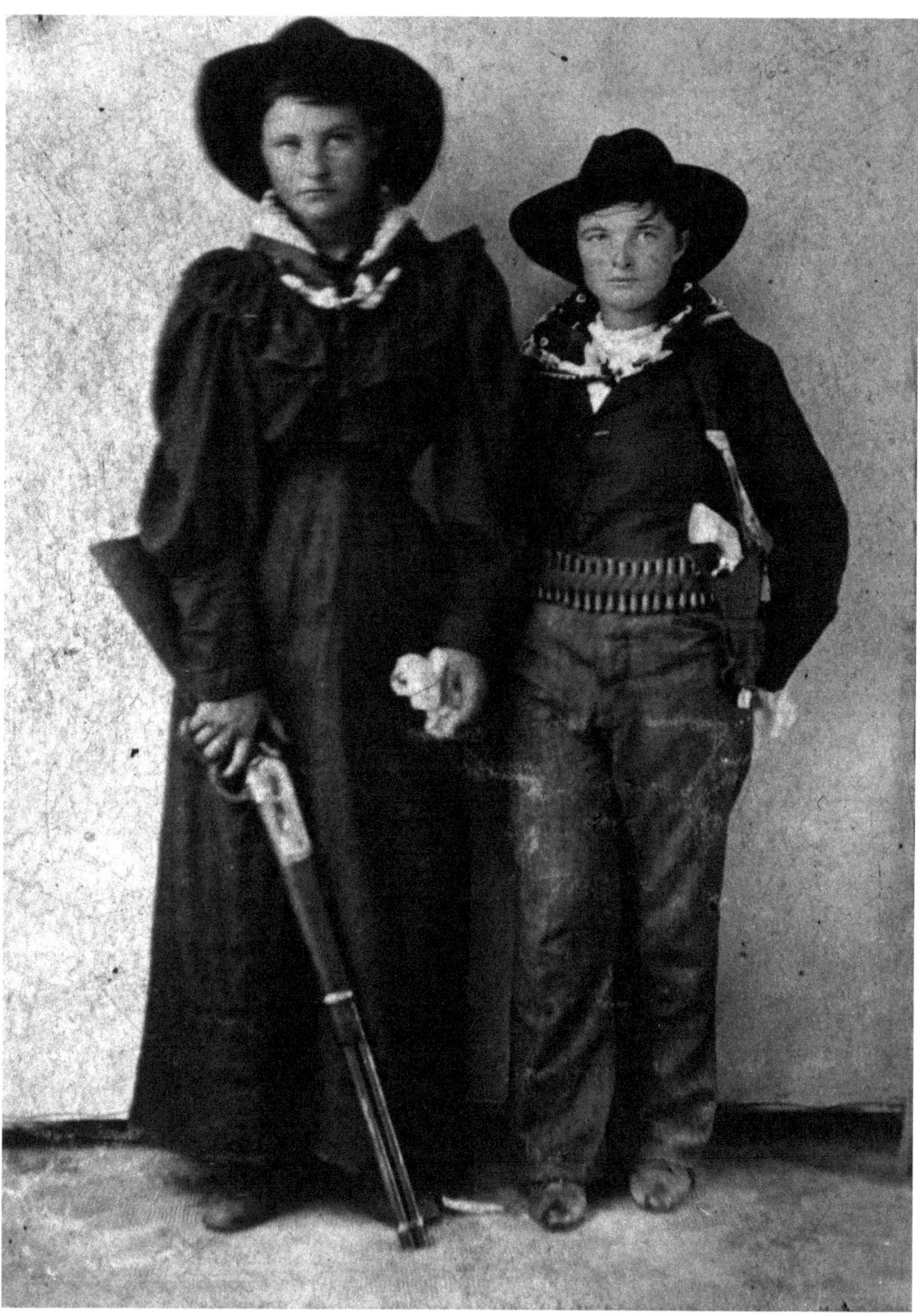

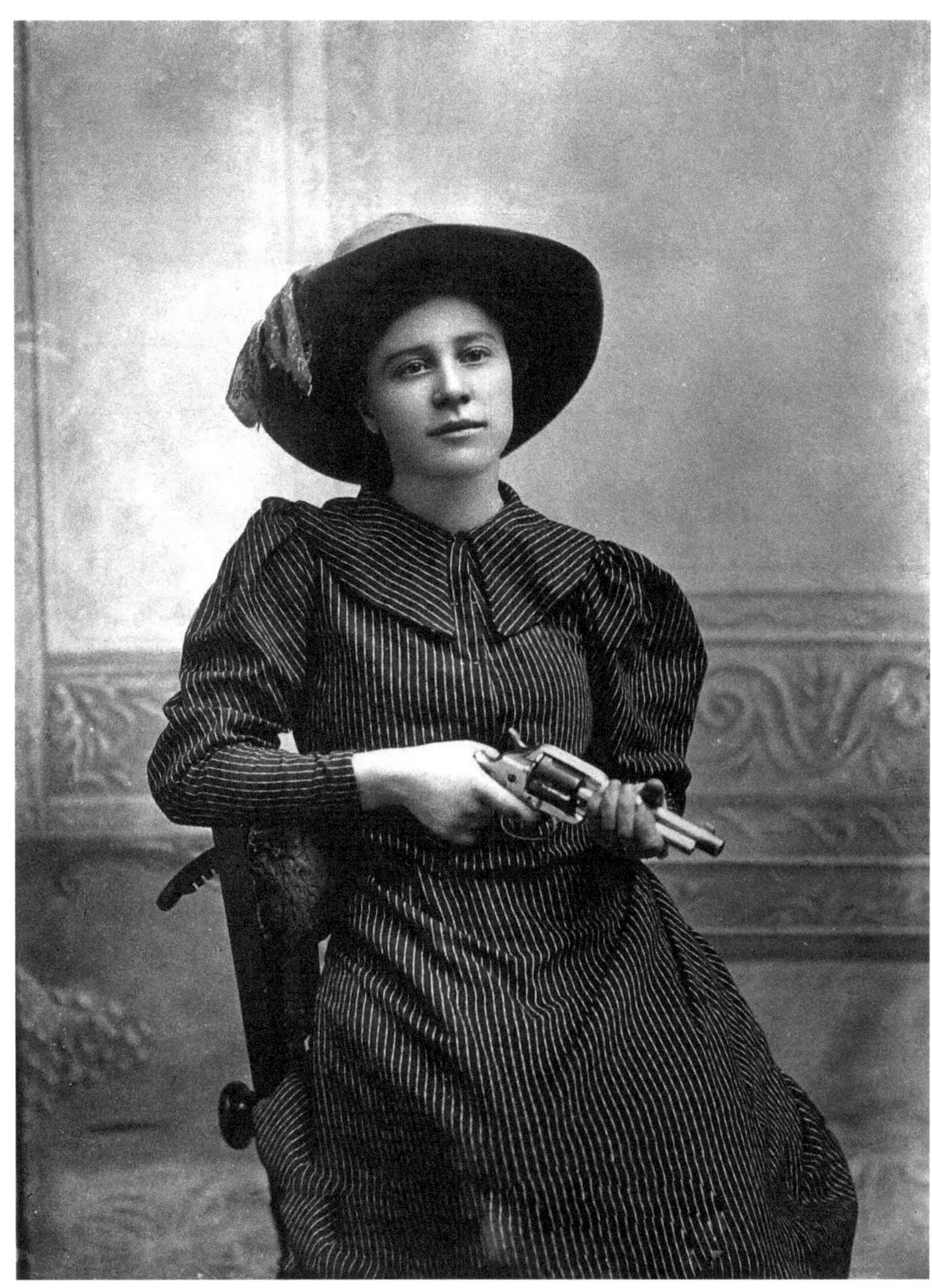

Although she was never fully accepted as a member of the Dalton gang, Jennie Metcalf was certainly capable of as much mayhem as they were. However, by most accounts, she found a higher purpose during her time in the Boston reformatory, where she and Annie were celebrities and went on to do mission work in the New York slums. She died of consumption (tuberculosis) soon after.

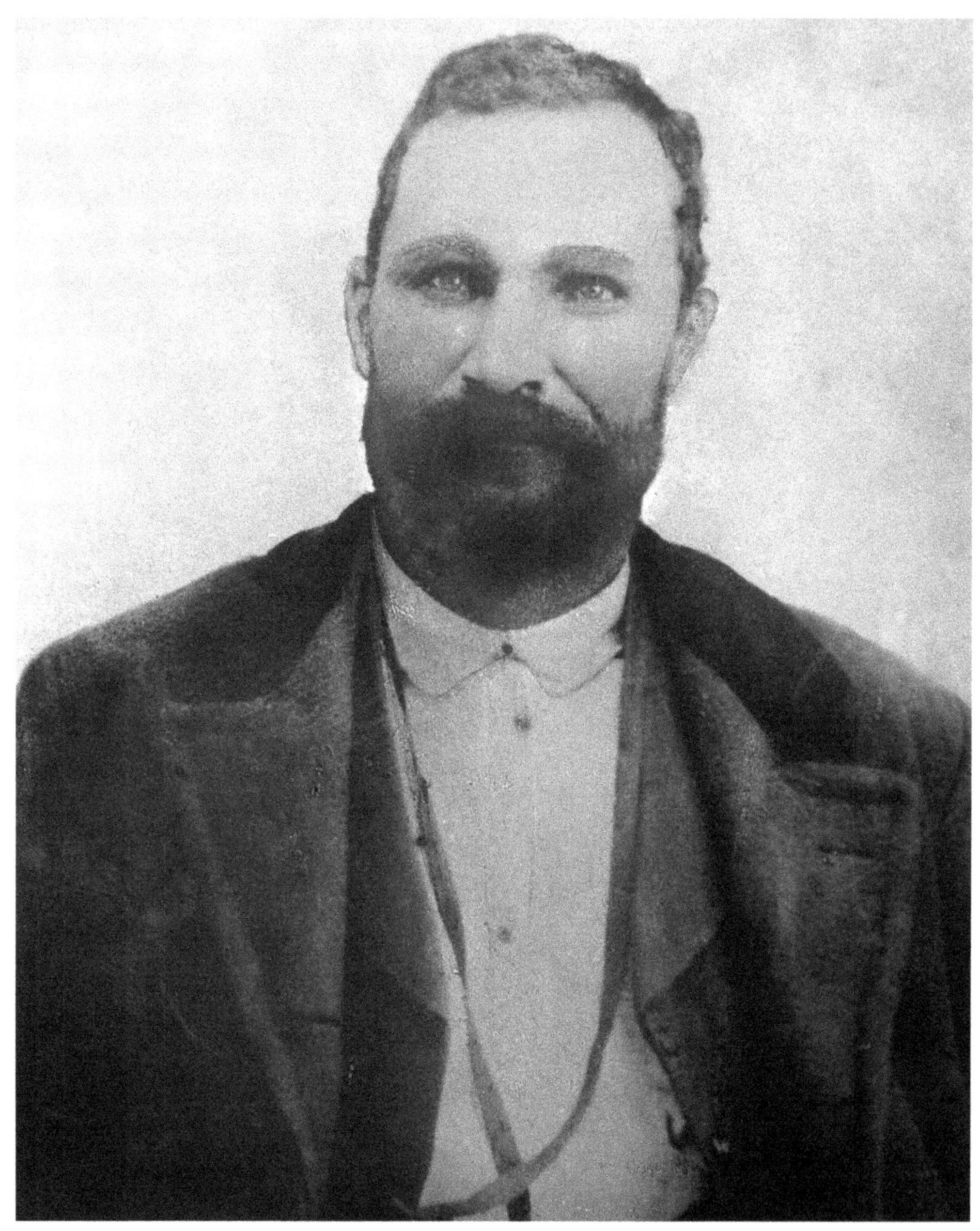

Confederate deserter John Selman led a stormy life, most of it in Texas on both sides of the law. A veteran of New Mexico's Lincoln County War and most notably the murderer of John Wesley Hardin, it was said of Selman at his death in an El Paso street in 1896, "When not drinking he was as gentle as a child, but he did not know what fear was, and has killed not less than twenty outlaws."

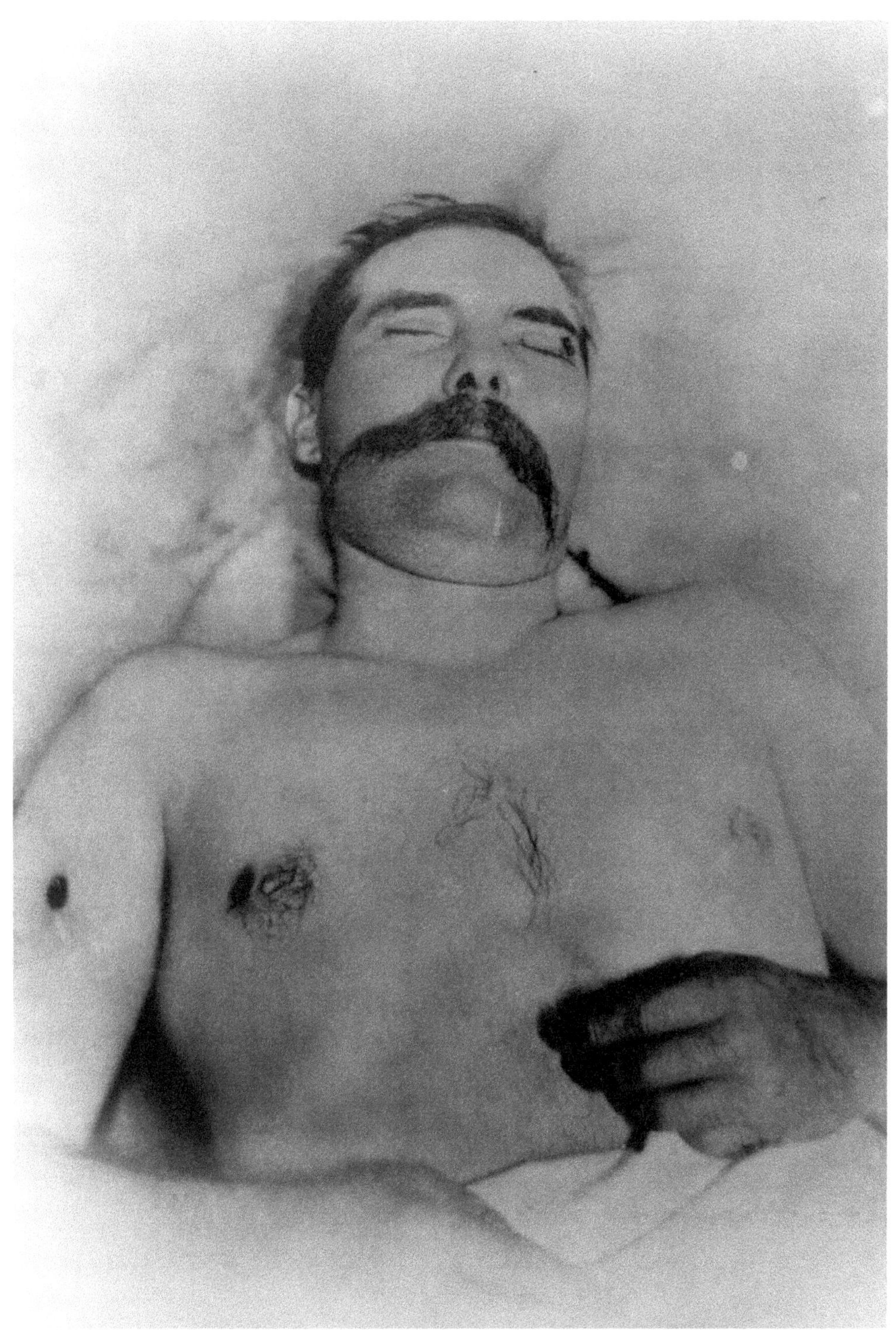

In the 1890s, John Wesley Hardin was released from prison and became a respectable attorney. However, after a series of personal tragedies he went into self-imposed exile in El Paso and fell back in with a bad crowd. In 1895, at the age of 42, he was shot in the back of the head at the Acme Saloon by John Selman, his two Colt .45 revolvers undrawn in their holsters.

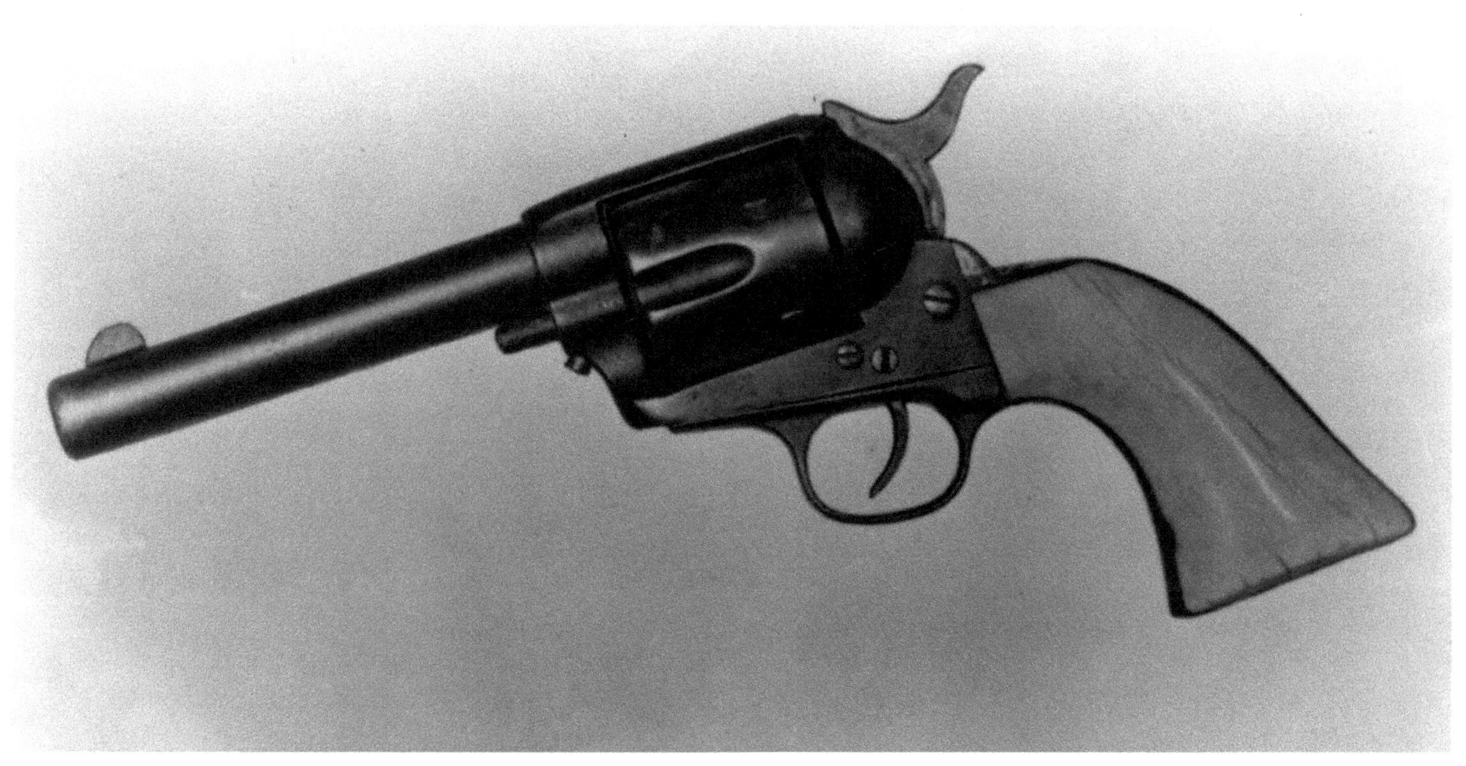

One of the two Colt .45 revolvers Hardin had on him at his death.

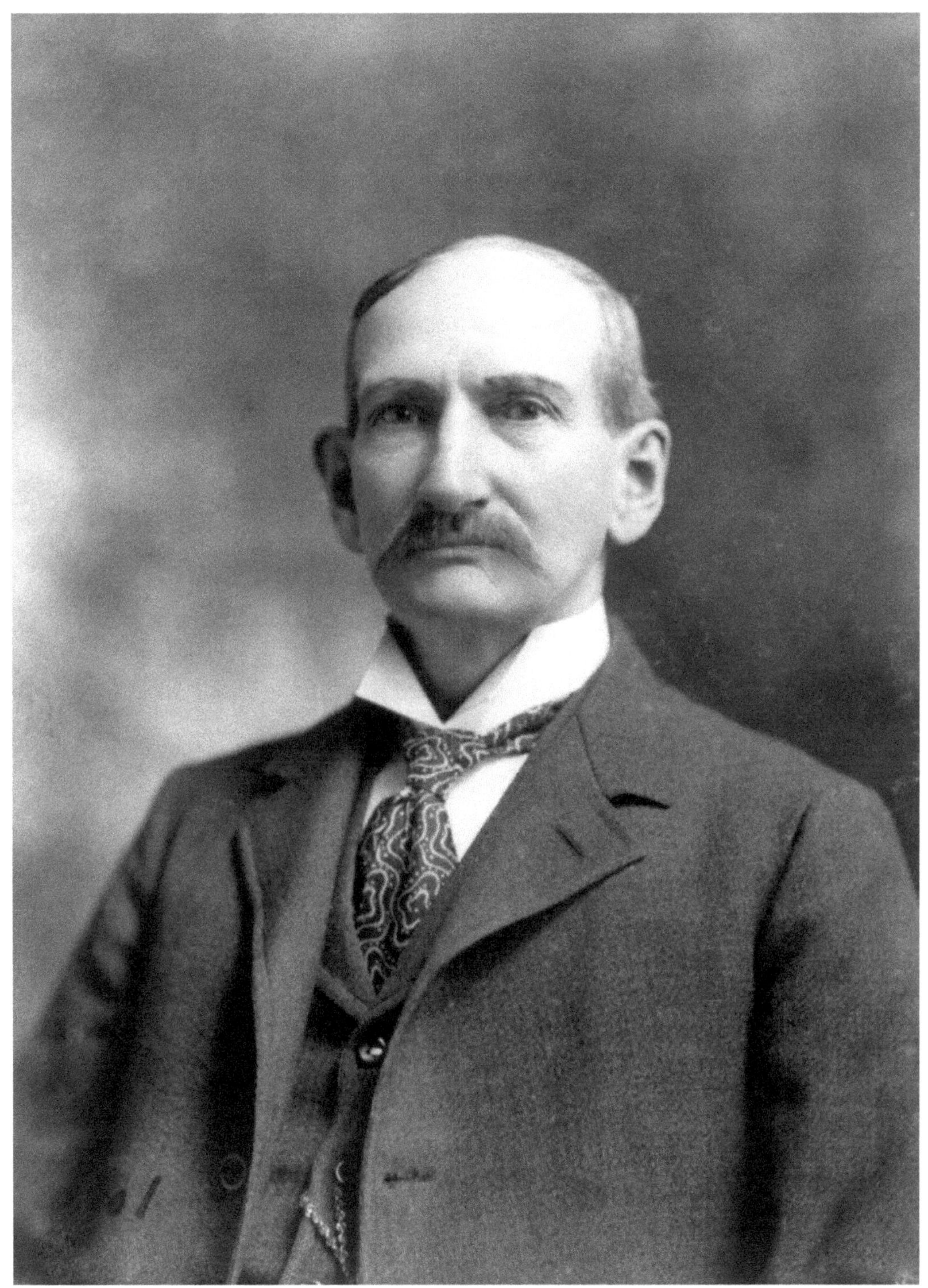

Even before Jesse James was killed in 1882, his brother Frank was looking to get out of the robbery business. After working out an amnesty deal with Governor Crittendon of Missouri, in which he would stand trial for only two of his crimes, he was acquitted of both. He's seen here in 1898, a year in which he bounced around between subsistence jobs in towns throughout the Midwest.

William "Tulsa Jack" Blake was one of Bill Doolin's most trusted lieutenants and as such took part in some of their gang's foremost exploits, including the Battle of Ingalls in 1893. Here Deputy Marshal William Banks (left) poses with Blake after his death in an ambush in 1895. Blake was the first big prize for U.S. Marshals in their push to deal an end to the Doolin gang.

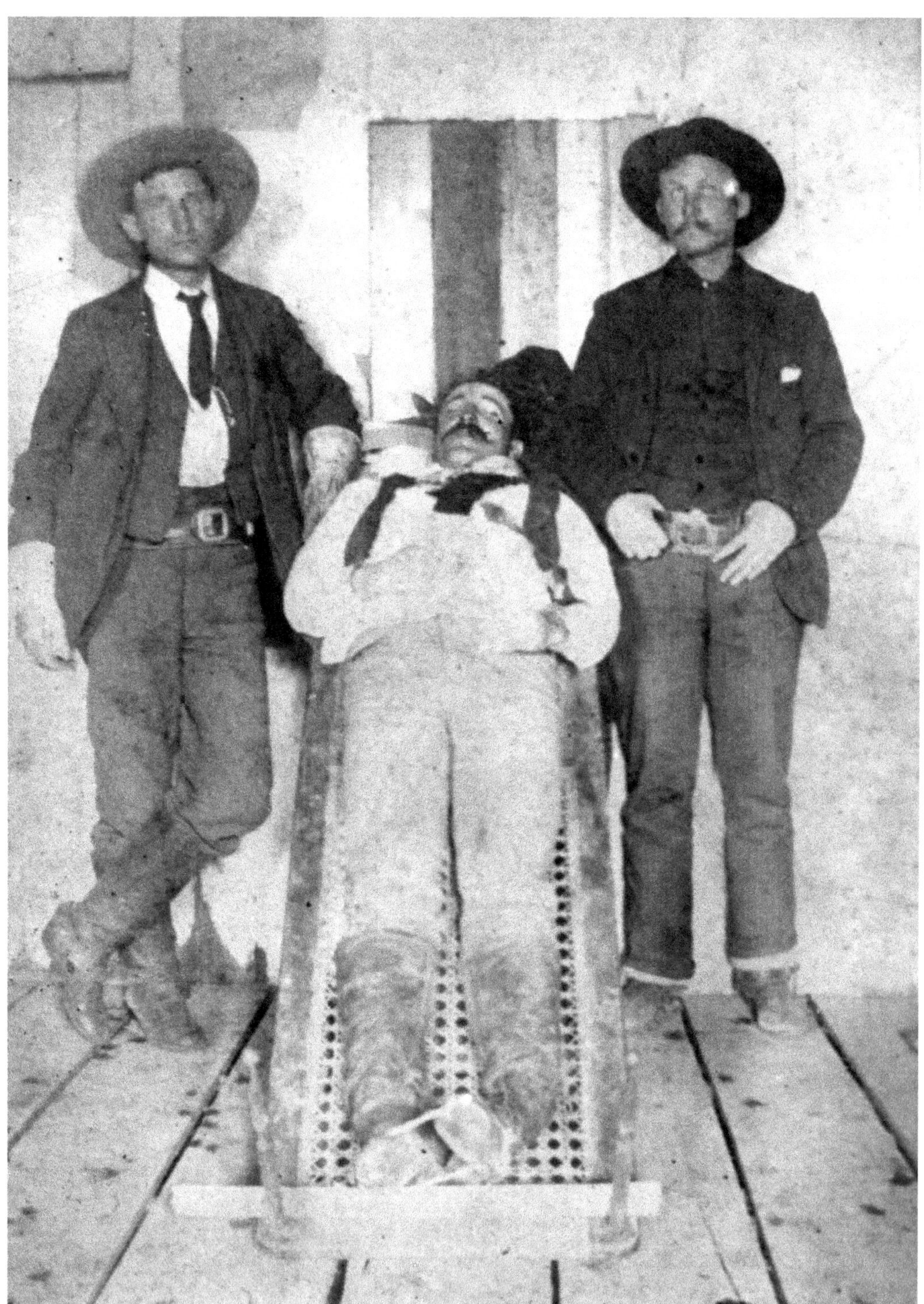

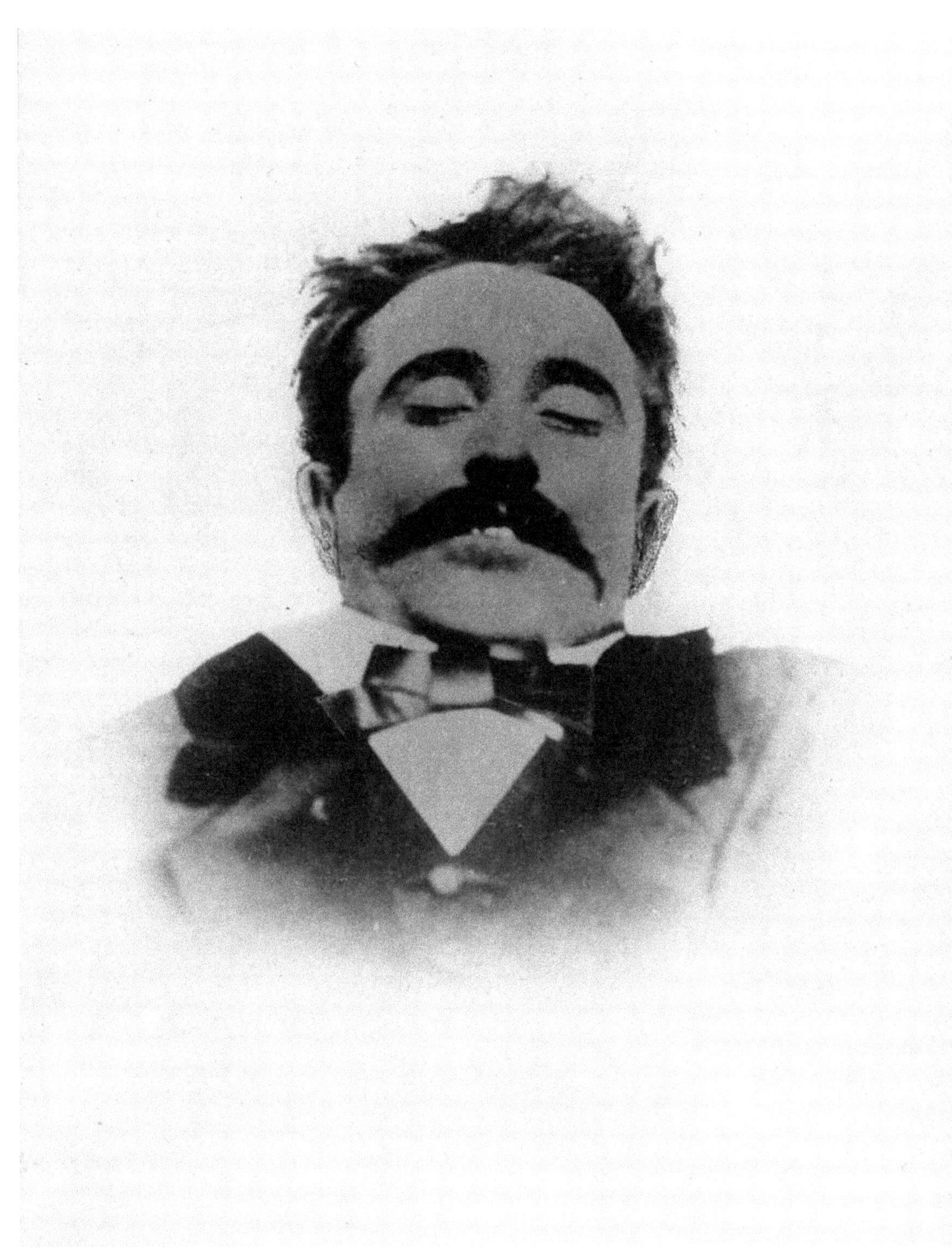

Another view of Tulsa Jack in repose. Blake and his men had just robbed a Rock Island train outside Dover in northwest Oklahoma and leisurely made their way to cover along the Cimarron River outside the town of Hennessey. Within hours of the robbery, Deputy Marshal Chris Madsen commandeered a train from the railroad, which deposited his large posse (including Deputy Marshal Banks) in the region.

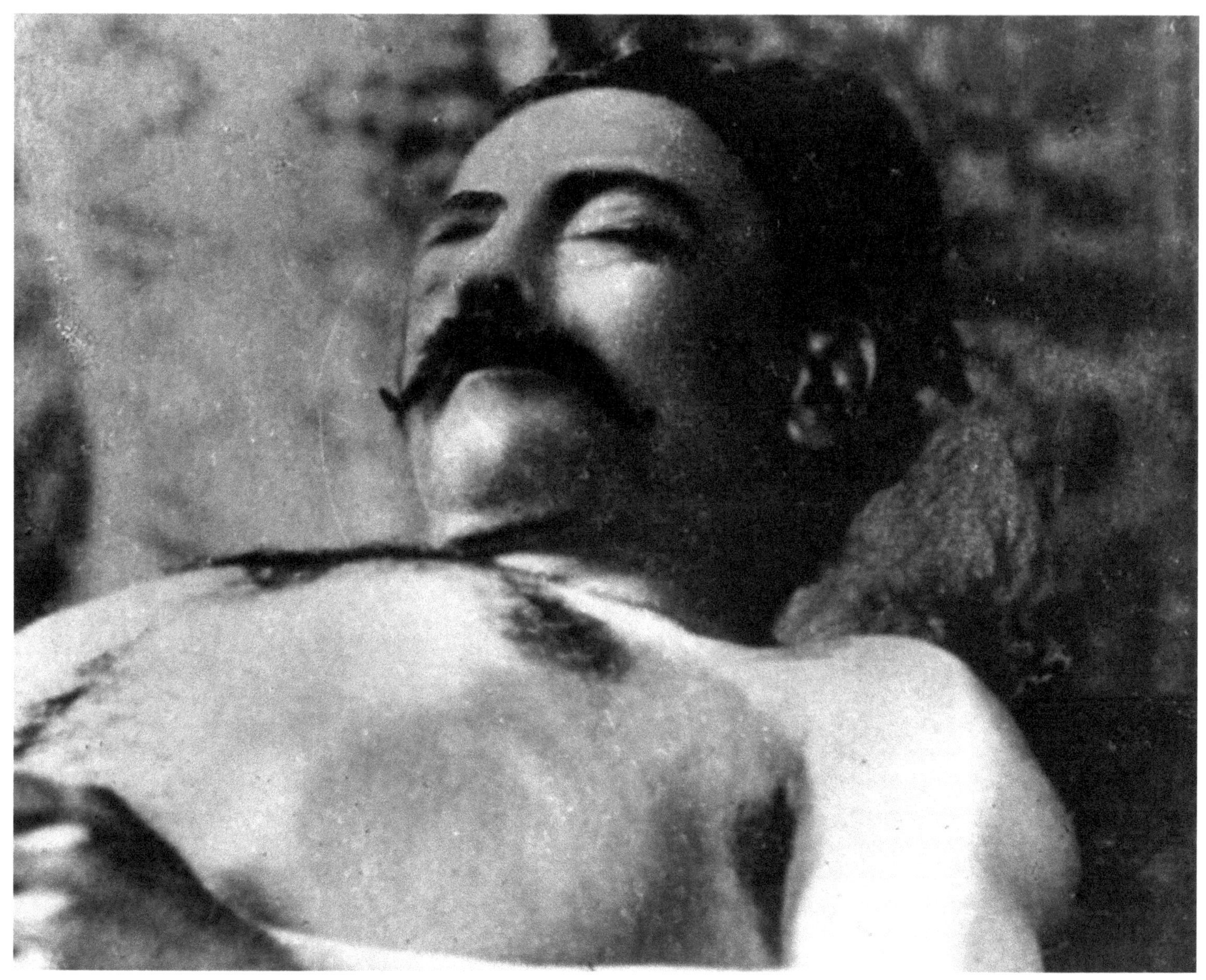

Cowboy George "Bitter Creek" Newcomb fell in with Bill Doolin and his gang rustling cattle in Indian Territory in the 1880s. More of a follower and not particularly audacious as a criminal, Newcomb took part in the Doolins' more famous exploits such as the Adair Raid and the Battle of Ingalls. Legend has it that he was ambushed by his teenage lover's bounty hunter brothers on the Cimarron River in 1895, and as his near lifeless body was transported to Guthrie for the reward, his gasping request for water was answered with a fatal bullet.

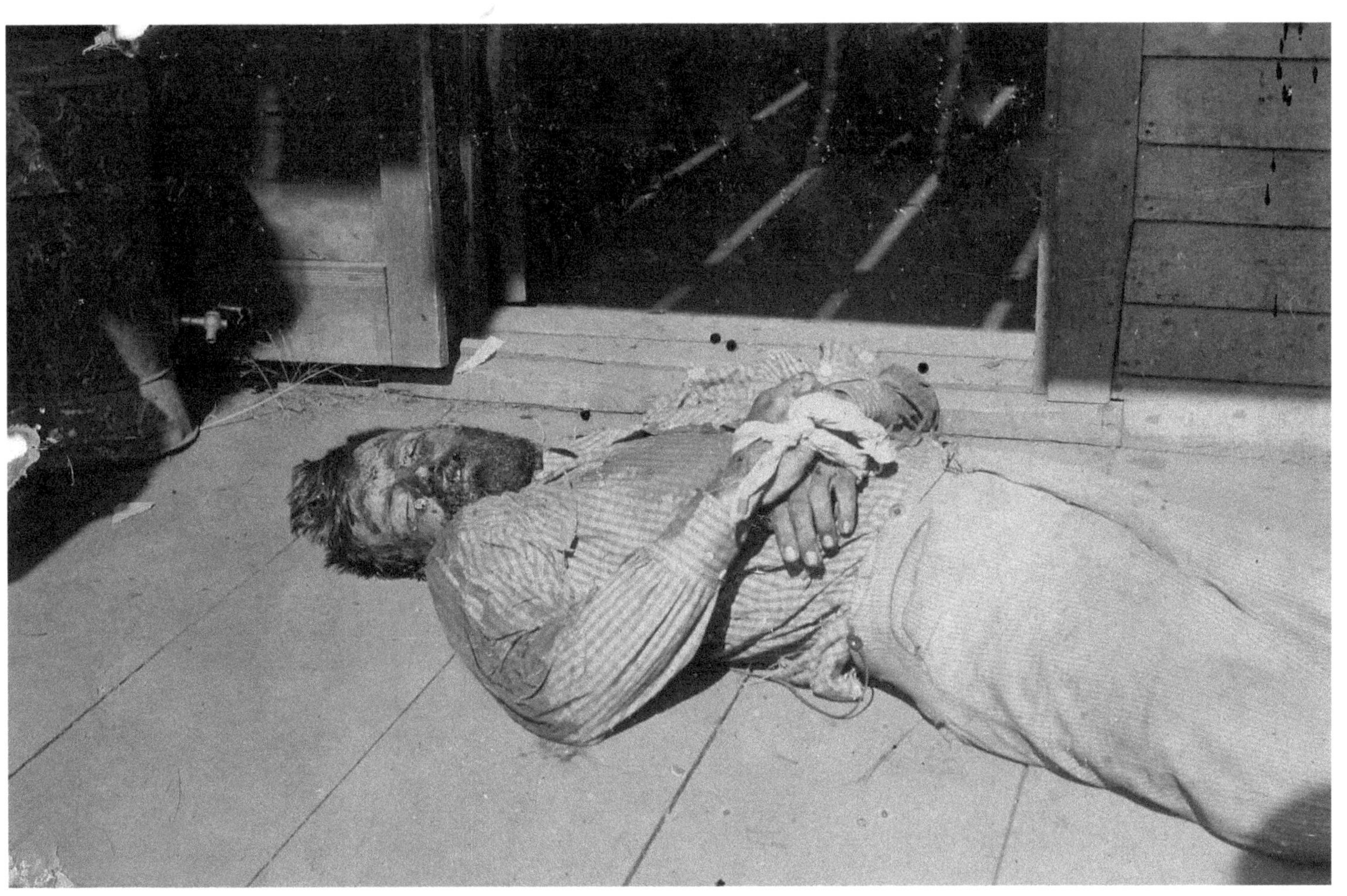

Ike Black and his partner Zip Wyatt were low-tier highwaymen in western Oklahoma in the 1890s. It was their brief association with the Doolin Gang during the 1895 robbery of a Rock Island express car near Dover, Oklahoma, that earned them the notice of Marshal Nix. Black was chased through the Gypsum Hills for three months until finally cornered at Alva. Here he lies in a makeshift morgue.

Bill Doolin and his Wild Bunch were the scourge of the Southwest throughout the 1890s, so much so that Marshal Bill Tilghman pronounced him "the king of Oklahoma's outlaws" when he escaped from the Guthrie jail in 1896. Six weeks later he was killed by lawmen during an ambush.

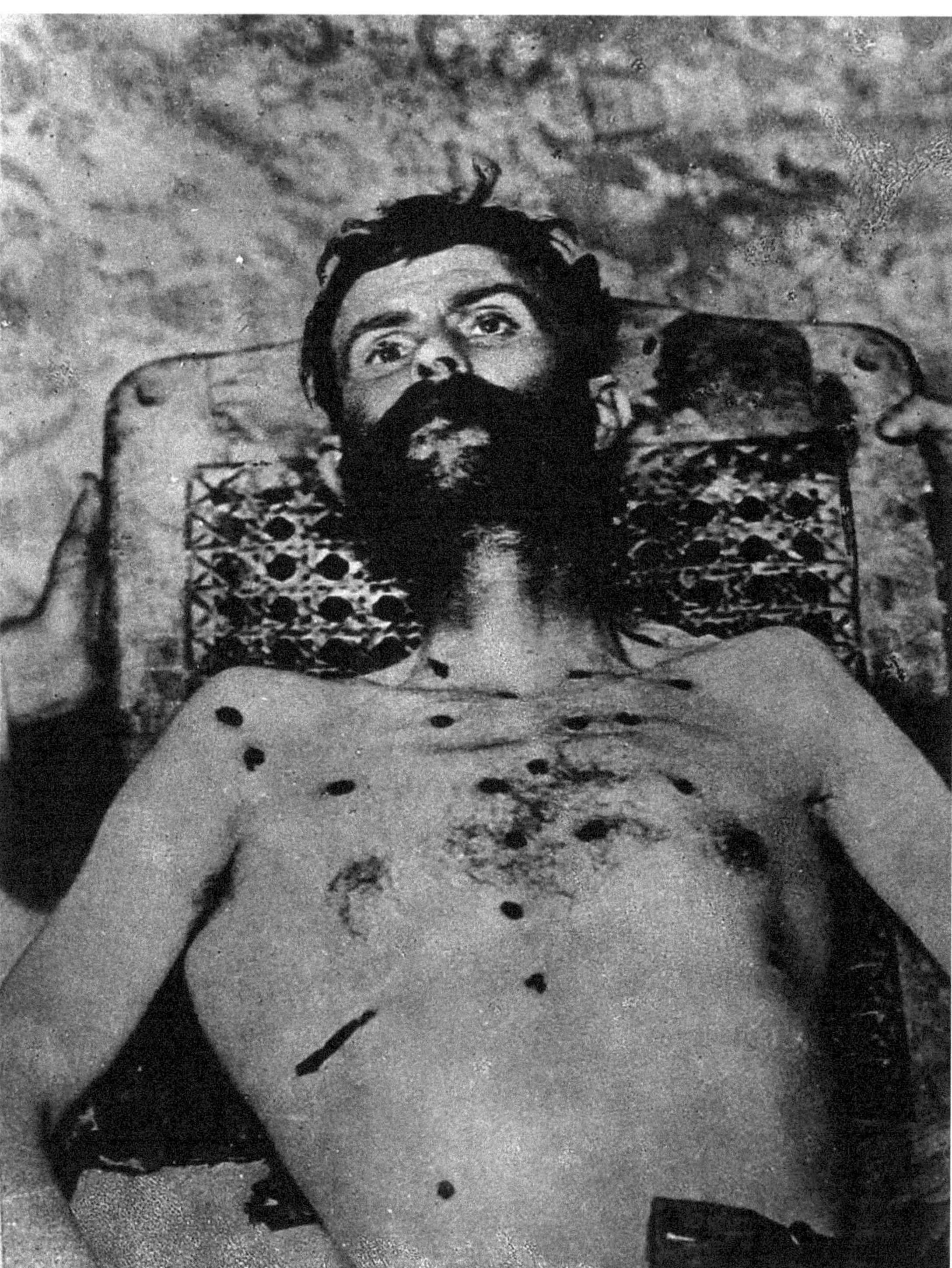

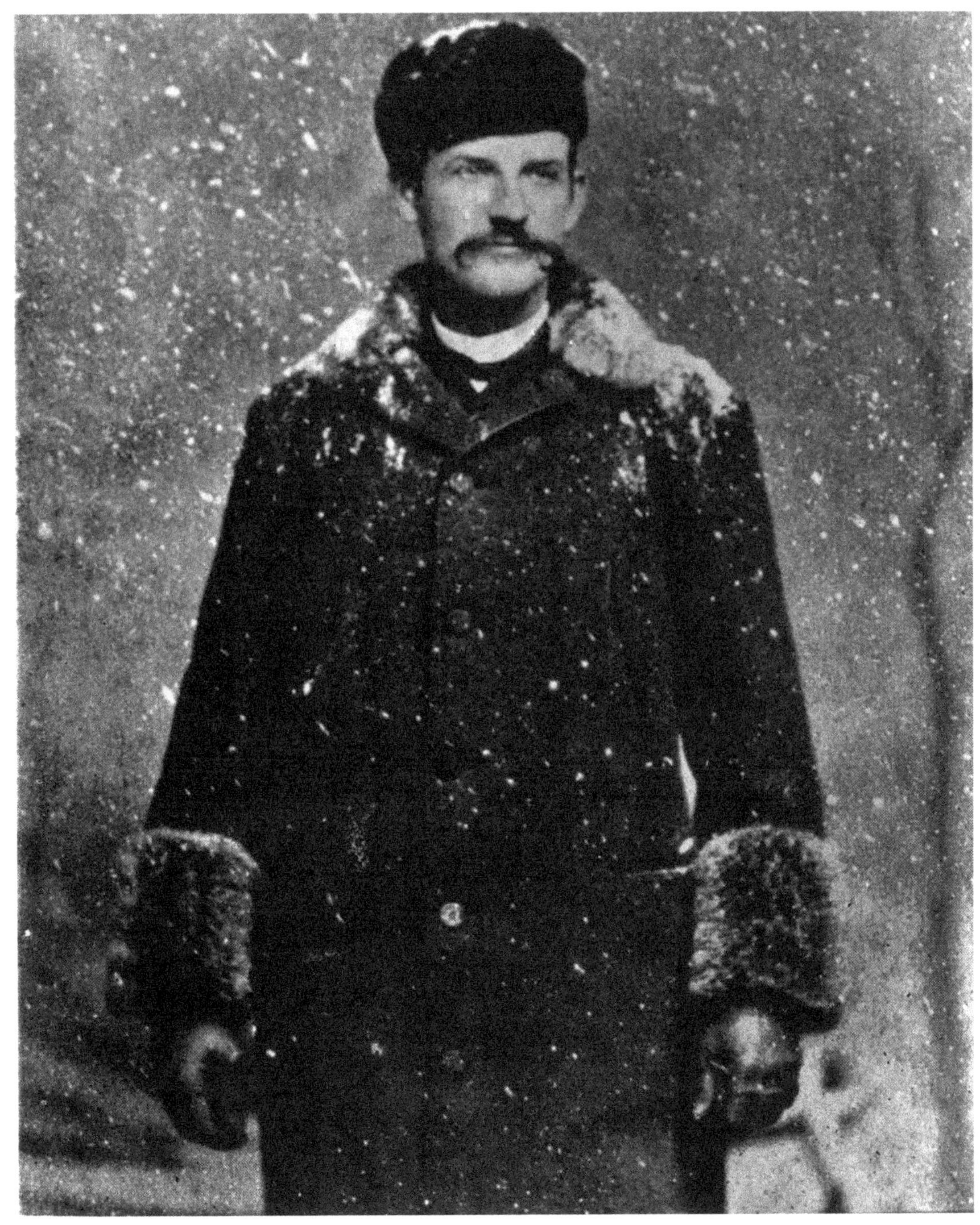

After a ten-year career of robbery and murder in the 1870s, Frank Canton (née Josiah Horner) took on a new identity as a cattle rancher, later becoming a sheriff and one of the Regulators in Wyoming's Johnson County War. Later he was a deputy U.S. marshal, a Klondike prospector (as seen here), and ultimately General of the Oklahoma National Guard. Canton would eventually confess his true identity before the governor of Texas, whereupon the governor, with in mind his service as a marshal, pardoned him.

Pearl Hart was a Canadian-born woman who became so infatuated with traveling Wild West shows that she left her husband and went to Arizona, where she became a camp follower in a mining area and eventually took up with miner Joe Boot. Reversals of fortune led the two to rob a stagecoach in 1898, believed by some to be the last stage robbery and the only one ever by a woman.

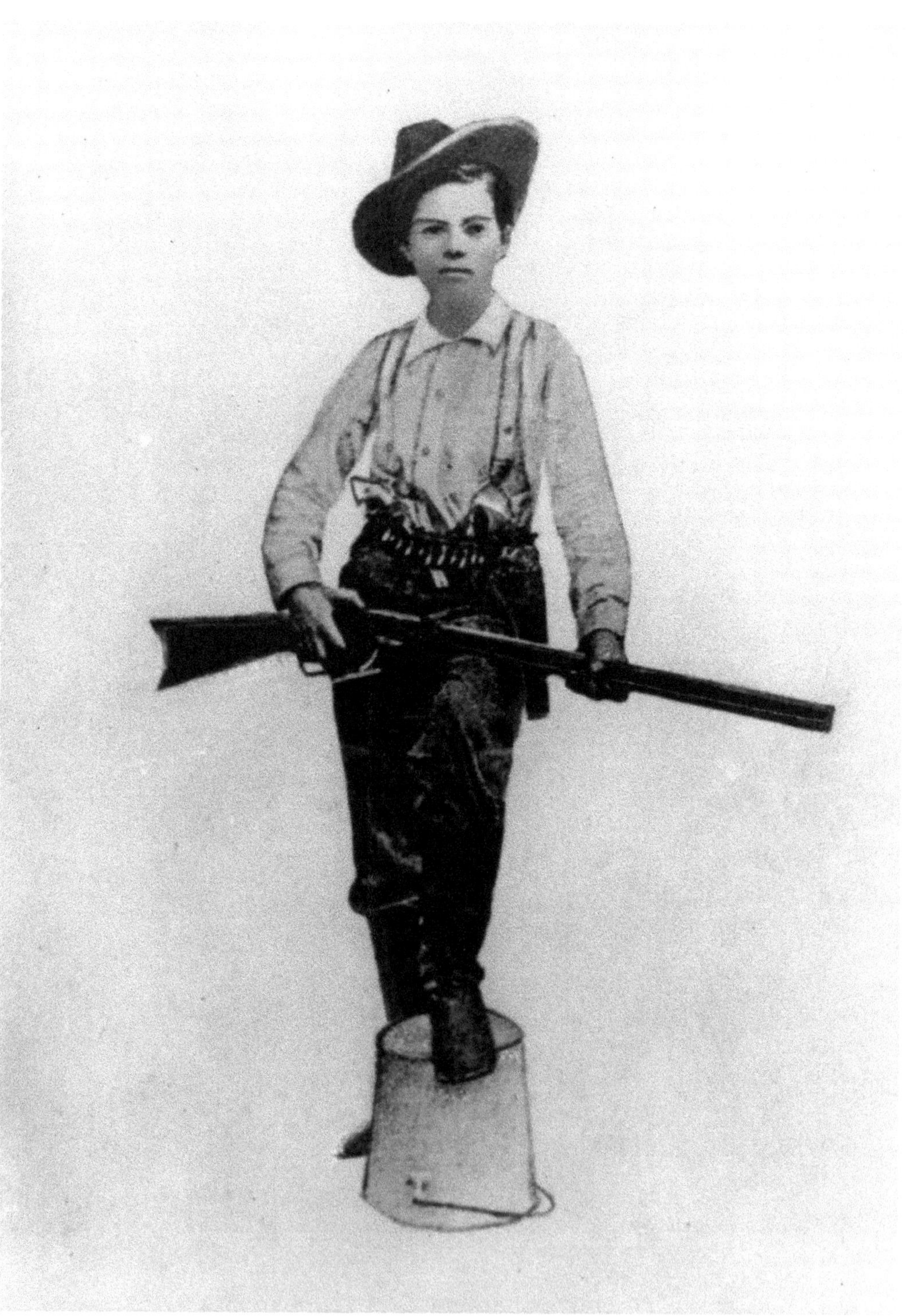

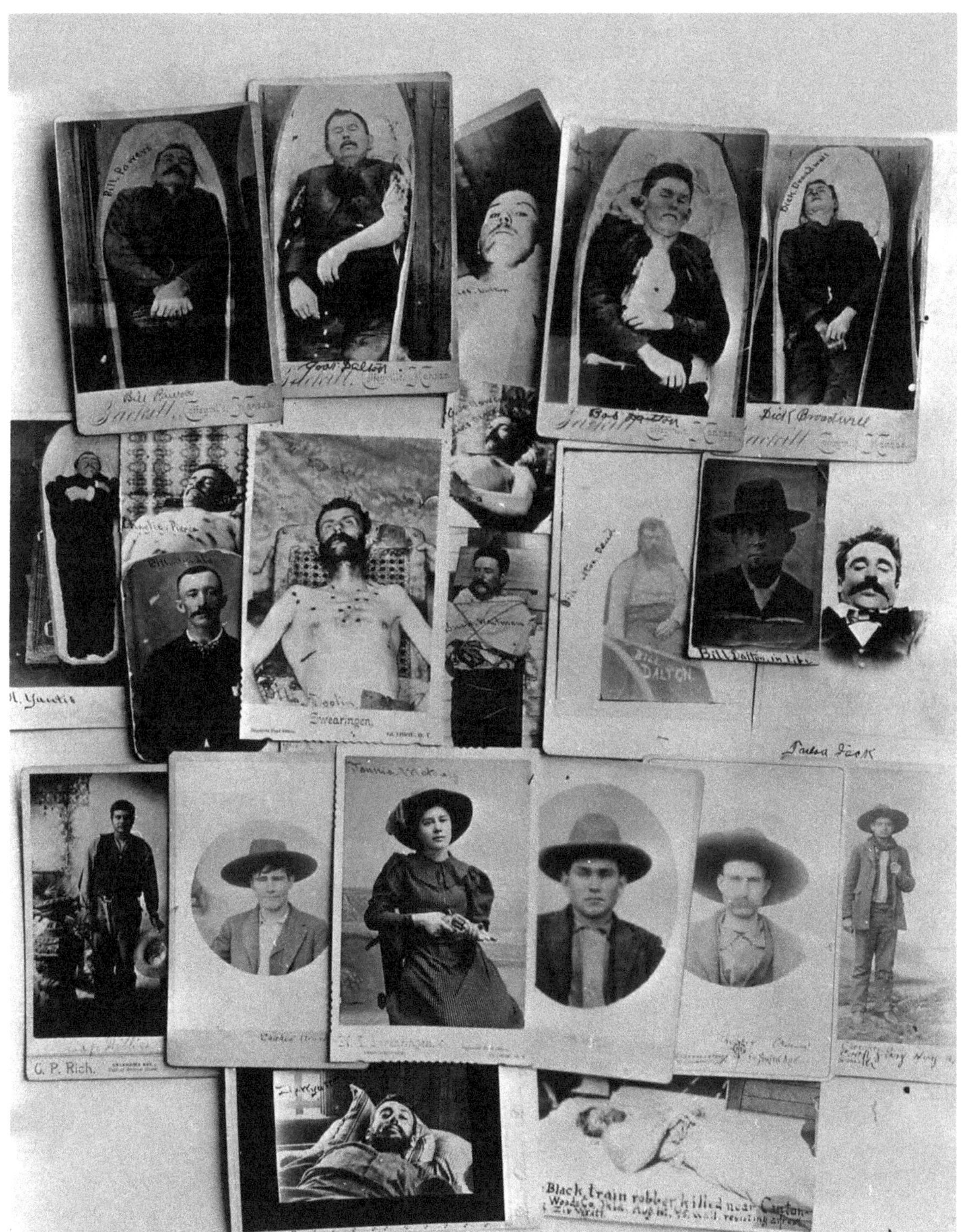

In the late 1890s, Guthrie, Oklahoma, photographer Harmon T. Swearingen created a series of collages of the outlaws captured or killed through the efforts of Marshal Nix and his famous deputies. Most notable in this collage are the slain Dalton Gang along the top row.

This collection depicts the Bill Cook Gang with Cook at the top followed by Thurman "Skeeter" Baldwin, Crawford Goldsby, Elmer "Chicken" Lucas, Henry Munson, and possibly Lon Gordon.

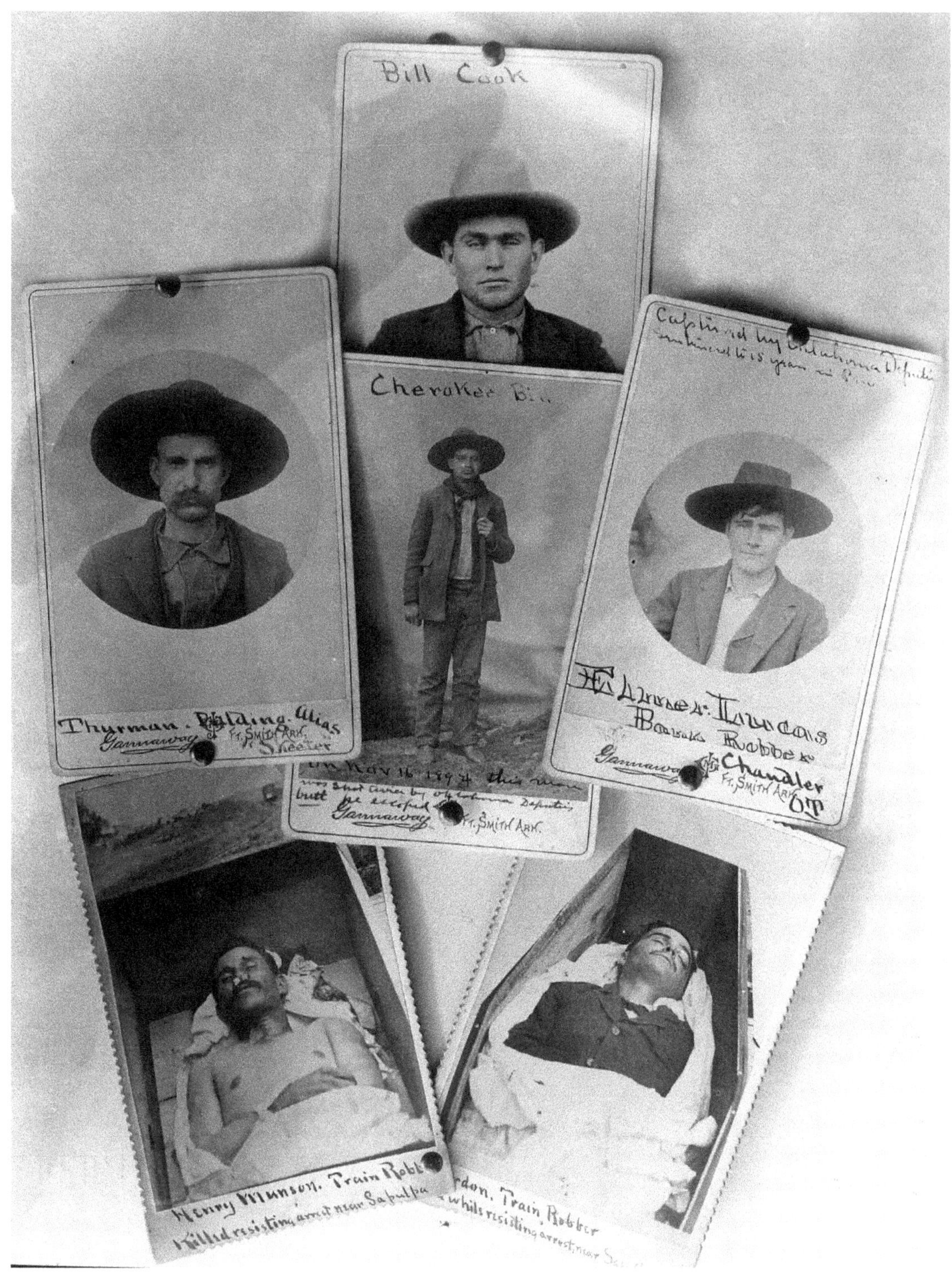

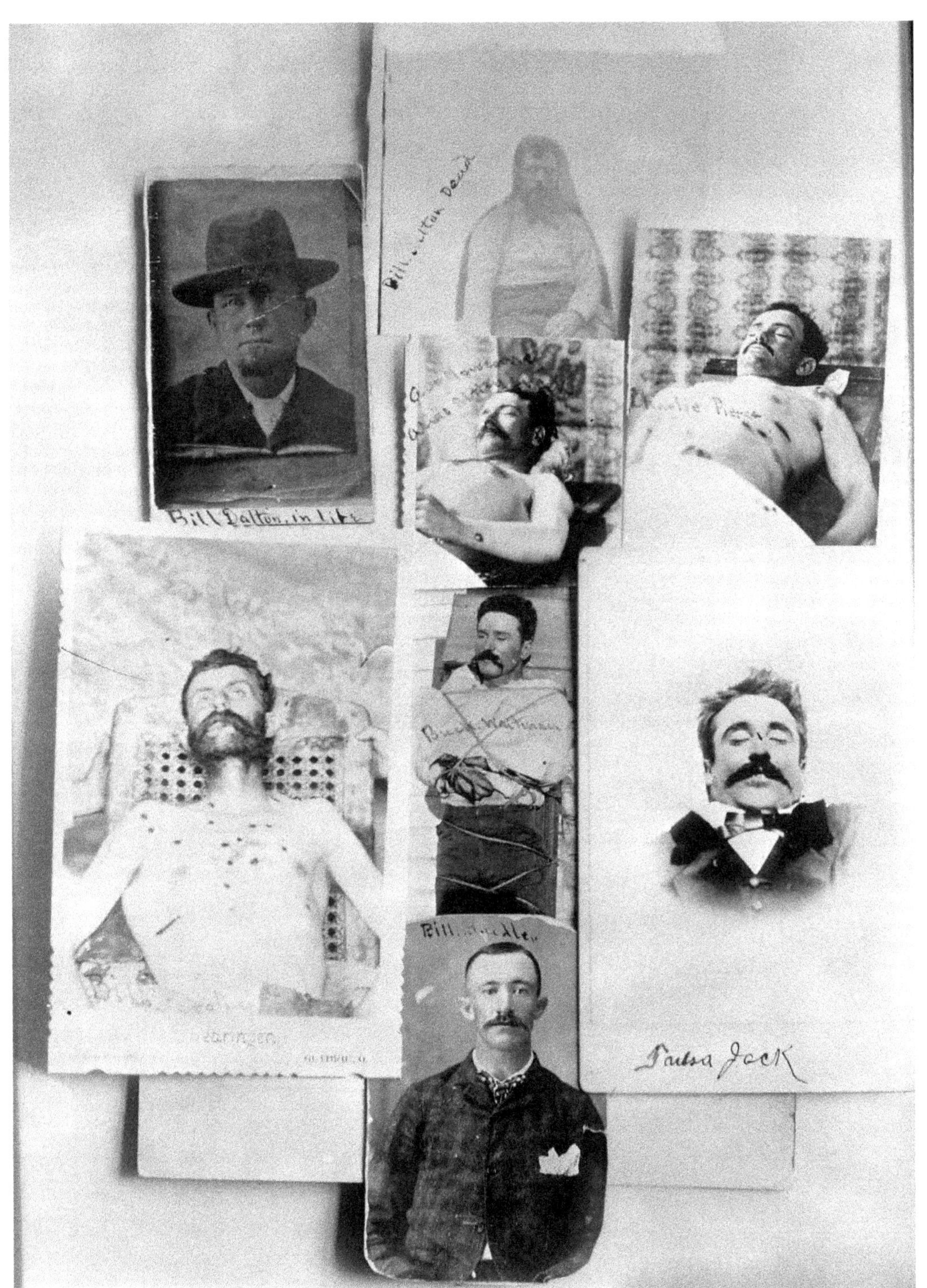

Yet another collage of deceased Oklahoma outlaws, this one adding Charlie Pierce in the upper right corner, a bound "Red Buck" Waightman in the center, and Bill Raidler below him.

Following Spread: The United States Prison was built near the military prison at Fort Leavenworth, Kansas, around the turn of the century to house criminals committing crimes against the federal government and some interstate crimes.

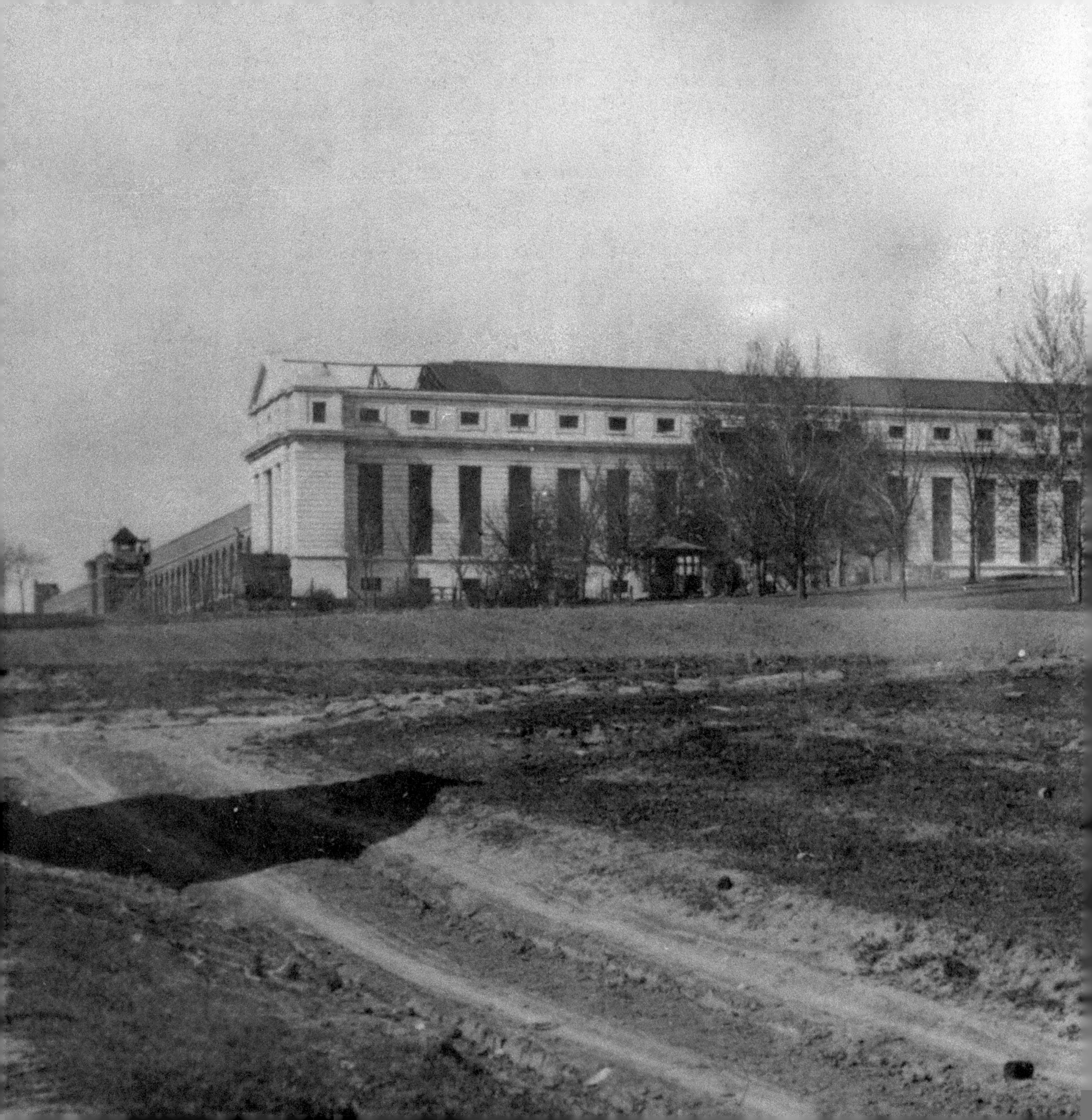

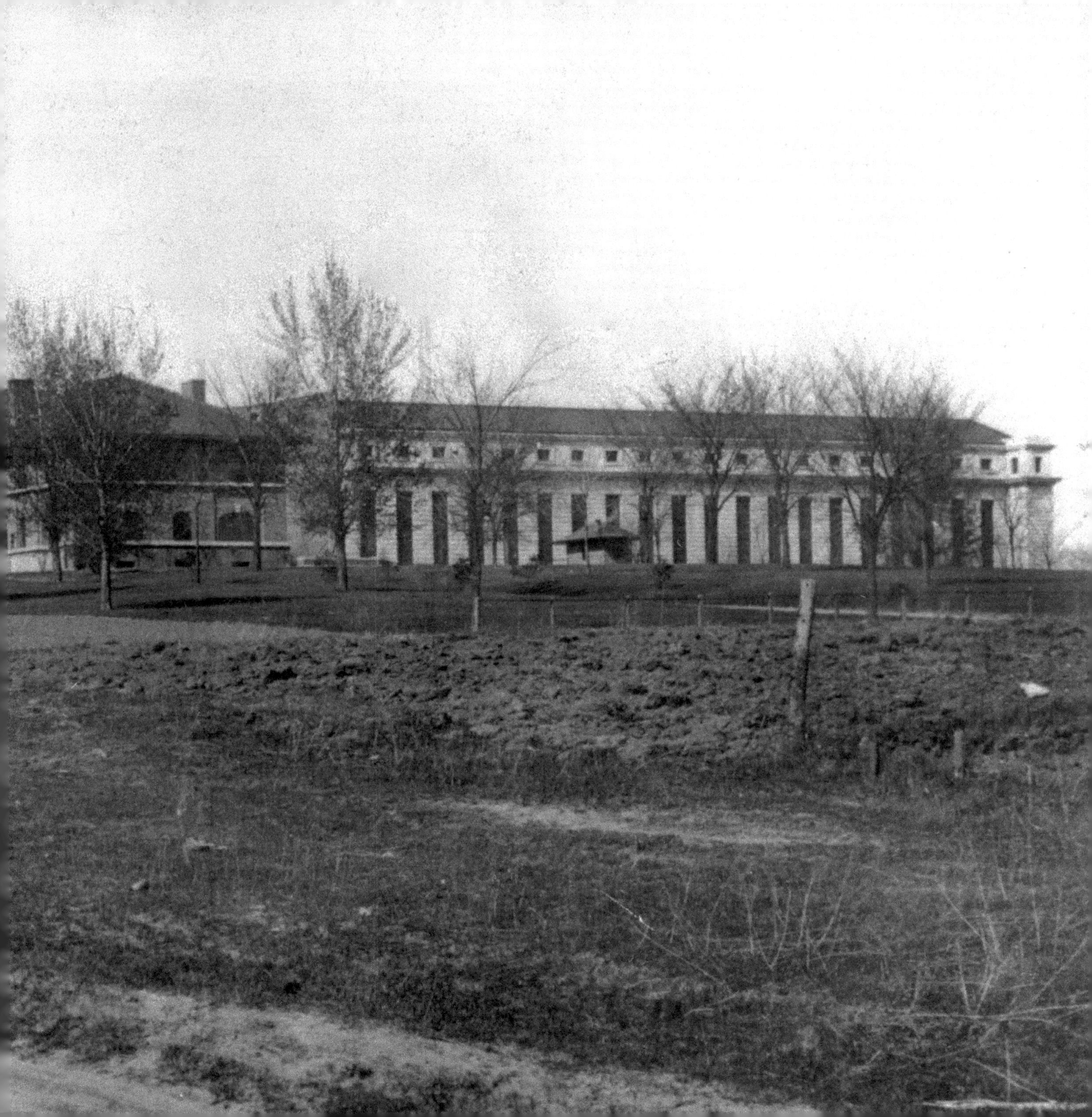

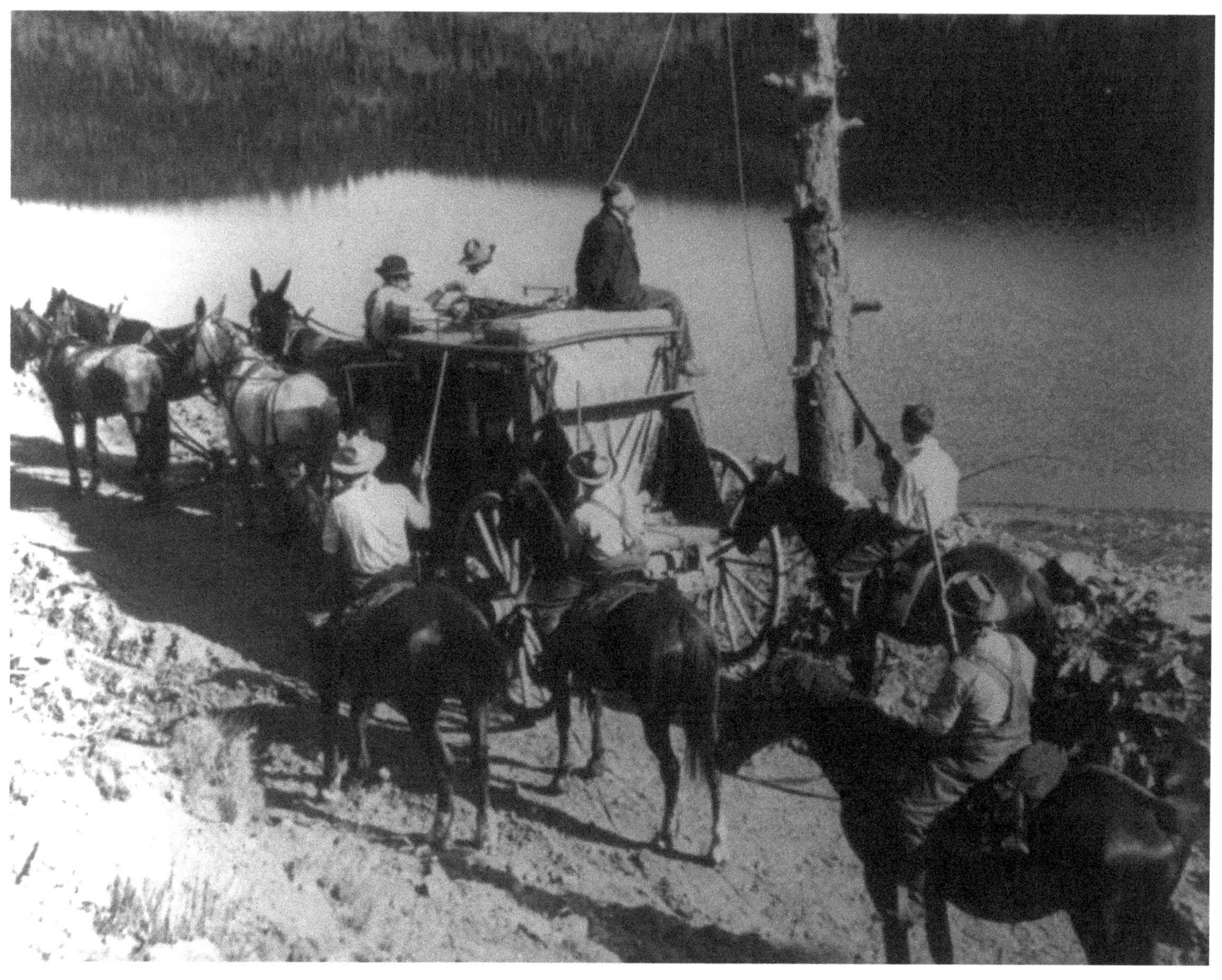

Not long after the Pearl Hart robbery, a photographer in Colorado snapped this reenactment of a foiled hold-up in which the bandit was overtaken and strung up by vigilantes.

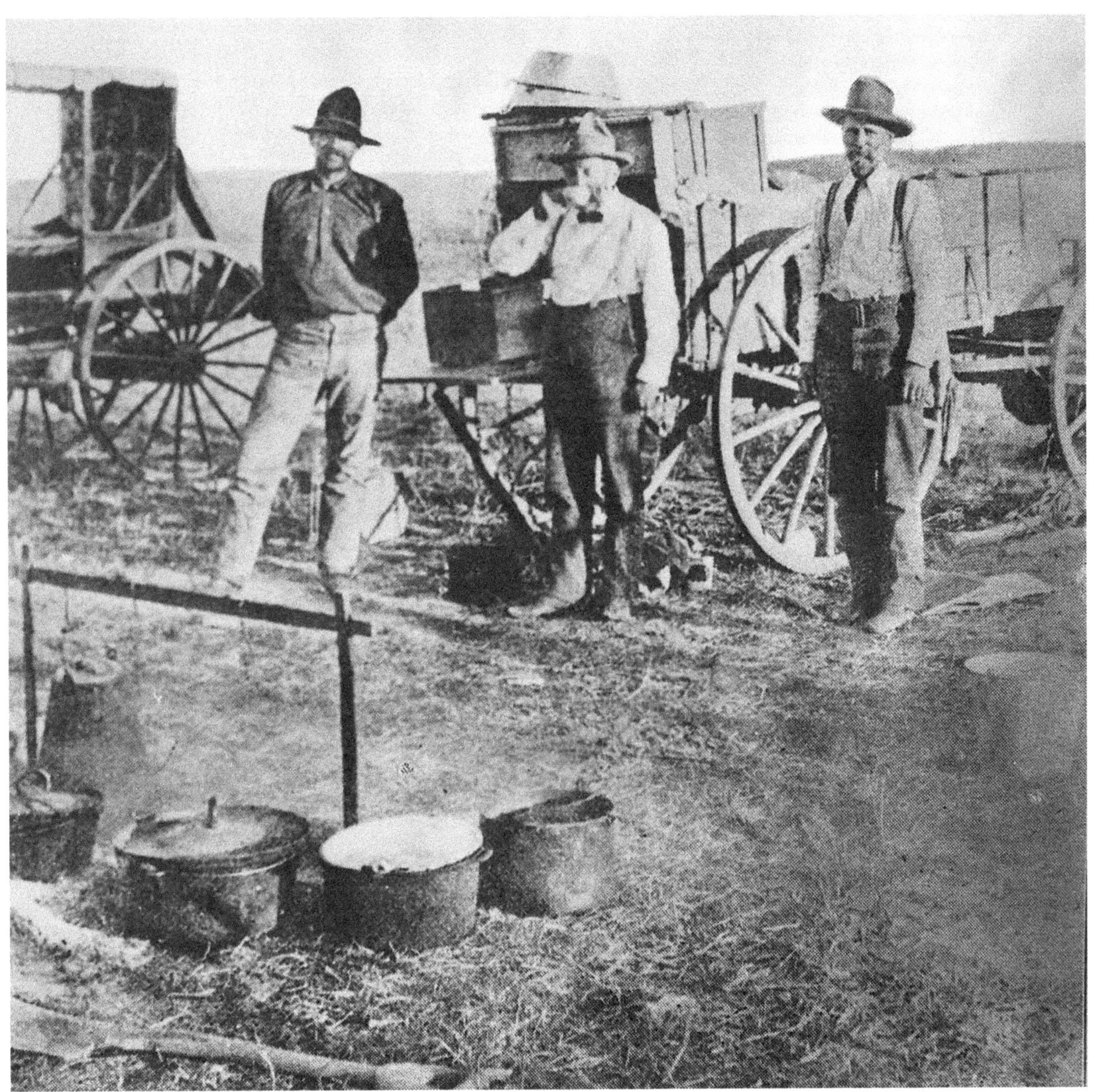

Doc Middleton (at right) appears here in his peaceful days after his lengthy prison term. Upon his release he toured with his own Wild West Show and then settled down and lived into his sixties—a rare feat for an outlaw—before being jailed again for bootlegging. Unable to pay the bootlegging fine, he seems to have died in jail from a communicable disease, possibly pneumonia.

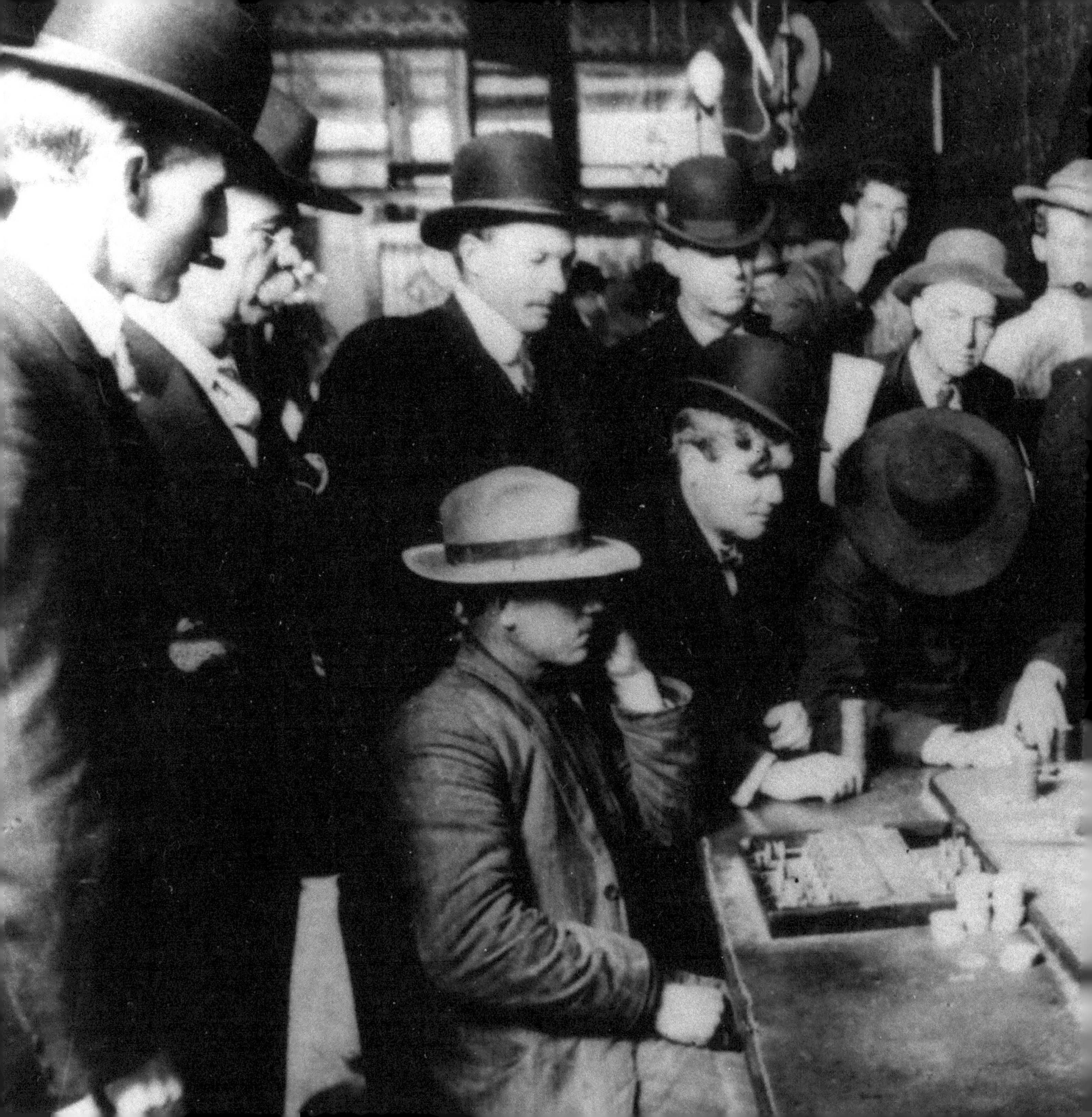

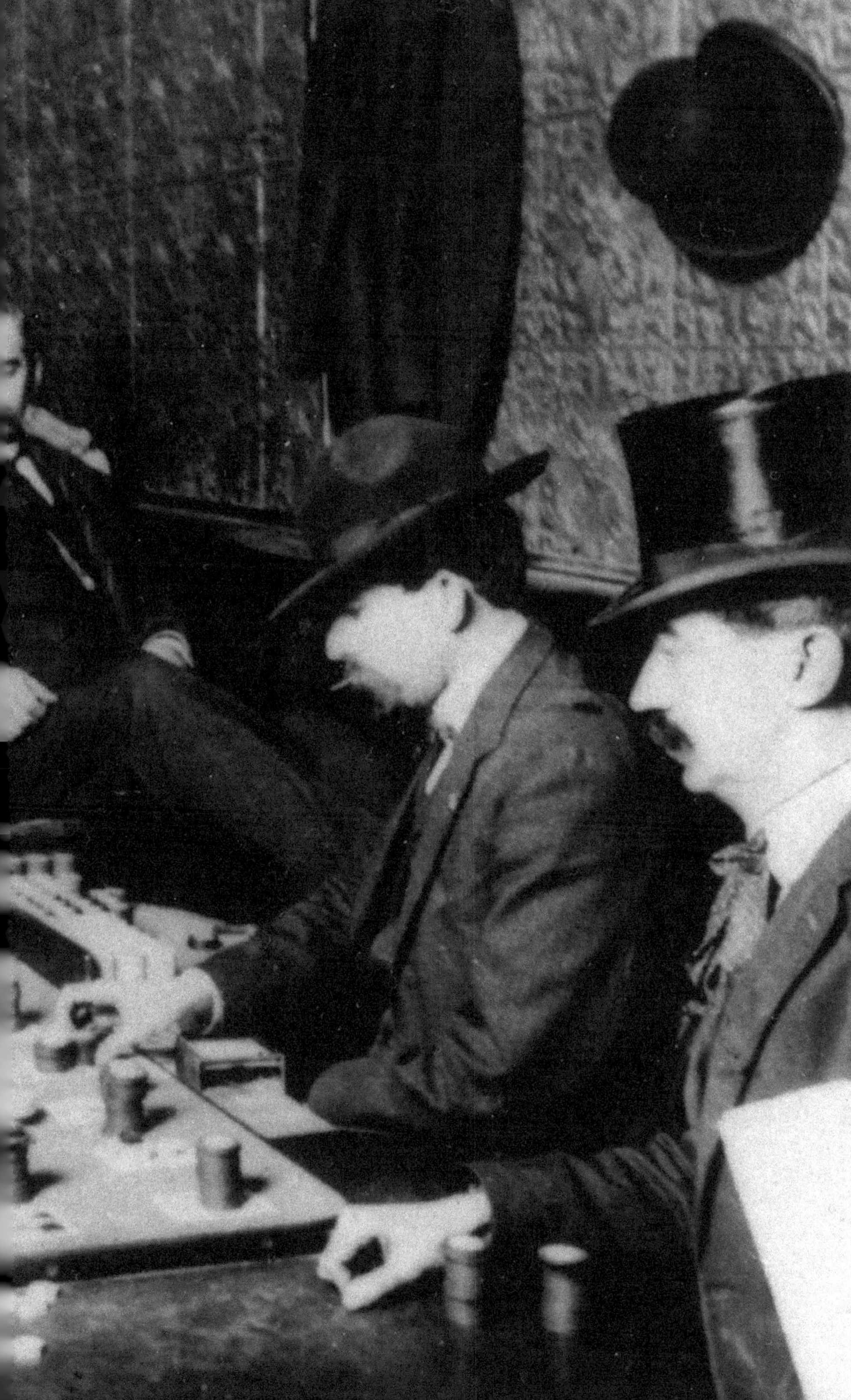

Unlike saloons in other rowdy towns like Dodge and Deadwood, the Orient Saloon in Bisbee, Arizona, was considered an oasis for miners, drifters, and travelers making their way across the desert. That's not to say that many fools came away from faro tables like this one with their stakes in hand.

Part-Cherokee Henry Starr began his career in crime at an early age and represents a transitional period of villainy in the West. He was contemporaneous with the last days of the famous Doolin-Dalton and Hole-in-the-Wall gangs and used similar tactics, but he also pioneered the use of automatic weapons and automobiles for a quick getaway. In this photograph, he is 22 and just released from his first prison stint.

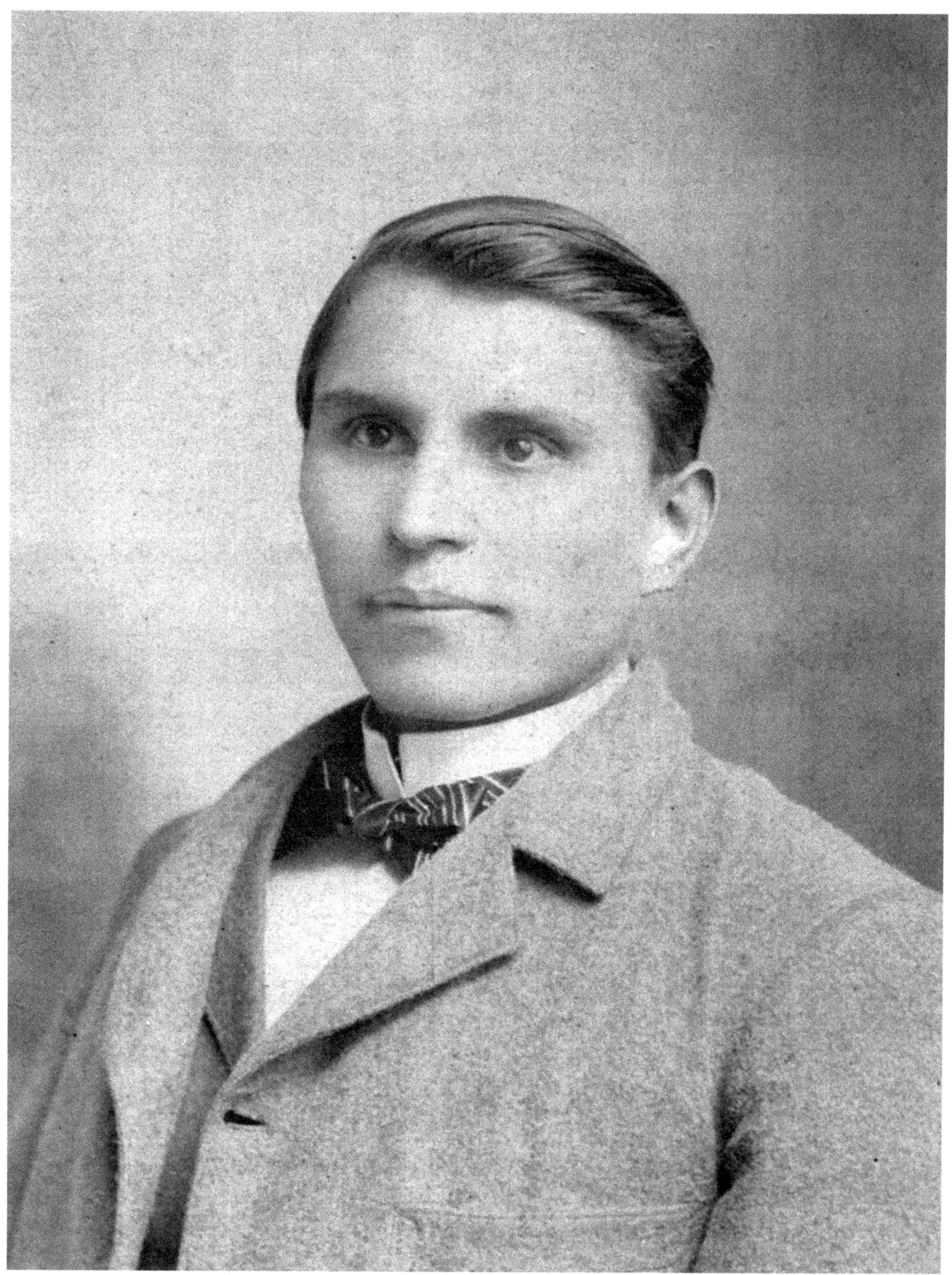

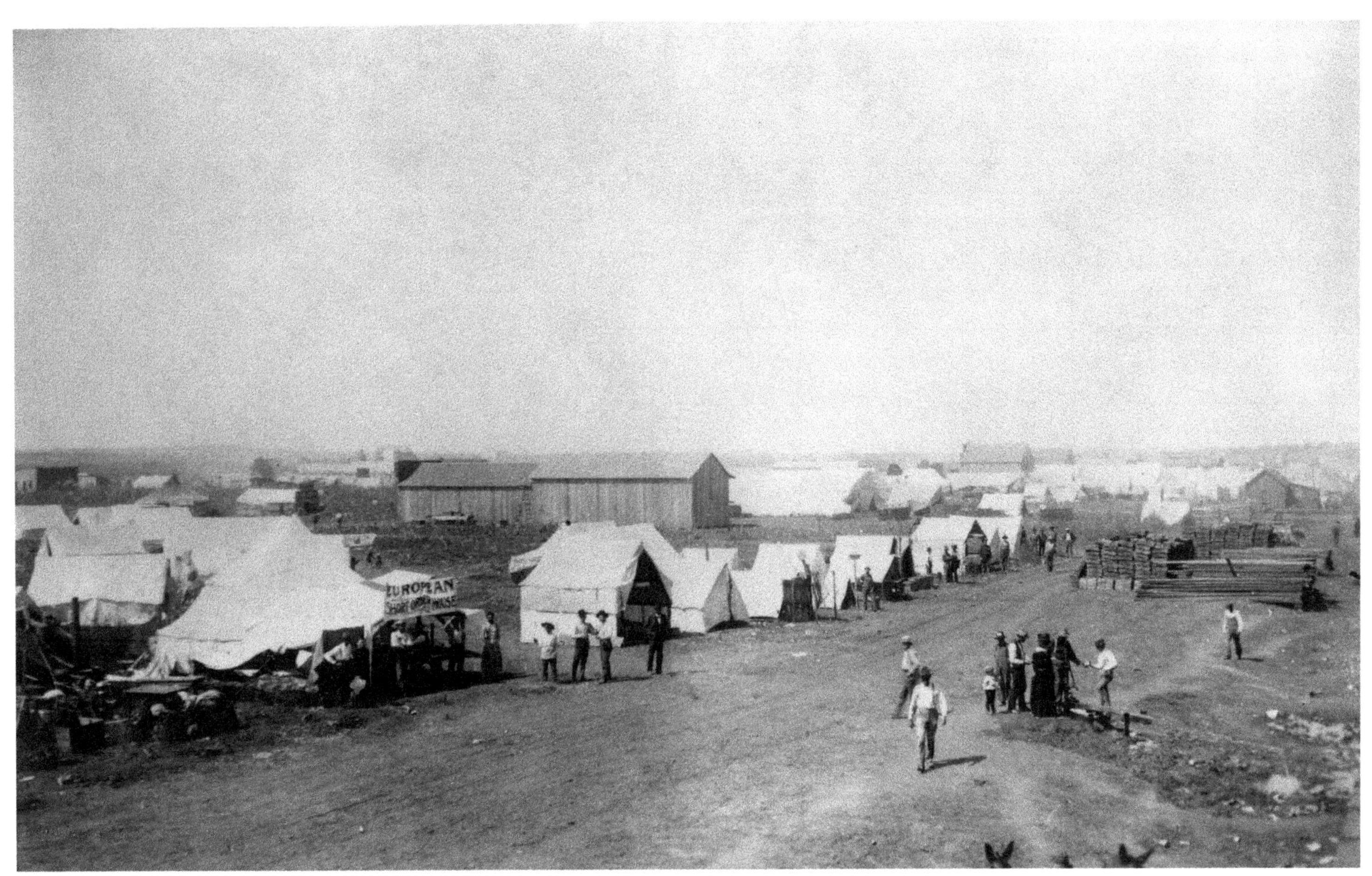

Soon after the Kiowa, Comanche, and Caddo lands were opened to white settlement in 1901, residents beseeched the Indian Agent at Anadarko to help protect the city from predatory gamblers. Anadarko was quite busy as a large settlement in southwestern Oklahoma, and regular traffic by soldiers from Fort Sill and Indian encampments nearby ensured that these officers rarely had a quiet day, but the agent had no authority to intervene.

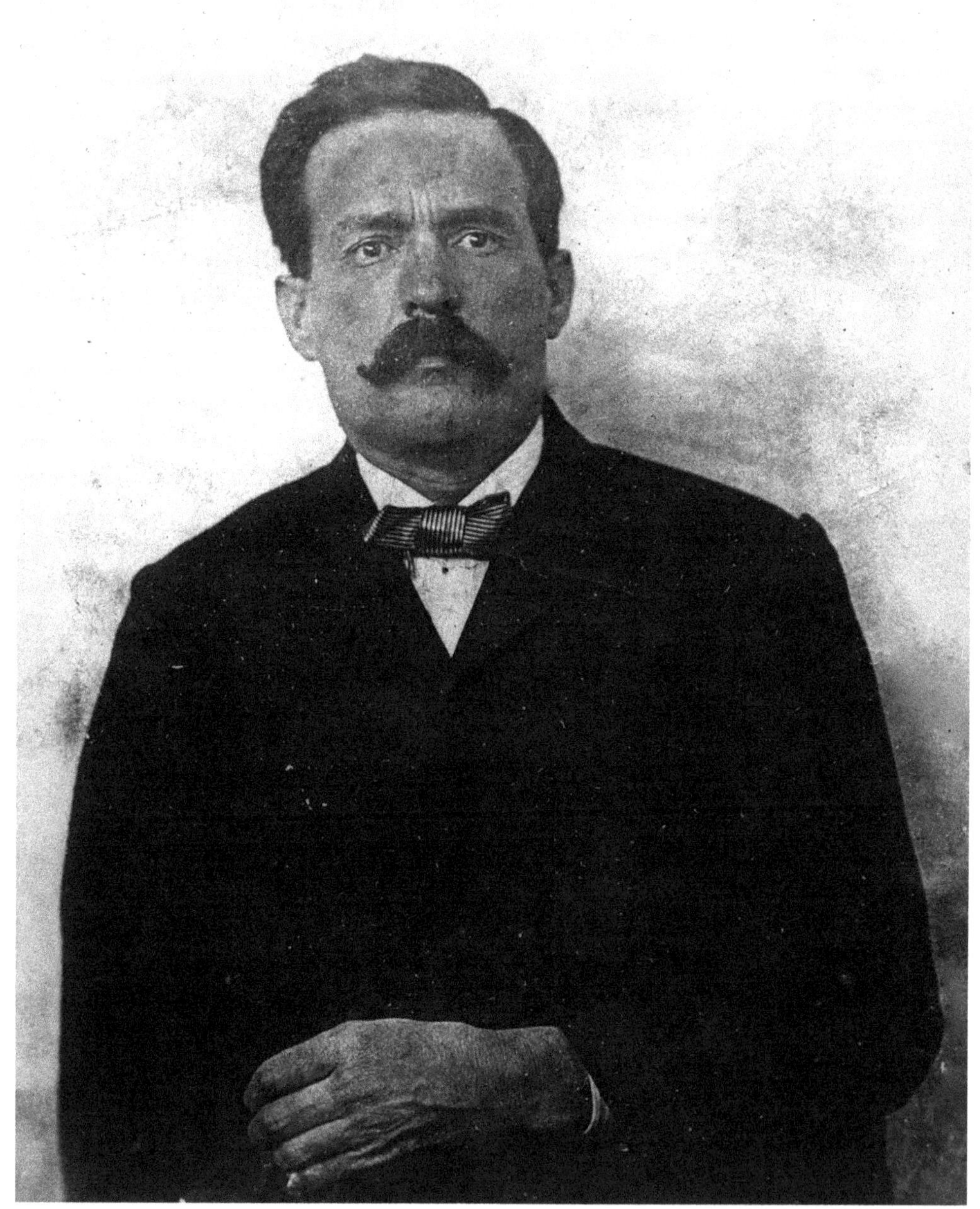

During an attempted robbery of a Southern Pacific Railroad express car outside Folsom, New Mexico, Thomas "Black Jack" Ketchum received a blast to his arm from the conductor's shotgun. He got away, but was soon captured. Blood poisoning had set in, and he lost the arm to amputation. Though undated, this photograph may have been taken after the event.

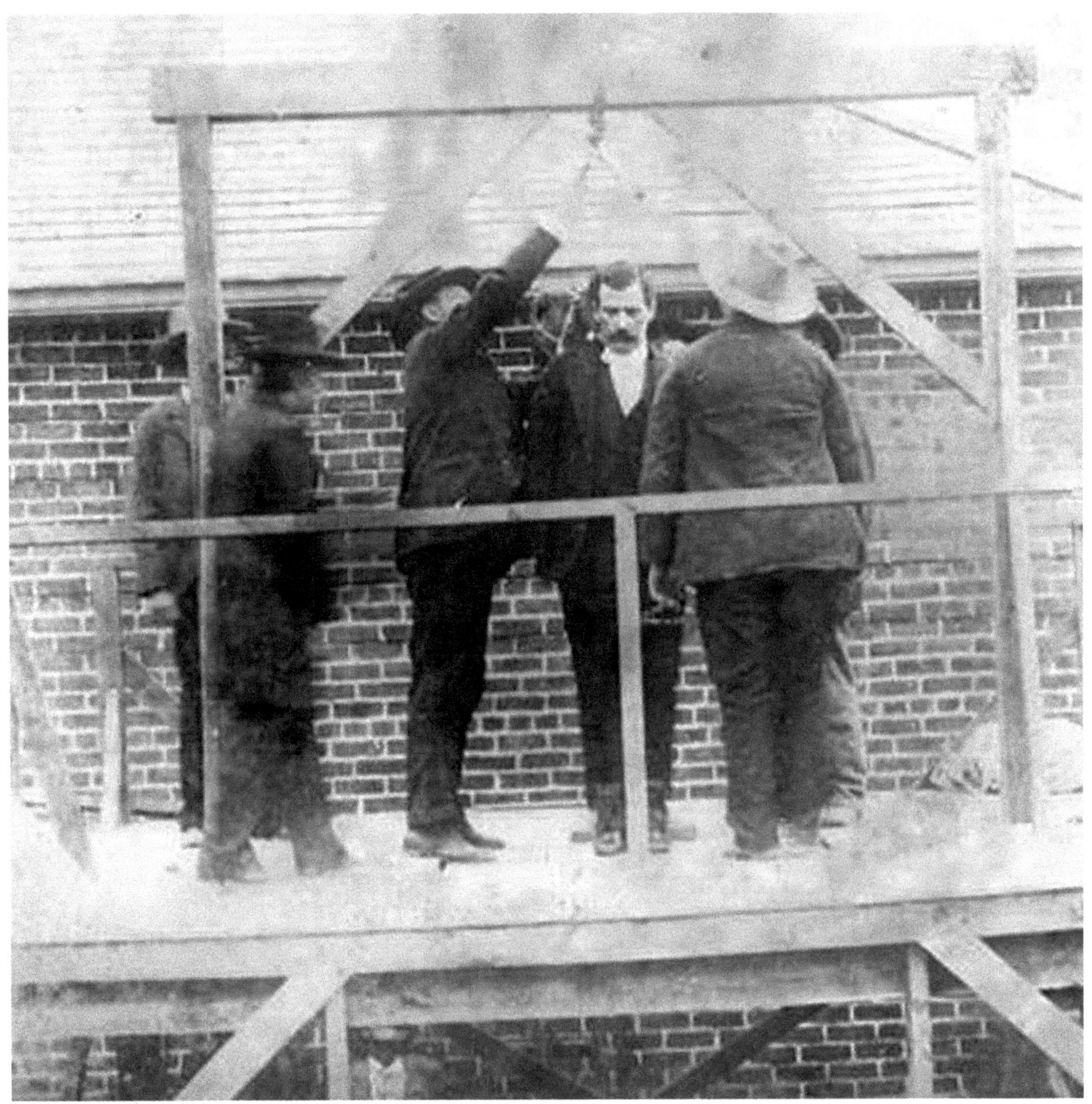

Local newspapers reported that Black Jack Ketchum was calm and collected on the gallows at Clayton, New Mexico. Here law enforcement officials and a priest prepare him for the drop in 1901. "Please dig my grave very deep," was Ketchum's final request to the sheriff.

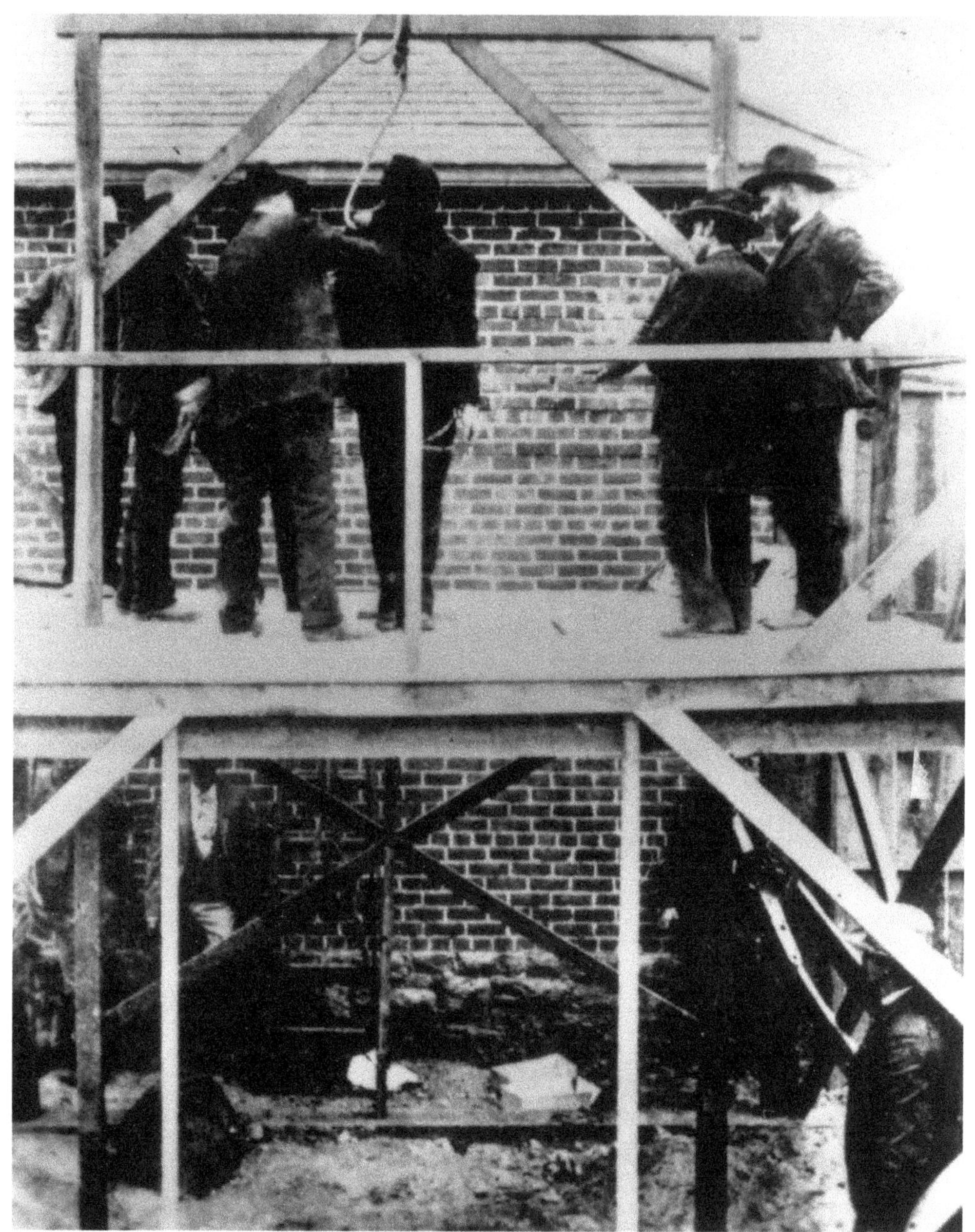

Black Jack Ketchum on the gallows at Clayton, New Mexico. After the hood was in place, he could be heard to say, "Let 'er go!" Because of an inexperienced hangman, 150 citizens looked on in horror as Ketchum's head was ripped from his body, which fell forward and splattered blood over those in front.

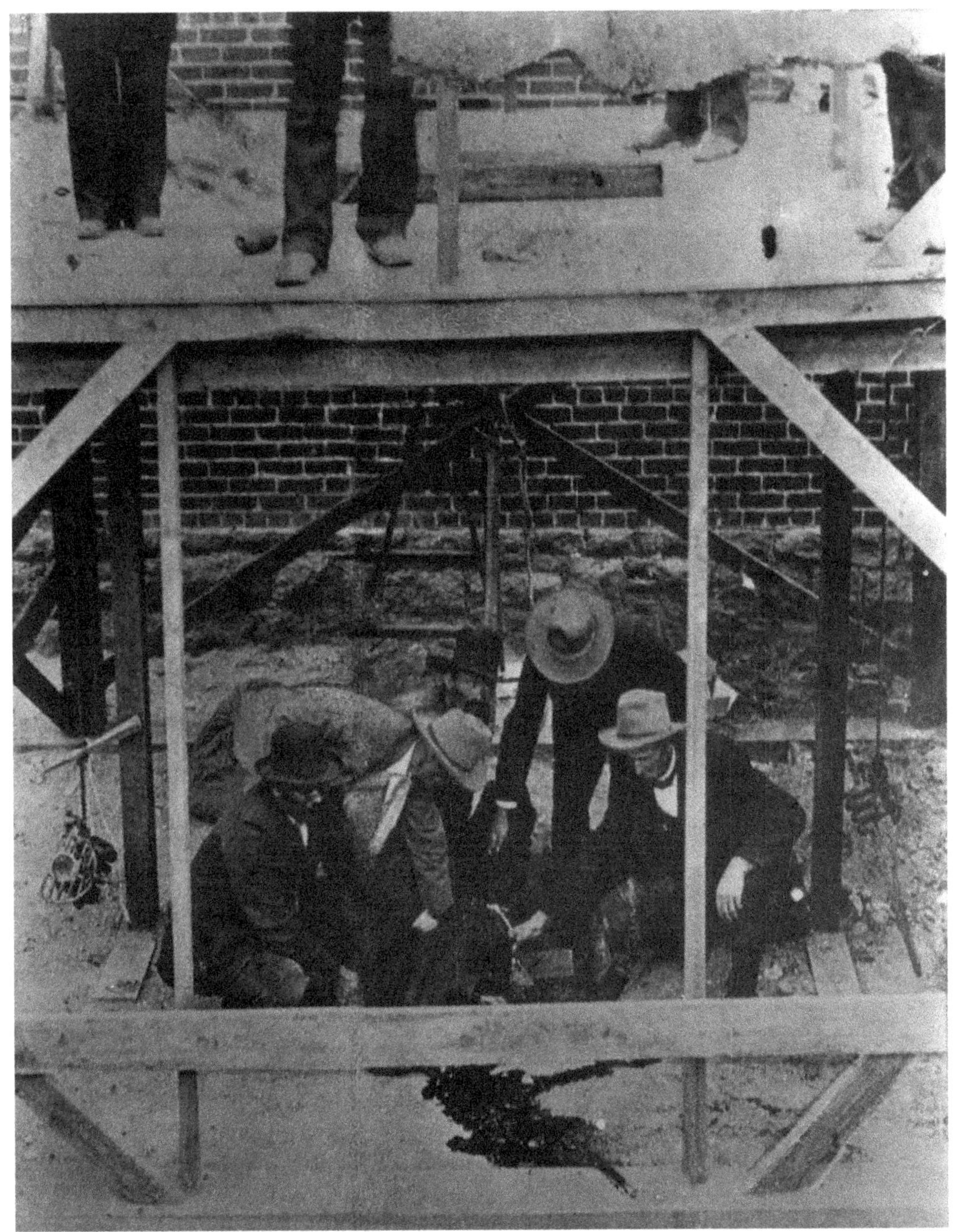

A reporter on the scene of the Ketchum execution reported, "For a few seconds the body was allowed to lie there half doubled up on the right side, with blood flowing in an intermittent streak from several arteries. Then the officers rushed down the scaffold and lifted the body from the ground."

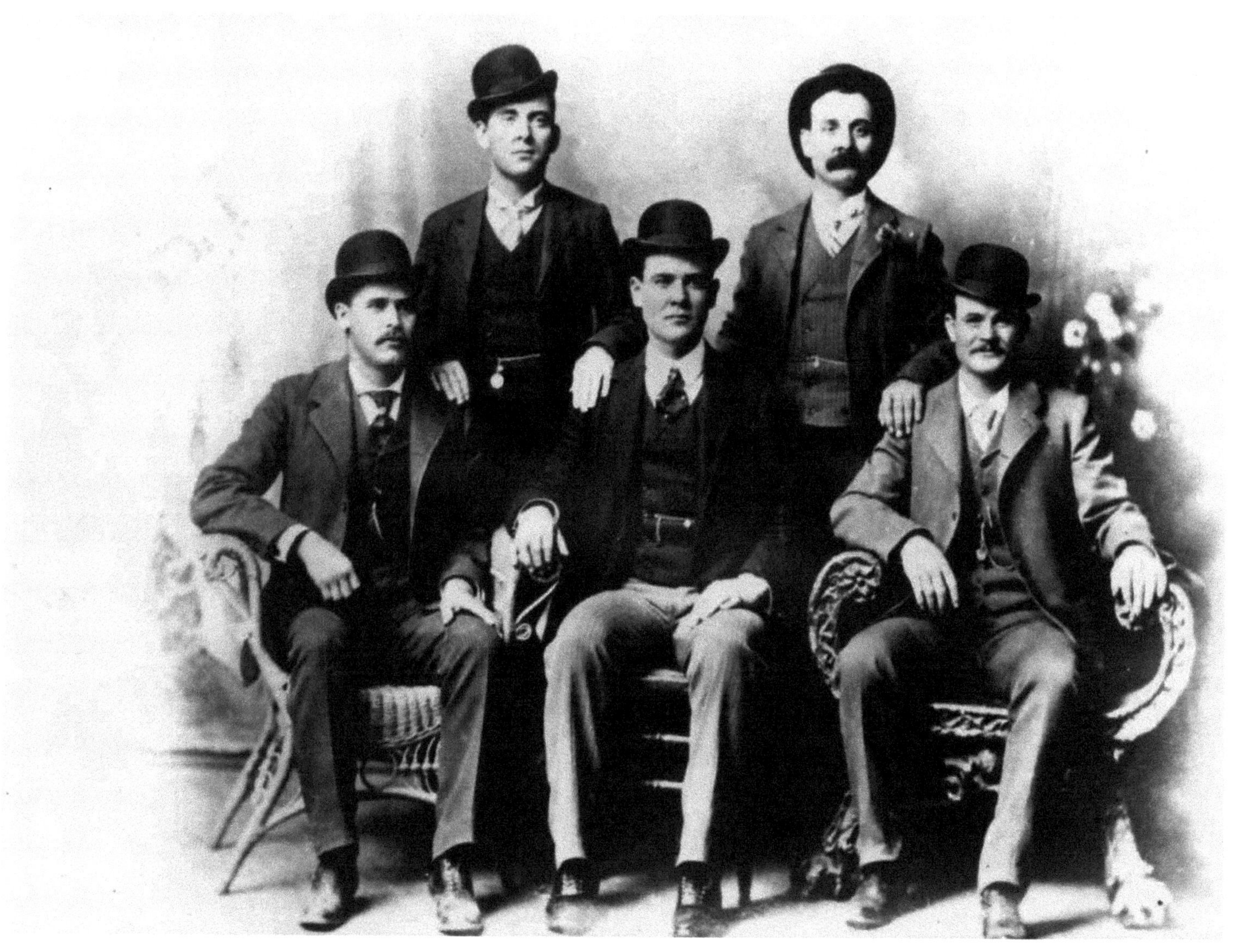

By the time this dapper collection of outlaws was photographed together at Fort Worth in late 1900, the Hole-in-the-Wall Gang (a.k.a. the Wild Bunch) had been hunted down all over the West and the widespread crime empire was near collapse. Standing (left to right) are Will Carver and Harvey Logan, and sitting are the Sundance Kid, Ben Kilpatrick, and Butch Cassidy. Cassidy once quipped, "If he'd just pay me what he's paying them to keep me from robbing him, I'd quit robbing him."

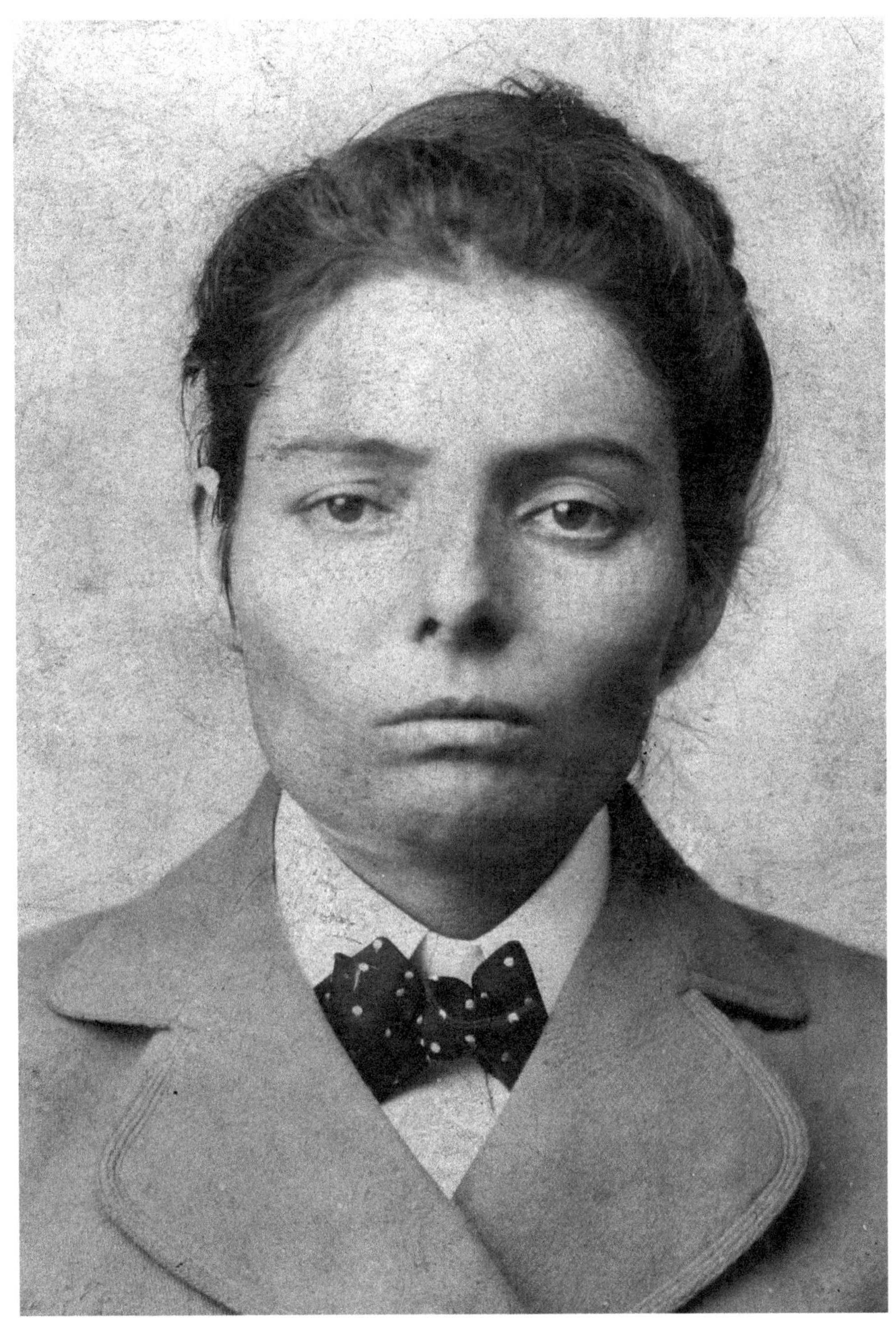

Not long after the Wild Bunch photos were made in Fort Worth, lawmen caught up with Ben Kilpatrick and his lover, Laura Bullion (her mug shot seen here), in St. Louis. Bullion was a prostitute who had grown up around the Ketchums, Will Carver, and Kilpatrick in Texas. She was a loyal camp follower for the gang and is known to have participated in at least one train robbery.

This formal photo of the Sundance Kid (together with an image of his lover Etta Place it was turned into a Souvenir card) was made about the same time as the famous group photo. Born Harry Longabaugh, the taciturn, quick-draw Sundance was Cassidy's closest friend and most trusted associate in the Wild Bunch. Conventional wisdom holds that, like Cassidy, he was killed during a shoot-out with Bolivian troops.

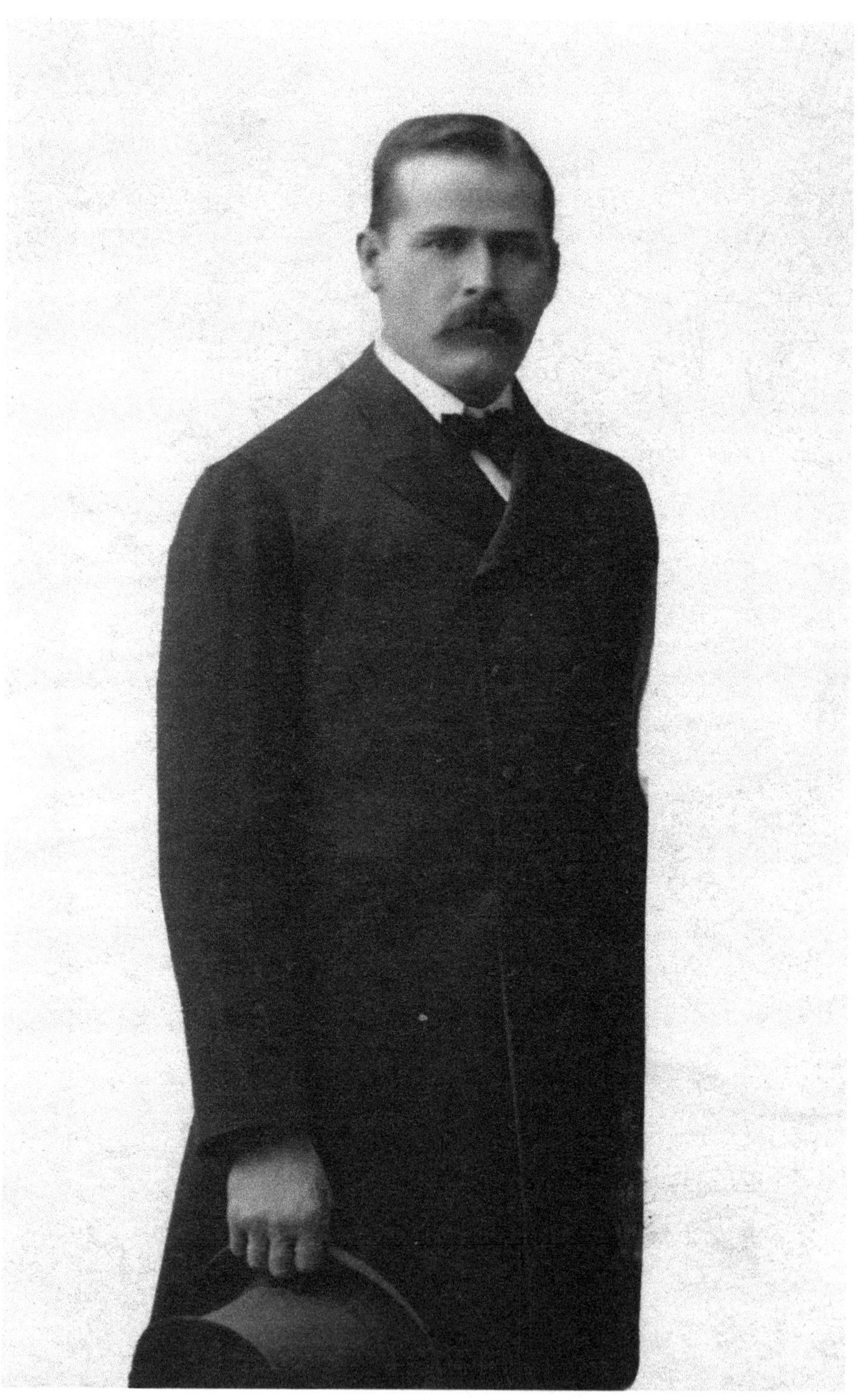

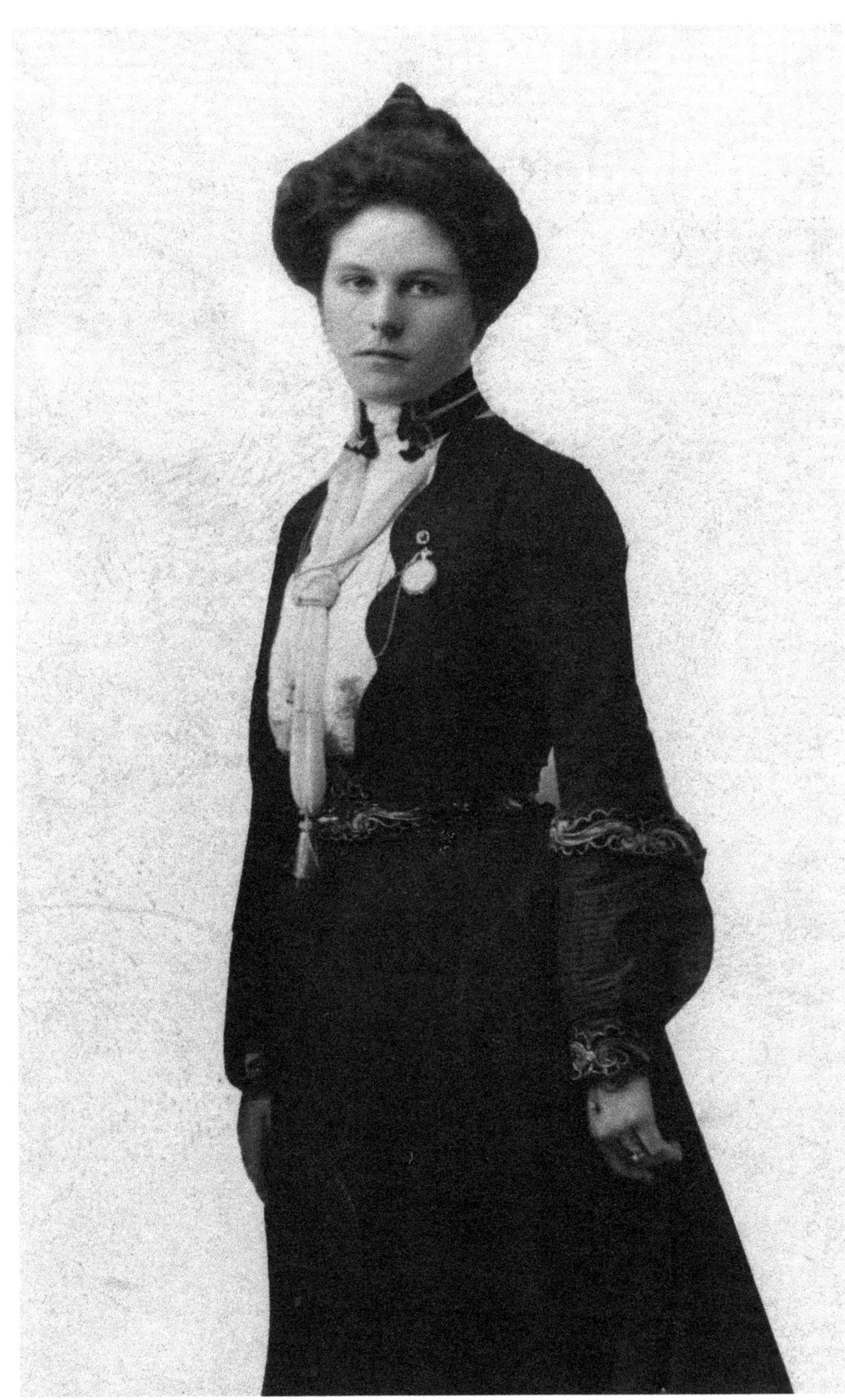

This companion photo depicts Longabaugh's wife, Etta Place. Etta's life is mired in even more mystery than surrounds that of Butch Cassidy's demise. Few documented facts exist about her origin or what became of her. In February 1901, they traveled by ship to South America with Butch Cassidy and the three of them operated a ranch in the foothills of the Andes.

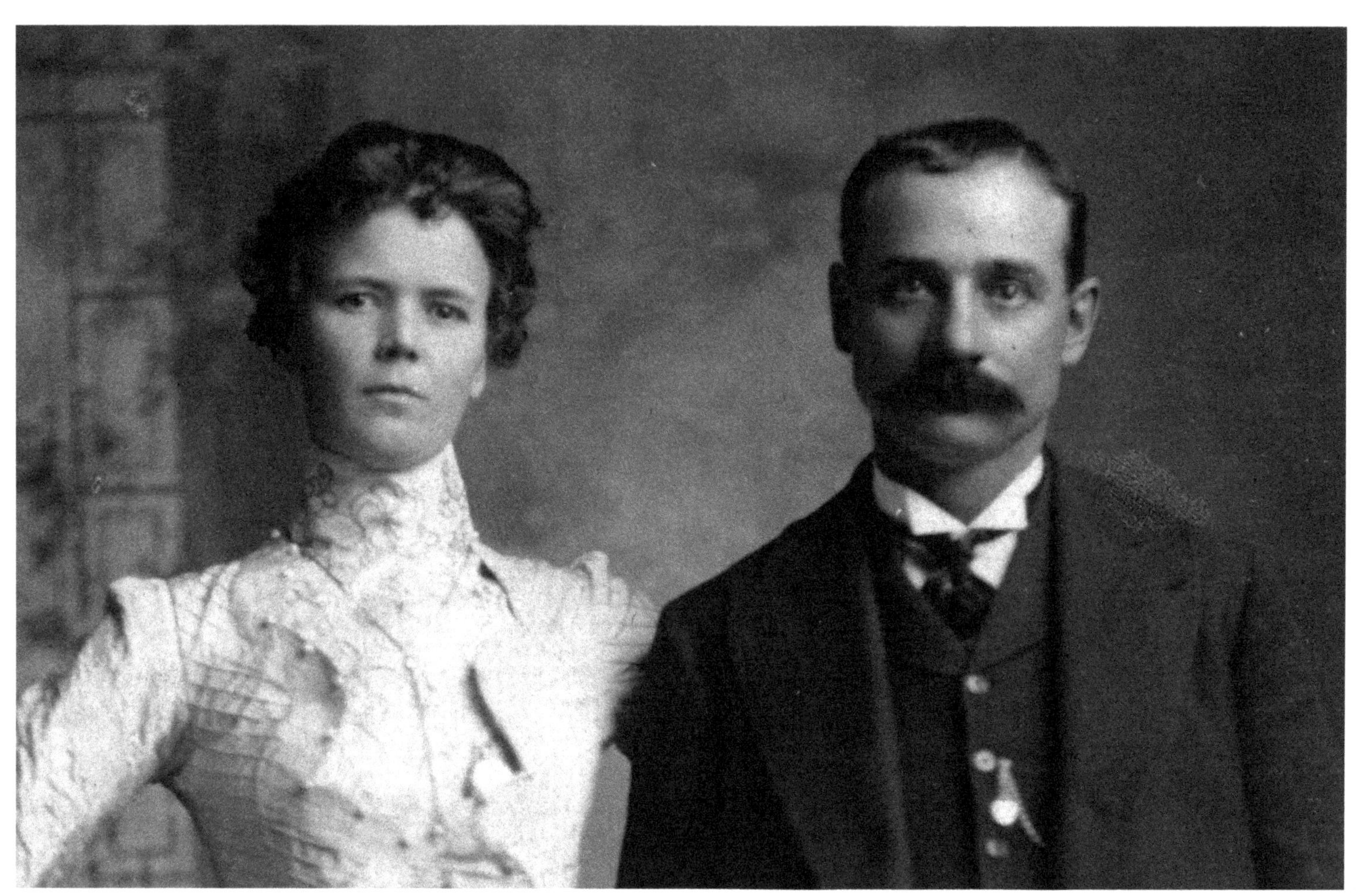

Just as the group photograph of the Wild Bunch in Fort Worth proved to be the gang's undoing (lawmen previously had no pictures of the gang to show informants), this photo linked Harvey Logan's lover Annie Rogers to him and his larcenous activities. She was a charming, literate, likable prostitute, but that wasn't enough to keep her out of prison when she tried to launder stolen cash in a Nashville bank in 1901.

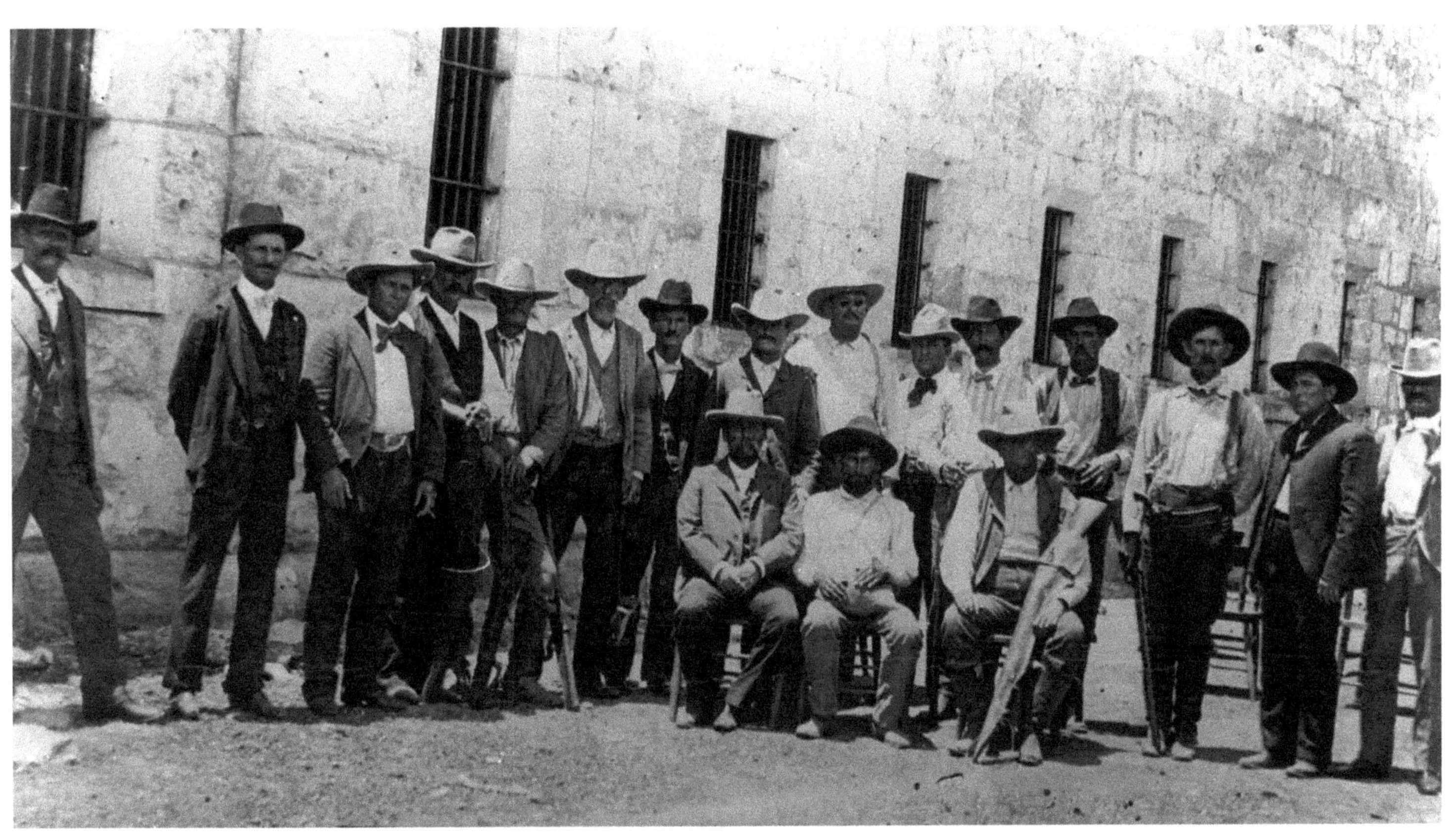

The manhunt for Tejano fugitive Gregorio Cortez became a phenomenon that forever cemented his place in the folklore of South Texas, much as Sam Bass did in the north. Cortez evaded capture by one of the largest manhunts in Texas history after a mistranslation caused a sheriff to kill his brother, which prompted Cortez to kill the sheriff. The phrase which polarized the Tejano and white communities? "No white man can arrest me."

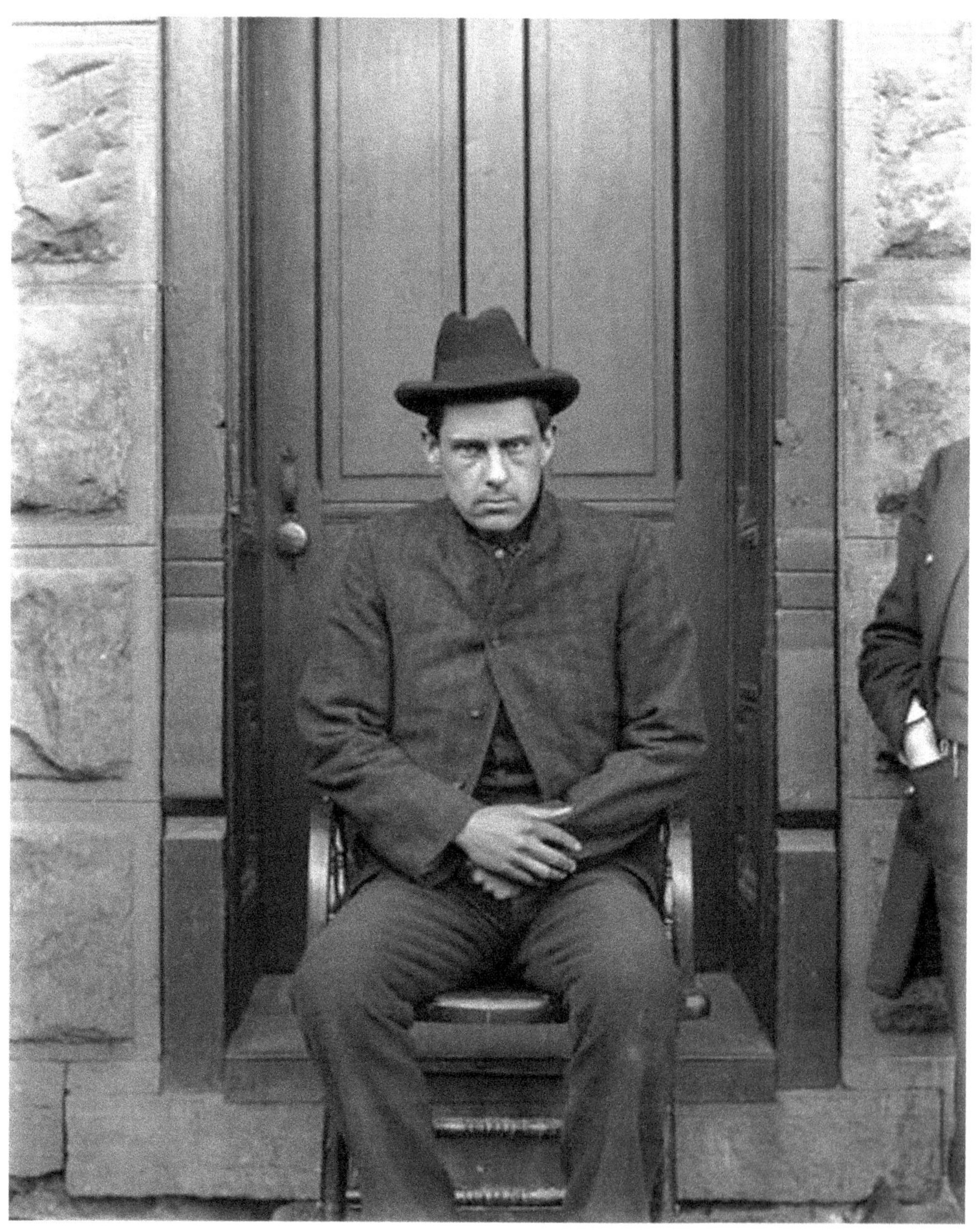

Though the circumstances behind this photograph of Colorado criminal J. W. Bond in 1902 are not known, it was probably taken at the Colorado State Prison in Canon City where the photographer, early filmmaker Harry Buckwalter, was known to have been working at the time.

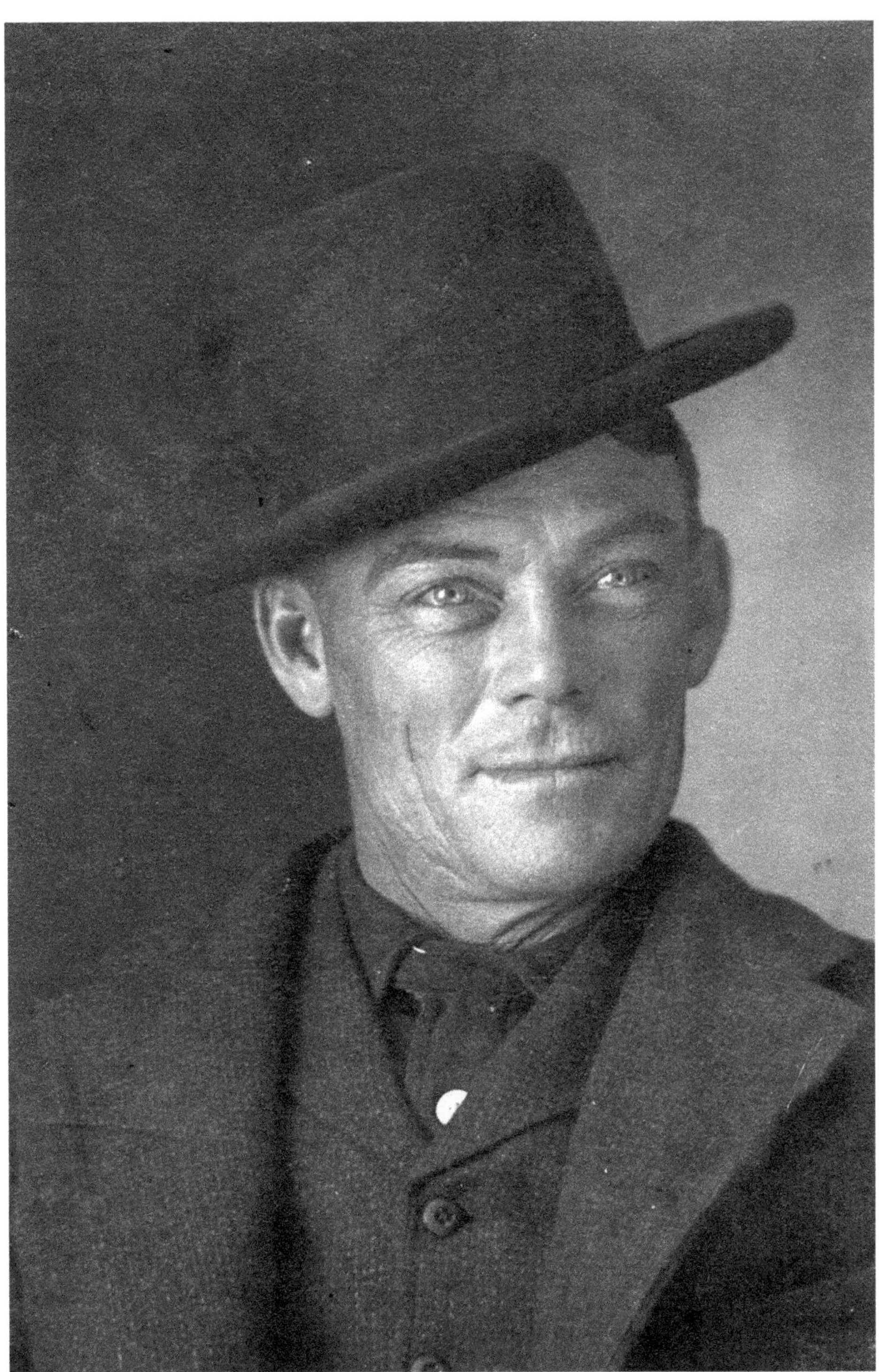

Jesse Linsley was a part-time robber loosely associated with the Hole-in-the-Wall Gang. In 1902, he took part in the robbery of the Stockgrowers' Bank in Bridger, Montana, with Patrick Murray and William Countryman. They made off with $2,338, but were quickly apprehended—Linsley got eight years in the prison at Deer Lodge.

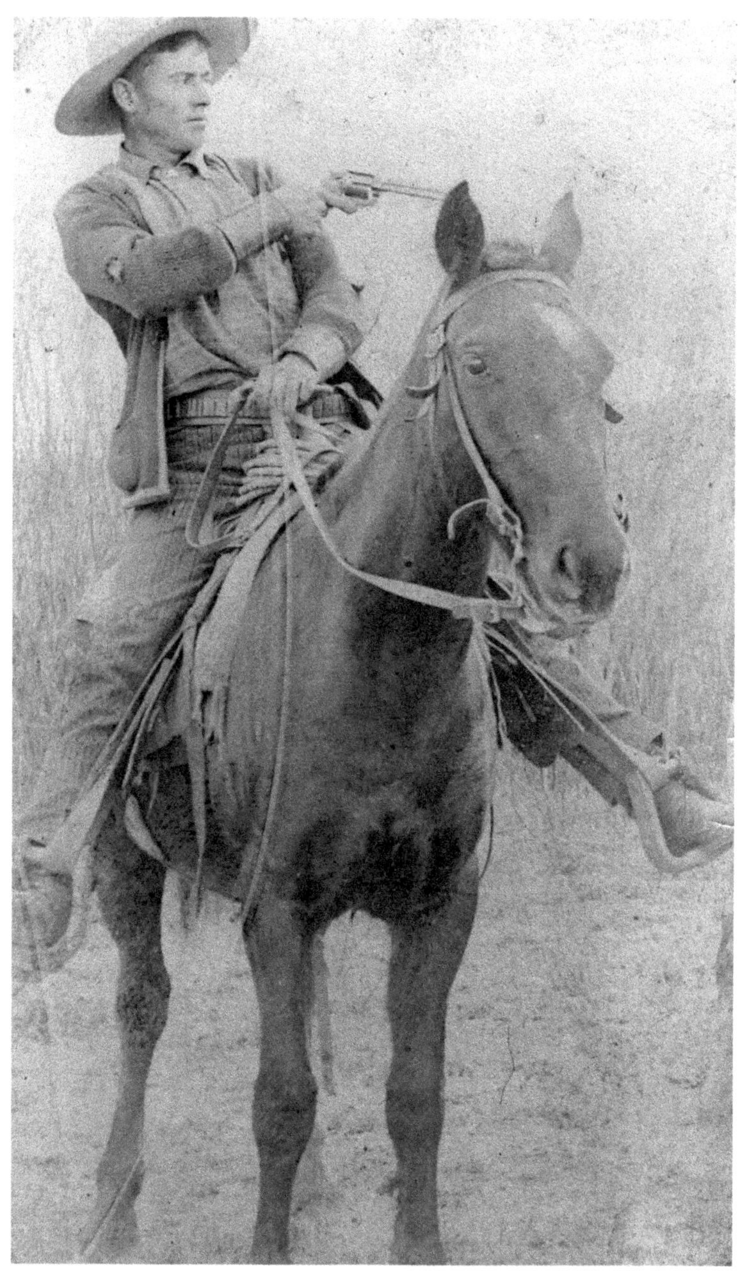

Details are sparse when it comes to the career of Will Roberts, a.k.a. Will Dixon, but evidence definitely links him to a handful of robberies by the Hole-in-the-Wall Gang around the turn of the century.

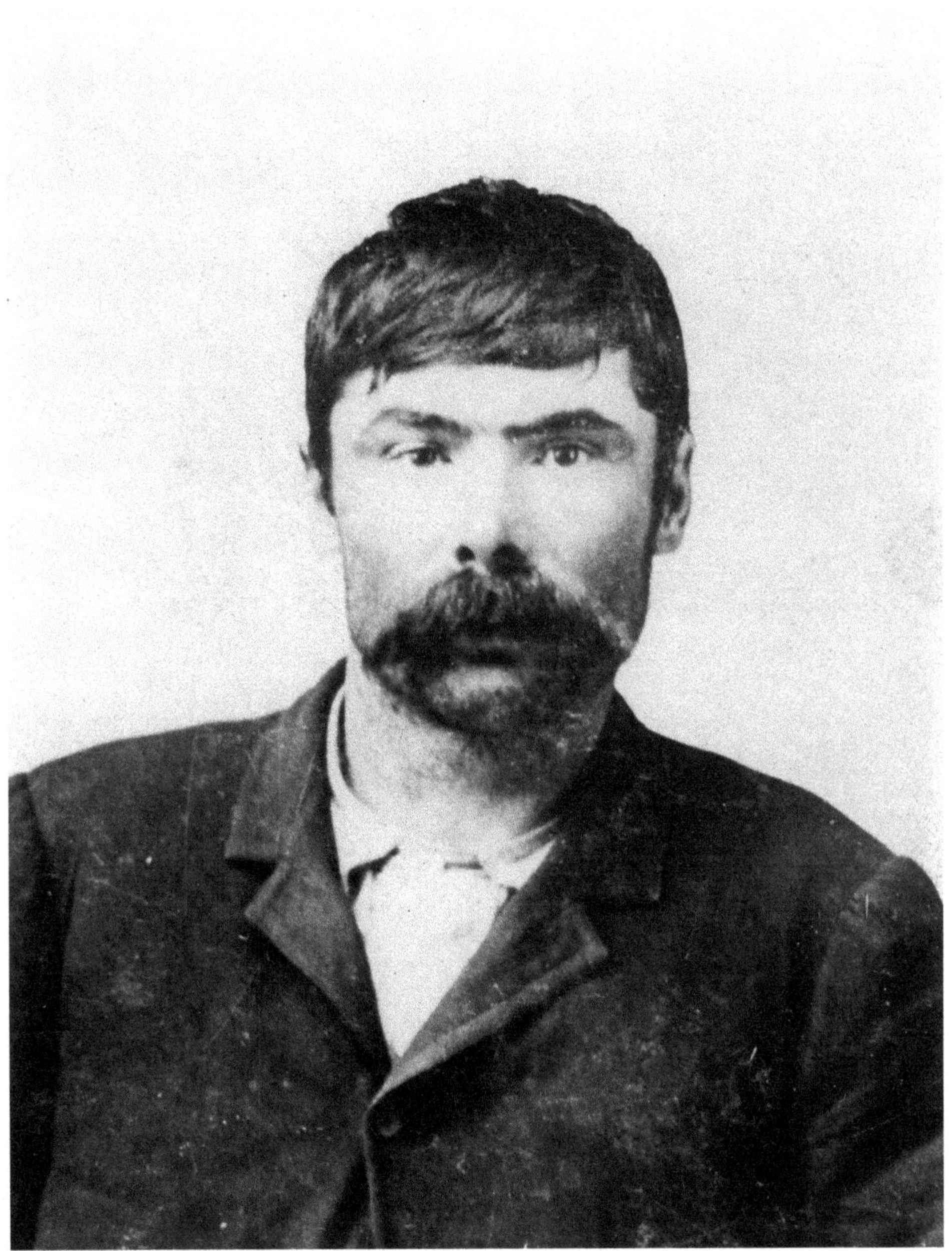

Iowan Tom O'Day was a secondary member of the Hole-in-the-Wall Gang associated with Kid Curry and generally operated in the northern plains and Wyoming. His hometown paper said he was "of a wild, harum-scarum temperament, fond of a fight and hard to whip." However, in late 1903 he was surprised by a sheriff while stealing horses and served a lengthy jail sentence.

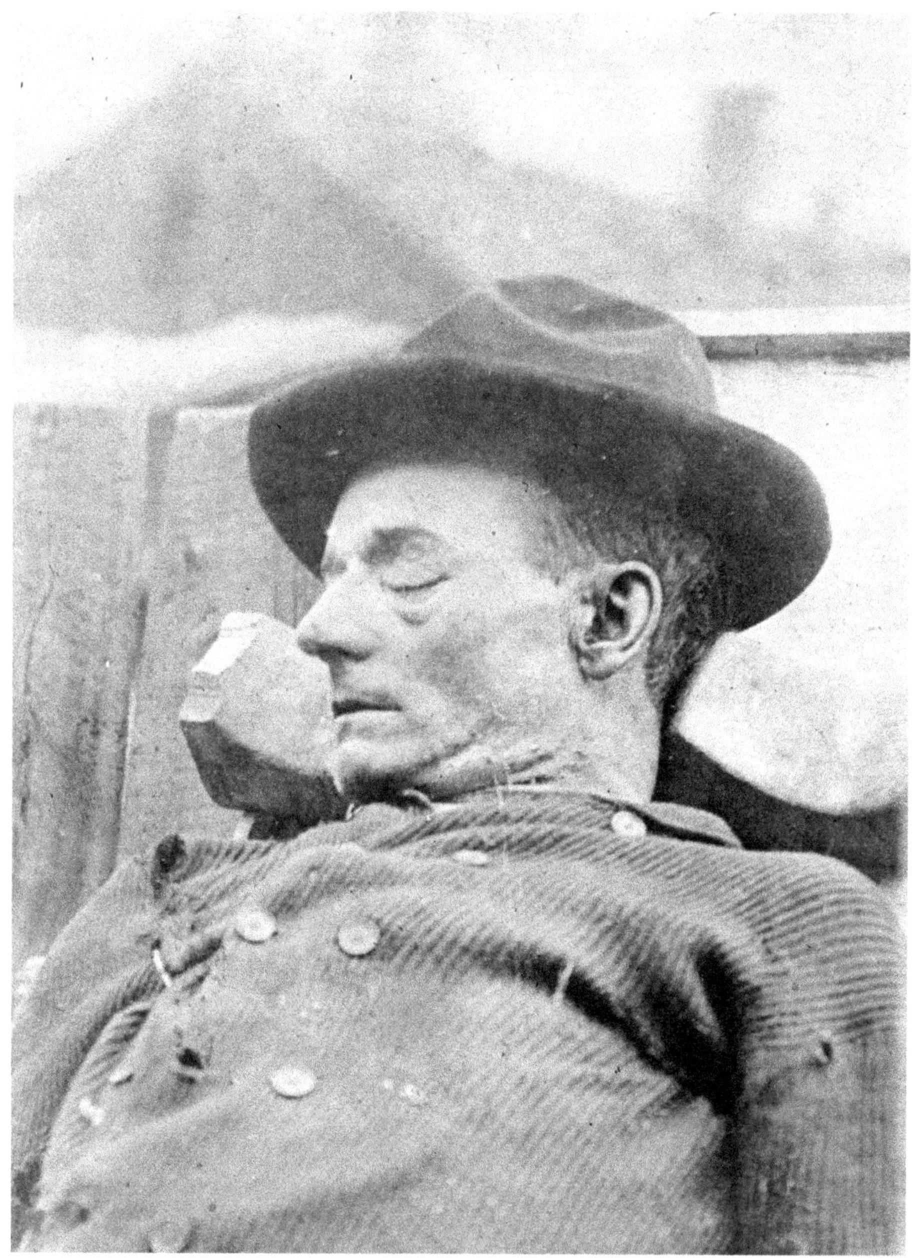

Harvey Logan, alias Kid Curry, has sometimes been called the "wildest of the Wild Bunch" because of his short temper and willingness to shoot anyone who got in his way. He was often at odds with Butch Cassidy because of his violent ways, but he was fearless and an expert marksman. Long having vowed never to be taken alive, he took his own life when wounded during a firefight in 1904.

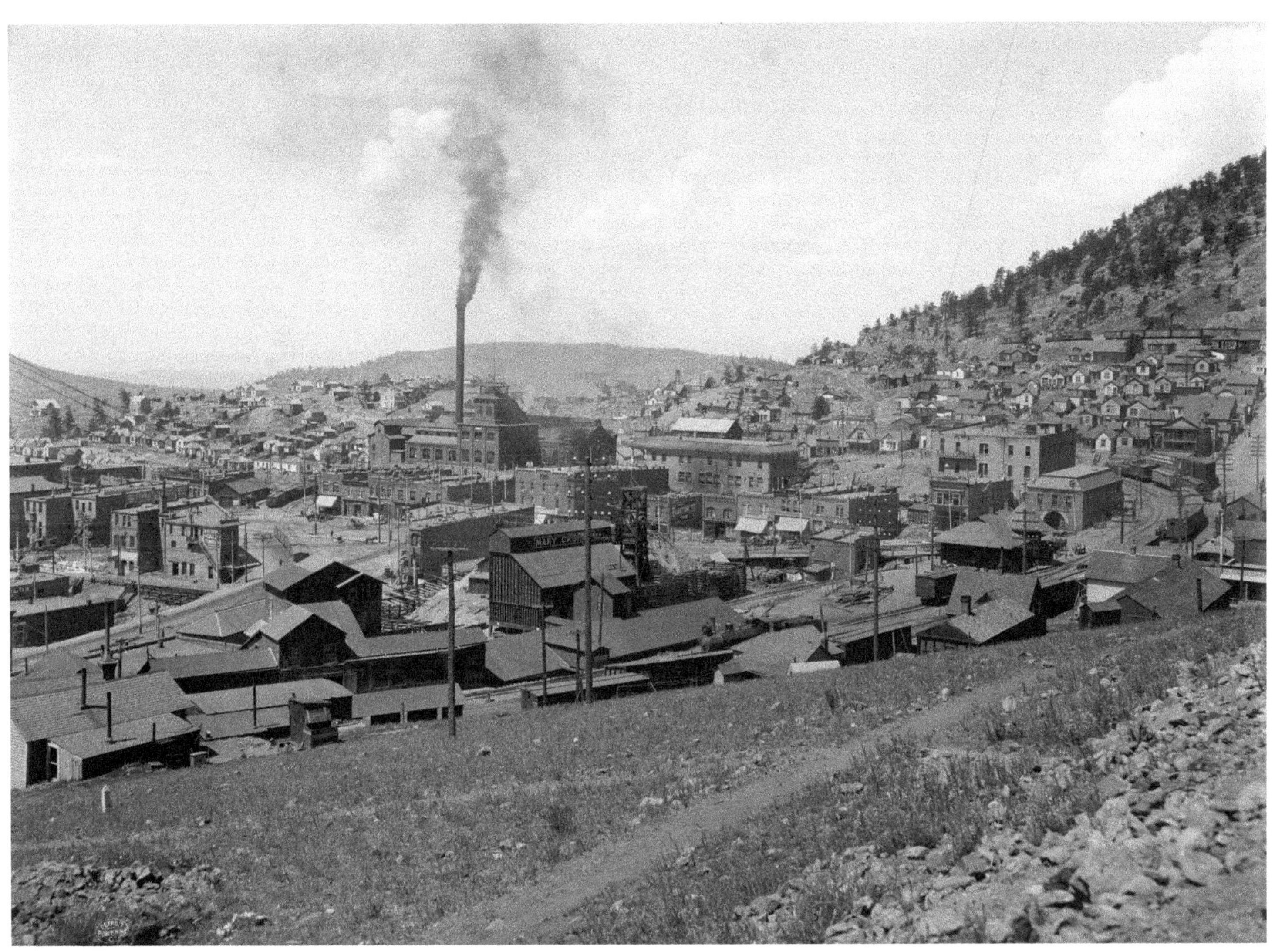

The Gold Coin Mine in the foreground of this view of Victor, Colorado, was the scene of the brutal murder of Martin O'Connor in 1905. The local sheriff's top suspect was Frank Buster, a known card sharp haunting Victor with no visible means of support. Despite uncovering information that Buster had murdered men and robbed banks across the West, he was released on a technicality.

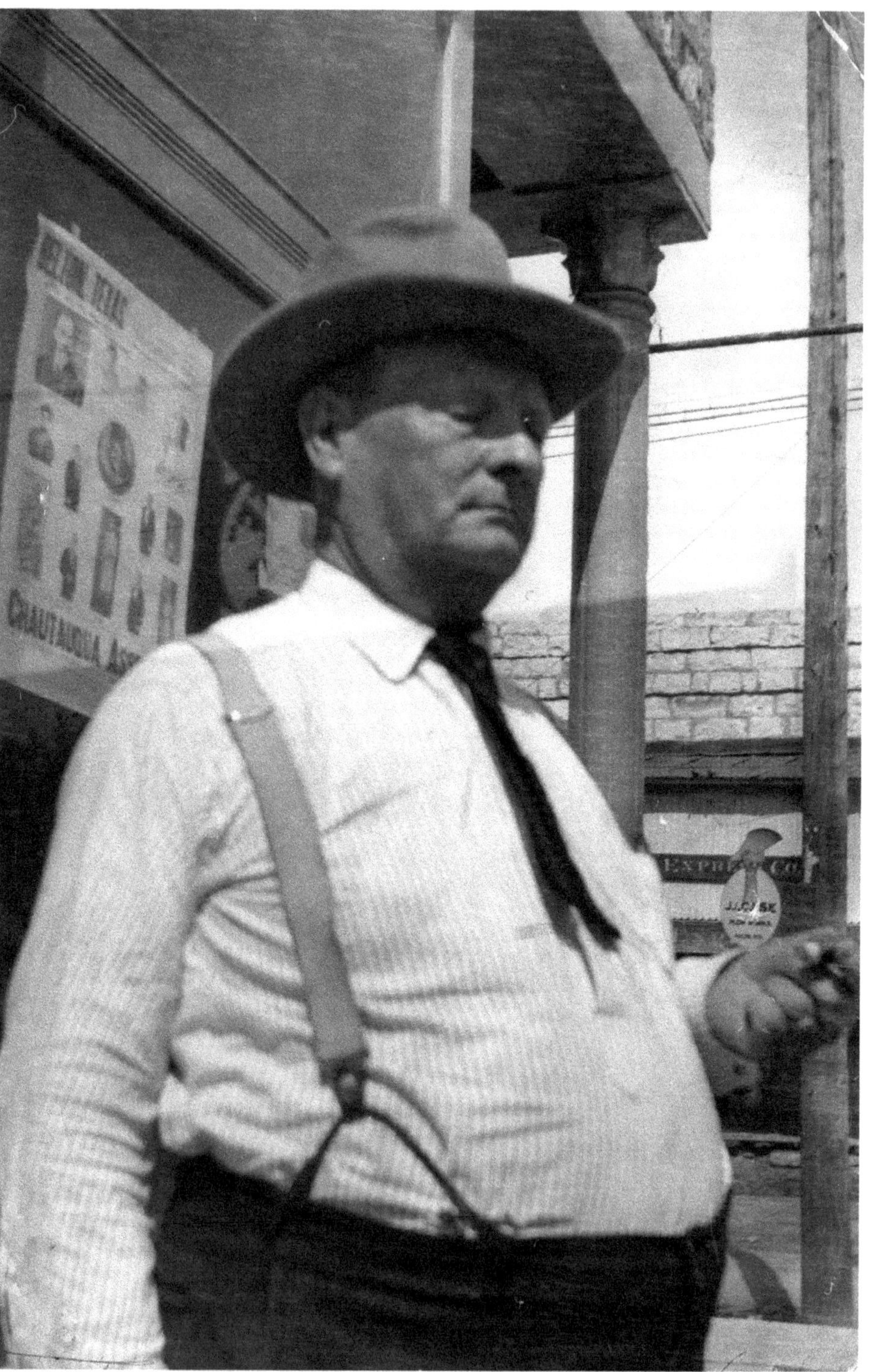

Thirty years after the Northfield raid and five years out of prison, Cole Younger paused for this photograph in 1906. After prison, he wrote his memoirs—in which he claimed to have committed only one crime—and toured the lecture circuit with Frank James, before dying in his hometown of Lee's Summit, Missouri, in 1916.

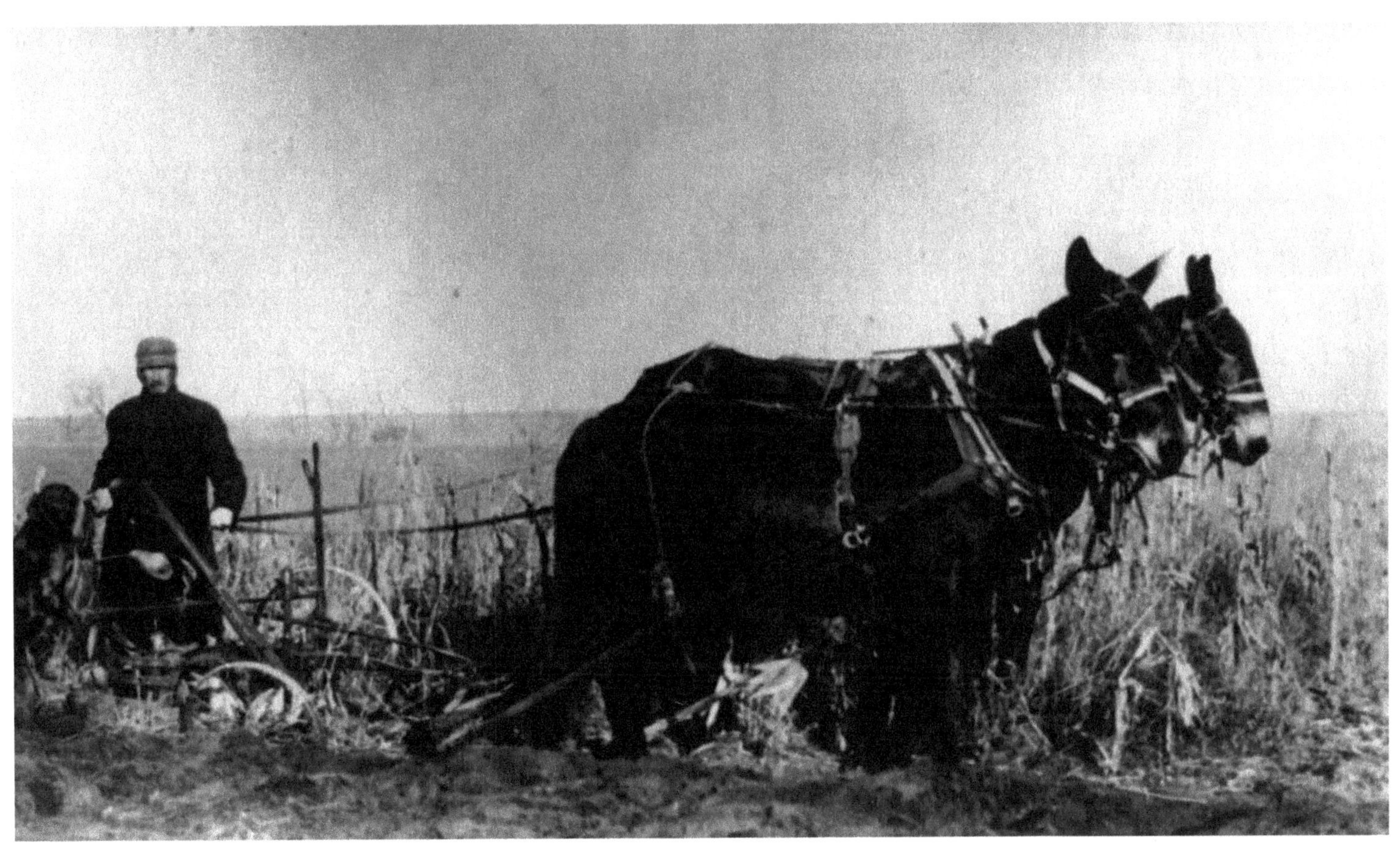

Frank James relocated to Fletcher, Oklahoma, sometime after the turn of the century. In 1911, a story ran in the *Daily Oklahoman* newspaper which reported that Frank's mother had died in a train carriage on her way home from her visit with Frank and his wife, Annie, at their farm in Fletcher. After her death he moved back to the family farm in Missouri where he died four years later.

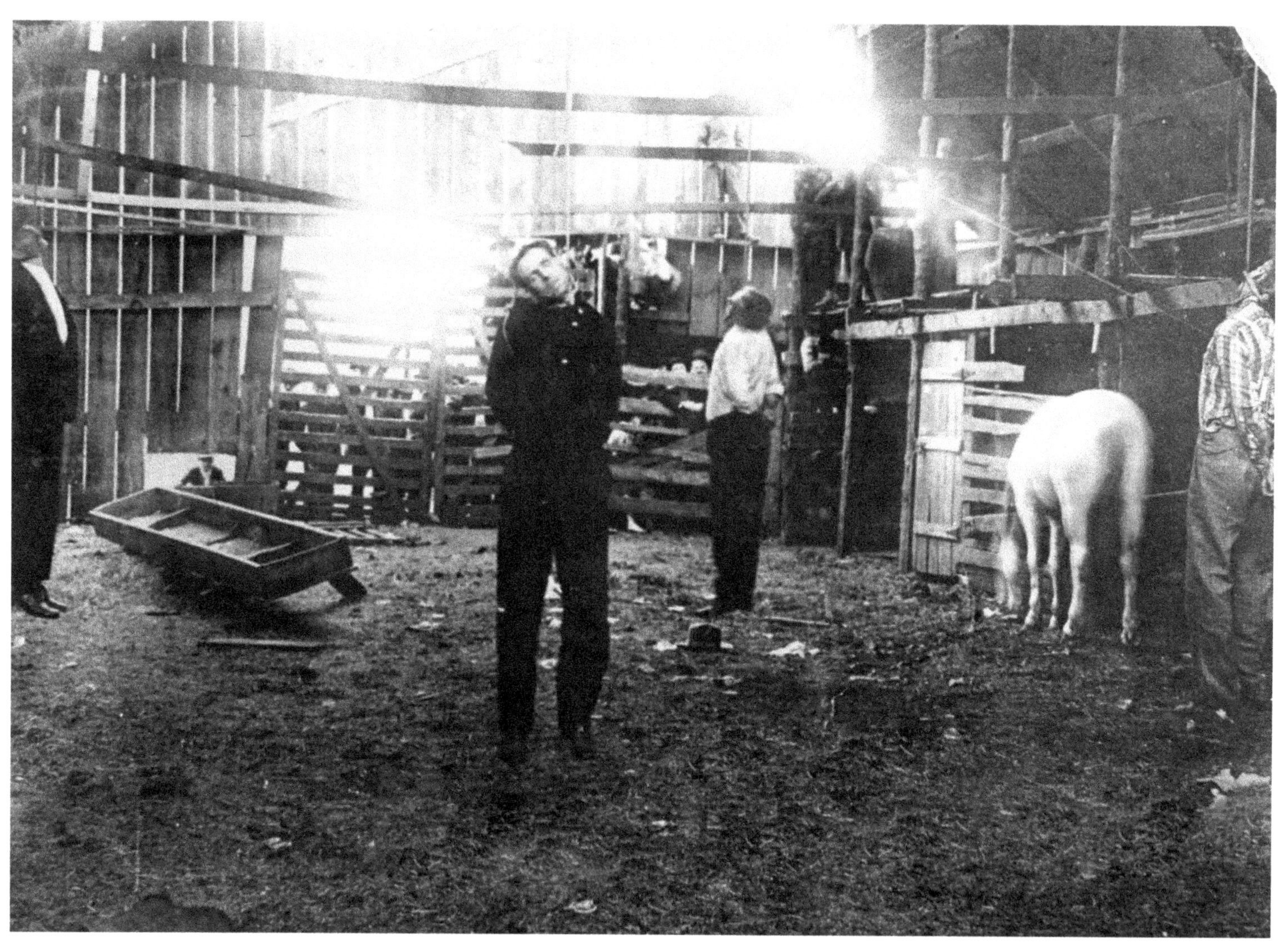

In April 1909, a sizable mob in Ada, Oklahoma, stormed the jail, removed the men imprisoned for the murder of former Deputy Marshal A. A. Bobbitt, and strung them up in a nearby stable. Though the details are still shrouded in mystery, "Deacon" Jim Miller (hanging at far-left) was undoubtedly the triggerman in the murder.

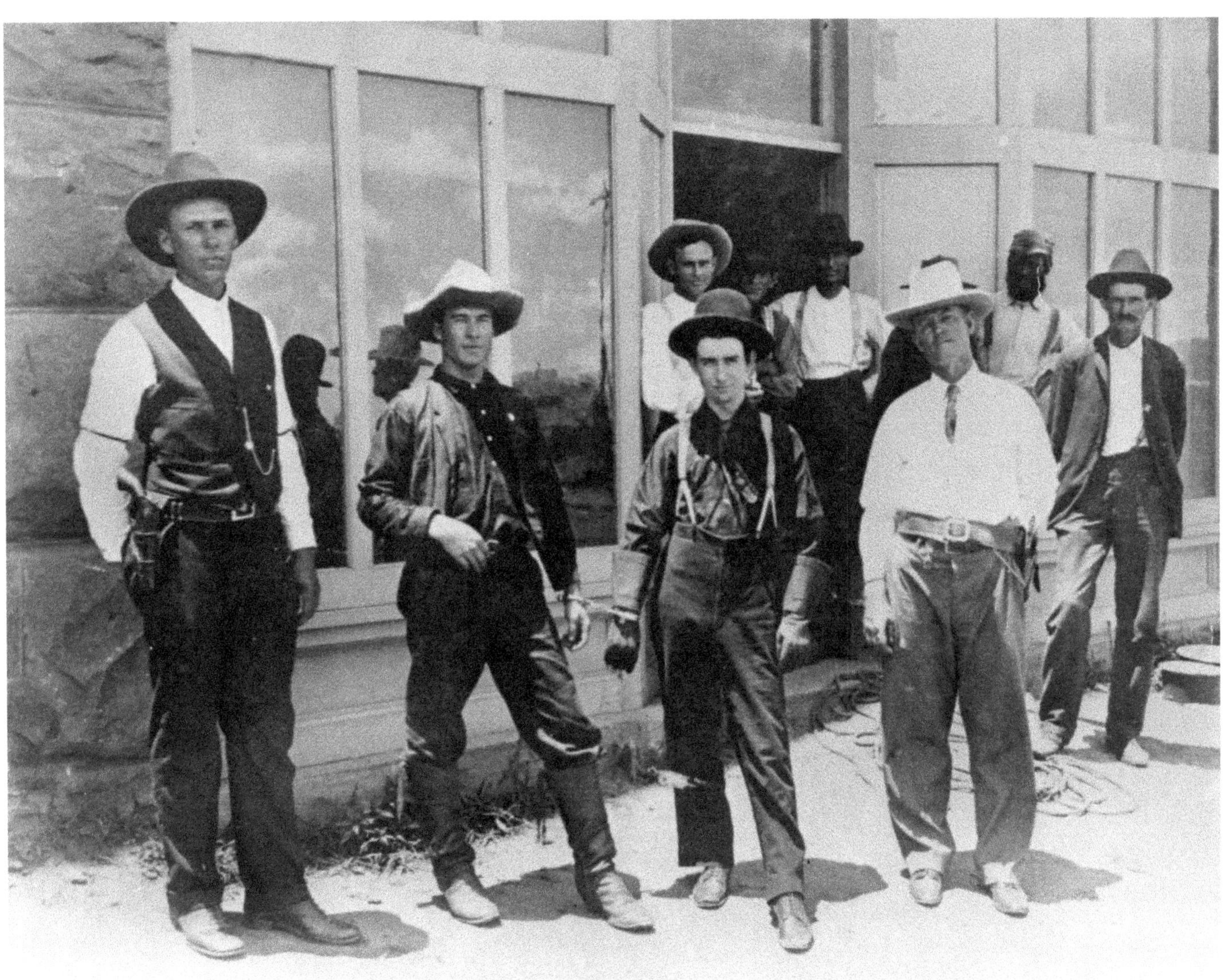

Okfuskee County, Oklahoma, deputy Bailey Wilson (in the foreground at left) and Sheriff William McCulley (at right) embark for McAlester to deliver the county's first inmates (sharing a pair of handcuffs) to the new Oklahoma State Penitentiary around 1909.

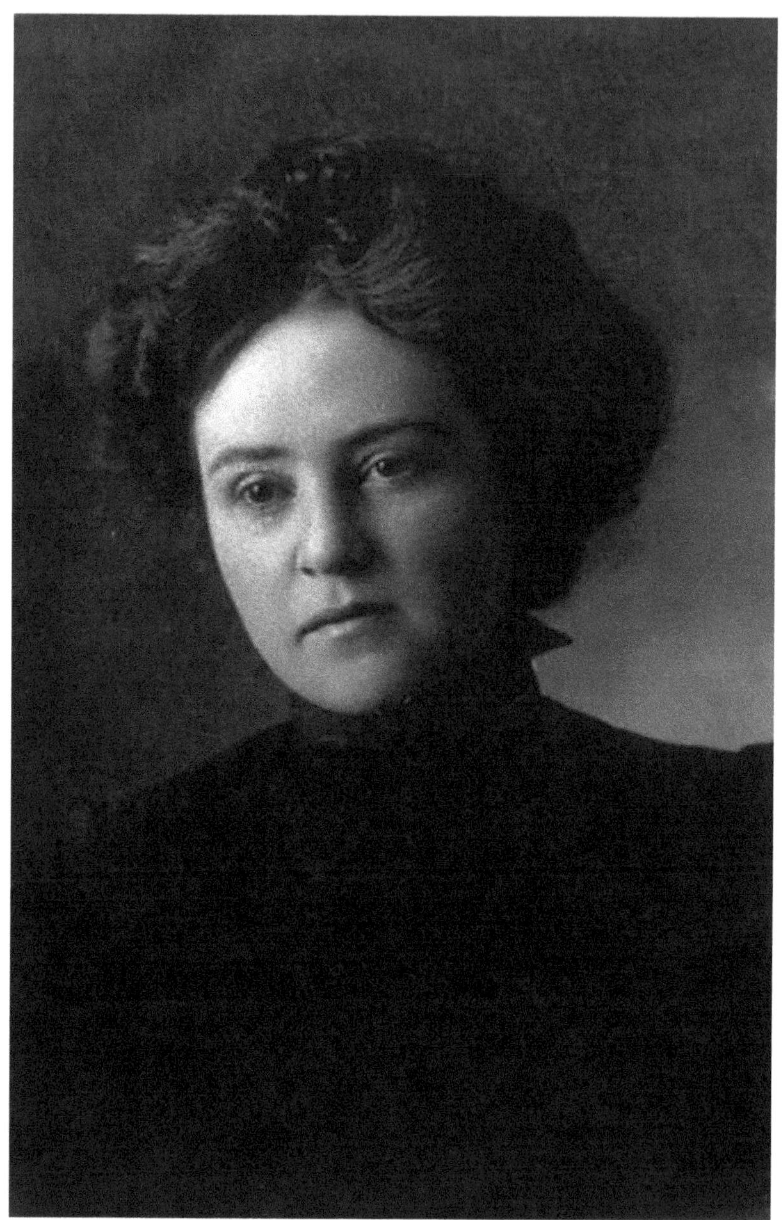

Ann Bassett was one of the most colorful women of the Old West, having practically been raised as a cowboy, but educated and refined in finishing schools. Known as "Queen Ann," she ran a large ranch in northwestern Colorado and was a known associate of Butch Cassidy and his gang. In 1911, she beat a rustling rap in court but in her memoir she said, "I did everything they said I did and more."

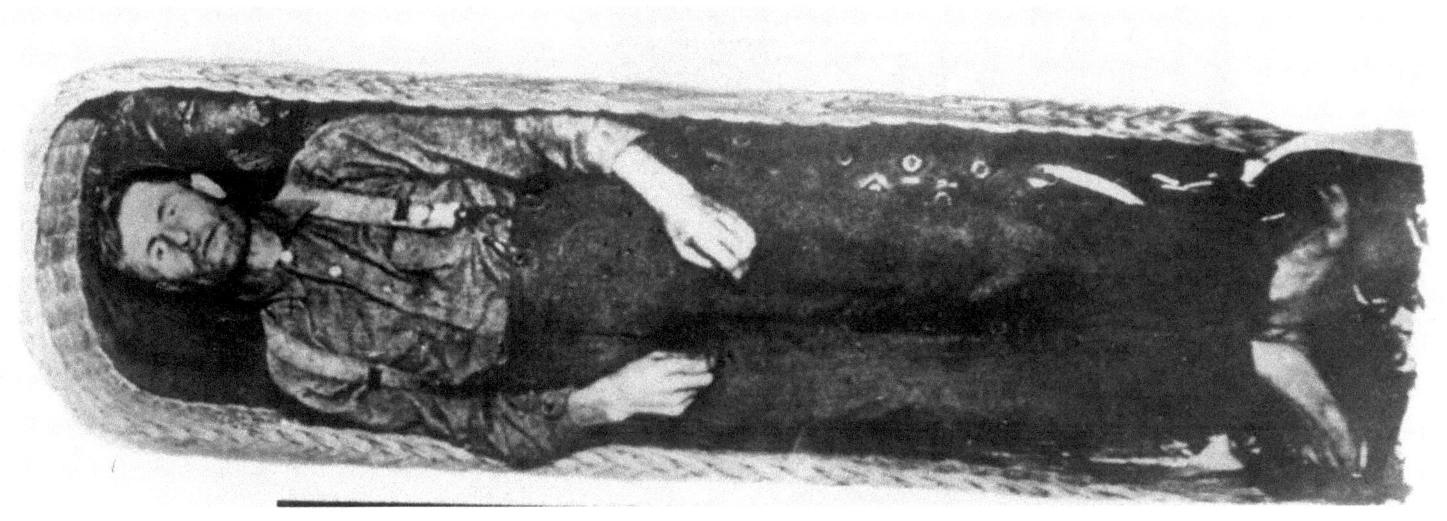

Elmer McCurdy was a two-bit lowlife who hung around the criminal element in Oklahoma. His specialty was a fondness and ineptitude for nitroglycerin and its use in cracking safes. In 1911, he was killed by a posse in Osage County following a train robbery, and when no one claimed his body, the undertaker put him on display and charged a nickel to view his corpse. Over the next 60 years his mummified body toured carnival shows before finally coming to rest in Guthrie, Oklahoma, in 1977.

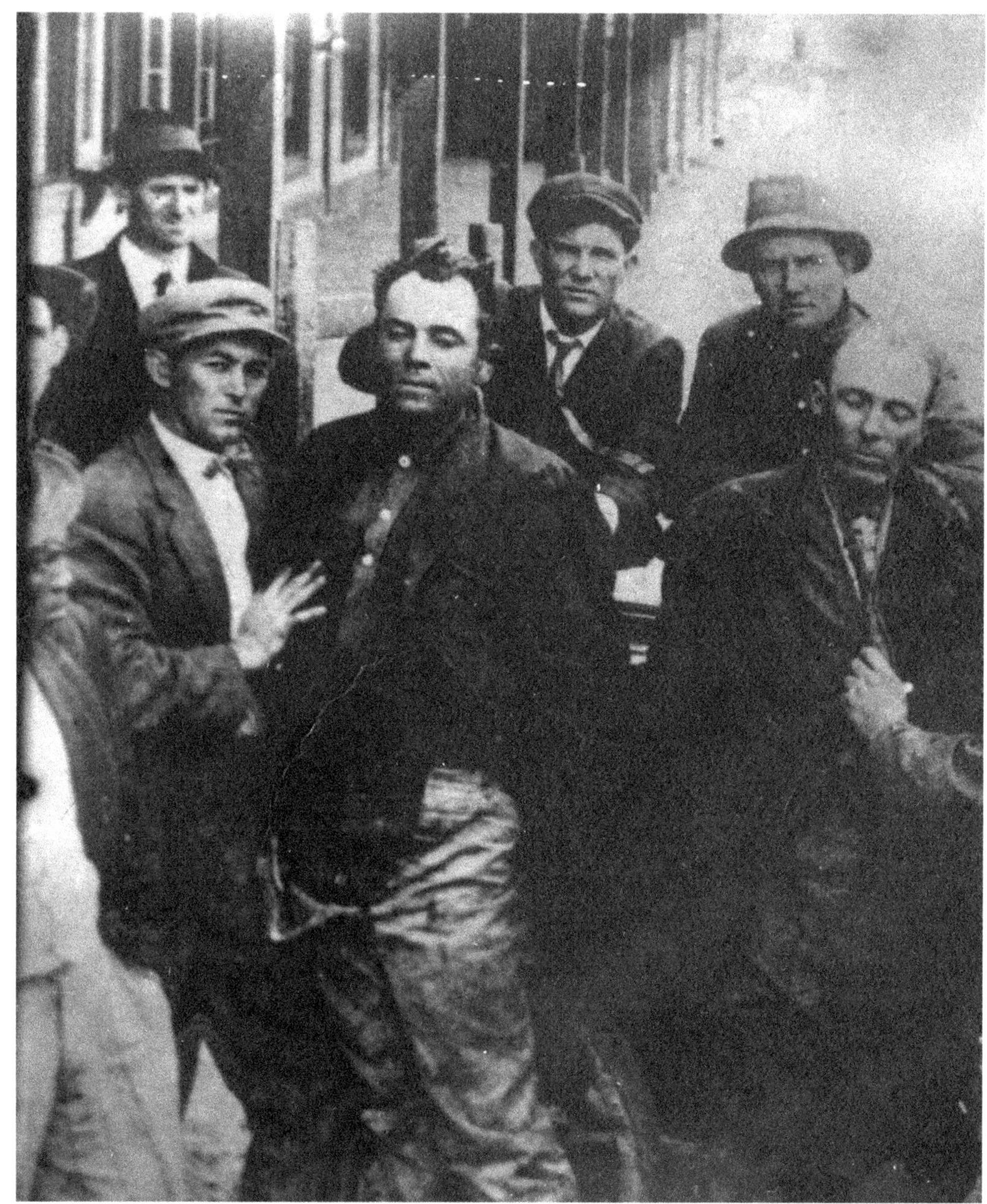

A ten-year prison stint did not deter former Wild Bunch member Ben Kilpatrick (the Tall Texan) from more robbery. In 1912, he and partner Ole Beck held up a Southern Pacific Express train near Sanderson, Texas. However, a crew member surprised Kilpatrick and split his head open with an ice mallet, then retrieved Ben's rifle and shot Beck to death.

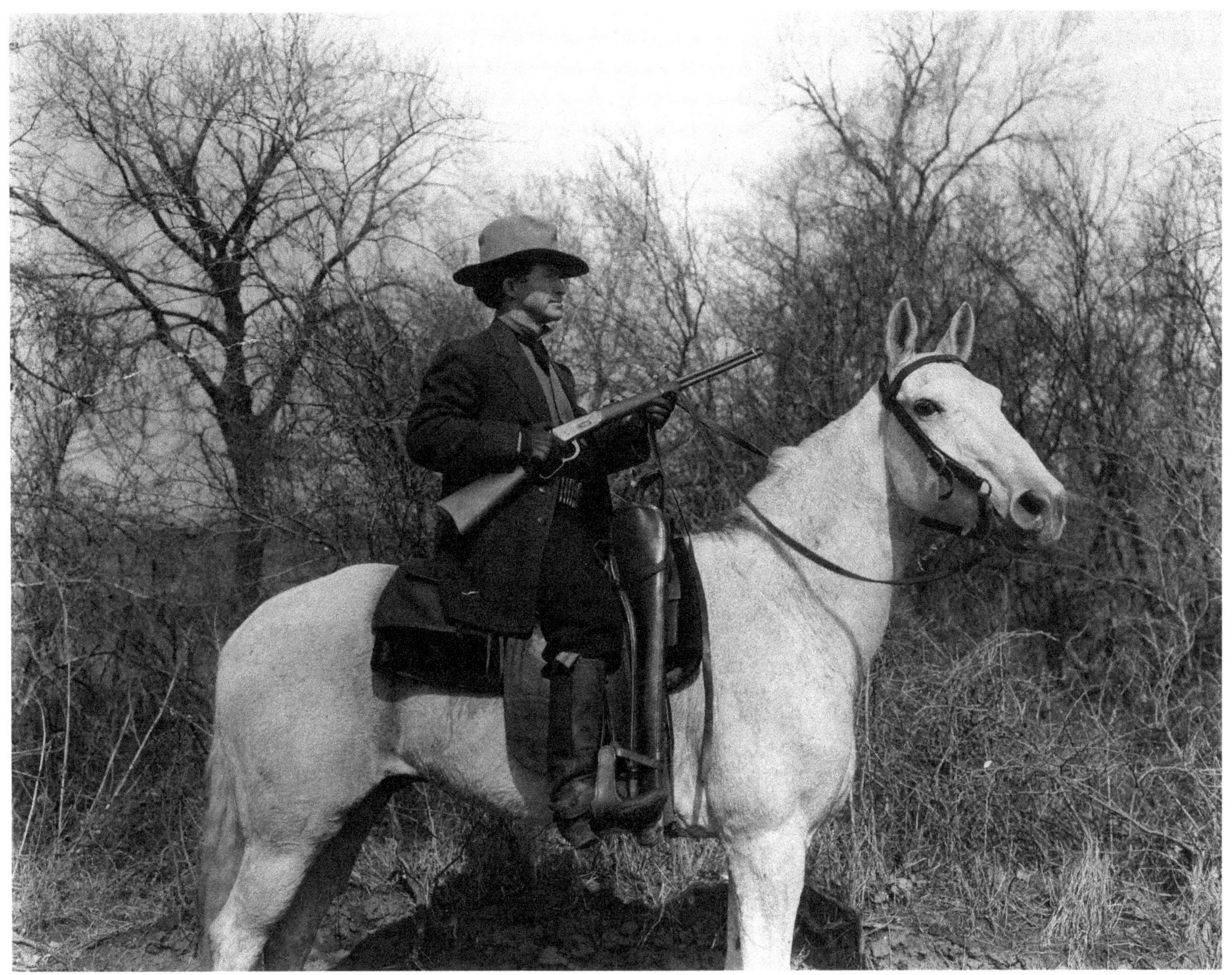

Al Jennings was something of a megalomaniac who started out as a lawyer in Oklahoma, but became enchanted with the outlaws roaming the territory and was sure he could do better. He assembled a gang and made a few robberies, including a botched train robbery in which Jennings was captured and sent to prison. After release, he ran unsuccessfully for political office and then became an advisor on western movie sets in Hollywood.

Henry Starr poses with his wife and child (probably near Tahlequah) around 1913. The historical record is not complete, but around this time Starr ended his second prison term only to learn that his wife had divorced him and left his son with his mother in Tulsa.

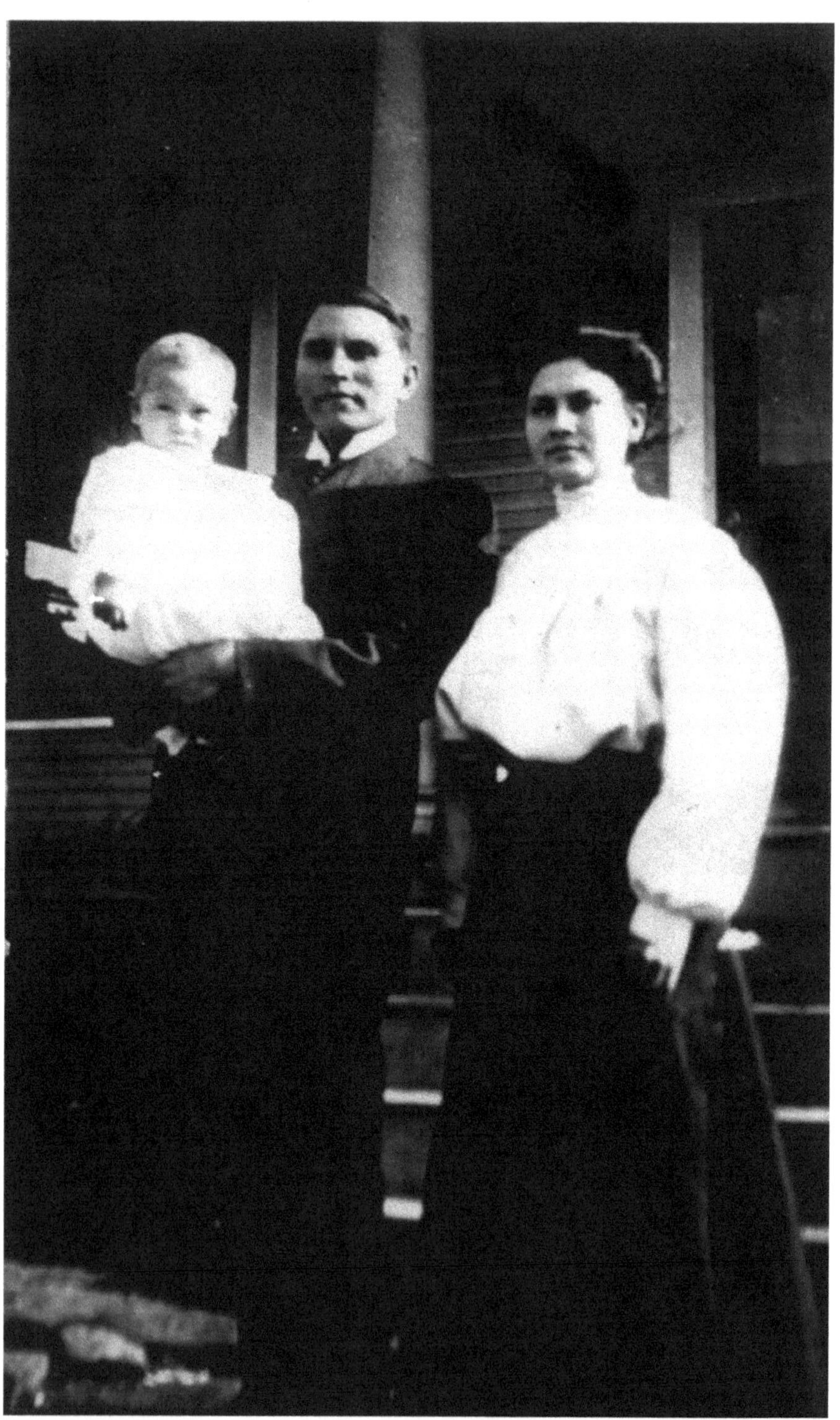

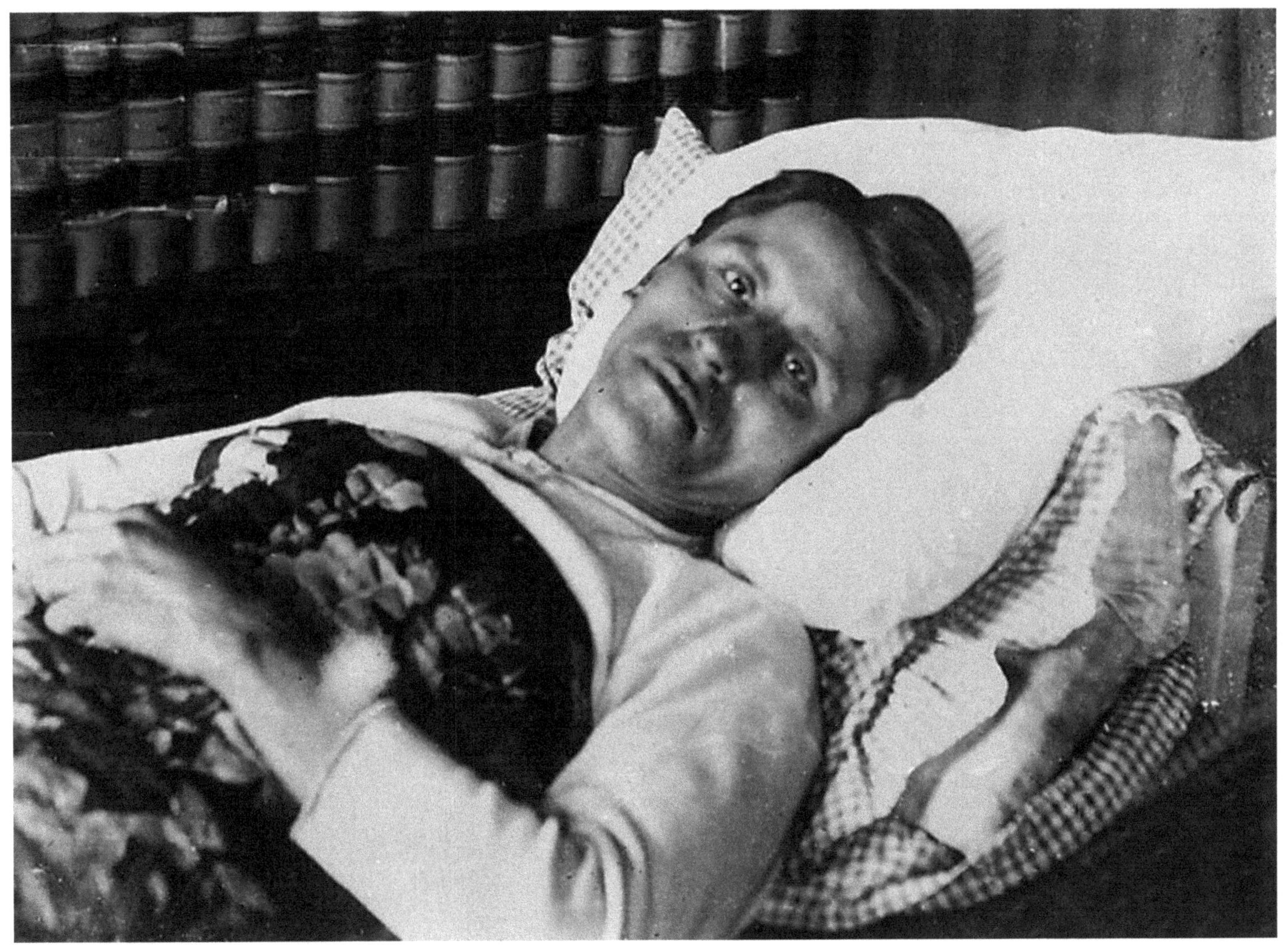

Minutes after Henry Starr and his gang pulled off the amazing feat of robbing two banks at once in 1915, he was wounded by Stroud, Oklahoma, teenager Paul Curry, who claimed a $1,000 reward for the capture. Starr would live to rob another day.

Following Spread: These heavily armed soldiers were rebels led by Mexican general Pancho Villa (center), a former bandit who became one of the central figures of the Mexican Revolution. More from desperation than strategy, Villa and his Villistas attacked Columbus, New Mexico, killing dozens of Americans and burning and pillaging much of the town. Among those chasing them back across the border were General John J. Pershing and a young George S. Patton.

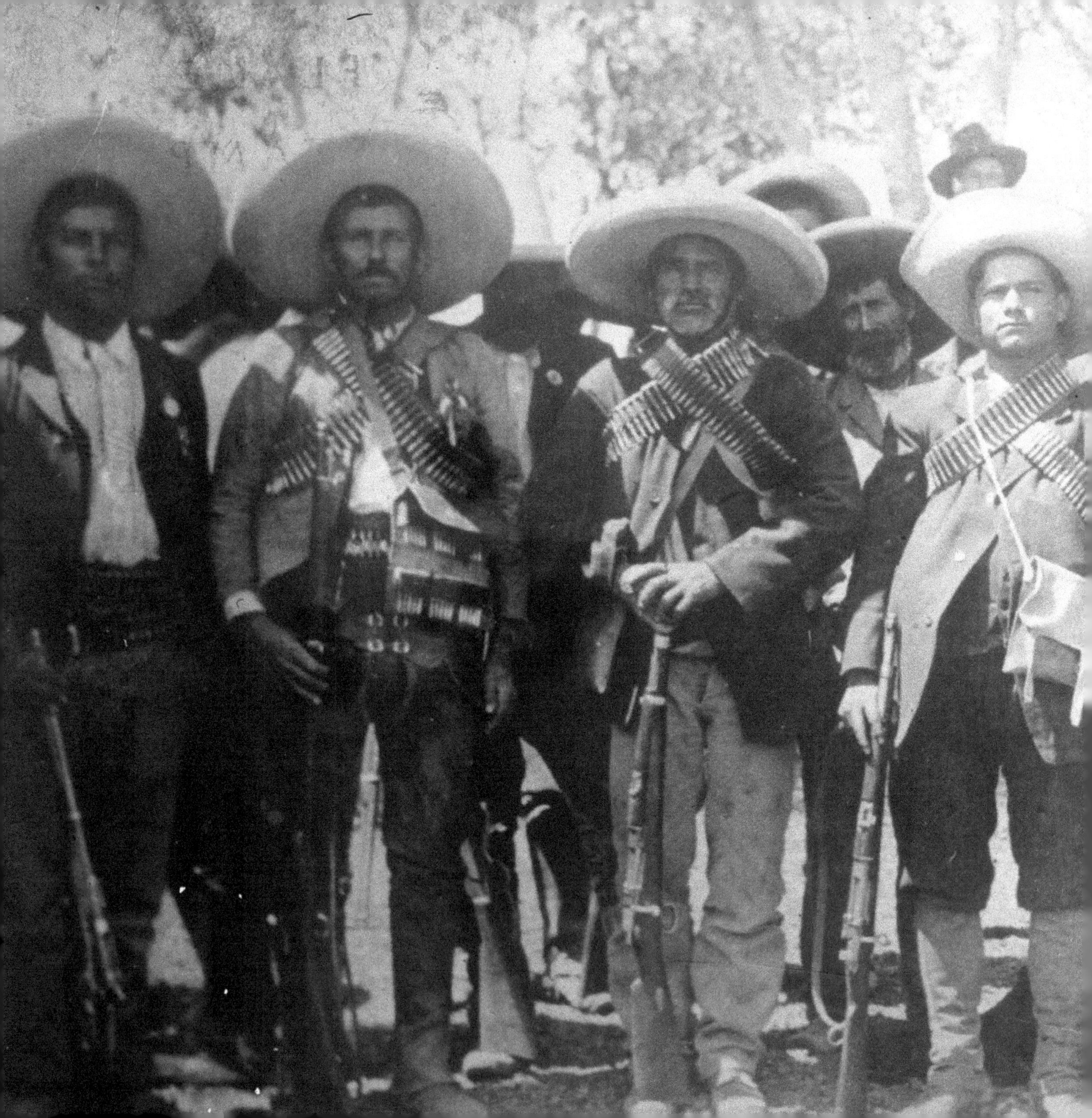

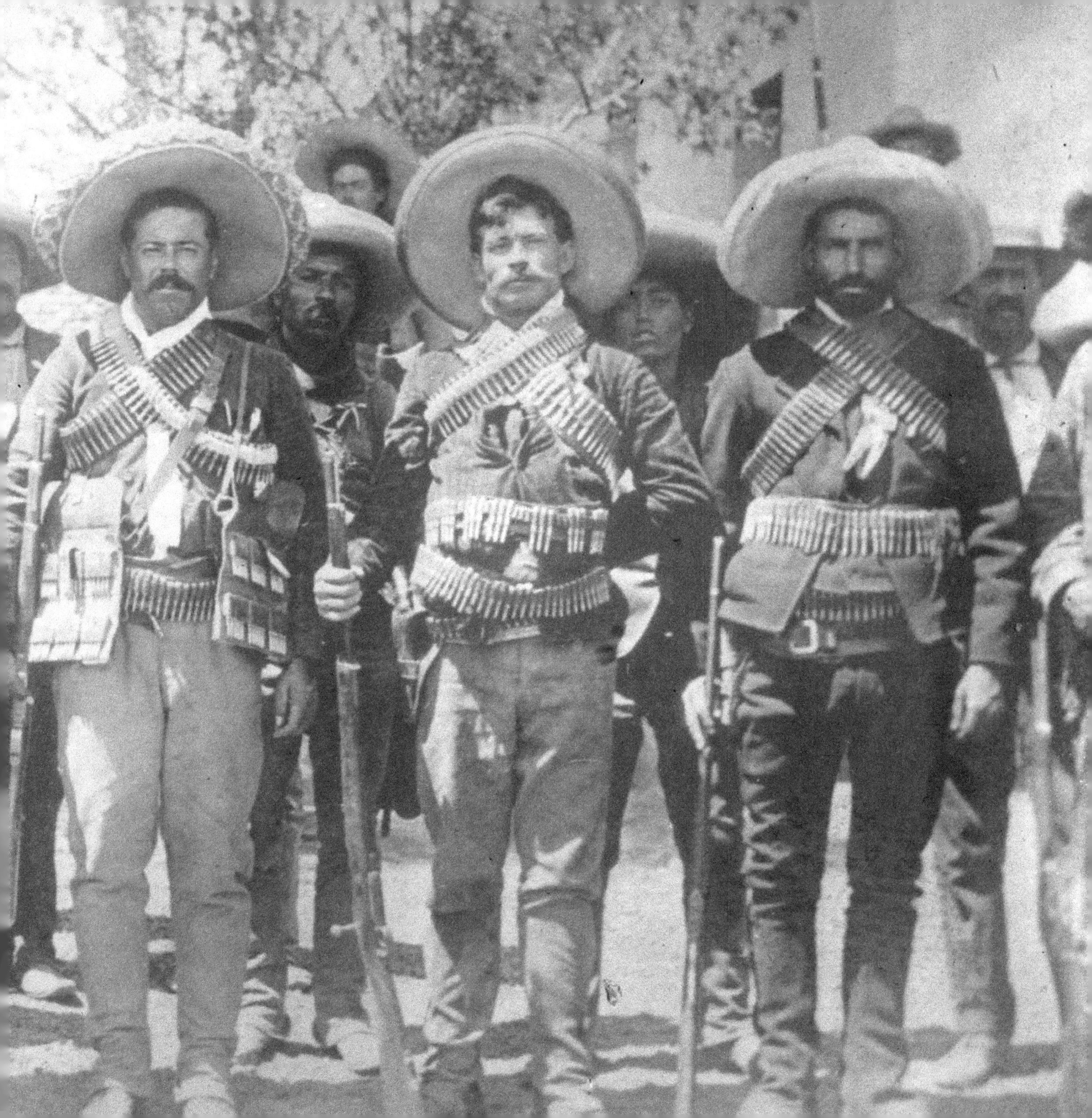

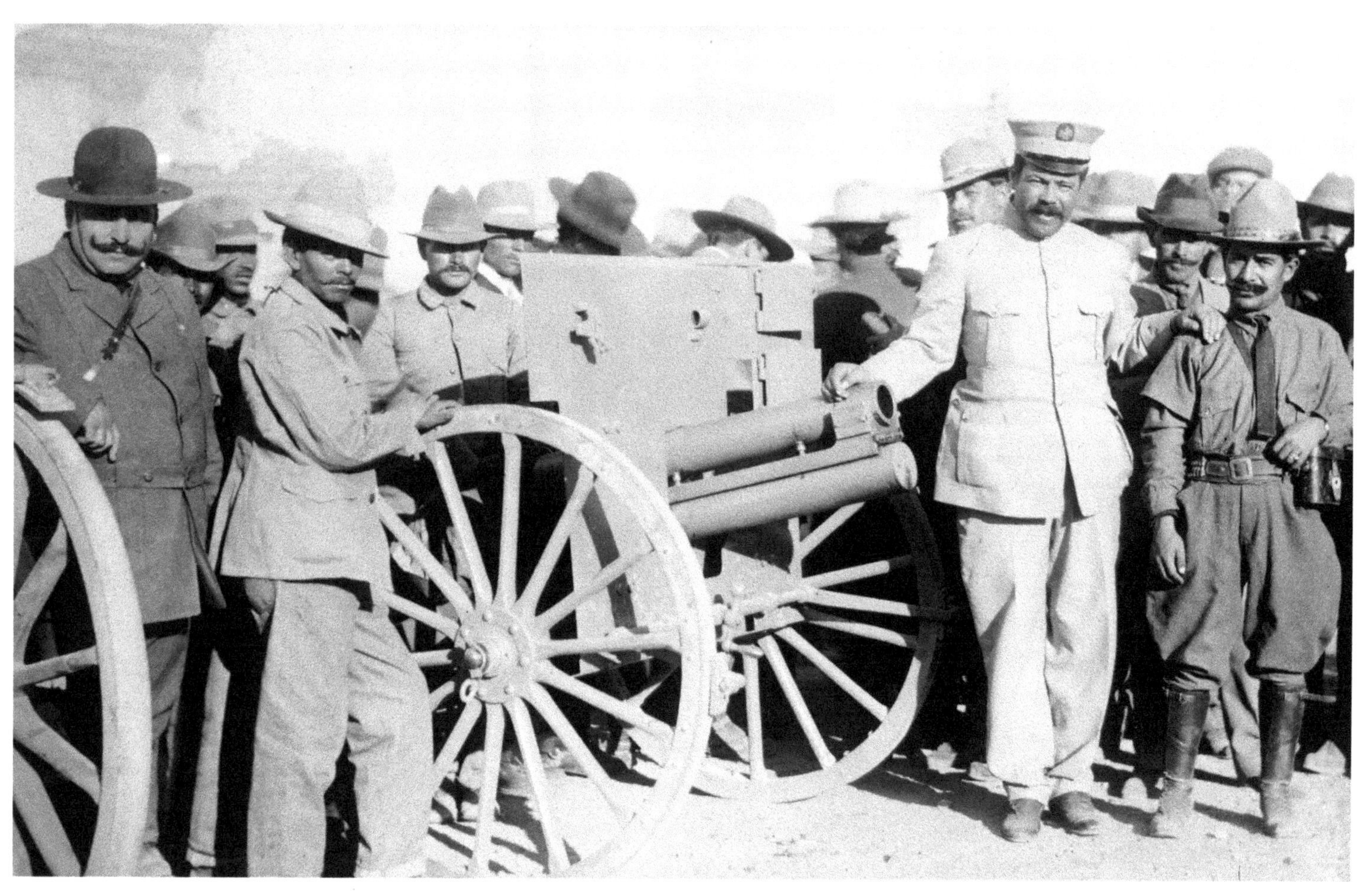

After what he defined as a betrayal by the United States government, Pancho Villa (hand on gun barrel) made several raids on U.S. border towns, among them the attack on Columbus, in which 500 Villistas participated.

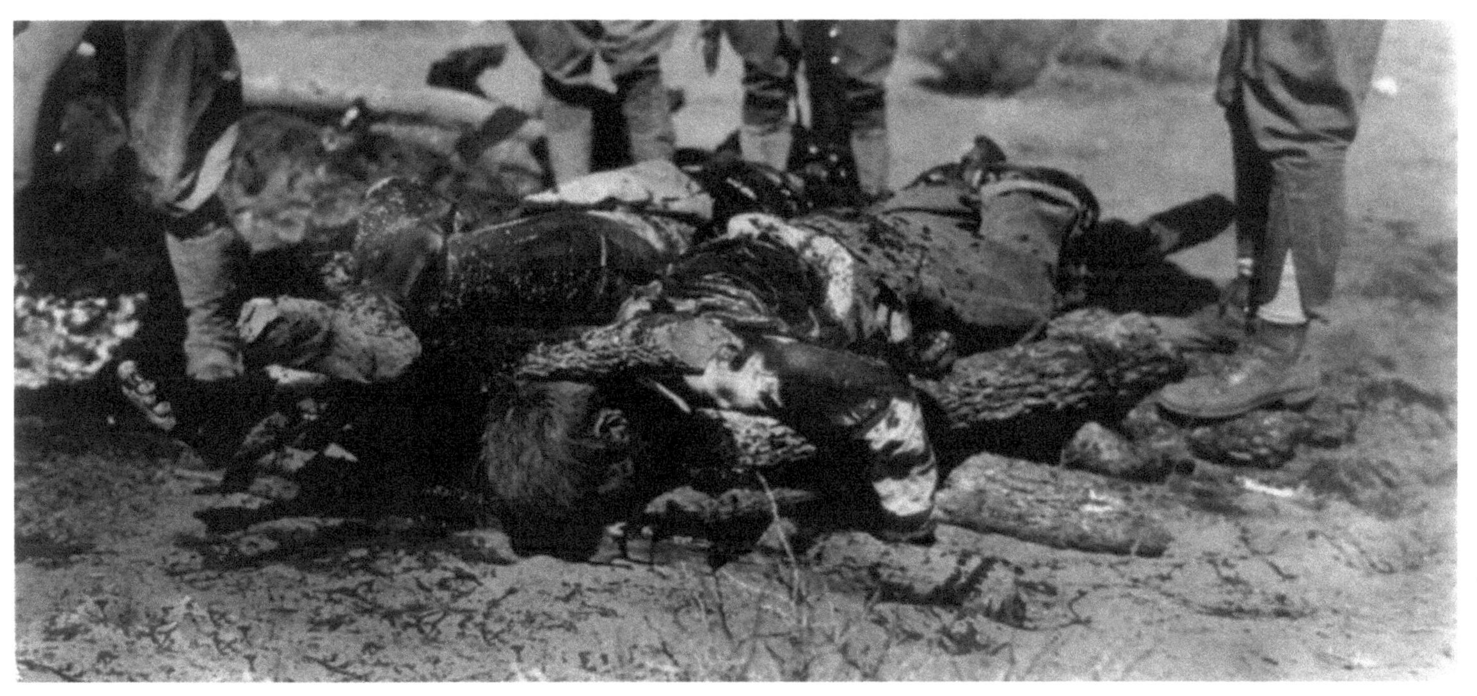

Following the Villista raid on Columbus, Colonel Herbert Slocum was put in charge of cleaning up the town. He later faced accusations of brutality after cremating the bodies of the bandits, some of whom may still have shown faint signs of life.

Recovered from his wounds, Henry Starr appears alongside the Chandler, Oklahoma, jail where he was held after his capture during the Stroud raid. In succeeding years he would portray himself in the film *Debtor to the Law* and continue robbing banks until he met his end at the long-in-the-tooth age of 48 during a bank robbery in Harrison, Arkansas, in 1921.

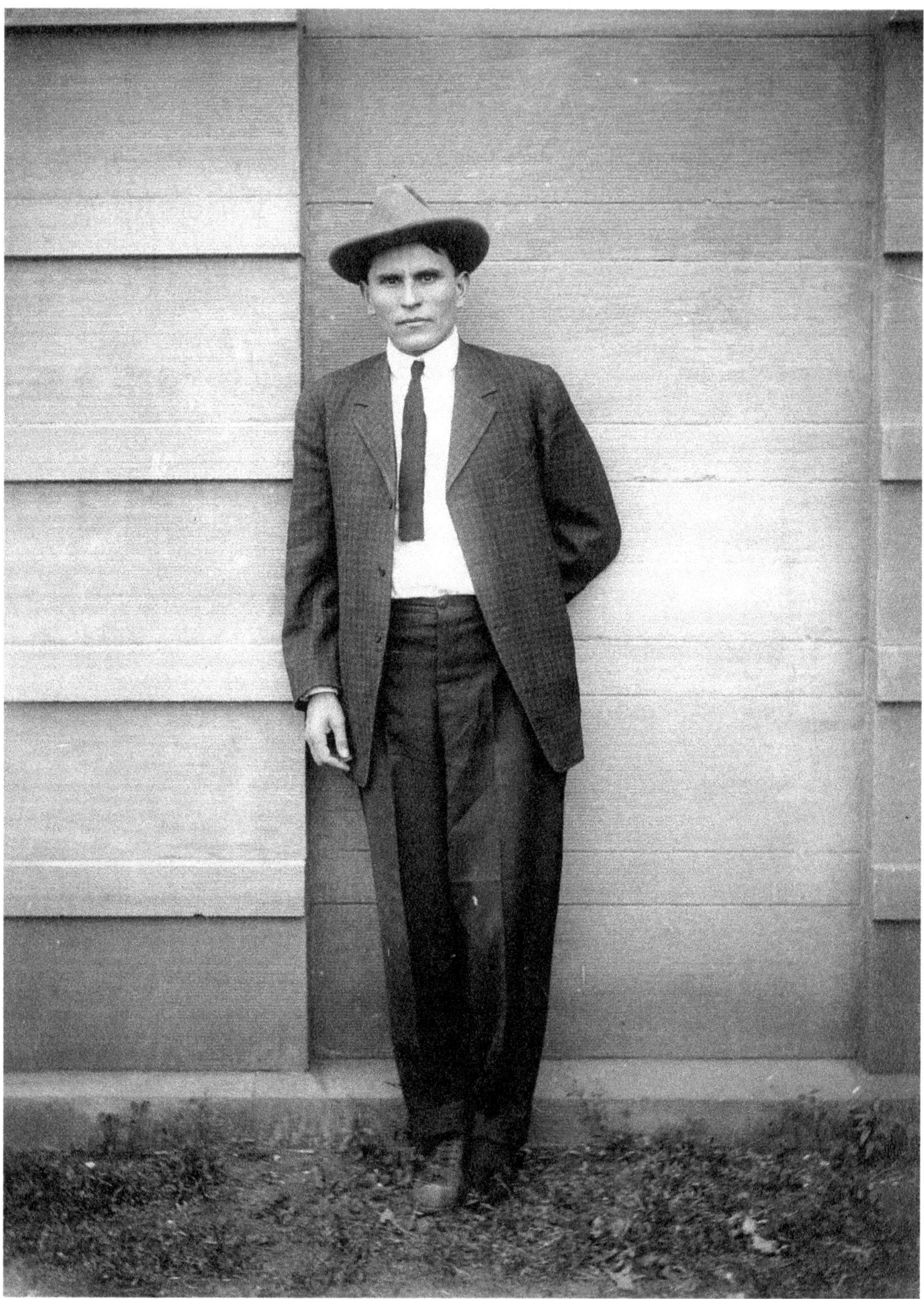

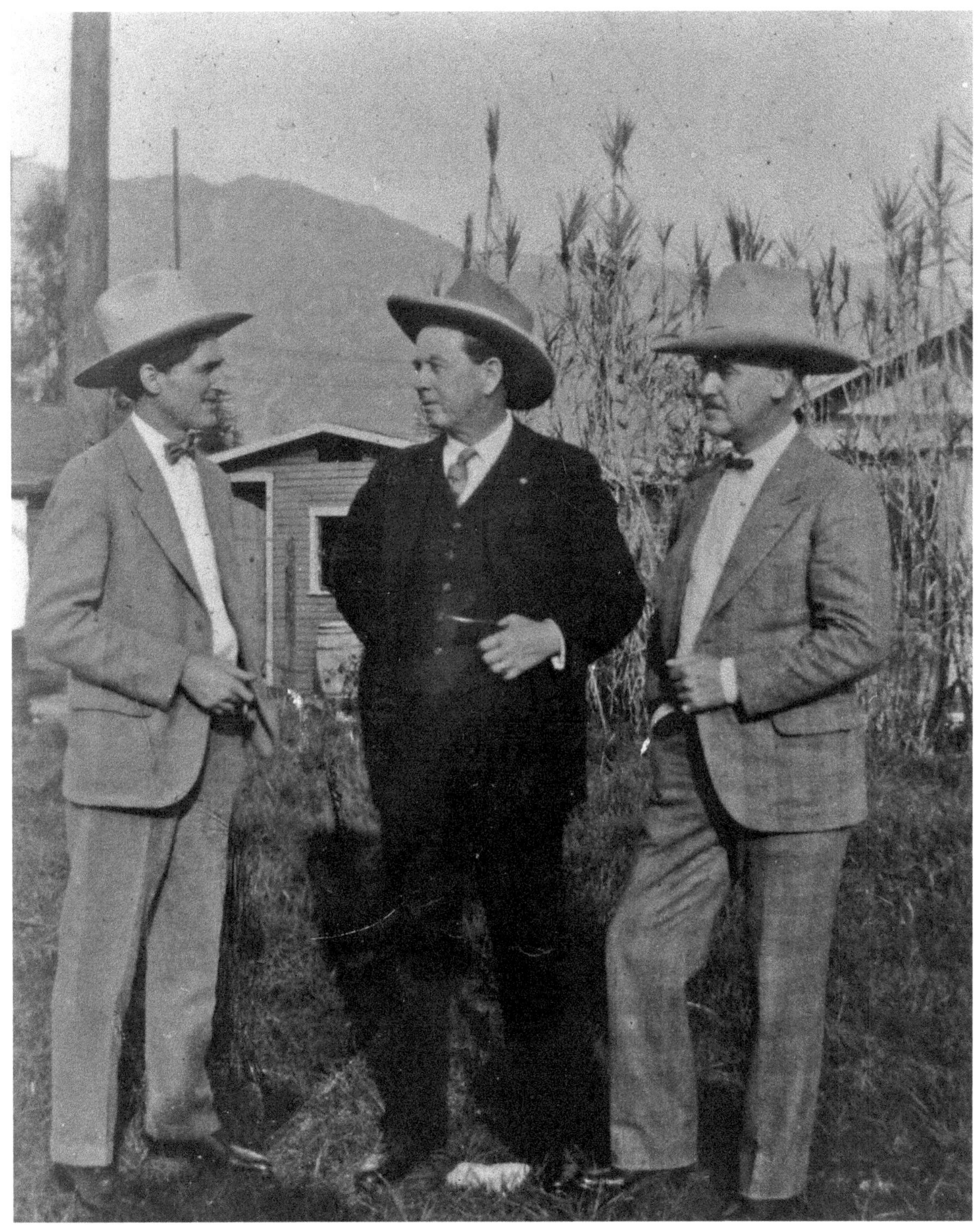

Emmett Dalton (center) shoots the breeze with noted Western artists Will James (left) and George T. Cole (right) at his home in Los Angeles in the 1930s. Survivors of the Old West's wildest days, Dalton among them, were invaluable to western writers and artists during the early twentieth century for the details and firsthand accounts they could impart.

Emmett was the sole survivor of the Coffeyville raid in which his brothers were killed, served his prison time, and finally became wealthy in California real estate. Here he is seen presenting a pistol from his former life to writer Chuck Martin.

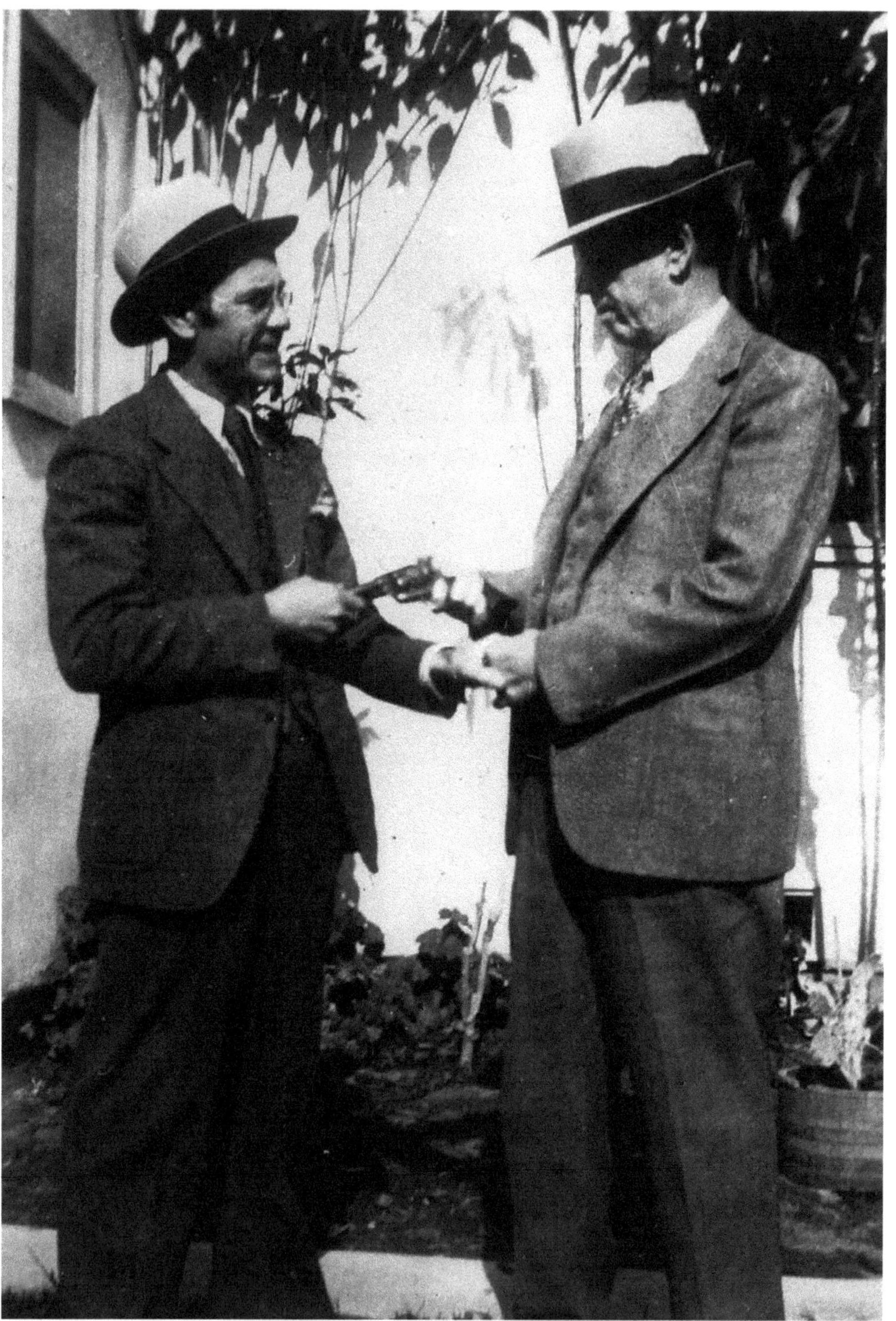

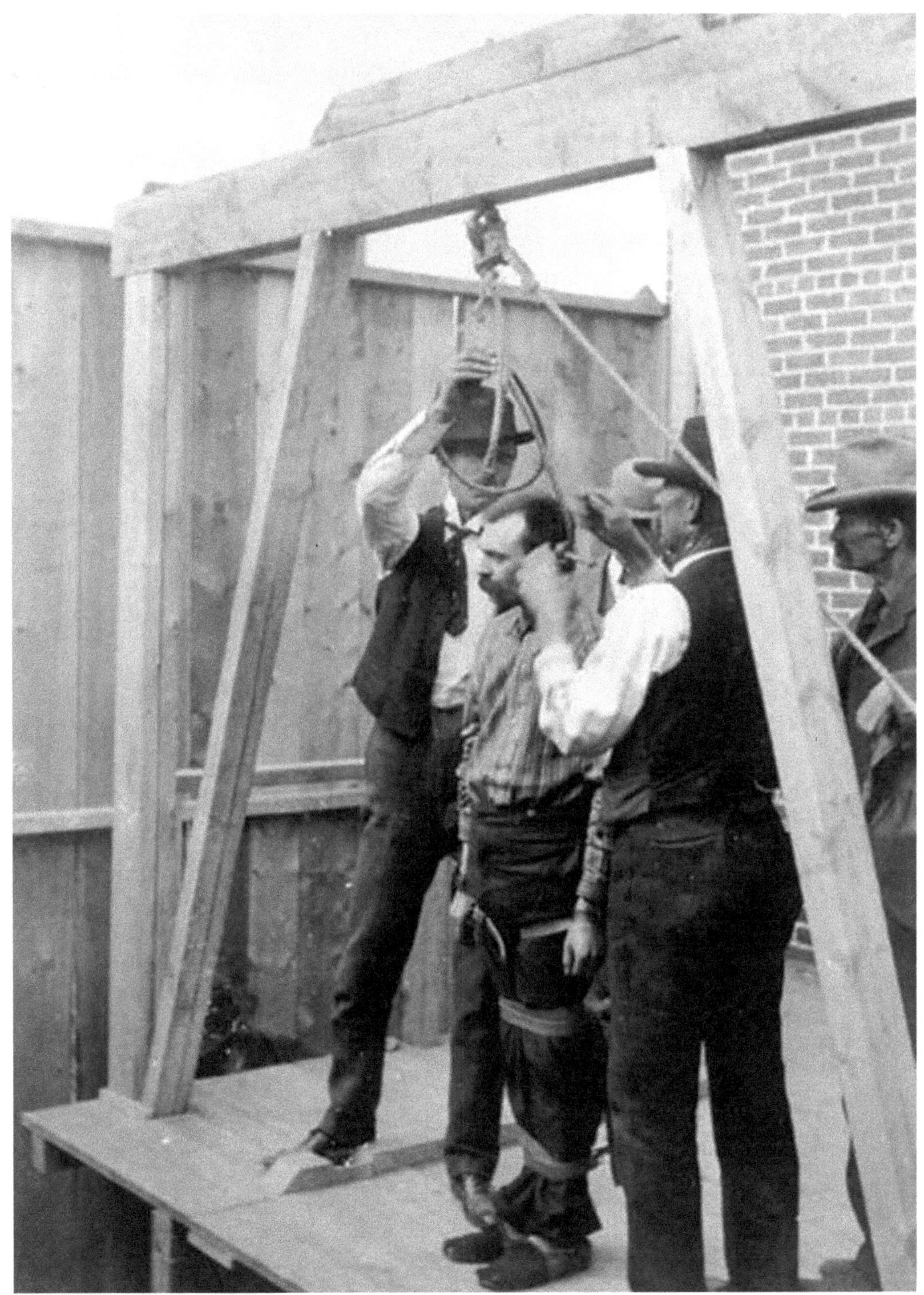

Despite receiving a death sentence, this criminal was actually fortunate to have the services of an experienced hangman rather than dying at the hands of a vigilante mob and strung from a tree. Generally, the prisoner was joined by the hangman, an officer of the court (i.e., a sheriff), and a clergyman. The legs were often strapped to prevent the body from flailing about.

Notes on the Photographs

These notes, listed by page number, attempt to include all aspects known of the photographs. Each of the photographs is identified by the page number, photograph's title or description, photographer and collection, archive, and call or box number when applicable. Although every attempt was made to collect all data, in some cases complete data may have been unavailable due to the age and condition of some of the photographs and records.

ii **Cheyenne, Wyoming, 1876**
National Archives, American West Collection
AW154

vi **Robbing a Stagecoach**
Denver Public Library, Western History Collection
Rufus Zugbaum
11003270

x **Order of the Day at Flagstaff**
National Archives, American West Collection
AW164

2 **Joaquin Murrieta**
Library of Congress
LC-USZ62-50204

3 **Ben Thompson, 1862**
Western History Collections, University of Oklahoma
Rose2146

4 **Marshall Cleveland**
Kansas State Historical Society
00079710

5 **William Clarke Quantrill**
Denver Public Library, Western History Collection
Crescent Photograph
10022139

6 **Destruction of Lawrence, Kansas, 1863**
Library of Congress
3c34452u

7 **Ruins of Lawrence**
Library of Congress
3c32750u

8 **Frank James, 1865**
Western History Collections, University of Oklahoma
Rose1965

9 **Santa Fe, New Mexico, 1866**
National Archives, American West Collection
AW151

10 **Clay Allison**
Western History Collections, University of Oklahoma
Rose2143

11 **Virginia City, Nevada, 1867**
National Archives, American West Collection
AW152

12 **Gold Hill, Nevada**
National Archives, American West Collection
AW120

13 **Drover's Cottage at Abilene, Kansas**
Library of Congress
3b04639u

14 **Ellsworth, Kansas, 1867**
Library of Congress
3a10445u

15 **Billy Brooks**
Kansas State Historical Society
00094133

16 **Zeke Proctor**
Courtesy of the Oklahoma Historical Society
17584.1

17 **Overland Stage at Fort Hays, Kansas**
Library of Congress
1s01630u

18 **Three Hangings at Laramie, 1868**
Denver Public Library, Western History Collection
Arundel Hull
11005808

19 More Vigilante Justice at Laramie
Denver Public Library,
Western History Collection
11005807

20 Murdering Mayor Attached to a Tree
Denver Public Library,
Western History Collection
11005786

21 Gallows at Lansing, Kansas
Kansas State Historical Society
d538

22 Davies Bank at Gallatin, Missouri
Library of Congress
LC-USZ62-41642

24 Jesse James, Holding Crossed Pistols, 1870
Courtesy of the Oklahoma Historical Society
20738.L.3.2

25 Billy Thompson, 1872
Western History Collections,
University of Oklahoma
Rose2145

26 At the Bender Farm near Cherryvale, Kansas
Kansas State Historical Society
00079704

27 Kate Bender
Kansas State Historical Society
00079691

28 John Bender
Kansas State Historical Society
00079684

29 Excavation of the Bender Pit
Kansas State Historical Society
00079701

30 Results of the Excavations
Kansas State Historical Society
00079700

31 Bender Grave Excavations
Kansas State Historical Society
d380

32 King Fisher, 1873
Western History Collections, University of Oklahoma
Rose2153_300

33 Wichita as a Wild Cow Town
Library of Congress
3b33897u

34 Luke Short
Western History Collections, University of Oklahoma
Rose2162

35 Belle Starr
Western History Collections, University of Oklahoma
rose2124

36 Henrietta, Cole, Jim, and Bob Younger
Library of Congress
3b05693u

37 Wells Fargo Reward Poster
Denver Public Library,
Western History Collection
11004533

38 Filomeno Gallotti and His Banditti
Denver Public Library,
Western History Collection
10018696

39 Lawman and Bad Man Jim McIntire
Western History Collections, University of Oklahoma
Rose2109

40 Central City, Colorado
Library of Congress
07820u

41 The James Farm in Kearney, Missouri
Library of Congress
3a24058u

42 Jesse James, 1876
Library of Congress
3a07300u

43 Northfield Bank the Day of the Robbery
Western History Collections,
University of Oklahoma
rose2018

44 Cole Younger
Western History Collections,
University of Oklahoma
Rose1984

45 Jim Younger
Western History Collections,
University of Oklahoma
Rose1986

46 Clell Miller
Western History Collections,
University of Oklahoma
Rose2016

47 Deadwood, South Dakota, 1870s
National Archives, American West Collection
AW155

49 Deadwood's Boom Town Lawlessness
National Archives, American West Collection
AW156

50 Deadwood, 1876
Library of Congress
1s00438u

52 Robbers' Roost Station
Denver Public Library,
Western History Collection
G. Dalgleish
10021890

53 **"Mysterious" Dave Mather**
Western History Collections, University of Oklahoma
Campbell606

54 **Billy the Kid at Apache Massacre**
Library of Congress
LC-USZ62-69941

55 **Bill Longley**
Western History Collections, University of Oklahoma
rose2139

56 **Sam Bass at Sixteen**
Western History Collections, University of Oklahoma
rose2155

57 **Kopperal's Store at Round Rock, Texas**
Western History Collections, University of Oklahoma
rose2156

58 **Sam Bass Grave and Marker**
Western History Collections, University of Oklahoma
Rose2157

59 **Paean to Sam Bass**
Western History Collections, University of Oklahoma
Rose2161

61 **Atchison Topeka and Santa Fe Depot at Las Vegas**
Denver Public Library, Western History Collection
Harry Lake
00120508

62 **Blazer's Mill, New Mexico**
Western History Collections, University of Oklahoma
Rose2174

63 **Billy the Kid**
Western History Collections, University of Oklahoma
Rose2169

64 **The Kid's Colt .44**
Western History Collections, University of Oklahoma
Rose2278

65 **Billy the Kid Grave at Fort Sumner, New Mexico**
Western History Collections, University of Oklahoma
Rose2176

66 **County Jail at Lincoln, New Mexico**
Western History Collections, University of Oklahoma
Rose2171

67 **Most Wanted Poster**
Western History Collections, University of Oklahoma
Rose2177

68 **The End of Gus Mentzer, 1882**
Denver Public Library, Western History Collection
Wm. White
11000335

69 **Arrival of Outlaws in Ortonville, Minnesota**
National Archives, American West Collection
AW191

70 **Benjamin Hodges**
Denver Public Library, Western History Collection
10021568

71 **Clifton, Arizona, Stone Jail**
National Archives, American West Collection
AW080

72 **Charles "Black Bart" Boles**
Western History Collections, University of Oklahoma
Rose2108

73 **Residence of Charles and Robert Ford**
Western History Collections, University of Oklahoma
Rose1992

74 **At the O.K. Corral in Tombstone**
Western History Collections, University of Oklahoma
rose1818

75 **Extravagant Coffins for the Killed**
Western History Collections, University of Oklahoma
Rose1820

76 **The James House at St. Joseph**
Western History Collections, University of Oklahoma
Rose1971

77 **Body of Jesse James, 1882**
Library of Congress
3a27360u

78 **Public Veneration of the James Brothers**
Library of Congress
3a15920u

79 **John Heith, Hanging Around in Bisbee**
National Archives, American West Collection
AW081

80 **King Fisher**
Western History Collections, University of Oklahoma
Rose2152

81 **Henry Newton Brown and Ben Wheeler**
Kansas State Historical Society
00089073

82 **Bank Robbers in Shackles**
Kansas State Historical Society
00089075

83 The Original Boot Hill at Hays, Kansas
Kansas State Historical Society
00114553

84 Booming, Lawless El Paso
Denver Public Library, Western History Collection
11000249

86 The Apache Kid
Western History Collections, University of Oklahoma
Rose910

87 A Three-man Team
Western History Collections, University of Oklahoma
Rose911

88 Apache Kid with Brigands
Western History Collections, University of Oklahoma
Rose913

90 Geronimo at Fort Bowie
Denver Public Library, Western History Collection
Frank Randall
10032891

91 Apache Prisoners near Nueces, Texas
National Archives, American West Collection
AW069

92 Brack Cornett
Western History Collections, University of Oklahoma
Rose2112

93 Belle Starr at Fort Smith
Courtesy of the Oklahoma Historical Society
1356

94 Belle Starr with Blue Duck
Western History Collections, University of Oklahoma
rose2124

95 Emmett Dalton
Western History Collections, University of Oklahoma
Wenner12

96 George D. Miller and Associates
Courtesy of the Oklahoma Historical Society
Outlaw Hookie Miller
14321

97 Bob Dalton, 1889
Western History Collections, University of Oklahoma
Rose2021

98 Abandoned Wyoming Jailhouse
National Archives, American West Collection
AW083

99 Deadwood Odd Fellows Parade, 1890
Library of Congress
02570u

100 Deadwood's Remarkable Resiliency
Denver Public Library, Western History Collection
S. D. Butcher & Son
11002551

101 Tom "Black Jack" Ketchum
Western History Collections, University of Oklahoma
Lillie228

102 Hilltop View of Nogales, Arizona
National Archives, American West Collection
AW163

104 Doc Middleton a.k.a. James Riley
Denver Public Library, Western History Collection
10031309

105 Tom Horn
Western History Collections, University of Oklahoma
Rose661

106 Grat Dalton
Western History Collections, University of Oklahoma
Rose2023

107 Scene of the Foiled Coffeyville Robberies
Western History Collections, University of Oklahoma
Ferguson823

109 Coffeyville Bank Bullet Holes
Western History Collections, University of Oklahoma
Ferguson824

110 Bob and Grat Dalton, Dead
Courtesy of the Oklahoma Historical Society
8957

111 Bodies Laid Out in the Livery Stable
Western History Collections, University of Oklahoma
Ferguson825

112 Dead Outlaws on Display
Wikimedia Commons
Dalton_Gary_memento_mori_1892

113 Dick "Texas Jack" Broadwell, Dead
Western History Collections, University of Oklahoma
Rose2033

114 Emmett Dalton, Model Prisoner
Kansas State Historical Society
00095817

115 Ned Christie, Dead
Western History Collections, University of Oklahoma
rose2064

116 Paden Tolbert and Posse with Body of Ned Christie
Western History Collections, University of Oklahoma
Hudson33

117 Scene at Creede After the Killing of Bob Ford
Western History Collections, University of Oklahoma
Rose1994

118 Bob Ford's Funeral
Western History Collections, University of Oklahoma
Huston33

119 Guthrie, Oklahoma, 1893
National Archives, American West Collection
AW160

121 Base of Operations for Marshal Nix
National Archives, American West Collection
AW173

122 Perry, Oklahoma, 1893
National Archives, American West Collection
AW142

123 Calamity Avenue in Perry
National Archives, American West Collection
AW143

124 Stephen A. Bowen
Western History Collections, University of Oklahoma
Ferguson361

125 Robert Leroy Parker a.k.a. Butch Cassidy
Library of Congress
10772u

126 Kelley's Bijou at Round Pond, 1894
National Archives, American West Collection
AW180

127 Chris Evans
Western History Collections, University of Oklahoma
Rose2095

128 John Sontag, Fatally Wounded
National Archives, American West Collection
AW086

129 Chris Evans Homestead at Visalia, California
Western History Collections, University of Oklahoma
Rose2098

130 Chris Evans in Prison
Western History Collections, University of Oklahoma
Rose2096

131 Cripple Creek, 1890s
Library of Congress
3c18650u

132 Bill Cook
Western History Collections, University of Oklahoma
rose2048

133 Thurman "Skeeter" Baldwin
Western History Collections, University of Oklahoma
Rose2050

134 Hell of a Court to Declare Guilty in
Western History Collections, University of Oklahoma
rose2049

135 Henry Munson, Dead
Western History Collections, University of Oklahoma
Rose2053

136 Cherokee Bill and Crowd
Western History Collections, University of Oklahoma
Ferguson765

138 Cherokee Bill on a Good Day to Die
Western History Collections, University of Oklahoma
rose2052

140 The Rufus Buck Gang
Western History Collections, University of Oklahoma
rose2073

141 Bud Newman
Western History Collections, University of Oklahoma
Rose2138

142 Little Britches and Cattle Annie
Western History Collections, University of Oklahoma
Ferguson106

143 Jennie Metcalf at Reformatory
Western History Collections, University of Oklahoma
rose2126

144 John Selman
Western History Collections, University of Oklahoma
Rose2137

145 John Wesley Hardin
Western History Collections, University of Oklahoma
Rose2136

146 Hardin Colt .45
Western History Collections, University of Oklahoma
Rose2279

147 Frank James, 1898
Library of Congress
3a38563u

148 William "Tulsa Jack" Blake, Dead
Western History Collections, University of Oklahoma
Ferguson359

149 Tulsa Jack in Repose, 1895
Western History Collections, University of Oklahoma
Rose2041 copy

150 George "Bitter Creek" Newcomb, Dead
Western History Collections, University of Oklahoma
Rose2047

151 Ike Black, Dead
Western History Collections, University of Oklahoma
Ferguson362

152 Bill Doolin, Dead
Western History Collections, University of Oklahoma
rose2040

153 Frank Canton
Western History Collections, University of Oklahoma
rose1780

154 Pearl Hart
Western History Collections, University of Oklahoma
Rose2125

155 Swearingen Collage of Outlaws
Western History Collections, University of Oklahoma
Swearingen130

156 Collage of the Cook Gang
Western History Collections, University of Oklahoma
Swearingen132

157 Collage no. 3
Western History Collections, University of Oklahoma
Swearingen134

158 Federal Prison near Fort Leavenworth
Kansas State Historical Society
d833

160 Reenactment of Foiled Hold-up
Library of Congress
3b13830u

161 Doc Middleton in His Peaceful Days
Western History Collections, University of Oklahoma
Rose2069

163 At the Orient Saloon in Bisbee
National Archives, American West Collection
AW185

164 Henry Starr at 22
Courtesy of the Oklahoma Historical Society
11118

165 Scene at Anadarko, Oklahoma, 1901
National Archives, American West Collection
AW147

166 Black Jack Ketchum
Kansas State Historical Society
00061998

167 Black Jack on the Gallows
Kansas State Historical Society
00185282

168 The Ketchum Hanging
National Archives, American West Collection
AW085

169 Ketchum Hanging Aftermath
Western History Collections, University of Oklahoma
Rose2242

170 The Hole-in-the-Wall Gang
Western History Collections, University of Oklahoma
rose2163

171 Laura Bullion
Library of Congress
10777u

172 Harry Longabaugh a.k.a. the Sundance Kid
Library of Congress
10770u

173 Etta Place of the Wild Bunch
Library of Congress
10771u

174 Annie Rogers and Harvey Logan
Library of Congress
07624u

175 The Manhunt for Gregorio Cortez
Western History Collections, University of Oklahoma
Rose2113

176 J. W. Bond
Denver Public Library, Western History Collection
20031265

177 Jesse Linsley
Library of Congress
10774u

178 Will Roberts
Library of Congress
10791u

179 Tom O'Day
Library of Congress
10776u

180 Harvey Logan a.k.a. Kid Curry
Library of Congress
07625u

181 Victor, Colorado, Scene of a Murder
Library of Congress
4a09194u

182 Cole Younger, 1906
Western History Collections, University of Oklahoma
Wessell33

183 Frank James at Fletcher, with Mules and Plow
Courtesy of the Oklahoma Historical Society
15788

184 Lynching of "Deacon" Jim Miller and Associates
Courtesy of the Oklahoma Historical Society
10493.A

185 Bailey Wilson and William McCulley with Prisoners
Western History Collections, University of Oklahoma
Payne10

186 Ann Bassett
Denver Public Library, Western History Collection
11000153

187 Elmer McCurdy, Dead
Western History Collections, University of Oklahoma
Rose2065.2

188 Ben Kilpatrick and Ole Beck, Dead
Library of Congress
10778u

189 Al Jennings
Courtesy of the Oklahoma Historical Society
2728

190 Cherokee Outlaw Henry Starr with Wife and Child
Courtesy of the Oklahoma Historical Society
8668

191 Henry Starr, Wounded and Recovering
Western History Collections, University of Oklahoma
Tilghman137a

192 Pancho Villa and Villistas
Library of Congress
29882u

194 Pancho Villa and Villistas no. 2
Library of Congress
19556u

195 Aftermath of the Villista Raid on Columbus
Library of Congress
3b38785u

196 Henry Starr at Chandler, Oklahoma
Western History Collections, University of Oklahoma
Tilghman153

197 Emmett Dalton with Western Artists, 1930s
Western History Collections, University of Oklahoma
Rose2027

198 Emmett Dalton with Chuck Martin
Western History Collections, University of Oklahoma
Rose2028

199 Hanged Right
Denver Public Library, Western History Collection
11002993

HISTORIC PHOTOS OF OUTLAWS OF THE OLD WEST

From our earliest history, Americans have had an uneasy affection for our outlaws, especially those from the romantic period of the Old West. Whether it is the fearlessness and freedom they represent or some other psychological need, we often overlook the misdeeds of these people in our fascination with them.

This book is about their photographs. Some of the mythology is perpetuated in the captions and some new truths put forth as well. Viewing these photographs allows us to look these fellows in the eye and assess their character—something we probably wouldn't have been allowed to do in real life and live to tell about it.

Historic Photos of Outlaws of the Old West includes nearly 200 photographs, reproduced in vivid black-and-white, with captions and introductions by writer and historian Larry Johnson. Here are the most legendary outlaws and many of the less infamous characters whose lives found a place in the story of the American West.

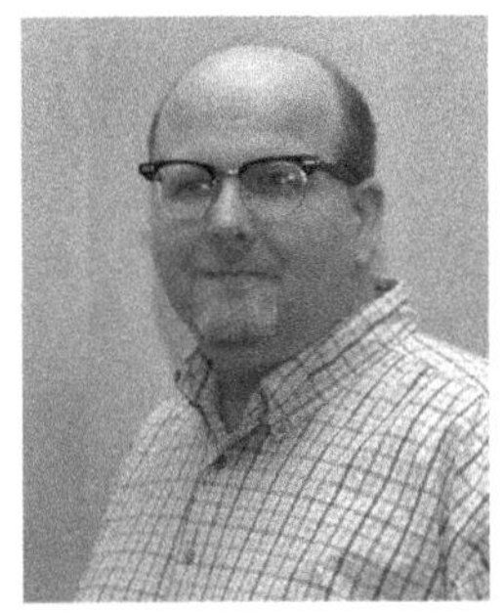

Larry Johnson holds a degree in history from Southern Nazarene University, a library degree from the University of Oklahoma, and a cherished certificate in Nuclear Disaster Preparedness from FEMA.

Johnson is a reference librarian for the Metropolitan Library System where he maintains the Oklahoma Room and the Oklahoma Images database. He is a frequent contributor to *Info* magazine and is the author of *Historic Photos of Oklahoma City, Historic Photos of Oklahoma, Historic Photos of Harry S. Truman,* and *Historic Photos of Oklahoma Lawmen,* all available from Turner Publishing.

He lives in Oklahoma City where he maintains an odd fascination with even numbers and baseball statistics.

WWW.TURNERPUBLISHING.COM

www.ingramcontent.com/pod-product-compliance
Lightning Source LLC
LaVergne TN
LVHW060606110826
845154LV00003B/44

* 9 7 8 1 6 8 4 4 2 1 1 8 3 *

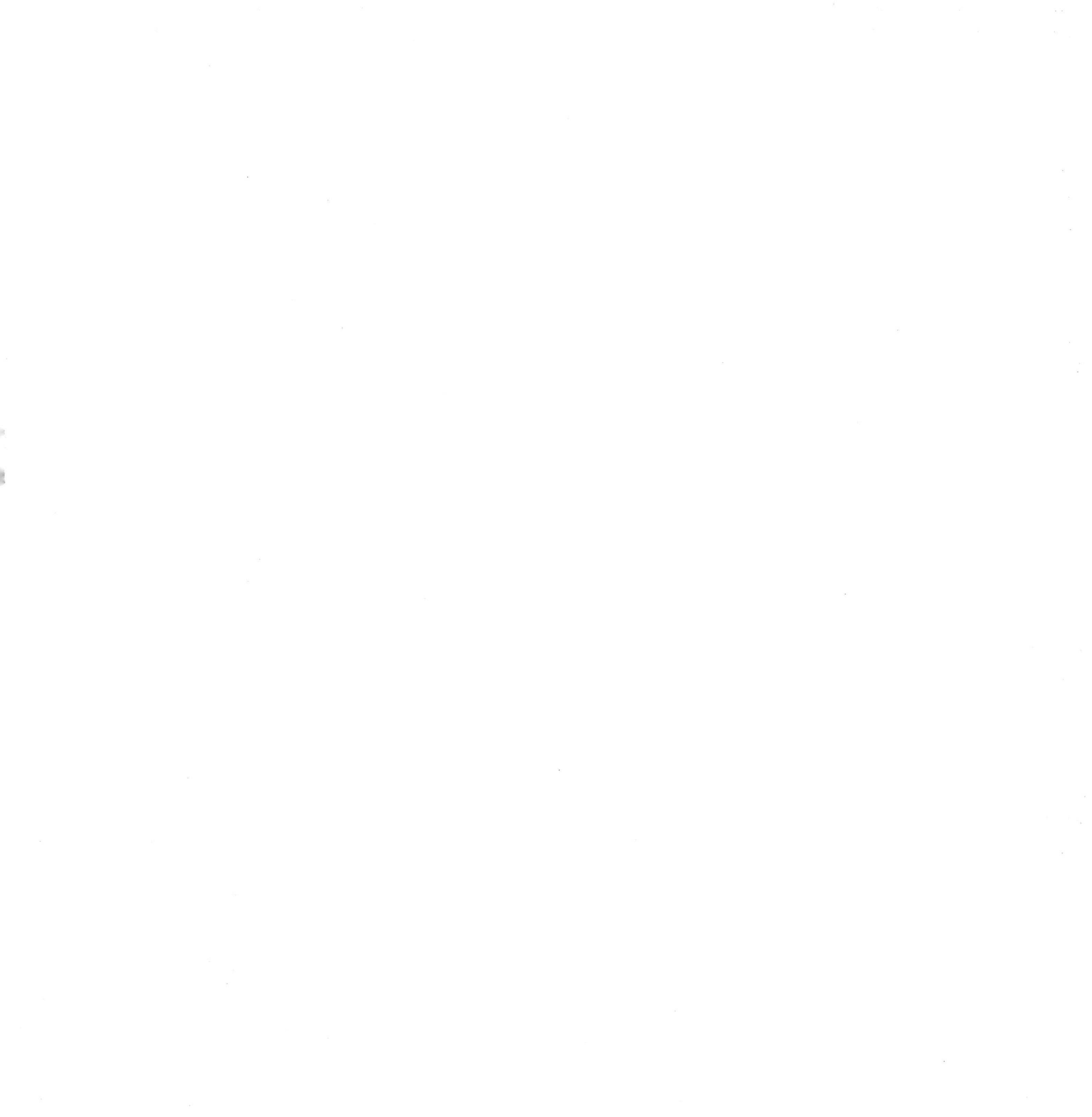